University of London Historical Studies

XXI

UNIVERSITY OF LONDON HISTORICAL STUDIES

CROWN AND CLERGY
IN COLONIAL MEXICO
1759–1821

Crown and Clergy in Colonial Mexico
1759–1821

The Crisis of Ecclesiastical Privilege

by

N. M. FARRISS

UNIVERSITY OF LONDON
THE ATHLONE PRESS
1968

Published by
THE ATHLONE PRESS
UNIVERSITY OF LONDON
at 2 Gower Street, London WC1
Distributed by Constable & Co. Ltd
12 *Orange Street, London* WC2

Canada
Oxford University Press
Toronto

U.S.A.
Oxford University Press Inc
New York

485 13121 8

Printed in Great Britain by
Alden & Mowbray Ltd
at the Alden Press, Oxford

In memory of my father

PREFACE

THE purpose of this work is to explore a relatively neglected aspect of the relations between Church and State in colonial Mexico—the exercise of royal control over the conduct and activities of the clergy, a function which the Spanish Crown considered as vital to the interests of the State as the more fully treated question of royal control over the Church's administration. I have concentrated on the last decades of Spanish rule as a period of crisis in relations between Church and State, marking the transition from the interdependence and close identification of interests of the Habsburg era to the open antagonism that has been so prominent a feature of Mexican history since independence. This crisis was provoked and sustained in large part by a basic conflict between the State's need to exert authority over a powerful and influential clergy and the latter's claim to exemption from that authority; and in tracing its development I have sought to shed some light on the social, political and economic role of the clergy in colonial Mexico, as well as to analyse the origin and consequences of the Spanish Crown's decision to curtail ecclesiastical power and privilege after centuries of encouraging their growth.

This study is based principally on primary sources in the archives and libraries of Spain, Mexico and England. The Archivo General de Indias in Seville provided the major part of the pertinent manuscript material, in particular the *expedientes* and correspondence on jurisdictional disputes in the sections *Audiencia de Guadalajara* and *Audiencia de Mexico*. Material on the formation of Charles III's ecclesiastical policy, as well as judicial and other colonial records, were found in the Archivo Histórico Nacional in Madrid, while the Archivo General de la Nación in Mexico was an indispensable source of material for the independence period (1808–21), when the flow of documents from the colony to Spain dwindled considerably. The smaller but more selective collections in Spain, such as the Biblioteca del Palacio, the manuscript section of the Biblioteca Nacional, and the Real Academia de la Historia, contain invaluable documents, often key pieces missing from *expedientes* in the general archives. The printed sources, many of them extremely rare (e.g., pamphlets, gazettes, and the works of lesser-known Spanish canonists and regalists) were consulted in the British Museum, the Biblioteca Nacional in Madrid and in Mexico, the libraries of the Universities of Madrid and Seville, and the *Colección Graíño* of the Instituto de Cultura Hispánica in Madrid.

I should like to express my gratitude to those who have aided my research: the directors and staff of the libraries and archives mentioned above, and those of the Escuela de Estudios Hispanoamericanos, the Biblioteca Pública de Toledo, and the Archivo Diocesano de Toledo; the Director and staff of the Comisión de Intercambio Cultural in Madrid; Dr Antonio Muro Orejón; Dr Guillermo Céspedes del Castillo; Sr Leandro Tormo, Sr Masae Sugawara, Fr Ernest J. Burrus, s.j., Fr Norman F. Martin, s.j., Dr J. F. Cummins, Lic Ernesto de la Torre Villar, Sra Angeles Flores Moscoso, Sr Antonio Muñiz, and Dr Nettie Lee Benson, all of whom provided archival and bibliographical information. I am deeply indebted to Sr Manuel Giménez Fernández, who gave generously of his time and knowledge to guide me through the labyrinths of canon law, ecclesiastical history, and the principal sources pertaining to them, and to Professor R. A. Humphreys and Dr John Lynch, who patiently supervised the writing of this book, originally a doctoral thesis of the University of London. The Fulbright Commission for Cultural Exchange between the United States and Spain, the American Association of University Women Educational Foundation, and the University of London Central Research Fund have provided the grants which enabled me to conduct the major part of my research. Finally, I wish to thank my husband for his unfailing support throughout the preparation of this book.

Kingston, Jamaica   N. M. F.
April 1966

CONTENTS

ABBREVIATIONS

A.G.I.	Archivo General de Indias, Seville
A.G.N.	Archivo General de la Nación, Mexico
A.H.N.	Archivo Histórico Nacional, Madrid
B.M.	British Museum, London
B.N.	Biblioteca Nacional (*Sección de Manuscritos*), Madrid
CIVM	*Concilio Cuarto Provincial Mexicano*, 1771
D.H.M.	*Documentos históricos mexicanos*, ed. by Genaro García (7 vols., Mexico, 1910)
H.A.H.R.	*Hispanic American Historical Review*
Ind. Gen.	Section *Indiferente General*, Archivo General de Indias
Novís. Recop. España	*Novísima recopilación de las leyes de España* (1805)
R.A.H.	Real Academia de la Historia, Madrid
R.C.	*real cédula*
R.O.	*real orden*
Recop. Indias	*Recopilación de leyes de los reynos de las Indias* (1681)

Introduction

RELATIONS between Church and State in Mexico in the years since independence have oscillated between the closest collaboration and a degree of religious persecution hardly surpassed in any other Catholic country. Both extremes, like the paradoxical compromise of recent times that permits the Catholic Church to flourish within the framework of an unequivocally anti-clerical constitution, are a heritage of Spanish colonial rule. During the three centuries of that rule the power and influence of the Church, already deeply embedded in Spanish life, were transmitted to Mexico, where they became accentuated in the more propitious climate of Mexican society. The clergy in Mexico represented the temporal authority of the Spanish Crown as well as the spiritual authority of the Christian deity to a conquered population that inherited a tradition of extreme reverence for the priestly class from the pre-Colombian past and that remained in a state of political and religious tutelage throughout the colonial period.[1] Consequently they exerted an even stronger influence over the thoughts and actions of the faithful there than in Spain, despite the fact that in proportion to total population peninsular ecclesiastics far outnumbered those in Mexico even at the end of the colonial period.[2]

This position of dominance was attained with the approval and encouragement of the Crown. Moved by sincere religious conviction and shrewd calculation of self-interest, the Spanish kings not only supported the clergy's missionary work, through which both Spanish rule and Christianity were extended, but also employed ecclesiastics as royal agents to check the abuses

[1] See *Recopilación de leyes de Indias* (1681), Libro 6, which outlines the Indian's status as ward of the State entitled to special protection. His religious status as neophyte is dealt with in the Fourth Mexican Provincial Council (1771), Libro 1, título 1, canon 4; Libro 3, título 3, cánones 2–4 & 7, published in J. Tejada y

I

or excessive independence of early colonists and officials.[1] The secular authorities were ordered to 'honour and favour' the clergy,[2] and their fulfilment of this command was one of the points included in the *juicios de residencia*, or investigations of an official's conduct in office—whether governor, *oidor*, or viceroy.[3]

The clergy's all-pervading influence in the lives of the colonial Mexicans rested mainly on religious and social rather than political foundations. The lives of the vast majority of the people, especially the urban and rural poor, centred around the Church, for religious festivals were usually the only relief in the monotonous existence of the masses, and the parish *cofradías* their only social organizations. The Church had a virtual monopoly of charity and education: most orphanages, hospitals, and schools were administered by the religious orders; the university faculties were composed mainly of ecclesiastics; and any instruction the lower classes received was generally limited to the catechism. The notable piety of the Mexicans and their almost superstitious veneration of the priesthood,[4] most extreme among the Indians but by no means limited to them, enabled the clergy to guide their actions and shape their ideas by direct

---

[1] The precedent was established in the appointment of Fr Bernado Boil to represent the Crown's interests in the newly discovered Hispaniola: see M. Giménez Fernández, *La política religiosa de Fernando V en las Indias* (Madrid, 1943), Chapter 2.

[2] See, e.g., R.C.'s to Audiencias of Mexico, Guatemala and New Galicia, 11 March 1543, in *Documentos inéditos ó muy raros para la historia de México*, edited by G. García and C. Pereyra (36 vols., Mexico, 1905–11), xv, 93.

[3] Point 4 in the 'Interrogatorios para la pesquisa secreta . . .': see A.H.N., Consejos 20716, Juicio de residencia del Marqués de Cruíllas, 1766 (viceroy); Consejos 20718, Eusebio Sánchez Pareja, 1777 (*oidor*); and Consejos 20723, Jacobo Ugarte y Loyola, 1788 (Governor of Puebla).

[4] See G. García and C. Pereyra, *Documentos inéditos ó muy raros*, vii, 'De la naturaleza del indio', by Juan de Palafox y Mendoza (seventeenth-century Bishop of Puebla), pp. 232–4. See also A.G.I., Mexico 1661, Archbishop of Mexico to the king, 25 June 1804.

Ramiro, ed., *Colección de cánones y de todos los concilios de la iglesia de España y de América* (6 vols., Madrid, 1849–62), vi, Part 1, 177–313.

[2] The entire Mexican clergy, including secular and regular priests, nuns and dependants, represented only 0.24 per cent of the population, according to F. Navarro y Noriega, *Memoria sobre la población del reino de Nueva España* (Mexico, 1820), appendix 'Estado de la población . . . 1810'; while in Spain the figure was 1.5 per cent in 1800, according to J. Vincens Vives, ed., *Historia social y económica de España y América* (5 vols., Barcelona, 1957–9), iv, 80.

intervention in their daily lives, as well as from the pulpit, the confessional, and the classroom.

The degree of clerical influence varied, but its greatest strength was in the rural areas, where the parish priest or *doctrinero* was usually the only Spaniard other than the local royal justice ('no hay más casta blanca que la del cura y la del justicia'),[1] who was often ignorant of Indian languages and whose authority could be challenged by an ecclesiastic using threats of excommunication and other forms of intimidation. The regular clergy, who impressed the people with their greater dedication and more exemplary lives,[2] generally gained predominance over the secular priests among the upper classes, for whose education they were responsible, and among the Indians, who had looked to their missionaries and *doctrineros* for protection since the time of Fray Bartolomé de las Casas.

Whatever its gradations, clerical influence was a strong force in colonial society, not only in Mexico but throughout the entire Indies, a force which had significant political and social implications in the history of the Spanish empire. Whether condemning or praising Spanish rule in America, both contemporary observers and present-day historians agree that a large share of the credit for maintaining this rule for almost three centuries belongs to the colonial clergy.[3] The peaceful subordination of a vast empire with only a token force of troops during most of that period was possible, it has been argued, because the priests and bishops constantly impressed upon the people their duty to render obedience and devotion to their temporal sovereign as well as to God.[4] According to an anonymous Mexican broadsheet, the most effective method of quelling any riot was to station a 'friar with a Holy Crucifix in the

[1] B.N., 12009, Representación del Obispo y Cabildo de Michoacán a S.M., 11 Dec. 1799, referring to the majority of the villages in the viceroyalty.

[2] H. Villarroel, *México por dentro y fuera bajo el gobierno de los virreyes. Ó sea enfermedades políticas que padece la capital de N. España* . . . (1785, published in Mexico, 1831), pp. 9–17.

[3] A.G.I., Mexico 1675, Alejo García Conde, Comandante General de las Provincias Internas, to the Minister of Ultramar, 6 Dec. 1819; *Mexican Political Pamphlets* (B.M., 14 vols.), vii, no. 136, Reverente representación de un ciudadano franco, 1823; *ibid.*, no. 137, Reflexiones sobre la reverente representación . . . de un ciudadano justo, 1823; J. L. Mecham, *Church and State in Latin America*

nearest plaza',[1] an opinion undoubtedly based on the experience of various tumults during the seventeenth century in which
regulars, exhorting the masses to disperse 'for the sake of their
souls and loyalty to the king', were successful in calming them
after soldiers had failed.[2] In the eighteenth century the importance of clerical support of Spanish rule in Mexico was illustrated by the effect of the expulsion of the Jesuit missionaries
on the northern frontier region. Despite the strengthening of
the military garrisons and the encouragement of civilian settlers,
no new areas were brought under colonization after the expulsion, and many that had been thriving deteriorated because the
Indians reverted to their former pagan and nomadic life and
became doubly hostile to Europeans.[3]

The Spanish government realized the extent of clerical
dominance over public opinion and sought to enlist it as an
instrument of royal policy.[4] When introducing an unpopular or
controversial measure (for example, the exaction of yearly
tribute from previously exempt Indian tribes), royal officials
were often instructed to gain the clergy's support, since their
methods of persuasion, it was thought, would be more effective
than the use of force.[5] But the government was also aware that
clerical influence, though one of the staunchest supports of
Crown and empire, could just as easily work against the

[1] *Mexican Political Pamphlets* (B.M.), vii, no. 136, Reverente representación, 1823.
[2] *Documentos inéditos ó muy raros*, x, 'Tumulto acaecido en la ciudad de México
1692', pp. 244–7; and 'Pacificación que hizo en Tehuantepec el Sr. D. Alonso de
Cuevas Dávalos, Obispo de Oaxaca', pp. 96–154.
[3] A.G.I., Mexico 1142, Informe sobre las misiones, 31 Dec. 1793, a detailed
history of the northern missions compiled under the direction of Viceroy Revill-
lagigedo; see also H. Bancroft, *History of Mexico* (6 vols., San Francisco, 1883),
iii, 721.
[4] 'Instrucción reservada', 8 July 1787, addressed by the king to the newly
created Junta de Estado, art. 86, published in *Obras originales del Conde de Floridablanca y escritos referentes a su persona* (Madrid, 1867); see also Biblioteca del Palacio,
Col. Ayala 31, Instrucción y noticias que se dieron al Marqués de Cruíllas, 1760.
[5] *La administración de D. Frey Antonio María de Bucareli y Ursúa* (Publicaciones
del Archivo General de la Nación, vols. 29 and 30, Mexico, 1936), ii, 7, Bucareli to
Pedro Corbalán, Governor of Sonora y Sinaloa, 12 Feb. 1772.

(Chapel Hill, 1934), p. 44; A. Toro, *La iglesia y el estado en México* (Mexico, 1927),
p. 31, condemns the clergy for having used their influence to that end.
[4] R.A.H., Colección de Mata Linares 76, Deán y Cabildo de Mexico to the
king, 28 Nov. 1799; A.G.I., Ind. Gen. 3027, Bishop of Puebla to the king, 30 Oct.
1799.

interests of the State: if, as the Crown asserted, 'the conduct of the people depends in large part on that of the clergy',[1] then obviously any anti-social or disloyal activities of the clergy would have extremely harmful consequences.

The ecclesiastic 'de mala vida' was recognized by the Crown as a contributor to public disorder from the early years of the Spanish empire.[2] Although the loyalty of the clergy as a whole was not seriously questioned until the end of the colonial period,[3] the Crown also realized that ecclesiastics without consciously seditious intentions could successfully oppose royal commands and even encourage civil disobedience by example and exhortation.[4] That the clergy went to this extreme only on rare occasions did not remove the fact that their enormous influence was a potential challenge to royal authority; nor did their full co-operation in the promotion of royal aims on most occasions eliminate the need for 'constant vigilance to preserve suitable conduct and healthy principles of obedience and love for Your Majesty among the clergy'.[5]

Although it entrusted the early missionaries with extensive authority for the task of evangelization and later encouraged the growth of clerical power as the conquered territories evolved into well-established colonies, the Spanish Crown was not willing to assume that the clergy would automatically act in its best interests any more than it was willing to trust its own civil servants without the myriad checks provided by the *visitas* and *juicios de residencia* and the close, often stifling, supervision exercised by the Council of the Indies. But the task of exerting royal control over the actions of individual ecclesiastics was infinitely more difficult and complex than the supervision of royal officials, for it had to take into account the institution of ecclesiastical immunity.

---

[1] 'Instrucción reservada', 8 July 1787, art. 30.

[2] *Recop. Indias*, ley 1, título 6; ley 12, título 7; ley 9, título 12, Libro 1, all based on royal *cédulas* of the mid-sixteenth century.

[3] See below, Ch. VI.

[4] For example, the tumults occurring in Mexico in 1624, when the archbishop clashed with and excommunicated the entire viceregal government and placed the capital under interdict. C. Ruyz de Cabrera, *Algunos singulares y extraordinarios sucesos* (Mexico, 1624) is the archbishop's version; and R.A.H., Colección Jesuítas 86, Sucesos del gobierno de D. Diego Pimentel, 1624, the viceroy's version.

[5] A.G.I., Ind. Gen. 3041, Consulta Extraordinary Council, 3 July 1768.

The personal immunity of ecclesiastics, as set forth in canon law, involved two basic privileges: the privilege of *fuero* and the privilege of the canon.[1] The first provided exemption from judicial actions by any but the ecclesiastical judges, even the summoning of a witness to give testimony, as well as summary investigation, prosecution and sentencing; the second protected the ordained ecclesiastic from any physical violence, which included arrest, torture, and any form of temporal punishment from imprisonment to the death penalty. Some canonists interpreted this immunity as an exemption from any form of vassalage to a temporal sovereign. But while most conceded that the clergy were obliged to obey all secular laws not in conflict with divine law, it was unanimously agreed by orthodox canonists that the State possessed no coercive authority over ecclesiastics to enforce compliance with these laws.[2]

Long established in the Spanish peninsula and recognized by Castilian monarchs centuries before the discovery of America,[3] the institution of ecclesiastical immunity was transferred to the Indies with the official sanction of the colonial law code, which prohibited secular magistrates from conducting any judicial proceedings against any member of the clergy.[4] Although determined to honour this prohibition in practice, the Spanish government was not prepared to renounce all authority over such an influential segment of society; rather it devised a complex system of indirect control to take the place of direct judicial and coercive power. Detailed legislation governing every aspect of the clergy's spiritual mission, royal control of ecclesiastical appointments, royal review of the Church's judicial decisions, and the extra-judicial measure of

---

[1] The two principal sources of canon law used during this period by both royal jurists and ecclesiastics were the *Decretum Gratiani*, see quaest. 1, causa xi; and the *Decretales* of Pope Gregory IX, see Lib. 2, tit. 1 and 2.

[2] See L. de Molina, *De justitia et jure* (3 vols., Cuenca, 1597–1600), i, Tract. 2, disput. 31; F. Suárez, *Defensio fidei catholicae et apostolicae adversus anglicanae sectae errores* (Coimbra, 1613), Lib. 4; and G. de Villarroel, *Gobierno ecclesiástico pacífico y unión de dos cuchillos, pontificio y regio* (Madrid, 1634), Part 2, art. 5, deals with ecclesiastical immunity and was frequently cited in colonial legal briefs. The author was Bishop of Santiago de Chile.

[3] *Las Siete Partidas del rey don Alfonso el Sabio* (3 vols., Madrid, 1807), Partida 1, título 6, leyes 56–61; Partida 3, título 2, ley 10.

[4] *Recop. Indias*, ley 8, título 12 and ley 73, título 14, Libro 1.

expulsion[1] were among the various methods used by the State to regulate clerical conduct without violating at least the letter of canon law, which the Crown had publicly pledged to support in the Indies.[2]

This system of control formed part of the *patronato* concept of relations between Church and State, formulated under the direction of Ferdinand of Aragon in the early years of colonization,[3] a reciprocal arrangement whereby the Crown fulfilled the duties of patron to aid the spread of Christianity and the maintenance of the Church, while the Church supported the Crown and submitted to royal intervention in ecclesiastical affairs. Ferdinand's Habsburg successors gradually developed a variation of the *patronato*, in which the king claimed the function of vicar as well as patron of the American Church in order to justify the supremacy of royal authority over ecclesiastical activities.[4] However, the fundamental nature of the system remained unaltered: royal control over the colonial clergy was extended under the *vicariato* system, but the Crown continued to channel this control through the ecclesiastical superiors and institutions, which were limited in independence but not in strength.

The colonial prelates on the whole acknowledged the supremacy of royal over ecclesiastical authority. Their dependence on the Crown's favour for any preferment within the ecclesiastical hierarchy naturally predisposed them to conform to royal policies,[5] but personal ambition is only a partial explanation of their attitude. They did not view royal supervision of ecclesiastical affairs as an encroachment on their own authority, since the theory that the king was the pope's representative in the Indies was commonly accepted even among the more conservative American canonists.[6] In addition, the Crown's general practice of regulating the clergy's activities through

[1] The indirect methods of royal control are discussed in Chs. I–III.

[2] Royal *cédula* of Philip II, promulgating the canons of the Council of Trent, 12 June 1564, quoted in M. Cuevas, *Historia de la iglesia en México* (5 vols., El Paso, 1928), ii, 94–5.

[3] See M. Giménez Fernández, *La política religiosa de Fernando V*, particularly pp. 37–41.

[4] See Ch. I, sect. 2, The royal *vicariato*.

[5] See below, pp. 17–18.

[6] B.N., 5806, Extracto compendioso de las actas del Concilio Provincial

their immediate superiors preserved at least the illusion of an independent ecclesiastical jurisdiction.

The *vicariato* system in particular received the full co-operation of the vast majority of the colonial bishops, mainly because several of its aspects coincided with their own aspirations. The system's Gallicanist idea of a national Church administered without papal intervention naturally appealed to those bishops who believed that a greater degree of independence from Rome would enhance their own authority. Francisco de Lorenzana, Archbishop of Mexico during the early years of Charles III's reign, echoed the current regalist eulogies of the Visigothic period (during which the Spanish Church had been virtually autonomous) and, like many royal ministers, regarded the Visigothic Councils of Toledo as a model for the type of partnership he envisaged between the Crown and the episcopate,[1] a partnership realized in the Mexican Provincial Council he headed under the Crown's direction.[2] This desire for greater independence from Rome was not universal among the colonial hierarchy—in 1778, for example, the Bishop of Yucatán objected to swearing an oath of obedience from which the pope's name had been deleted, leaving only the king's[3]— but it was clearly discernible in the favourable opinions voiced by many colonial prelates on the *vicariato* concept and other royal challenges to papal supremacy, such as the royal *exequatur*.[4]

Even more eagerly than they endorsed the Crown's challenge to papal supremacy, the colonial bishops supported another aspect of *vicariato* policy, pursued with particular vigour under Charles III, that curtailed the privileges of the religious orders in the Indies.

The traditional rivalry between the secular hierarchy and

[1] Biblioteca Pública de Toledo, Col. Borbón-Lorenzana, vol. 178, no. 3, Escrito del Arzobispo de Mexico, 16 April 1768.

[2] See below, pp. 32–8.

[3] A.G.I., Mexico 2628, Expediente sobre el juramento de sumisión y fidelidad, 1779.

[4] See *CIVM*, cánones 1 and 3, título 3, Libro 1. For a discussion of the royal *exequatur*, see below, pp. 61–4.

Mexicano, 1771, contains many references to the king as head of the Church and ultimate guardian of the canons in America.

the supra-diocesan religious orders, common to all Catholic countries, was especially strong in the Spanish colonies because of the special powers and exemptions that had been granted the regulars early in the colonial period to aid them in their task of evangelizing the conquered territories.[1] The colonial bishops, who had long complained of these privileges, could count upon the full support of the Bourbon monarchs in their efforts to exert more control over the religious orders, since by the middle of the eighteenth century the Crown had also come to view this independence as excessive, and even sought to resurrect seventeenth-century papal bulls rescinding the regulars' privileges, which at the time of their promulgation had remained unpublished in the Indies by royal order.[2] By submitting the religious orders to the authority of the secular hierarchy, which was more dependent on the State, the Crown could extend its own authority and eliminate a major restraint on royal absolutism.[3]

The regulars did not of course acquiesce wholeheartedly in the curtailment of their privileges, but open resistance was imprudent. The official doctrine that the initial establishment of the religious orders in the Indies had been authorized on the condition that they contribute to the public good (as interpreted by the Crown) and that their continued presence there was contingent upon the fulfilment of this condition[4] contained a veiled threat of expulsion, which was realized in the case of the Jesuit order in 1767.[5] Thus the regulars accepted these royal policies without protest, though they sometimes sought to evade their application—especially the intervention of the diocesan authorities, considered more onerous than that of the government.

In general the acceptance of royal control by both the regular and secular clergy, although unqualified in theory, depended

[1] See, e.g., papal bull 'Omnimoda', by Adrian VI, 1522, published in F. Hernáez, ed., *Colección de bulas, breves y otros documentos relativos a la iglesia de América y Filipinas* (2 vols., Brussels 1879), i, 382–4.

[2] A.G.I., Ind. Gen. 62, Marqués de los Llanos to Thomás de Mello, 11 Sept. 1767, instructing him to search the files for these bulls, among them one issued in 1622, which had been revoked in 1625 at the request of Philip II.

[3] A.G.I., Ind. Gen. 3041, Consulta Extraordinary Council, 3 July 1768.

[4] *Ibid.*

[5] For material on the expulsion of the Jesuits, see below, pp. 51–2, 136.

in practice on the particular agents and methods by which it was exercised. The more closely related the methods were to judicial and coercive power over the clergy, and the further removed the royal agent was from the immediate authority of the Crown, the greater the degree of ecclesiastical resistance. Thus the prelates might accept the Crown's right to control ecclesiastical appointments or to order them to chastise a delinquent subject, but they often objected to secular interference in their correction of the delinquent, in the form of summary inquiries into his conduct or a demand for his removal from office.[1] Similarly, they might willingly renounce their authority in favour of the king but did not always welcome supervision from his subordinates in the Indies, whom they considered rivals for power and influence. The king, as head of the Church in America (in practice at least) as well as of the State, was supposed to be an impartial master over the representatives of both, and this dual function helps to explain why the bishops were willing to accept the king's intervention and even to appeal to him to adjudicate their jurisdictional disputes with the colonial officials, at the same time that the most regalist among them would accuse an official of usurping ecclesiastical jurisdiction when he was merely exercising the authority granted him by royal law.

The complex system of regulating the clergy's actions within the framework of ecclesiastical institutions continued to function throughout the Bourbon reigns until the end of the colonial period, but during the latter decades of the eighteenth century the Spanish Crown promulgated a series of laws subjecting the clergy to the jurisdiction of the secular courts in many civil and criminal cases. This new system of control by-passing the ecclesiastical superiors did not entirely replace the traditional indirect methods (these at the same time were modified in the direction of greater stringency), but was used to reinforce them whenever circumstances required more drastic action.[2]

The legislation curtailing ecclesiastical immunity formed part of a general programme of reform, initiated under Charles III,

---

[1] See below, Ch. I, sect. 1, and Ch. II, sect. 1.

[2] See below, Chs. VII and VIII, for a discussion of the new laws and their application in Mexico.

which was designed to strengthen the economic and political foundations of the State. Charles's ministers opposed many traditional Spanish institutions that they considered obstacles to the fulfilment of this programme, but ecclesiastical privileges came under especially vigorous attack. The clergy's immense power and influence caused their exemption from the State's judicial and coercive authority to be viewed as a major challenge to royal absolutism, in the same way that their immunity from taxation and the privileged status of the large amount of property in ecclesiastical mortmain were believed to impede material prosperity in general and to limit royal revenues in particular.[1]

The Crown's new policy towards ecclesiastical privilege was both stimulated and reinforced by indications that the old methods of indirect control were inadequate. Colonial officials asserted that the negligence and inefficiency of the ecclesiastical superiors, together with the restrictions placed on the State's authority by ecclesiastical immunity, encouraged immorality and crime among the clergy. Presented with evidence of a notable breakdown in ecclesiastical discipline in this period, the government became convinced that the preservation of ecclesiastical immunity was incompatible with the Crown's responsibility to protect public order and to ensure that equal standards of justice were applied to all royal subjects.[2]

The application of the Caroline programme of ecclesiastical reform was incomplete and its direct effect relatively short-lived, since only part of the revised law code, or *Nuevo Código de las leyes de Indias*,[3] which embodied the programme, was published, and most of the new laws were promulgated at the end of the colonial period. But the indirect effect of the innovations that were introduced, principally the curtailment of ecclesiastical immunity, was more lasting. Conceived as a means of extending royal power, the Caroline programme contributed to the complete destruction of that power in Mexico by alienating first a large portion of the lower clergy and pious

[1] Ch. IV contains more detailed background on the Caroline programme of reform.
[2] See Ch. V on the problem of ecclesiastical discipline.
[3] A.G.I., Mexico 1159, Borradores del Nuevo Código de las leyes de Indias, 1790. See also below, pp. 105-6.

laity and later the majority of the hierarchy also. Willing to accept the more subtle indirect methods of control, the clergy were alarmed by these direct attacks on ecclesiastical immunity, which they considered the main source of their power and prestige, and many of them believed that in sanctioning these attacks the Crown had broken the traditional bonds between Church and State and forfeited any claim to their loyalty. Able to foment widespread opposition to these reforms because of their influence over public opinion, the clergy helped to bring an end to Spanish rule and to restore ecclesiastical privilege in an independent Mexico.[1]

[1] For a discussion of the role of the clergy and ecclesiastical immunity in the independence movement, see Ch. IX and the Conclusion.

PART I

Indirect Control of the Clergy

CHAPTER I

Methods of Control under the
Patronato System

I. THE PREROGATIVES OF THE 'PATRONATO REAL'

ALTHOUGH the reformist ministers of Charles III sought to limit ecclesiastical immunity and to place the clergy in a position more equal to the Crown's lay subjects, ecclesiastics had by no means been exempt from royal control during the Habsburg and early Bourbon reigns. The Habsburg kings had steadily amplified the original papal concession of the *patronato*, made in the early years of the colonial period,[1] into a complex system of royal intervention in the affairs of the American Church,[2] a system that included a variety of methods by which the clergy could be controlled even without the drastic measures outlined in the Caroline programme of reform.

The Church had been permitted and even encouraged to gain immense influence and power in the social, economic, and political life of the colonies, but this did not mean that the Crown was prepared to relinquish authority over its American subjects and to permit the colonies to become a vast theocracy. On the contrary, the prerogatives claimed by virtue of the *patronato real* were designed to ensure that the Church functioned as an auxiliary to the Crown and to transform the clergy into a branch of the civil service that could be relied upon to execute royal commands faithfully.

Royal control of the clergy under the title of patronage

---

[1] The basic patronage concessions were made in the bull 'Universalis ecclesiae', by Julian II in 1508, published in F. Hernáez, *Colección de bulas y breves*, i, 24-5.

[2] *Recop. Indias*, Libro I, is almost entirely devoted to ecclesiastical matters, in addition to scattered laws in other sections.

prerogatives, which the second Count of Revillagigedo described as 'the functions that most enhance the authority of the viceregal office',[1] took three main forms: presentation to benefices, adjudication of patronage litigation, and the removal of unsatisfactory beneficiaries. All ecclesiastical beneficiaries were in effect appointed by the king, or by the viceroys and governors acting as his vice-patrons. Although royal nominations were technically subject to approval by either the pope (in the case of bishops) or the diocesan authorities (in the case of lower beneficiaries), this approval was virtually automatic. Many bishops-elect governed their dioceses before receiving the papal bulls of confirmation, which were considered a mere formality, but which were often delayed by slow communications.[2] The confirmation of curates and prebendaries was also almost invariably automatic. On the rare occasions when bishops refused canonical collation they did so for purely technical reasons, such as the candidate's failure to appear within the prescribed time limit, and they were usually overruled by the Council of the Indies.[3]

The prerogative of presentation could be an effective means of ensuring clerical support of royal authority and policies. Certainly the Crown's general policy was to select the most co-operative ecclesiastics, especially for the higher positions of archbishop, bishop, and canon.[4] These dignitaries were presented directly by the Madrid government, and it was the task of the colonial vice-patrons to keep the Crown informed of the qualifications of candidates residing in the Indies. A royal *cédula* in 1766 ordered all viceroys and governors to conduct investigations 'with the greatest secrecy and care' into the conduct and character of the ecclesiastics in their areas and to

---

[1] Count of Revillagigedo II (Juan de Güemes Pacheco y Padilla), *Instrucción reservada que dió a su sucesor en el mando el Marqués de Branciforte* (1794; published in Mexico, 1831), p. 176.

[2] For material on presentations to the bishoprics of Guadalajara and Durango, for example, see A.G.I., Guadalajara 536, 546.

[3] See, e.g., A.G.I., Guadalajara 348, Expediente sobre el recurso que ha interpuesto D. Nicolás de Monserrate, 1784.

[4] See G. García, ed., *Documentos históricos mexicanos* (7 vols., Mexico, 1910), iii, 'Semanario patriótico' (an insurgent newspaper), 31 Oct. 1812; and *Memorias de Fray Servando Teresa de Mier*, edited by Alfonso Reyes (Madrid, n.d.), pp. 206–7, for Creole criticism of this policy.

send the information to the Secretary of the *Despacho de Indias* for incorporation into permanent files on the colonial clergy.[1] It is not certain that these dossiers were in fact compiled, although reports on the vices, talents, and attitudes of the secular clergy in several dioceses were sent to Madrid and usually contained evaluations of the clerics' suitability for promotion.[2]

An intelligence system covering all the ecclesiastics in so vast an area was bound to be imperfect, even when information was available. For example, in 1785 a canon of Durango was advanced to the more prosperous diocese of Michoacán, despite the fact that the Council of the Indies was examining charges against him of having defied the authority of the *Audiencia* of Guadalajara.[3] However, by the time he applied for promotion to the archdiocese of Mexico two years later, word of his misconduct had filtered down to the Secretary of the Indies, and another candidate was presented to the vacant benefice, though he was a Creole, and the canon a peninsular.[4] This use of the prerogative to punish unco-operative or unruly ecclesiastics was common and even included demotion to less lucrative benefices,[5] just as promotion was used as a reward for particular zeal in the service of the Crown.[6]

Even if the Crown had never exerted pressure in such a blatant fashion, the mere awareness that any advancement in their careers depended on royal favour could be sufficient to induce co-operation from the clergy. As one Mexican bishop explained:

In the Indies the secular officials and the clergy serve the same superior, which is the King, our Master (*nuestro Amo*). From his royal hand I have received three curacies, two prebends, and, lastly, his generosity has raised me to the high position of bishop. . . .

[1] A.H.N., Códices 696, R.C. circular, 5 Dec. 1766.
[2] See, e.g., Guadalajara 566, Informe secreto sobre el clero de esta diócesis, sus vicios y talentos, . . ., 1768.
[3] A.G.I., Guadalajara 244, Respuesta Fiscal, Council of the Indies, 14 Aug. 1785.
[4] A.G.I., Mexico 2534, Consulta Council, 1 Oct. 1787, with an undated *real resolución*.
[5] See, for example, below, p. 26, note 2.
[6] See below, p. 35, for the promotion of the prelates who led the Fourth Mexican Provincial Council in 1771.

C

The Dean, canons and curates all serve by his royal will. How then could we fail to observe his adorable commands?[1]

Presentation to the less important benefices was the exclusive responsibility of the vice-patrons. Candidates for vacancies appeared before the cathedral chapters for qualifying examinations,[2] and the vice-patron was expected to act on the chapter's recommendations, presenting the person who received the most votes, but an *asistente real* always attended the examinations and submitted an independent report along with his opinion of the candidates.[3] If there seemed to be glaring irregularities in the voting, the vice-patrons could order a re-examination of the applicants, although in the recorded examples of the occasions when this was done, they acted only at the behest of dissenting members of the chapters.[4]

Thus civil control over these appointments was more relaxed than that over the higher benefices. The Crown's main concern was the preservation of the *patronato* forms and prerogatives rather than the actual choice of the candidates, and in practice this control was even less effective than the laws would indicate. If the bishop or dean had a favourite candidate, he could publish the notice of a vacancy too late for other priests to appear for the examinations.[5] Bishops could also fill vacant curacies on a temporary basis, name coadjutors, and authorize exchanges of benefices without the intervention of the vice-patron. These appointments 'defraud the royal *patronato*', according to one governor, who asserted that the interim curates were in fact permanent beneficiaries and that the coadjutors assumed all the duties and authority of the absent incumbents.[6] Other officials made the same complaints and

[1] A.G.I., Guadalajara 341, Bishop Tamarón of Durango to Viceroy Croix, 2 Aug. 1768.

[2] *Recop. Indias*, ley 24, título 6, Libro 1.

[3] *Ibid.*, ley 37, título 6, Libro 1. See also *Papeles tocantes a la iglesia española 1625–1790* (B.M.), No. 53, R.C. circular, 17 June 1799, describing the duties of the *asistente real*.

[4] A.G.I., Mexico 1271, Bucareli to the king, 12 Oct. 1773; for other disputes over these examinations, see Guadalajara 341, 369, 533, 534.

[5] A.G.I., Guadalajara 345, Expediente sobre la publicación de vacancias . . ., 1780–7.

[6] A.G.I., Mexico 3053, Antonio de Zayas, Governor of Yucatán, to Julián de Arriaga, 18 Oct. 1767. See also Guadalajara 569, Dictamen del Asesor General de las Provincias Internas, 30 Sept. 1791.

also wrote that beneficiaries frequently exchanged their patronage living for a private *capellanía* and a fee.[1] But the Madrid government does not seem to have viewed these practices as a serious threat to patronage authority as long as standard procedure was followed in the presentation of candidates: in answer to the complaints the Crown merely instructed bishops in the Indies to keep the vice-patrons informed of any temporary appointments and exchanges, but did not insist on the need for obtaining their prior consent.[2]

The religious orders in America were less affected by patronage control, although they were still subject to royal supervision. The closest approximation to royal presentation was the right the Crown had obtained from the Holy See to control the selection of missionaries,[3] none of whom could travel to the Indies nor return from there without royal permission.[4] But the regular superiors in America had sole responsibility for filling specific mission posts, and these superiors were also elected by the members of the order without royal presentation. Even the religious who held curacies in Indian parishes were appointed by the provincials, although these curacies, or *doctrinas*, were technically benefices under royal patronage.[5] The vice-patron was supposed to be informed of these appointments, but in practice even this formality was generally ignored.[6]

The later Bourbon kings were opposed to the high degree of independence enjoyed by the regular clergy, but instead of trying to extend patronage control over them, they preferred to transform the missions and *doctrinas* into ordinary parishes administered by the secular clergy. This policy, although supported wholeheartedly by the secular hierarchy, was only partially successful. A number of *doctrinas* and missions were

[1] See M. de Amat y Junient (Viceroy of Peru), *Memoria de gobierno* ... (1776; published in Seville, 1947), pp. 60–1; and A.G.I., Mexico 3068–9, Expediente sobre la permuta de curatos en Yucatán, 1782–7.

[2] A.G.I., Ind. Gen. 62, R.C. circular, 25 Aug. 1765; Mexico 3069, R.C. circular, 3 Oct. 1787.

[3] F. Hernáez, *op. cit.*, i, 382–4, papal bull 'Exponi nobis', of Adrian VI, 1522.

[4] *Recop. Indias*, leyes 4, 15 and 90, título 14, Libro 1.

[5] *Ibid.*, ley 28, título 15, Libro 1.

[6] For an example of the numerous *cédulas* in answer to vice-patrons' protests, see A.H.N., Códices 691, R.C. circular, 12 Nov. 1697.

secularized during the latter half of the eighteenth century, but the lack of secular priests willing or able to exist on the meagre livings these new parishes produced forced the government to curtail the programme and, in some cases, even to return secularized parishes to the religious orders.[1]

This shortage of priests was in fact a major obstacle to the effective use of the Crown's patronage prerogative. Most parishes in the viceroyalty of New Spain were poor and remote, except in the relatively well-populated nucleus of each diocese. Incumbent curates would congregate in the capitals, leaving their parishes in the charge of coadjutors, and in many cases the bishops were forced to appoint interim curates because no one wanted the less attractive livings on a permanent basis.[2] Thus if the Crown often had little real choice in the selection of these lower beneficiaries, material conditions were largely responsible, and not the patronage laws themselves or deliberate attempts to circumvent them.

The right of presentation was the basic prerogative from which were derived a number of corollary powers that enabled the Crown to intervene in many aspects of ecclesiastical administration. The most comprehensive of these powers was the right to decide 'all controversies emanating directly or indirectly from the universal *Patronato*', as stated in a royal *cédula* of 1765.[3] The relationship between some types of patronage litigation and the original papal concession is clear: the disputes over impediments to the canonical possession of a benefice[4] and those concerning the synodal examinations of candidates for curacies are directly related to the right of presentation; and secular jurisdiction over disputes concerning the amount and payment of ecclesiastical stipends can be considered

---

[1] A.G.I., Guadalajara 369, Expediente sobre las doctrinas de la provincia de San Francisco de Jalisco, 1768. For viceregal correspondence and other material on the secularization of *doctrinas* in this period, see Mexico 2189, 1424, 2622–6, 2633, 2637 and 2665.

[2] B.N., 12009, Representación del Obispo y Cabildo de Michoacán a S.M., 11 Dec. 1799, according to which this problem was universal throughout the viceroyalty.

[3] R.A.H., Col. Mata Linares 9, R.C. to Audiencia of Santo Domingo, 14 July 1765.

[4] See, e.g., A.G.I., Mexico 2630, Expediente sobre el recurso que hizo D. Antonio López Portillo . . ., 1762.

a logical corollary to another papal concession, the donation of ecclesiastical tithes to the Spanish Crown.[1] But patronage jurisdiction was not limited to these two clearly defined areas; it extended over a variety of questions, such as conflicts over diocesan and parochial boundaries and the divisions of benefices,[2] which had an extremely remote connection with either appointments or livings. Ecclesiastics were even obliged to bring all litigation over property attached to a benefice before the vice-patron: for example, a lawsuit in 1760 between the order of St Augustine and a secular priest over possession of a convent, which the latter had appropriated when a *doctrina* was secularized.[3]

This broad interpretation of patronage litigation was a significant limitation of ecclesiastical immunity; for, in addition to suits over property, appointments, and livings, the vice-patron could decide all controversies over the fulfilment of a beneficiary's duties (including any ecclesiastic on the staff of an institution, such as a *colegio mayor*, hospital, or university, under royal patronage)[4] and could call him to account for negligence or misconduct in office.[5] Without their connection, however tenuous, with the royal *patronato*, all these suits, which involved ecclesiastical defendants and plaintiffs, would normally have been settled in the diocesan courts without any intervention from the civil magistrates.[6]

The execution of royal laws concerning patronage jurisdiction, like those concerning other aspects of relations between Church and State, depended to a great extent on the relative zeal with which the ecclesiastical and civil authorities defended their respective jurisdictions. In many cases the vice-patron's intervention in diocesan affairs was welcome. Arguments and conflicts among the cathedral canons, for instance, were frequent and exasperating for the bishops to handle, because the

---

[1] *Recop. Indias*, ley 17, título 7, Libro 1.

[2] See A.G.I., Mexico 2621, Expediente sobre división de la sacristía mayor de la Metropolitana de Mexico, 1771.

[3] A.G.I., Mexico 2531, Consulta Council, 25 Feb. 1761.

[4] A.H.N., Códices 691, R.C. to Audiencia Mexico, 11 June 1709.

[5] A.G.I., Mexico 2630, Testimonio de la apelación que hizo D. Juan de Viera, mayordomo del Colegio de San Ildefonso, 1781.

[6] For a discussion of *fuero* in civil suits, see Ch. VII.

disputing parties had enough wealth and influence to prolong them indefinitely by making innumerable petitions to higher courts and by sending representatives to the Spanish Court. It is not surprising, then, that the bishops were content to let the civil authorities decide questions of precedence, protocol and other minor disputes. Sometimes the prelates referred them directly to the king or sometimes via the vice-patrons, who seemed equally eager to forward these annoying squabbles to Madrid.[1]

At times capitular squabbles went further than petty questions of protocol, especially when there was no bishop to restrain the canons, which unfortunately was all too frequently the case.[2] In 1772 the *sede vacante* Chapter of Michoacán divided into two factions, mainly over the issue of the recent examinations for curacies, which each side accused the other of manipulating in favour of relatives and friends. Although by canon law the Metropolitan Archbishop of Mexico had jurisdiction over this case, he was glad to leave the decision to the viceroy, who ended the dispute by calling for new examinations.[3]

But the ecclesiastical magistrates were not always so willing to relinquish their jurisdiction to the vice-patrons. If they felt that the State's intervention was not required in a particular case or that it constituted a more serious violation of ecclesiastical immunity—for example, in the controversies involving a beneficiary's conduct in office—they often attempted to initiate proceedings in the diocesan court or to summon (*avocar*) a case already under the cognizance of the vice-patron.[4]

The extent to which patronage prerogatives infringed the personal immunity of the clergy was the primary consideration in the hierarchy's reaction to them. Thus colonial prelates accepted the State's control over ecclesiastical appointments

[1] A.G.I., Guadalajara 243, 315, 348, 356, contain many patronage disputes sent by the bishops and vice-patrons to the Council of the Indies from 1771–90.

[2] Any list of colonial bishops, such as J. Bravo Ugarte, *Diócesis y obispos de la iglesia mexicana 1519–1939* (Mexico, 1941), will reveal the frequency and duration of these vacancies.

[3] A.G.I., Mexico 1271, Bucareli to the king, 12 Oct. 1773.

[4] For examples of ecclesiastical resistance to patronage jurisdiction, see A.G.I., Mexico 2661, Provisor of Oaxaca to the king, 14 Sept. 1773; and Mexico 2645, Expediente del pleito seguido ante el Provisor de Mexico, 1791–2.

and, in varying degrees, its jurisdiction over patronage litigation, but they were less inclined to accept its authority over the
removal of an unsatisfactory curate once he had taken office—
another prerogative claimed by the Crown as a corollary to the
right of presentation.

Secular intervention in the removal of beneficiaries was the
most direct method of controlling the conduct of individual
ecclesiastics under the *patronato* system. An ecclesiastical incumbent did not hold his benefice in perpetuity but could be
deprived of his living by the vice-patron and bishop,[1] and
removal proceedings could be instituted against him for
general misconduct (e.g., causing a public scandal by his
immoral behaviour[2] or usurping the authority of the local
royal justice[3]), as well as for neglecting his ministerial duties
(e.g., unauthorized absence from his parish and extortion of
parochial fees[4]). The vice-patrons interpreted the royal law
that established this joint procedure for removal as authorizing
them at the very least to judge the merits of each case,[5] and
many believed that they had the right to initiate a joint trial
of any incumbent who misbehaved: under either interpretation
the prerogative constituted secular jurisdiction over ecclesiastics
in criminal cases,[6] a much more obvious encroachment on
ecclesiastical *fuero* than the adjudication of patronage suits.

This prerogative functioned smoothly as long as the bishop
and vice-patron agreed on the need for removal and, on that
basis, it could be an effective means of reforming the conduct
of unruly ecclesiastics, as illustrated in a case arising in Yucatán
in 1776. The bishop and governor decided that a curate in
Tabasco, who had usurped the authority of the local *alcalde
mayor* and publicly defamed the characters of other royal
officials with charges of corruption, was a disruptive element in
the district and should be removed, but within several years

---

[1] *Recop. Indias*, ley 38, título 6, Libro 1.
[2] A.G.I., Mexico 3053, Testimonio de autos formados en la causa de Bernardo
de Echeverría, 1768.
[3] A.G.I., Mexico 3072, Testimonio de autos contra José Perdomo, 1792.
[4] A.G.I., Mexico 3064, Testimonio de autos contra el cura de Umán, 1783.
[5] M. de Amat y Junient, *op. cit.*, pp. 69–70.
[6] This intervention was considered abusive by J. de Solórzano Pereira, *Política
indiana* (Madrid, 1647), Libro 4, cap. 15, no. 30.

both the governor and the bishop were sufficiently convinced of the priest's reformation to reinstate him in his benefice.[1]

However, the prescribed method of removal, requiring the concurrence of the two authorities, presupposed a state of harmony that did not always exist and meant in practice that either dissenting party could obstruct proceedings successfully. In two similar cases in Yucatán, one in the 1760's and the other in the 1790's, a governor requested that a curate be removed for unsatisfactory behaviour, but a bishop tried the accused in the diocesan court and reached the conclusion that there were no grounds for removal in either case.[2] The two governors were convinced, on the basis of their own secret inquiries, that the curates should not have been acquitted and asserted that, under such circumstances, bishops were obliged to defer to the vice-patrons' demands. But the bishops resisted this extreme interpretation of the law in both cases, and the governors were warned that in challenging the judicial decisions of the diocesan court with evidence gathered by a secular magistrate they committed an offence against ecclesiastical immunity that risked the penalty of excommunication.[3]

The prelates clearly had the upper hand in these cases, unless the Crown decided to give the vice-patrons decisive judicial authority, and this it was unwilling to do: despite urgent requests from both governors, the Council upheld the bishops' original verdicts and declined to revise the existing procedure.[4]

The law's failure to define the limits between ecclesiastical and secular authority in this procedure resulted in many disputes, which the Council of the Indies often resolved with inconsistent rulings that merely added to the confusion. Sometimes the impasse in proceedings was caused by vice-patrons who conducted their own inquiries and decided that the beneficiary had given no cause for complaint. In 1759 the Council fined the Governor of Quito for this 'unauthorized

---

[1] A.G.I., Mexico 3063, Bishop of Yucatán to Ventura de Taranco, 23 July 1783.

[2] A.G.I., Mexico 3053, Testiminio de autos . . . Echeverría, 1768; Mexico 3072, Testimonio de autos contra José Perdomo, 1796.

[3] *Ibid.*, Provisor Agustín de Echano to governor, 5 Aug. 1767; Mexico 3072, Bishop of Yucatán to governor, 13 April 1792.

[4] A.G.I., Mexico 3054, Acuerdo Council, 30 June 1768; Mexico 3072, Acuerdo Council, 23 June 1796.

action' and issued a general *cédula* declaring that the vice-patron's consent was unnecessary for removal if the incumbent had been convicted by his superior, whose decision was to be final.[1] Yet when an almost identical dispute arose in Durango in the 1770's, the Council reversed this *cédula*, approved the vice-patron's investigation, and upheld his decision to refuse consent for a curate's removal.[2]

The Council's resolutions could actually be an obstacle to the law's application even when the civil and ecclesiastical authorities co-operated. In 1784, for example, it overruled the Bishop and Governor of Yucatán, who had removed a delinquent curate before the completion of his trial in order to prevent further delay from his constant appeals to higher courts.[3] This new ruling, made applicable throughout the Indies in 1795, contradicted an earlier one of 1769, according to which a formal trial was unnecessary as long as the two authorities concurred,[4] and virtually nullified the basic law as well, for any incumbent could contest the simple procedure of concurrence and demand a trial if the loss of the benefice would cause him 'considerable hardship'.[5]

If this prerogative was not always an effective method of controlling the clergy, the Crown itself was in large measure to blame. It had created a procedure which was open to abuse from impatient vice-patrons and to obstruction from determined prelates, while the Crown's organ of judicial review, the Council of the Indies, contributed to the law's ambiguities and even hindered well-intentioned colonial authorities in cases where the procedure could have functioned efficiently.

Though the authority derived from the patronage concession was most frequently exercised over the lower clergy, it extended over the bishops in the Indies as well. It was acknowledged that the pope was the spiritual head of the American Church,

[1] A.H.N., Códices 691, R.C. circular, 5 April 1759.
[2] A.G.I., Guadalajara 343, R.C. to Bishop of Durango and Audiencia of Guadalajara, 19 Sept. 1777.
[3] A.G.I., Mexico 3064, Testimonio de autos . . . cura de Umán, 1783; Acuerdo Council, 22 Dec. 1784.
[4] *Ibid.*, R.C., 11 Dec. 1769 (copy).
[5] A.G.N., Bandos y Ordenanzas 18, R.C. circular, 1 Aug. 1795, inserted in bando, 24 Feb. 1796.

but in most other aspects of administration the Spanish Crown was the prelates' *de facto* superior, and even the acts embodying episcopal subordination, such as the *visita ad limina*, or report made to the Holy See by a new bishop on taking possession of his see, and the episcopal oath of 'submission and fidelity', were transferred from pope to king during the reign of Charles III.[1]

Royal policy concerning the actual extent of patronage jurisdiction over the colonial bishops is not clear, especially in its most extreme manifestation: deposition. The Crown certainly felt that a bishop's conduct in office was a matter of royal responsibility, but other forms of pressure could be brought to bear on an unco-operative or unsatisfactory prelate, such as transfer to a less attractive see[2] or public reprimand,[3] which did not require any judicial authority. There was no provision in royal law for the removal of a bishop, but one regalist author sought to establish the Crown's coercive power over bishops in its capacity of patron of the Church,[4] and there is reason to believe that Charles III included the right of deposing a bishop among his patronage prerogatives.

The Fourth Mexican Provincial Council, which met in 1771, was to take cognizance of any crimes committed by its members, according to the royal instructions ordering its convocation.[5] Although canon law reserves jurisdiction over any serious crimes of bishops to the Holy See,[6] two Council judges were in fact appointed and carried out a secret trial of the Bishop of Durango, José Vicente Díaz Bravo, the records of which they sent to Charles III for his decision. The Archbishop

---

[1] A.G.I., Mexico 2622, R.C., 1 July 1770, and Relación del estado material y formal de la iglesia de la Puebla de los Angeles, 2 Dec. 1772, report *ad limina mayorem* submitted by the Bishop of Puebla, in accordance with the 1770 *cédula*.

[2] Usually to a minor see in the peninsula, e.g., Badajoz, to which Archbishop Manso y Zúñiga of Mexico was demoted in 1630 for insubordination. See A.G.I., Mexico 3, Expediente sobre la estancia . . ., 1630–4.

[3] P. de Leturia, *Relaciones entre la Santa Sede e Hispanoamérica* (3 vols., Rome, 1959–60), i, 329–31, deals with the public reprimand given to St Toribio de Mogrovejo in Lima in 1594.

[4] A. Álvarez de Abreu, *Víctima real legal* (Madrid, 1726), p. 59.

[5] 'Tomo regio para los concilios provinciales', 21 Aug. 1769, punto 3, published in F. Tejada y Ramiro, *Colección de cánones*, vi, Part 1, 315–17.

[6] Council of Trent, sess. 13, cap. 8 *de reform.* and sess. 24, cap. 5 *de reform.* The Council is published in Spanish translation in F. Tejada y Ramiro, *op. cit.*, iv.

of Mexico, Francisco de Lorenzana, admitted later that this regalist action, among others, would be a serious obstacle to obtaining the Pope's approval of the Council.[1]

The precise charges brought against the bishop are not known, since the documents prepared in Mexico were passed on to the king's confessor and do not appear in the official files. What is certain is that several of Díaz Bravo's fellow bishops, and not the government in Madrid, instigated the proceedings. He apparently incurred the wrath of Archbishop Lorenzana by objecting to his dictatorial methods of conducting the Council sessions and accusing him of having prepared all the canons in advance.[2] Soon after the Council convened, rumours abounded that Lorenzana had commissioned his two loyal followers, the Bishops of Puebla and Yucatán, to make a secret inquiry into Díaz Bravo's conduct and gather evidence against him which was to be used only in the event that he became too difficult to control by more subtle means.[3]

Lorenzana and the two judges sent frequent reports and letters to Madrid begging the king to take action to 'prevent further scandal'[4] and were soon rewarded by a royal *cédula* summoning Díaz Bravo to Spain, where he was to be held in custody and urged to renounce his bishopric. In case he should refuse, the Council judges were instructed to continue the trial and produce sufficient evidence to justify his deposition.[5]

Since Díaz Bravo's 'sudden and unforeseen' death on board the ship carrying him back to Spain[6] closed the case before it was resolved, there is no record of what procedure would have been followed in the likely event that he had refused to

[1] A.G.I., Ind. Gen. 3026, Lorenzana to Arriaga, 19 Nov. 1774.
[2] B.N., 5806, Extracto Compendioso de las actas del Concilio IV Provincial Mexicano, 1771.
[3] *Ibid.*, Diario de las operaciones del Concilio Provincial por uno de los individuos que lo componen . . . 1771, 10 Jan. and 13 Jan. 1771. Internal evidence indicates that the author was Dr Antonio Ríos, delegate of the Bishop of Valladolid, who could not attend.
[4] Biblioteca Pública de Toledo, Col. Borbón-Lorenzana, vol. 178, no. 15, Extracts of letters from Lorenzana, 26 Jan. 1771; Bishops of Puebla and Yucatán, 28 Jan., 2 March, 28 March, 28 May and 30 June 1771.
[5] A.G.I., Guadalajara 545, Dictamen del Padre Confesor, 15 May 1771; R.C.'s to Lorenzana, Díaz Bravo and Viceroy Bucareli, 24 May 1771.
[6] *Ibid.*, death certificate signed by the *Escribano* on the ship *Nuestra Señora de la Begoña*, 24 April 1772.

resign: whether the king would have deposed him solely on his authority as patron, or whether he would have sought a papal brief confirming the act is a matter of conjecture. It is clear, however, that Charles treated the case in essentially the same manner as the removal of an unsatisfactory curate, and this extension of royal authority, even if existing only as a threat, was a notable contribution to royal control over the clergy under the title of patronage prerogatives.

This case is the only one on record in which the Crown attempted to depose a consecrated bishop. The Bishop-elect of Michoacán, Manuel Abad y Queipo, was recalled to Spain and deprived of his bishopric in 1814.[1] However, he had only been nominated, without yet receiving his papal bull of confirmation, and it was argued that he was not legally in possession of his see. The king ignored Abad y Queipo's protests that only the pope had the power to depose him and merely presented another candidate in his place.[2]

2. THE ROYAL 'VICARIATO'

In addition to the prerogatives emanating more or less directly from the royal right of presentation, the Spanish Crown had created a much more comprehensive system of control over ecclesiastical activities based on the regalist doctrine that the Spanish kings had the function of God's vicar general in the American Church.[3] First tentatively expressed by the seventeenth-century jurist Juan de Solórzano Pereira[4] and developed to an extravagant degree by regalist authors of the following century,[5] the *vicariato* doctrine possessed two rival theories con-

---

[1] A.G.I., Mexico 2571, R.O. to Abad y Queipo, 15 Sept. 1814.

[2] *Ibid.*, Consulta Council of the Indies, 29 Nov. 1815.

[3] A. de Egaña, *La teoría del regio vicariato español en Indias* (Rome, 1958), traces the development of this theory from the beginning of the colonial period.

[4] J. de Solórzano Pereira, *op. cit.*, Libro 4, cap. 2, no. 24.

[5] Especially A. Álvarez de Abreu, *Víctima real legal*, and A. de Ribadeneyra y Barrientos, *Manual compendio del Regio Patronato Indiano* (Madrid, 1755). The first author was rewarded for his defence of royal prerogatives with the title Marqués de la Regalía and a pension: A.G.I., Ind. Gen. 60, R.C., 24 June 1738; the second author with a grant of 4,000 *pesos*: F. Osores, *Noticias bío-bibliográficas de los alumnos distinguidos del colegio de San Ildefonso* (2 vols., Mexico, 1908), ii, 185–6.

cerning its legal origin: one theory, influenced by foreign works on the divine right of kings,[1] asserted that the authority of vicar general was derived directly from God as an inherent right of temporal sovereignty; and the second theory based this authority on the *patronato* concession of the early sixteenth century. Although the first theory, by declaring that the *patronato* concession was superfluous and merely recognized rights already granted to the Crown,[2] had the obvious advantage of eliminating any dependence on the Holy See, the Crown preferred to base this claim in public statements on the papal bulls, which provided a more convincing appearance of legitimacy but which could be interpreted to suit the needs of royal absolutism.

Whether derived directly from God or via apostolic delegation, the purpose of the *vicariato* was the same: to extend royal power at the expense of papal authority. Indeed, the Crown's official sanction of this regalist concept, expressed in a royal *cédula* of 1765, stated that the pope's authority in the Indies actually devolved upon the king in all areas of ecclesiastical jurisdiction except for the *potestad de orden*, or those powers acquired through ecclesiastical ordination, which by their nature cannot be transferred to laymen.[3]

Although the patron's responsibility to protect his ecclesiastical foundation had always been considered an adjunct to his right of presentation,[4] the Spanish kings, by replacing the pope as head of the American Church, could regulate almost every aspect of colonial life that pertained to the Church's spiritual mission. In particular they could exercise an almost unlimited authority over the clergy through the ecclesiastical superiors, since they maintained that a missionary's or curate's conduct was as much the responsibility of the royal patron or vicar as the provision of a sufficient number of parish churches and

---

[1] For an excellent study of the introduction of divine right theories into Spanish colonial jurisprudence, see M. Góngora, 'Estudios sobre el Galicanismo y la "Ilustración Católica" en la América española', *Revista Chilena de Historia y Geografía*, no. 125 (1957), pp. 102–9, 117–20.

[2] A. de Ribadeneyra y Barrientos, *op. cit.*, particularly p. 57, where the author claims to find origins for the *patronato* and *vicariato* in the Book of Genesis.

[3] R.A.H., Col. Mata Linares 9, R.C., 14 July 1765.

[4] See W. Ullmann, *The Growth of Papal Government in the Middle Ages* (London, 1955), pp. 69–70, for the origin of the patron's role as *defensor ecclesiae*.

endowments for cathedral fabrics.[1] This concept did not originate with the Spanish colonial empire, since from medieval times the worldly lord had considered it his duty to call upon the bishop to ensure the amendment of a delinquent ecclesiastical subject. But it was developed by the Spanish Crown into a theory of secular control over ecclesiastical discipline in which the independent jurisdiction of the Church was preserved only in appearance and the ecclesiastical superiors were mere executors of royal decisions.

Two cases of forgery in 1787, one in Peru and the other in Mexico, illustrate the application of this theory. A Mercedarian friar in Lima, accused of forging a royal *cédula*, was sent by the Viceroy to Spain, where the King ordered the Mercedarian General to sentence the culprit to imprisonment in the royal fortress in Ceuta, with the condition that he should not be released after serving his term without express royal permission.[2] The general complied. In the second case, a Franciscan from the province of Zacatecas in New Spain, who had re-written part of a royal *cédula*, was interrogated by a royal magistrate, deported by the viceroy to Spain, and kept in the custody of the Council of the Indies until sentence was pronounced on him. Here too, the Spanish *comisario general* of the order promptly obeyed the Council's order to confine the friar in a corrective monastery until the king should order his release.[3] Except for the rubber-stamp intervention of the ecclesiastical superiors and the absence of a formal arraignment in both cases, there is little to distinguish the treatment of these two friars from that of the Crown's lay subjects.

It was clearly out of the question for the central government in Madrid to take full judicial responsibility for every case of ecclesiastical misconduct in so vast an overseas empire. In some cases similar to the two involving forgery, the Council of the Indies did take formal cognizance of an ecclesiastic's offence

---

[1] For a résumé of royal *vicariato* powers, see B.N., 10653, Respuesta Fiscal, Council of the Indies, 16 Aug. 1774.

[2] A.G.I., Ind. Gen. 563, Consulta Council, 19 Oct., 1787, and real resolución 14 Jan. 1788.

[3] A.G.I., Guadalajara 357, Viceroy Revillagigedo to the king, 27 March 1790; Consulta Council, 3 Jan. 1792; Comisario General to Ventura de Taranco, 7 Feb. 1792.

on the basis of substantial evidence forwarded from the colonies.[1] But in many others the Crown left greater discretion to the ecclesiastical superiors, ordering them to investigate more fully certain allegations made to the government in Madrid, although specifying what punishment should be imposed if the accused were found guilty.[2]

A co-operative and efficient prelate could solve a disciplinary problem in full accordance with royal will and with a minimum of fuss. But at times the prelate was either unable or unwilling to correct his subordinates, and the Crown was then compelled to intervene more decisively by passing judgement and imposing a suitable penalty itself. Between 1788 and 1800 the Crown commissioned three different prelates to take action against several canons of the Michoacán chapter accused of unruly and scandalous behaviour. The first prelate, the Bishop of Michoacán, declined to call the canons to account, fearing the turmoil and further scandal they would create because of their 'very aggressive and belligerent characters'.[3] The Archbishop of Mexico, next to be commissioned, died before he could begin his task; and the Bishop of Guadalajara, who did conduct an inquiry into the matter, wrote to the Crown that he saw no need for any corrective measures in what he termed 'one of the usual conflicts prevalent in ecclesiastical chapters',[4] even though the inquiry had revealed that one of the canons was a notorious profligate, that another had attacked a fellow canon with a dagger, and that all of them were noted for violent tempers and troublemaking. Since these excesses continued unchecked, the Council finally decided to intervene directly and sentence two of the worst offenders to supernumerary status at half pay.[5]

---

[1] See, for example, A.G.I., Mexico 2614, Respuesta Fiscal Council, 19 Feb. 1769, and R.C. to the Bishop of Málaga, 12 March 1769, concerning an ecclesiastic deported from Mexico; and Guadalajara 358, Respuesta Fiscal, 17 March 1794, and Franciscan Comisario General to the Council, 14 July 1794.

[2] A.G.I., Mexico 2628, R.C. to Archbishop of Mexico, 22 Jan. 1770; Carta acordada to Archbishop of Mexico, 20 Oct. 1778 (concerning another case); and Guadalajara 315, Real orden to Bishop of Guadalajara, 17 March 1803.

[3] A.G.I., Mexico 2637, Bishop of Michoacán to Ventura de Taranco, 17 June 1788.

[4] A.G.I., Guadalajara 315, Bishop of Guadalajara to Antonio Caballero, 16 April 1802.

[5] A.G.I., Mexico 2544, Consulta Council, 17 Nov. 1802.

The American prelates were accustomed to regard the king as the effective head of the American Church even before the *vicariato* concept received its fullest expression in the middle of the eighteenth century. For this reason they willingly executed royal judicial sentences without considering that these sentences violated ecclesiastical immunity much more directly than the intervention of the vice-patrons in patronage litigation and in the removal of beneficiaries, to which many of them objected so strongly.[1]

The *vicariato* prerogatives were not limited to the control of individual ecclesiastics in specific cases, but extended, under the absolutist rule of Charles III, to the supervision of legislative and administrative reforms affecting the American clergy as a whole. Charles III conducted two major experiments in the reform of ecclesiastical discipline in the Indies through the medium of the ecclesiastical hierarchy: the provincial councils and the reforming *visitas* of the religious orders. Both experiments are particularly relevant to a study of the Mexican Church, for they were inspired by two prelates from the viceroyalty of New Spain, Archbishop Lorenzana of Mexico and Bishop Francisco Fabián y Fuero of Puebla, and were most vigorously pursued in that area.

In order to gain the Crown's interest in their proposals for reform, the two prelates submitted reports early in 1768 on what they termed the 'deplorable state' of the colonial clergy.[2] Although they admitted that disorderly and immoral conduct was unfortunately prevalent among the secular clergy, they emphasized the decadence of monastic discipline and, making an exception of the communities of Descalzed Carmelites, they accused the other religious orders in New Spain of having completely abandoned their vows of poverty, chastity, and obedience. These reports, reinforced by similar allegations

[1] See, for example, A.G.I., Guadalajara 339, Representación del Obispo de Durango a la Audiencia, 19 April 1771.
[2] A.G.I., Ind. Gen. 3041, Respuesta Fiscal Campomanes, 26 June 1768, quotes letters from Archbishop Lorenzana and Bishop Fabián y Fuero to the king's confessor, dated 25 and 29 March 1768. See also Biblioteca Pública de Toledo, Colección Borbón-Lorenzana, vol. 178, nos. 3, 4, Escrito del Arzobispo de Mexico, 16 April 1768, and Relación enviada por el Obispo de Puebla, 21 April 1768.

from other sources,[1] convinced the king and his ministers that the American clergy were in need of drastic reform on the lines of the pre-Tridentine measures carried out by Cardinal Cisneros in the sixteenth century. Whether or not the alarming reports were accurate, there is no reason to doubt the sincerity of the Crown's belief that ecclesiastical morals and discipline in the Indies had degenerated greatly. However, the existence of such conditions was certainly convenient for the promotion of specific royal aims: the extension of royal authority over ecclesiastical administration and the clergy, especially the religious orders.

Lorenzana's and Fabián y Fuero's proposals were submitted to an extraordinary Council, composed of an equal number of peninsular prelates and royal councillors headed by the Count of Aranda, and were endorsed with enthusiasm. Under the conditions stipulated by the Council the reforms became royal projects whose primary end would be to further the Crown's interests, and they were to be carried out by the ecclesiastical superiors under the strict supervision of the State. It was not even necessary, according to the Council (nor, it might have added, expedient), to seek the prior consent of the pope, since the king, 'as patron and protector of the Church', had sufficient authority to take any measures that would 'lead the clergy back to the path of virtue from which they had strayed'.[2]

Royal authority over these reforms could hardly have been more complete had they been carried out by the Crown's own officials. Both the provincial councils and the *visitas* were ordered by the king,[3] who also decided their precise content. The four *visitadores* from each religious order (for the Philippines and the viceroyalties of Peru, New Granada and New Spain) were furnished with detailed instructions on the specific reforms the king desired and the methods they were to follow in

---

[1] A.G.I., Ind. Gen. 3041, Respuesta Fiscal, 26 June 1768, also mentions letters in the same vein from the Archbishop of Manila, 30 June 1767, and from Visitador José de Gálvez, 28 March 1768.

[2] *Ibid.*, Consulta Extraordinary Council, 3 July 1768.

[3] *Ibid.*, R.C. to all metropolitan archbishops in the Indies and the Philippines, 21 Aug. 1769; and Ind. Gen. 3040, R.C. to generals of all religious orders in the Indies, 27 July 1769.

D

imposing them.[1] Similarly, the Crown dictated in advance a general outline, called the 'Tomo regio', of the legislation that was to be enacted by the provincial councils,[2] and also expressly prohibited the discussion of certain topics that might prove 'harmful to the *regalías*', especially any disputed areas of jurisdiction such as ecclesiastical immunity.[3] Not only were the ecclesiastical superiors instructed what to do and how to do it, but the proper fulfilment of these instructions was to be ensured by placing the reform projects under the immediate supervision of the colonial officials in each area and by subjecting them to royal review, for neither the canons passed by the provincial councils nor the measures imposed by the *visitadores* were to be considered valid until submitted to the Crown for confirmation.[4]

The ostensible purpose of these projects—the restoration of ecclesiastical discipline—although not abandoned, was subordinated to the purely political aims of the Crown. The underlying purpose, according to the extraordinary Council, was 'to preserve healthy principles of love and obedience to Your Majesty among the clergy',[5] who in turn were to instill these principles in the king's lay vassals 'by example and exhortation'.[6] Some of the measures dictated by the Crown, such as the establishment of diocesan theological seminaries and the restoration of community life among the regulars, had the laudable aim of improving the morals of the clergy and encouraging the proper performance of their spiritual duties. But many of them were clearly designed to curtail the independence of the clergy, particularly the regulars, who were subjected to increased control from both the diocesan authorities and the State,[7] and to strengthen secular authority over ecclesiastical administration in general.

The ecclesiastical superiors co-operated fully in executing the

---

[1] A.G.I., Ind. Gen. 3040, Instrucción para visitadores-reformadores, 26 May 1771.

[2] 'Tomo regio', dated 21 Aug. 1769, published in J. Tejada y Ramiro, *op. cit.*, vi, Part i, 315–17.

[3] A.G.I., Ind. Gen. 3041, Minuta de cédula, 24 July 1769.

[4] *Ibid.*, Consulta Extraordinary Council, 3 July 1768.

[5] *Ibid.*, Consulta, 3 July 1768.

[6] 'Instrucción para visitadores-reformadores', punto 7; 'Tomo regio', punto 8.

[7] 'Tomo regio', punto 17; 'Instrucción para visitadores-reformadores', punto 8.

royal orders. The Mexican bishops, the first to obey the *cédula* convoking the provincial councils, met in January 1771 and, under the vigorous (one delegate described it as 'tyrannical')[1] leadership of Archbishop Lorenzana, dutifully followed the agenda dictated by the Crown. The intervention of the *asistente real*, or royal observer appointed by the viceroy, was completely superfluous, since Lorenzana and Bishop Fabián y Fuero of Puebla had already drafted the canons in conformity with the 'Tomo regio':[2] they were passed with scarcely any debate, and that usually limited to a discussion of which royal laws should be cited in support of particular canons.[3] Fabián y Fuero protested against the *asistente's* constant interruptions with the well-justified statement that the bishops were fully as zealous as he in defending the Crown's prerogatives,[4] and in some instances they took an even more regalist position than the royal ministers who had drafted the 'Tomo regio'. The Council had merely been instructed to encourage loyalty to the Crown among the clergy, but the bishops were so eager to demonstrate their zeal that they created two canons on their own initiative which prescribed the penalty of excommunication for anyone, layman or ecclesiastic, who acted or spoke against the king or failed to show respect for his commands.[5] Charles III expressed his appreciation of these efforts by promoting the two key figures in the Council, Lorenzana and Fabián y Fuero, to the sees of Toledo and Valencia in Spain shortly before the Council's conclusion.[6]

---

[1] Bishop Díaz Bravo of Durango, see above, p. 27, note 3.

[2] The Fourth Mexican Provincial Council (*CIVM*) is published in J. Tejada y Ramiro, *op. cit.*, vi, Part 1, 177–313. The original manuscript is located in the Biblioteca Pública de Toledo, Col. Borbón-Lorenzana, vol. 62. For an analysis of the Council's adherence to the 'Tomo regio', see M. Giménez Fernández, *El Concilio IV Provincial Mejicano* (Seville, 1939), pp. 111–19.

[3] B.N., 5806, Extracto compendioso de las actas del Concilio . . ., especially sessions 13 Jan., 19 Feb. and 14 March 1771.

[4] *Ibid.*, Diario de las operaciones del Concilio . . ., by Dr Ríos, quotes the bishop's speech in the entry of 10 March 1771. For a record of the *asistente's* many speeches and objections, see B.N., 19199, 19200, Compendio de todo lo trabajado durante el Concilio Provincial Mexicano, 6 May 1772, by Antonio de Ribadeneyra (also author of *Manual compendio del Regio Patronato Indiano*).

[5] *CIVM*, cánones 2, 8, título 16, Libro 1.

[6] B.N., 10653, Respuesta Fiscal, Council of the Indies, 16 Aug. 1774, mentions these promotions as proof that the king was 'well pleased' with the Council.

The co-operation of the secular hierarchy in these projects is not surprising. Mindful of their dependence on royal favour, the bishops also regarded royal policies as a means of enhancing their own authority at the expense of papal supremacy and the independence of the religious orders and, even if some of the reforms involved increased royal control over their own activities, under the *vicariato* system the kings were careful to preserve the appearance of an equal partnership between the episcopate and the Crown. What is surprising is that the regular superiors were almost equally obliging. Far from resenting the king's initiative or the fact that he claimed the right to choose the *visitadores*, the generals of the religious orders endorsed the project fully and submitted their lists of nominees. The Augustinian General even suggested that the king should select the *visita* secretaries as well.[1] They were unlikely to object to the item in the general instructions for the *visitas* calling for the encouragement of holy studies, but neither did they question the Crown's right to meddle in the internal administration of the orders and to authorize the viceroys to regulate the number of friars and monasteries in each province.[2]

The regulars were far more disposed to submit to royal authority than to that of the bishops. The local superiors attending the Mexican Provincial Council as observers objected to the canons which placed many of their activities under diocesan control,[3] but they and the *visitadores* accepted without a murmur the intervention of the viceroy in all aspects of the *visitas*, from his preliminary investigation of the general state of each order, which were used as the basis of the reforms, to his supervision of the specific measures taken. The peninsular *visitadores*, entrusted with a difficult task in unfamiliar surroundings, understandably welcomed the added support of the viceroy's authority and were eager to let him settle the many disputes that arose between them and the local superiors and other friars.[4] They also submitted their final reports to the

---

[1] A.G.I., Ind. Gen. 3040, General of the Augustinians to the king, 14 Sept. 1769; see also Consulta Extraordinary Council, 27 Oct. 1769.

[2] *Ibid.*, 'Instrucción para visitadores-reformadores', 1771, puntos 4, 5.

[3] B.N., 5806, Extracto compendioso, particularly sessions 10 and 12 October 1771.

[4] For viceregal adjudication of conflicts during the *visitas* of the Franciscan and

viceroy, who had the responsibility of deciding whether the *visitas* had been concluded in accordance with the Crown's instructions before forwarding the reports to Madrid for royal confirmation.[1]

If these ambitious projects produced few tangible results, it was obviously not because of any resistance from independent-minded prelates. The vast size of the colonies, their distance from the centre of power, and a natural reluctance to change deeply rooted habits inevitably weakened the impetus of any reform programme. But one of the most important obstacles to the success of these particular projects was the excessive amount of secular intervention. The Fourth Mexican Provincial Council had little or no effect on ecclesiastical administration in New Spain. By insisting on royal confirmation as a pre-requisite for its validity, the Crown condemned the Council to years of drifting from one government office to another, while different *fiscales* and ministers examined each canon for possible infringements of royal prerogatives.[2] Archbishop Lorenzana had already expressed doubts concerning the reception of the Council's proposals in Rome, in view of the regalist tenor of many of the canons and the State's supervision through the 'Tomo regio' and the *asistente real*;[3] and the Spanish Minister in Rome, finally entrusted in 1792 with the task of obtaining papal approval, without flatly refusing to try, indicated that such an attempt would be completely fruitless.[4] Thus, lacking

[1] See for example, B.N. 2706, Visita-reforma de la Provincia de Nueva España (Mercedarian order), 1771–9. For similar material concerning other religious orders, see A.G.I., Mexico 2743, Expediente sobre la reforma de la Orden de S. Juan de Dios, completed in 1785; Mexico 2744, Expediente sobre la reforma de S. Hipólito Mártir, completed in 1791; Mexico 2747, reform of the Dominicans, 1786; Mexico 2748–9, Agonizantes (San Camilo Lelis), 1787; Mexico 2750–1, Bethlemites, 1804.

[2] The numerous *respuestas* and *consultas* of the Council from 1772 to 1803 are contained in A.G.I., Mexico 2711, Expediente sobre la aprobación del Concilio Cuarto Provincial Mexicano, 1772–1803. See also B.N. 10653, Respuesta Fiscal, 16 Aug. 1774; and Biblioteca del Palacio, 1439, Consulta Council, 5 March 1776.

[3] A.G.I., Ind. Gen. 3026, Lorenzana to Arriaga, 19 Nov. 1774.

[4] A.G.I., Mexico 2711, José de Azara to Ventura de Taranco, 28 March 1792.

Bethlemite orders, see *Administración de Bucareli*, ii, 290–1, 298–301, 311–14, Bucareli to Arriaga, 27 May 1773, Bucareli to the king, 27 Oct. 1773, and 27 Oct. 1774.

either royal or papal confirmation, the Council's enactments were never even promulgated in the viceroyalty, much less put into effect.

The reform *visitas* met with little more success, dragging on for years—one into the nineteenth century—and long before their completion the king conceded that they were not accomplishing the reforms that had been outlined.[1] Aside from the almost impossible scale of the task, the main reason for this failure was the ultra-regalist system of administration in the Indies, which made available almost unlimited opportunities for obstruction to those friars who were unwilling to accept the new restrictions made by the *visitadores*. Since any onerous provision could be appealed to the viceroy (and sometimes to the *audiencia*), the enactment of reforms could at the very least be delayed, if not prevented entirely. Thus the civil encroachments on the Church's jurisdiction, which were so energetically advanced by the regalists, were the main obstacle to their cherished reform programme. This conflict was in fact the major defect of the *vicariato* system in general: under this system, royal control of the clergy was channelled in the main through the ecclesiastical superiors, yet the many forms of secular interference in ecclesiastical administration (such as executive intervention and judicial review of ecclesiastical cases,[2] in addition to the patronage prerogatives) undermined the prelates' authority and actually hindered the effective control of their subordinates.

---

[1] 'Instrucción reservada', 8 July 1787, art. 90, in *Obras originales del Conde de Floridablanca*, p. 226.

[2] See Chs. II and III for a discussion of executive intervention and judicial review in *visitas* and other areas of ecclesiastical jurisdiction.

CHAPTER II

Control of the Clergy by
Executive Intervention

I. ADMINISTRATIVE DECREES AND THE
'PROCESO INFORMATIVO'

ROYAL CONTROL over the actions of individual ecclesiastics through the *patronato* prerogatives was far from complete, since it depended for the most part on the Church's own jurisdiction. Unwilling to rely entirely on these prerogatives, the Habsburg kings devised another method of dealing with their ecclesiastical subjects which, although resting on different principles in respect to royal authority over the clergy, did not replace the *patronato* system, but was exercised alternately or in conjunction with it, whatever the specific case might require.

This method, which can be described as executive intervention, employed various administrative rather than judicial measures, such as secret inquests, sentence by executive decree, and exile, procedures which in effect amounted to trial and punishment, but which Spanish jurists, by legalistic juggling of terms, could claim did not infringe the ecclesiastical privilege of immunity. The comparatively modern theory of the separation of powers was not even recognized in Spanish jurisprudence, since the king was considered to be the source of all authority—legislative, judicial, and executive[1]—and all three powers were exercised in varying circumstances by the same representatives of the Crown. The *audiencias*, for example, were primarily judicial bodies, but they often performed administrative functions and passed legislation in the form of *provisiones reales*.[2] However, a useful if not always apparent distinction

---

[1] A. García Gallo, *Historia del derecho español* (2 vols., Madrid, 1941), i, 245, 462.
[2] For an analysis of the audiencia's different functions, see J. H. Parry, *The*

39

was made between the king's judicial and his executive, or 'economic',[1] authority when dealing with his ecclesiastical subjects, since royal jurists could argue that any measure taken under the latter did not violate the clergy's judicial immunity.

This concept of the *poder económico* was developed during the seventeenth century, primarily by two jurists serving the Crown in Peru, Pedro Frasso and Juan Luis López,[2] and continued without alteration as a major source of royal policy until the end of the colonial period. Both jurists, as well as later regalist authors,[3] produced several different theories (usually in the same work) to justify this system of control over the clergy: either it was another corollary to the papal concession of the *patronato*; or ecclesiastical immunity was a royal grant, not a privilege contained in divine law, and therefore rescindable; or this authority was part of the royal *poder económico*, supposedly inherent in the nature of temporal sovereignty. This last theory was the most convenient, since it excluded any dependence on papal concessions (which in theory could also be rescinded) and avoided a direct clash with canon law by ignoring the question of ecclesiastical immunity altogether.

López and Frasso both based their argument on the principle that ecclesiastics did not cease to be royal subjects when they took holy orders, so that the king had the right to regulate all their actions not directly related to their sacramental functions.[4] And in order to ensure that they obeyed the laws of the realm,

---

[1] The use of this term as synonymous with administrative was derived from the original definition of *económico*, 'pertaining to the administration of property'. Real Academia de la Lengua, *Diccionario de la lengua castellana* (Madrid, 1780).

[2] P. Frasso, *De regio patronatu indiarum* (Madrid, 1677), Libro 1; J. López (Marqués del Risco), *Discurso jurídico, histórico-político en defensa de la jurisdicción real* (Lima, 1685).

[3] See A.G.I., Mexico 2617, Respuesta Fiscal de lo Civil, 5 March 1763; and Biblioteca del Palacio, 1492, Defensa de la jurisdicción real, by (Antonio) Joaquín de Ribadeneyra, Mexico, January 1763, two lengthy apologies of executive intervention based on the theories of Frasso and López.

[4] P. Frasso, *op. cit.*, Libro 1, cap. 45, nos. 1–3; J. López, *op. cit.*, cap. 9.

Audiencia of New Galicia in the Sixteenth Century (Cambridge, 1948), Part II. T. Esquivel Obregón, *Apuntes para la historia del derecho en México* (4 vols., Mexico, 1937–47), ii, 88, 335–41, 423–5, discusses the interchange of functions in the different governmental bodies in the colonies.

he could submit them to certain purely administrative measures by virtue of his 'economic' authority.

In practice there was often nothing to distinguish this 'economic' authority from the State's judicial and coercive authority except the terminology used by the royal officials. There were, for example, numerous disputes among cathedral canons or between them and their bishops which the viceroys settled by executive decree, but which were otherwise identical with the patronage suits they heard in their capacity of vice-patron.[1]

Executive intervention, however, had the advantage of a wider scope of action than the patronage prerogatives, so that more drastic measures could be taken if adjudication did not prove successful. In 1771, for example, Viceroy Carlos de Croix (Marqués de Croix) commissioned an investigation into the bitter disputes among the members of the cathedral chapter of Durango, which he had tried unsuccessfully to settle several times in the past.[2] The investigation indicated that the dean was the main cause of the dissension, and he was confined by viceregal order in a monastery in Mexico until Croix's successor, Viceroy Antonio de Bucareli, issued another executive decree ordering his release six months later.[3]

Both viceroys emphasized the extra-judicial nature of their intervention. Croix ignored the dean's protest that he had, in effect, been sentenced to imprisonment and denied him permission to appeal to the archdiocesan court in Mexico since, in the opinion of the viceregal *asesor general*, the viceroy had not taken judicial cognizance of the case.[4] Bucareli also denied permission to appeal the original decree and declined to hear the dean's defence, but simply released him after deciding that six months of confinement had chastened him sufficiently.[5]

[1] For examples of executive intervention in patronage disputes, see A.G.I., Mexico 2627, Expediente de los pleitos entre el Revdo. Obispo de Puebla y su Venerable Cabildo, 1778; and *Instrucciones que los virreyes de Nueva España dejaron a sus sucesores* (2 vols., Mexico, 1873), ii, 754–60 (Félix Berenguer de Marquina, 1803). See above, pp. 20–2, for judicial intervention in patronage suits.

[2] A.G.I., Guadalajara 341, Expediente de la pesquisa secreta hecha contra el Deán de la Sta. Iglesia de Durango, 1770. Guadalajara 566 contains material on a series of disputes between members of the Durango Chapter, 1754–68.

[3] A.G.I., Guadalajara 545, Bucareli to Arriaga, 20 Dec. 1771.

[4] A.G.I., Guadalajara 341, Dictamen Diego de Cornide, 20 Sept. 1771.

[5] A.G.I., Guadalajara 545, Bucareli to Arriaga, 20 Dec. 1771.

The efficiency of the various methods of executive intervention lay precisely in the possibility of avoiding the judicial
formalities which were equally cumbersome in the ecclesiastical
and civil courts.[1] One viceroy of Peru, in recommending
administrative measures to his successor, assured him that 'there
would never be sufficient time to attend to the multitude of
claims, allegations, objections, and other interpellations that
the ecclesiastics plead in their favour', if judicial procedures
were followed.[2]

Usually the only distinction between judicial and administrative acts was that the ecclesiastic in question was deprived of
the due process of law in either the ecclesiastical or civil courts
and was actually in a worse position than one of the Crown's
lay subjects. The *proceso informativo*, or summary inquiry, for
example, was carried out in secret without even notifying the
accused, who was thus prevented from testifying in his defence
and kept ignorant of the charges against him.[3] The *proceso
informativo* was the most legally ambiguous administrative
measure. Although the canonists protested that these inquiries
clearly violated the subject's privilege of *fuero*,[4] civil jurists
argued that the *proceso* only resembled the initial stage of a
criminal trial, but its purpose was solely information, not indictment, and that, since neither prosecutor, defendant, verdict,
nor sentence was involved, it was an extra-judicial process.[5]

The usefulness of such a procedure is obvious: royal officials
could investigate the actions of any ecclesiastic without having
to rely on his superior, who might be either incompetent or too
lenient, and they could then force the superior to take action
based on this evidence, or they could use the evidence themselves

[1] J. de Hevia Bolaños, *Curia Philipica* (Madrid, 1615), is the most thorough
contemporary work on the Spanish judicial system. See Parts I, 'Juicio civil',
and III, 'Juicio Criminal', for forensic procedure.

[2] M. de Amat y Junient, *op. cit.*, pp. 9–10.

[3] See, e.g., the petition from the Dean of Durango to the viceroy, 18 Sept.
1771, asking to be told the charges against him and to be heard in defence, in
A.G.I., Guadalajara 341.

[4] D. de Avendaño, *Thesaurus indicus* (2 vols., Antwerp, 1668–77), i, título 2,
cap. 11, part 2. See also 'Ofensa y defensa de la libertad eclesiástica', commissioned
by the Archbishop of Lima, 1685, published as an appendix to and refuted in
J. López, *Discurso jurídico*.

[5] J. de Solórzano, *op. cit.*, Libro 4, cap. 27, nos. 34 and 36; J. López, *Discurso
jurídico*, cap. 7.

to justify more rigorous intervention. In 1778 the *Comandante General* of the Provincias Internas in northern New Spain commissioned several subordinates to conduct a secret inquiry into the administration of the Franciscan missions in Parral. For years the Franciscan provincial in Zacatecas had been countering the *comandante*'s demands for reform with assurances that the new *custodio* of the missions was eliminating all the abuses. But the evidence obtained in the inquiry revealed, on the contrary, that this same *custodio* was the major cause of the abuses: he had been enriching himself by appropriating the stipends of the other friars (which in turn forced them to extract unpaid labour from the Indians), by raising cattle on land stolen from the Indians, and by selling them goods for exorbitant payments in kind.[1] A massive report based on the inquiry was sent to the Crown and, although subsequent royal orders to the Franciscan superiors for a thorough reorganization of the missions may not have produced spectacular results,[2] at least the *comandante* was able to justify his order expelling the offending *custodio* and confiscating all illegally held mission property.[3]

Executive intervention in ecclesiastical affairs was often a necessary means of preserving public order. The frequent disputes among ecclesiastics required secular adjudication and even the use of force, especially in the number of violent disturbances created by the regular clergy in this period. The main cause of disputes among the regulars was the rivalry for power between the Creoles and peninsular Spaniards in each order.[4] They were supposed to alternate in the higher offices, but in practice those in power would try to ensure re-election, often by sentencing members of the opposing faction to loss of vote or by sending them to the missions immediately before the *capítulos*, or biennial meetings to elect superiors.[5] Viceregal

[1] A.G.I., Guadalajara 545, Extracto de autos preparados por D. Galindo Navarro y D. Francisco de Campos de orden del Comandante General . . . en 7 cuadernos, 17 Nov. 1778.
[2] A.G.I., Guadalajara 243, Consulta Council, 14 Aug. 1783.
[3] A.G.I., Guadalajara 545, Comandante General Teodoro de Croix to the king, 23 May 1780.
[4] See A.H.N., Códices 717, Real instrucción al Presidente de Guatemala, 23 Sept. 1779, para. 20.
[5] See *Administración de Bucareli*, ii, 310, Bucareli to the king, 27 Oct. 1774.

admonitions and arbitration were often sufficient to restore order, but at times the friars became so turbulent that members of the *audiencia* had to supervise the voting in person,[1] and on two occasions, one in 1780 and another in 1787, the viceroy called out troops to pacify brawling friars armed with sticks and to rescue members of the losing faction.[2] These public disturbances were only the noisiest incidents in the seemingly endless squabbles that destroyed much of the effectiveness and good name of the religious orders towards the end of the colonial period. Almost every order was embroiled in upheavals, following a similar pattern of election disorders, accusations and counter-accusations of different crimes, and a general laxity of monastic discipline.[3] Some of these upheavals lasted for years, but the hospital order of Bethlemites was perhaps the most persistently troublesome: from the 1770's until the end of the colonial period successive viceroys were harrassed with a 'multitude of denunciations and *expedientes* concerning scandals, excesses, and internal discord'[4] and continual petitions requesting them to use their authority either to force recalcitrant friars to obey their superiors or, conversely, to prevent the superiors from oppressing their subordinates.[5] The peace-keeping tasks of the civil government had certainly become more difficult since the middle of the eighteenth century, when one viceroy assured his successor that the minor differ-

---

[1] *Documentos para la historia de México* (4 series, 20 vols., Mexico 1853–7), i, vii, 'Diario de José Gómez 1776–98' (an officer in the royal halberdiers stationed in the capital), p. 44, referring to the 1778 *capítulo* of the order of San Juan de Diós. See also Revillagigedo II, *Instrucción reservada* (1794), pp. 7–8, on *capítulos* of the Franciscans and Augustinians; and Biblioteca del Palacio, 3078, Instrucción del virrey Miguel José de Azanza a su sucesor Félix Berenguer de Marquina, 24 April 1800, on recent *capítulos* of the Franciscans, *Dieguinos*, and Dominicans.

[2] 'Diario de José Gómez', pp. 89–92, 284.

[3] *Administración de Bucareli*, ii, 311–14, Bucareli to the king, 27 Oct. 1774; and A.G.I., Mexico 1285, Expediente sobre las desavenencias . . ., 1785, on the Franciscan order; Mexico 2540, Expediente sobre los desórdenes . . . en la orden de San Hipólito Mártir, 1787–91; and for material on civil intervention in the disturbances arising during the various reform *visitas*, see the sources cited on p. 37, note 1.

[4] *Instrucciones que los virreyes* (Berenguer de Marquina, 1803), ii, 650–3.

[5] A.G.I., Mexico 2604, Bucareli to Lorenzana, 27 Aug. 1773; *Administración de Bucareli*, ii, 299–302, Bucareli to the king, 27 Oct. 1773; A.G.I., Mexico 1150, R.C.'s to Archbishop and Viceroy of Mexico, 22 Sept. 1801, 23 Feb. 1803 and 22 May 1805.

ences arising during the elections of regular superiors were easily smoothed over.[1]

Executive intervention was clearly an encroachment on the clergy's immunity and the judicial jurisdiction of their superiors, no matter how much royal jurists tried to disguise the fact with terms like 'paternal corrections' and 'preventive measures'.[2] Yet ecclesiastical opposition was far from universal. The regulars did not object to secular intervention in their quarrels. In fact, their constant petitions and denunciations forced the royal officials to take the roles of magistrate and constable and were a source of exasperation to the civil government rather than a welcome opportunity to exert secular authority over the clergy.[3] Ecclesiastics often protested if an administrative measure happened to favour an opponent in a dispute or checked their ambitions in some way, but they were less likely to challenge the measure's fundamental legality than to request a reversal of the decision or try to influence the State to shift its support to their side in a dispute.[4]

Oscillating royal support actually prolonged the disputes in many cases. A good example was the struggle between the Bishops of Puebla and the various orders of nuns in that diocese over the attempted reforms of convent life, a struggle that kept the city in turmoil for over ten years (1770–81). It was impossible to settle the issue definitely, because the king sent a series of conflicting *cédulas* to the colonial officials, ordering secular intervention that alternately favoured the nuns and their reformers, in accordance with the latest petition he had received from the disputants.[5]

The colonial bishops acknowledged the legality of executive intervention as long as it was used in support of, or at least did not conflict with, their own authority. They agreed that a secular official could gather evidence and take provisional

[1] *Instrucciones que los virreyes* (Count of Revillagigedo I, 1754), i, 370–1.

[2] A.G.I., Mexico 2617, Respuesta Fiscal de lo Civil, 5 March 1763.

[3] See Biblioteca del Palacio, Col. Ayala 31, Instrucción del virrey Cruíllas al Marqués de Croix, 1766; and M. de Amat y Junient, *op. cit.*, pp. 90–1.

[4] See, e.g., Mexico 2641, Comisario General de San Juan de Diós to Matías de Gálvez, 16 Sept. 1784, asking him to use his executive authority to 'punish the real culprits', i.e., his opponents.

[5] A.G.I., Mexico 2604, Expediente sobre la vida común de las monjas de Puebla . . ., 1770–81.

action against a delinquent ecclesiastic, but only if there were no ecclesiastical judge in the vicinity,[1] and a bishop might even ask the viceroy to confine or deport a subordinate, explaining that he had no means other than persuasion and reprimands to discipline him and had to rely entirely on the civil authorities whenever coercion was necessary.[2] But the bishops were quick to raise the standard of ecclesiastical immunity whenever an administrative measure was neither solicited nor convenient.

Such was the case in a *competencia* that arose in Guadalajara in 1778 over the *audiencia*'s use of the *proceso informativo*. The curate of one of the mining towns in the district, who showed signs of insanity, had assaulted his coadjutor and created a public disturbance while resisting efforts to conduct him to the bishop in the capital.[3] Royal law authorized civil magistrates to inquire secretly into crimes committed by ecclesiastics if there were any danger of public scandal, for the purpose of informing the ecclesiastical courts,[4] yet the investigation commissioned by the *audiencia* in this case fulfilled none of the law's requirements: there was no further danger of public scandal, since the unfortunate curate was in the bishop's custody before the *audiencia* even heard of the matter; nor was it necessary to gather information for the benefit of the ecclesiastical court, which had already begun proceedings.

The *audiencia* represented its refusal to call off the inquiry, even after the Bishop had threatened to excommunicate the *oidores* for usurping his 'exclusive jurisdiction',[5] as a courageous defence of royal authority.[6] But the Council of the Indies failed to see the case in that light and informed the *audiencia* of the king's 'extreme displeasure' at their imprudent actions, which were ascribed to 'ignorance or excess of zeal'.[7]

The colonial officials were not always sure of either the nature or the extent of their 'economic' authority over the

[1] *CIVM*, canon 14, título 11, Libro 2.
[2] A.G.I., Guadalajara 545, Bishop of Durango to the king, 2 June 1771.
[3] A.G.I., Guadalajara 343, Testimonio de autos formados por orden de la audiencia, 1778; and Guadalajara 310, Cuaderno de autos mandados por el Revdo. Obispo de Guadalajara, 1778. Both versions agree on the facts of the case.
[4] *Recop. Indias*, ley 73, título 14, Libro 1.
[5] A.G.I., Guadalajara 343, Bishop Antonio Alcalde to the king, 7 Dec. 1778.
[6] *Ibid.*, Audiencia to the king, 11 Dec. 1778.
[7] A.G.I., Guadalajara 533, Consulta Council, 16 Nov. 1780.

clergy. Even in secular matters the boundary between their administrative and judicial functions lacked clear definition, although the law code attempted to distinguish between the two,[1] and the officials rarely agreed, for example, on the subject of which viceregal measures were judicial and could, therefore, be appealed to the *audiencias*.[2] The laws regarding executive control of the clergy were equally vague, and the central government's inconsistent interpretation of them, as in many other areas of colonial jurisprudence, only added to the confusion.

A case in the 1780's illustrates the chaos created by this lack of a clearly defined and consistent policy. Several members of the order of San Juan de Diós appealed to Viceroy Matías de Gálvez to assist them in suspending their *comisario general* from office so that they could try him for simony and embezzling.[3] Instead, the viceroy decided to take cognizance of the case himself in an administrative capacity and he ordered the *comisario* to be confined in a monastery in Puebla for the duration of the inquiry. But when the *audiencia* assumed the viceroy's functions after Gálvez's sudden death, the *oidores* decided that Gálvez had exceeded his authority. They declared themselves incompetent to continue the inquiry and ordered the release and reinstatement of the *comisario*.[4]

The conflicting views held by the viceroy and *audiencia* on the legality of these executive measures were mirrored in the contradictory opinions of the Madrid government. In 1785 the Crown sent a royal order, issued by the Ministry of Marina y las Indias, approving of the viceroy's actions and instructing his successor to continue the *proceso informativo*.[5] Yet less than a year later the Council of the Indies condemned these same actions in a *carta acordada*. The Council's rebuke was reserved for the viceroy's advisers, the *fiscal de lo civil* and the *asesor general*, whose recommendations he had merely endorsed. They

[1] *Recop. Indias*, leyes 32–8, título 15, Libro 2.
[2] See A.G.I., Mexico 1142, Consulta Council, 8 March 1806, concerning a particular disagreement between the viceroy and *audiencia* and lamenting the frequency of these disputes throughout the colonies.
[3] A.G.I., Mexico 2641, Expediente en tres partes de las diligencias . . ., 1784–5.
[4] *Ibid.*, Audiencia governadora to the king, 24 April 1785.
[5] *Ibid.*, R.O. to the Viceroy of New Spain, 22 Sept. 1785, por la vía reservada.

were informed that the measures taken against the *comisario*, which amounted to a criminal trial *in absentia*, would be considered illegal even against a lay subject, and that in recommending them both advisers had shown 'a culpable ignorance of both royal and canon law'.[1] The fact that the two directives were issued by different royal agencies helps to explain the opposing interpretations of the law—the royal councils tended to favour a more cautious, legalistic policy than the individual ministers (and this particular minister, José de Gálvez, would be even more inclined to support the actions of the deceased viceroy, who was his brother). But the Mexican government was understandably 'perplexed over which of Your Majesty's commands should be carried out'.[2]

It is impossible to determine what form of intervention would have been appropriate in this case. The viceroy's measures had only increased the disturbances and public scandal they were supposed to prevent: the public learned of the order's internal problems as a result of the *comisario*'s notorious arrest and exile,[3] and in his absence the instigators were able to increase the chaos by implicating their other enemies in the secret inquiry. The *audiencia*'s policy (confirmed in the Council's *carta acordada*) of supporting the *comisario*'s attempts to prosecute his accusers completed the process of disintegration of discipline within the order, and the turmoil diminished gradually only after the *comisario*'s death and the arrival of a new *visitador* from Spain in 1791.[4]

2. EXPULSION

The *proceso informativo* was often used in conjunction with another executive measure: expulsion. The Spanish Crown claimed the exclusive authority to regulate all travel to and

---

[1] *Ibid.*, Carta acordada to the viceroy, the fiscal and the asesor, 12 April 1786.

[2] *Ibid.*, Archbishop Núñez de Haro (interim viceroy after the death, also sudden, of Bernardo de Gálvez, Matías's son) to the king, 20 June 1787.

[3] 'Diario de José Gómez', p. 192, entry for 4 Sept. 1784 mentioning the rumours and speculations set off by the arrest and exile under military escort of the *comisario*, in *Documentos para la historia de México*, I, vii.

[4] A.G.I., Mexico 2641, General of San Juan de Diós to the king, 28 April 1786, and to the Council, 18 May 1787; Fr Pedro de Jesús Medina, visitador, to the king, 2 Oct. 1793.

from the Indies, which included the right to expel any person, whether layman or ecclesiastic, whose presence there was deemed undesirable.[1] However, as Solórzano Pereira wrote, even the most humble lay vassal should not be expelled without good reason and, since royal officials could not justify the expulsion of an ecclesiastic in a formal trial, an extra-judicial investigation, or *proceso informativo*, would have to be substituted.[2]

The responsibility for dealing with a deported ecclesiastic once he arrived in Spain devolved upon the Council of the Indies, which required the evidence gathered in the *proceso informativo* in order to decide what further actions should be taken against him and also to judge whether this additional burden to its duties was in fact necessary. The apparently blanket law authorizing the expulsion of any ecclesiastic 'whose presence could result in scandal, sedition, or disturbances or could otherwise prove harmful to the republic'[3] obviously was not intended for use against every cleric who committed a crime or made a nuisance of himself; and the requirement that every deportee be accompanied by a report of the proceedings against him[4] served as an important check on the indiscriminate use of the measure. If the Council decided that the ecclesiastic's crime was not serious enough to warrant expulsion, it would send him back to the Indies with a reprimand to the colonial authorities.[5] One report, sent ten years late from Mexico, revealed that an unfortunate deportee, who had been kept in the prison of the *Casa de Contratación* in Cádiz since his arrival, had committed no crime at all but had been sent to Spain only because his religious order had expelled him for some minor infraction of the rules. The official responsible for this negligence received the customary notification of royal displeasure and the friar was set free.[6]

Thus, unless the colonial officials were willing to risk a royal

[1] J. de Solórzano Pereira, *Política indiana*, Libro 4, cap. 27, no. 7; G. de Villarroel, *Gobierno eclesiástico pacífico*, Part II, cap. 18, art. 3, maintained that expulsion was not a punishment and therefore did not violate ecclesiastical immunity, even though the author was a bishop.

[2] J. de Solórzano Pereira, *op. cit.*, Libro 4, cap. 27, no. 34.

[3] *Recop. Indias*, ley 1, título 6, Libro 1.

[4] *Ibid.*, ley 144, título 15, Libro 2.

[5] See, e.g., A.H.N., Códices 691, R.C. to Viceroy of Peru, 28 Feb. 1762.

[6] A.G.I., Ind. Gen. 68, Consulta Council, 6 Feb. 1783.

E

rebuke, they had to demonstrate that an expulsion order was both legal and expedient. Viceroy Croix's expulsion of two Mercedarian friars in 1770 fulfilled both requirements and accordingly received the Council's full approval. Croix had forbidden the Mercedarian provincial to attend the biennial *capítulo*, after receiving evidence from several sources that he was responsible for much of the strife and degeneration of morals within the order.[1] Disobeying this order, the provincial secured through bribery the election of his protégé, and together they proceeded to commission a *juez conservador* to investigate the viceroy's 'interference in the order's internal administration'.[2]

Since the Mercedarian *visitador* was unwilling to prosecute the two offenders in Mexico for fear of further scandal and dissension, the only alternative was to send them to Spain where the Council and the general of the order could punish them. The royal law ordering the expulsion of any regular who disrupted his order's *capítulo*,[3] which the viceroy cited in his decree, was perhaps only marginally applicable in this case, but the friars' disobedience and their challenge of the State's 'economic' authority supplied ample justification for this measure in the opinion of the Council.[4]

Royal officials were also authorized to expel apostate friars and any other ecclesiastics who resided in the Indies without royal permission. Apparently immigration regulations were not enforced very strictly, and it is likely that most of the ecclesiastics expelled under this rule would have escaped notice had they not violated other laws during their stay. The illegal entry in 1787 of a Spanish Carmelite, who had deserted the ship on which he was serving as chaplain, was discovered four years later only after the viceroy began to investigate certain reports about a friar who had been causing public disturbances in Puebla, Oaxaca, and Chiapas.[5] Similarly, a priest who had

[1] B.N., 2706, Testimonio de los autos hechos a consulta del Revdo. Obispo de Puebla, 1770, also containing a report from the Mercedarian *visitador*.

[2] A.G.I., Mexico 2618, Expediente sobre los motivos que tuvo el virrey de Nueva España . . ., 1770.

[3] *Recop. Indias*, ley 61. título 14, Libro 1.

[4] A.G.I., Mexico 2618, Consulta Council, 30 Oct. 1770.

[5] A.G.I., Mexico 1476, Testimonio de lo conducente del religioso carmelita Fr Nicolás de Guerrero, 1791–4, Cuaderno 1; Cuaderno 2 is located in Mexico 2646.

been expelled from the Capuchin order and entered Mexico in 1737 masquerading as a layman, managed to live there undetected until he was arrested by the civil authorities on the charge of concubinage in 1766. He was deported as soon as he revealed his true identity (in order to claim ecclesiastical immunity) and it was discovered that he had left Spain without royal permission.[1]

The original laws regarding the expulsion of ecclesiastics from the Indies were first promulgated ostensibly for the purpose of protecting the Indian neophytes from the harmful example of delinquent missionaries. But this executive measure soon became one of the most important instruments of royal control over the American clergy and an invaluable means of protecting the political interests of the State. The expulsion of ecclesiastics who had committed no specific offence, but whose mere presence was considered a danger to the State, was the most dramatic application of the Crown's 'economic' authority in the eighteenth century. On 25 June 1767 the members of the Society of Jesus, scattered in colleges and missions throughout most of New Spain, were suddenly notified of a Pragmatic Sanction ordering their immediate expulsion from the viceroyalty and all other royal dominions.[2] With the 'greatest submission to the King's will' they travelled under military escort to the port of Veracruz to embark for the Papal States,[3] where most of them were to die in exile. Many authors have dealt with the expulsion of the Jesuits from Spain and the Spanish colonies;[4] yet it is surprising, considering the wealth of opinions proffered about the motives behind this act and its

[1] A.G.I., Mexico 2614, Testimonio de los autos criminales fhos. contra Fr. Francisco de la Zerda . . ., 1768.

[2] *Decretos reales tocantes a la iglesia* (B.M.), no. 20, R.C., 5 April 1767, containing the Pragmatic Sanction of 2 April 1767.

[3] C. de Croix, *Cartas del Marqués de Croix* (Brussels, 1884), pp. 20–1, letter to his brother in Lille, 30 June 1767.

[4] Most histories of the reign of Charles III, such as A. Ferrer del Río, *Historia del reinado de Carlos III* (4 vols., Madrid, 1856), ii, 117–69, deal extensively with this topic. For details of the expulsion from Mexico and its consequences, see V. Rico González, ed., *Documentos sobre la expulsión de los Jesuitas y ocupación de sus temporalidades en Nueva España* (Mexico, 1949); and A. Pradeau y Avilés, *La expulsión de los Jesuitas de las provincias de Sonora, Ostimuri y Sinaloa en 1767* (Mexico, 1959), particularly pp. 25–120. For a discussion of the Crown's motives for this measure, see below, pp. 125–9, 137.

consequences, that the question of its legality has been ignored. Ruling over dominions in which adherence to canon law was largely taken for granted and over a population noted for its religious orthodoxy, Charles III could not be totally indifferent to popular reaction against a seemingly blatant violation of the canons relating to ecclesiastical immunity. Although he chose not to reveal the 'urgent, just, and necessary' reasons for the expulsion, he deferred to considerations of legality in his Pragmatic Sanction by claiming the familiar 'supreme economic authority' for the protection of his subjects and his crown.[1] The phrase was not invented for the occasion but had long served regalist jurists and ministers who sought ways to circumvent rather than abolish ecclesiastical immunity. Developed in the seventeenth century and realized in its most extreme form as an instrument of eighteenth-century royal absolutism, this concept of the *poder económico* was explained and justified by a contemporary Mexican bishop, who defended the expulsion of the Jesuits as a 'legitimate use of the rights which God gave the king along with his crown'.[2]

Charles's declaration that he was acting to protect his subjects and the State may seem a transparent subterfuge, but an element of genuine fear underlying royal policy towards the clergy in this period cannot be entirely discounted. Whether justified or not, the Crown believed that certain segments of the clergy were a danger to the security of the State, if not actively disloyal.[3] Several months after the expulsion of the Jesuits in 1767, the king wielded his 'supreme economic authority' again to order the immediate expulsion of all foreign ecclesiastics from the Indies.[4] Owing to incomplete documentation on this expulsion, it is impossible to determine either the number of foreign clergy residing in the colonies at that time or whether the order was carried out strictly. But unless the colonial officials were very lax—certainly the elaborate and thorough arrangements for the expulsion of the Jesuits were not repeated

---

[1] Pragmatic Sanction, 2 April 1767.

[2] R.A.H., Col. Jesuítas 28, Carta pastoral, Bishop Fabián y Fuero of Puebla, 28 Oct. 1767.

[3] See below, Chapter VI, for a discussion of these suspicions and their origin.

[4] A.G.I., Mexico 3053, R.C. circular, 17 Oct. 1767, employing the same phrase used in the Pragmatic Sanction expelling the Jesuits.

in this case—it appears that there were in fact few foreign ecclesiastics, at least in New Spain and the Caribbean area. The official report on Santo Domingo, for example, records only one, a French Dominican,[1] and in Guadalajara the local justices commissioned to carry out the order reported that no foreign clergy, secular or regular, resided in that district.[2]

The Crown made a charitable exception in the case of four Genoese Bethlemites from Mexico, whose superiors submitted dutifully to the order but complained that the meagre resources of the order, which existed only in New Spain, could not support the friars if they lived outside the cloister, and added that all four of them were too old to fend for themselves.[3] The king's decision to permit them to return to Mexico[4] was also influenced by the fact, pointed out by the Council of the Indies, that none of the friars posed any real threat to the security of Mexico: no suspicions had been cast on their conduct during their forty-year residence there, nor did Genoa have 'even the remotest intention of undertaking an aggressive expedition against that kingdom [New Spain]'.[5]

The State's 'economic' authority, obviously a useful method of dealing with delinquent or potentially dangerous members of the clergy, was also regarded by the royal officials in the Indies as an indispensable means of counteracting the immense power and influence of the Church. Rivalry for power was inevitable between the clergy and the civil officials, the two ruling classes in the colonies, who often co-operated but just as often clashed, each side accusing the other of defying or usurping its authority. Many royal officials found the distinction between judicial and administrative functions very convenient in the frequent struggles for local hegemony; for executive measures were often the only weapons they had against their ecclesiastical rivals, whose immunity protected them from the standard forms of coercion.

[1] A.G.I., Mexico 3051, Auto Dean and Chapter of Santo Domingo, 8 Jan. 1768.
[2] A.G.I., Guadalajara 335, Audiencia to the king, 14 June 1768.
[3] A.G.I., Mexico 2534, Respuesta Fiscal Council of the Indies, 30 June 1768, quoting a letter from the Bethlemite Definitorio to the Council, 23 March 1768.
[4] Ibid., Real resolución, Consulta Council, 11 Dec. 1769.
[5] Ibid., Consulta Council, 15 July 1768.

Relations between the civil and ecclesiastical authorities were especially chaotic in the more isolated provinces, since both sides were relatively free from the restraining influence of the viceroy and the *audiencias*. The Provincias Internas, one of the most remote areas in the viceroyalty of New Spain, was the scene of many conflicts during this period, ranging in severity from petty squabbling over protocol to fully-developed *competencias*.[1] This almost continual strife reached a crisis in 1793 when the Bishop of Durango commissioned his nephew, the parish priest of Chihuahua, to conduct a secret inquiry into the conduct of the *Comandante General* of the Provincias Internas and his *asesor general*, both of whom, the Bishop alleged, led such scandalous lives that the morals of the entire community were endangered.[2] The *comandante* did not learn of the investigation until after it had been completed and, when a diligent search of the priest's quarters failed to uncover the incriminating documents, he swiftly deported him in secret to a frontier fort.[3]

A curious struggle followed between the bishop and the *comandante*, during which the unfortunate priest was held incommunicado as a hostage for the documents, while the bishop refused to admit the existence of such documents, and the *comandante* refused to admit his motive for detaining the priest. The *comandante* countered the bishop's accusation that he had violated ecclesiastical immunity with the argument that he had merely exercised his executive authority to protect public order.[4] But the *comandante's* actions exceeded even the broadest interpretation of executive authority. Even if the priest's investigation had presented a 'grave threat to the image of royal authority',[5] as he alleged, he could legally do

[1] See, for example, material on a long and bitter *competencia* with the Governor of Durango, 1780–7, in A.G.I., Guadalajara 568; also the series of charges and counter-charges made by the governor and the bishop between 1762 and 1770, scattered in Guadalajara 334, 335, 341, and 563.

[2] A.G.I., Guadalajara 569, Bishop of Durango to Viceroy Revillagigedo, 14 March 1794.

[3] *Ibid.*, Oficio Comandante General Pedro de Nava, 26 Feb. 1794. The circumstances of the arrest are described by the priest, Juan Isidro Campos, in a letter to the *sede vacante* Chapter of Durango, 2 March 1795, in Guadalajara 563.

[4] *Ibid.*, Pedro de Nava to the Dean of Durango, 20 May 1794. All the correspondence between the bishop and the *comandante* was carried on through third parties, the viceroy and the dean.

[5] *Ibid.*, Nava to Antonio de Llaguno, 2 April 1795.

no more than deport the offender to Spain, but he naturally had no intention of giving the priest the opportunity to carry tales about his private life to the government in Madrid. And in the end his audacity succeeded. As long as his nephew was being held prisoner, the bishop dared not disclose the results of the investigation, nor even excommunicate the *comandante*. Although his complaints to the Crown eventually secured an order for the priest's release, its arrival coincided with the bishop's death and the matter ended there. The *comandante* had achieved his goal of suppressing the investigation at the relatively small price of a royal rebuke for having exceeded his authority.[1]

The Governor of New Mexico had resorted to similar tactics the previous year against a Franciscan friar whom he suspected of instigating a plot in Santa Fe to have him removed from office.[2] However, in this case, the governor used his executive authority in strict adherence to the law,[3] since the friar's arrest and expulsion were preceded by a *proceso informativo* in which the governor had been able to obtain evidence (whether under pressure or not is another question) of the friar's drunkenness and other excesses, which he sent, along with the friar, to the Franciscan Provincial of Zacatecas.[4] Though aware of the governor's real motives for removing the friar from Santa Fe, the Bishop of Durango was unable to gather evidence himself because of the great distance involved and thus was powerless 'to protect the Holy Habit of St Francis and the honour of the Church against this vile aggression'.[5]

The viceroy, ordered to report on both cases to the king, was correct in attributing the discord to the remoteness and almost total independence of the Provincias Internas.[6] But his suggestion to place ecclesiastical matters there under direct viceregal jurisdiction was hardly a solution, for the authorities in

[1] *Ibid.*, R.O., to Nava, 29 Sept. 1794.
[2] *Ibid.*, Governor of New Mexico, Fernando de la Concha, to Pedro de Nava, 22 and 24 Aug. 1793.
[3] *Recop. Indias*, ley 73, título 14, Libro 1.
[4] A.G.I., Guadalajara 569, Franciscan Provincial to Concha, 8 Oct. 1793, acknowledging receipt of the report.
[5] *Ibid.*, Bishop of Durango to the Franciscan Custodio in Santa Fe, 7 Jan. 1794.
[6] *Ibid.*, Branciforte to the king, 30 June 1797.

Mexico, dependent on whatever information the local officials chose to send, had no more direct knowledge of events in the area than did the government in Madrid.

Yucatán was another isolated province of the viceroyalty (indeed it is only within the last few decades that direct overland communications between Yucatán and the rest of Mexico have been established) with a large proportion of Indians under ecclesiastical tutelage, two conditions favourable to rivalry and discord between the local representatives of Church and State. The royal officials were convinced that the clergy were, in the words of one governor, 'accustomed to ruling everyone and everything, especially in the remoter areas',[1] and it is true that the clergy seems to have fared better here in the power struggle than in the Provincias Internas. Faced with ecclesiastical intimidation or meddling, the governors seemed unable or unwilling to exercise their executive authority to any effect. In 1792, for example, a Franciscan friar circulated a virulently libellous attack against Governor Lucas de Gálvez, but Gálvez did nothing more than protest to the bishop and then commission a *proceso informativo* to send to the king when the bishop refused to punish the offender.[2]

One priest from Campeche who repeatedly excommunicated local royal justices and interfered in civil administration was able to avoid expulsion for over forty years, even though the two expulsion orders (one in 1732 and the other in 1761) came directly from the king.[3] The diocesan authorities used the standard formula, 'obedezco pero no cumplo' (I obey but do not execute), to evade the *cédulas* and tried to justify the priest's actions in a series of letters and reports to the Crown.[4] But official indifference and administrative inefficiency were the priest's main allies: the governor, despite reminders from the

[1] A.G.I., Mexico 3072, Governor Lucas de Gálvez to the king, 18 May 1792.
[2] *Ibid.*, Expediente formado con motivo de pretender Fr. Casimiro Villa . . ., 1792.
[3] A.G.I., Mexico 3051, Consulta Council, 17 Oct. 1761, mentioning R.C., 15 Oct. 1732, 'que no consta porqué no tuvo efecto'; and R.C. to Governor of Yucatán, 15 Dec. 1761.
[4] *Ibid.*, Expediente sobre la buena conducta y arreglados costumbres del Pe. José de Nájera, 5 Sept. 1763; Dean and chapter to the king, 6 Sept. 1763; and Nájera to the king, 19 Sept. 1765.

Council, made no attempt to execute the order, nor even to make the necessary summary inquiry that was the legal preliminary to expulsion; and then the file was misplaced in Madrid for over thirty years, so that when it finally reappeared (in 1799), the Council decided that 'no further action is necessary'.[1]

Disputes over the use of executive measures were not confined to the peripheral provinces, nor were the ecclesiastical authorities limited to the use of pleas and protests: they had more drastic weapons in the form of canonical censures. The most violent clash between Church and State in New Spain during the reign of Charles III arose over the viceroy's exercise of his executive authority against an Italian Servite friar suspected of spying for the British during the Seven Years War. The viceroy's genuine but exaggerated concern for the colony's safety led him to take measures that violated ecclesiastical immunity, and the archbishop's similar concern for protocol and the privileges of the Church led him to the imprudent step of excommunicating almost the entire government.

The friar's arrival in Campeche in October 1762 from British-occupied Havana had been preceded by reports warning of his intention to gather information on the viceroyalty's defences. He was arrested immediately upon arrival, brought in chains to the royal prison in Mexico for interrogation, and then deported to Spain under military escort.[2] If the viceroy had simply deported the friar without notifying the archbishop, there would have been no dispute, but he foolishly forwarded all the documents to the ecclesiastical curia as a gesture of courtesy. The archbishop did not challenge the concept of executive intervention or the decision to send the friar to Spain, but he objected to the fact that the measures were carried out without his consent or even his knowledge and was determined that the royal officials should acknowledge his privative jurisdiction over the case. Without any warning he placed a notice of public excommunication on the great doors of the cathedral against the *asesor general*, the *auditor de guerra* and two *oidores*

---

[1] *Ibid.*, Respuesta Fiscal Council, 18 April 1799.
[2] A.G.I., Mexico 2617, Instrumentos hechos a motivo de la prisión del fraile servita Fr Juan de Annovacio, cuaderno 1, 1762.

for having carried out the viceroy's orders and, when the latter came to their defence, threatened him with the same.[1]

The various *dictámenes* and *respuestas* which the excommunicated officials presented to both the *audiencia* and the diocesan court in this case covered most of the points that canonists and regalists disputed concerning executive authority and ecclesiastical immunity: whether the royal magistrates had the right to register and identify ecclesiastics who entered the country; at what point a *proceso informativo* became a formal trial; and, the most hotly contested issue of all, whether an ecclesiastic could be deported without the consent of his superior. The ecclesiastics held that the king's economic authority was not independent of, but only an adjunct to, ecclesiastical jurisdiction. Civil officials could not act without instructions from an ecclesiastical judge, and only if he failed in his duty could they arrest, interrogate, or deport an ecclesiastic on their own initiative.[2] The royal jurists refused to admit any connection between these measures and the privilege of immunity and would concede only that the ecclesiastical judge should be notified of a deportation order.[3] Royal law was no real criterion in the dispute, since the typically vague wording calling for co-operation between the two jurisdictions made no mention of whose opinion was to prevail in the likely event that they disagreed.[4]

It is obvious that the royal officials had not been motivated by any desire to destroy the privileges of the Church, despite allegations that they were in the habit of persecuting the clergy 'under the guise of executive authority, the welfare of the State, or other frivolous pretexts'.[5] Although with hindsight the Italian friar may have seemed fairly harmless, word had been received from Havana that he was working for Lord Albemarle, the British commander, who was undoubtedly interested in

[1] A.G.I., Mexico 2617, Decree Archbishop Manuel Rubio y Salinas, 12 Jan. 1763; Oficio Rubio y Salinas to Viceroy Cruíllas, 14 Jan. 1763.

[2] *Ibid.*, Respuestas Promotor Fiscal (of the metropolitan curia), 7 Jan. and 30 April 1763.

[3] *Ibid.*, Respuestas Fiscal de la Audiencia, Manuel Velarde, 20 Dec. 1762 and 5 March 1763; also Defensa de la jurisdicción real, January 1763, (Antonio) Joaquín de Ribadeneyra, in Biblioteca del Palacio, 1492.

[4] *Recop. Indias*, ley 8, título 7, Libro 1; leyes 84 and 85, título 14, Libro 1.

[5] A.G.I., Mexico 2617, Respuesta Promotor Fiscal, 7 Jan. 1763.

learning of the fortifications and defences on the Mexican coast.[1] The exaggerated and somewhat garbled arguments in favour of extreme executive authority were brought forth only after the archbishop had reacted so violently and were basically a means by which the officials defended themselves against the peremptory canonical censures. They were so convinced that their actions were legal that they wrote to the king complaining that the archbishop had acted only out of vengeance because they had prevented royal authority from being usurped by the ecclesiastical courts in other recent cases.[2]

Although the *audiencia* nullified the archbishop's decree of excommunication, and the *fiscales* and the majority of the Council of the Indies upheld this decision,[3] the officials and later their descendants continued to petition the king to declare their action justified in order to erase this blot against their honour.[4] But the king did not consider it necessary or convenient to issue the general rule that both sides requested. The boundary between legal executive intervention and violation of the clergy's immunity remained unresolved and continued to cause disputes throughout the colonial period, even after direct judicial intervention was authorized by royal law.

[1] *Ibid.*, Letters from the Bishop of Havana and the Rector of the Jesuit College in Havana to the Captain General of Campeche, 14 and 22 Oct. 1762.

[2] *Ibid.*, Oidor Domingo Valcárcel to Arriaga, 22 April 1763; Oidor Domingo de Trespalacios to the king, 7 May 1763.

[3] *Ibid.*, Auto de fuerza, Audiencia, 6 May 1763; Respuestas Fiscales, Council, 19 and 22 Sept. 1763; and Consulta Council, 14 Nov. 1763. Two councillors upheld the archbishop's position in a long dissenting vote inserted in the *Consulta*.

[4] *Ibid.*, Ribadeneyra to the king, 11 Feb. 1764; and Mexico 1127, Antonio de Valcárcel (son of the now deceased *asesor general*) to the king, 6 March 1768.

CHAPTER III

Control of the Ecclesiastical Judicial System

I. ROYAL REVIEW OF ECCLESIASTICAL CASES

THE CHURCH in Spain and the Indies, as in all Catholic countries, had its own system of courts, complementary to the civil judiciary, with exclusive jurisdiction over spiritual matters as well as over all persons of ecclesiastical status. While the Spanish Crown acknowledged the Church's claim to this extensive judicial authority as a necessary means to achieve its end, the salvation of souls,[1] it was not prepared to permit the completely independent functioning of this authority as set forth in the canons.

In order to establish firm control over the ecclesiastical courts, the Crown had first to isolate them from the powerful Roman Curia, a policy that proved particularly successful with the American Church because of the area's geographical isolation and also because of early papal co-operation. In 1573 Pope Gregory XIII granted a bull to Philip II establishing a system of judicial appeals whereby all ecclesiastical cases were to terminate in the Indies.[2] The first appeal was to be made to the metropolitan and, if he did not concur with the original decision, then the second and final appeal was to be decided by the nearest suffragan instead of by a Roman congregation, ordinarily the final appellate court. The logic of this method was obvious, granted the great expense and long delay entailed in referring cases from America to Rome, but the bull represented a triumph for the royal policy of subordinating the Church to the State.

---

[1] Council of Trent, sess. 7, cap. 14; sess. 8, cap. 1 *de reform.*; sess. 25, cap. 3 *de reform.*

[2] F. Hernáez, *op. cit.*, i, 188–9, Constitution of Gregory XIII, 'Exposcit', 1573.

The bull of 1573 did not ensure the total isolation of the American ecclesiastical courts, for it did not expressly prohibit appeals to Rome, nor did it apply to the special cases over which the Roman Curia reserved jurisdiction in the first instance. Realizing that any further papal concessions were extremely unlikely and that the American ecclesiastics could and did find ways to defy the royal laws prohibiting direct communication with Rome, the Spanish kings decided instead to nullify the effect of these appeals by subjecting all papal rescripts to royal review.[1]

The *pase regio* or royal *exequatur*, which enabled the Crown to exercise a veto power over papal legislation, also transferred supreme judicial authority over ecclesiastical cases from the pope to the king since, when an appellant obtained a decision from a Roman court, he had to present the brief to the Council of the Indies before it could have legal force in America. His lawyers had to convince the councillors that the appeal was necessary in the first place and that the decision was just and in accordance with royal law.[2] The Crown took upon itself the authority to supervise even exclusively spiritual matters of the *fuero interno*, even though papal briefs concerning these matters were not supposed to be subject to the *exequatur*. It judged, for example, whether papal dispensations of canonical impediments to marriage or ordination were valid,[3] and in one case decided to retain a papal brief granting absolution to a Peruvian friar who had committed murder, on the grounds that it might influence the trial in his favour and also encourage other potential murderers,[4] even though the absolution simply meant that the friar could be readmitted to the sacraments.

It is surprising that the *pase regio* did not discourage these appeals altogether, considering the additional expense and delay suffered by the parties even if they were finally able to

---

[1] *Recop. Indias*, ley 55, título 7; leyes 2–4 and 8, título 9, Libro 1.

[2] See A.G.I., Ind. Gen. 2915 and 2916, Expedientes sobre pases de bulas, breves y patentes, 1770–80.

[3] See, e.g., A.G.I., Guadalajara 339, R.C. to Bishop of Durango, 22 Feb. 1769; and Guadalajara 343, R.C., 19 Sept. 1777, concerning papal dispensations of canonical impediments to ordination.

[4] A.G.I., Ind. Gen. 1653, Juntas del Nuevo Código, 19 May, 2 June and 10 Dec. 1783.

obtain the *pase*. But they continued, and during the reign of Charles III the Crown issued several regulations designed to create new obstacles: first, all rescripts were to be subject to the *exequatur* of the vice-patrons in the Indies in addition to the Council's;[1] and, more important, all petitions required the Council's *fiat* prior to being forwarded to Rome, otherwise the resultant rescripts would be automatically invalidated.[2]

The Crown's purpose in issuing the latter regulation, as stated by the fiscal, was 'to avoid any unintentional errors on the part of the Roman Curia by examining the evidence beforehand', since the Spanish government was in a better position to detect fraudulent claims and irresponsible appeals.[3] Following this principle, the Council in 1787 denied the *pase regio* to a judicial sentence pronounced by the Augustinian general in a case originating from Michoacán and advised him to reverse his verdict, because the local bishop had reported that the friar's appeal contained false evidence. If the appeal had been submitted to the Council initially, it was argued, the general could have made the 'appropriate decision' in the first place.[4]

The popes naturally never accepted the principle of the *pase regio*, but there was little they could do to oppose its use, especially since the colonial bishops acknowledged the king's supreme judicial authority in the Indies. They usually appealed to Madrid rather than to Rome for the settlement of disputes that ordinarily would have come under the jurisdiction of the papal courts and agreed with the regalist doctrine that no papal rescript could be legally valid in the Indies without receiving the *pase regio*.[5] One Mexican bishop justified his support of this prerogative, which was one of the Crown's principal instruments for subordinating the Church to the State, by claiming that the popes themselves had granted the privilege of royal review.[6]

The regular clergy were more inclined to resist the Crown's efforts to isolate the American Church. With the exception of

---

[1] *Decretos reales tocantes a la iglesia* (B.M.), no. 35, R.C. circular, 23 Nov. 1777.
[2] *Ibid.*, no. 42, R.C. circular, 21 Nov. 1778.
[3] A.G.I., Ind. Gen. 66, Respuesta Fiscal Council of the Indies, 16 Aug. 1774.
[4] A.G.I., Mexico 2538, Consulta Council, 24 Nov. 1787.
[5] *CIVM*, cánones 1 and 3, título 3, Libro 1.
[6] A.G.I., Guadalajara 339, Bishop of Durango to the Audiencia, 1 Oct. 1770.

the Franciscans, the major religious orders in the Indies had resisted royal pressure to establish a national *comisariato general* in Madrid, which would have placed them under royal supervision, and continued to be governed directly by their generals in Rome.[1] One of the major points, therefore, in the Crown's policy of strengthening royal authority over the American clergy was to reduce the regulars' judicial dependence on Rome and to subject the individual provinces to the jurisdiction of the local diocesan courts, over which the State had greater control.

One method of reducing this contact was through the royal laws regulating travel to and from the Indies, since the regulars usually carried their appeals to Rome in person. The colonial authorities were exhorted to be especially vigilant in preventing friars from embarking without royal licence,[2] and in 1774 the Crown ordered the arrest and confinement of any regulars apprehended on the way to Rome without permission.[3] There is, of course, no record in government files of those who managed to travel undetected but, aside from the risk of discovery *en route*, there was always the problem of trying to apply the sentence obtained from a papal court or from the order's general without the royal *exequatur*, and the bishops were apparently eager to denounce any clandestine appeals, especially if they circumscribed their own powers.[4]

The colonial bishops co-operated with the Crown to prevent direct communication between the American regulars and Rome. In some cases their common efforts were directed against abuses of this communication—for example, the numerous appeals to the Congregation of the Penitentiary for release from religious vows. Friars could and did obtain briefs of secularization under false pretences simply because they had tired of monastic life.[5] Despite the deterrent of possible arrest, these

---

[1] P. de Leturia, *op. cit.*, i, 74, 91.

[2] A.H.N., Códices 700, R.C. to Viceroy of Mexico, 26 Feb. 1767.

[3] A.G.I., Ind. Gen. 66, Expediente sobre averse venido sin licencias y por colonias extranjeras dos religiosos mercedarios, 1773; Respuesta Fiscal, 17 Feb. 1774; and Consulta Council, 20 April 1774.

[4] See, e.g., Mexico, 2638, Diocesan Provisor of Michoacán to José de Gálvez, 6 May 1783, denouncing a papal brief produced in a dispute with the Congregation of the Oratory.

[5] See A.G.I., Mexico 2696, Archbishop of Mexico to the Pope, 25 Nov. 1803, (copy) giving a number of examples.

appeals increased in number (the friars resorted to travelling via the French Antilles and France) and, by the end of the eighteenth century, the Council was receiving alarming reports from American bishops that many monasteries had to be abandoned for lack of members.[1]

Next the Crown decided to subject petitions for secularization, which (like all those concerning matters of conscience) had been exempt from royal review, to the prior approval of the Council and to the subsequent *exequatur*, and to require that they be accompanied by favourable reports from the bishops, who could best judge their merits.[2] But the resourceful friars found means of circumventing even this control. The problem intensified towards the end of the colonial period, perhaps reflecting the general degeneration of monastic life already noted,[3] and the large number of vagabond ex-friars without means of support, who still enjoyed ecclesiastical immunity but who were no longer under the supervision of the regular superiors, created serious disciplinary problems for both the diocesan and civil authorities.[4]

Efforts to place the regular clergy under the direct authority of the local bishops were not much more fruitful than the attempt to prevent their appeals to Rome. During the latter part of the eighteenth century, the Crown was able to persuade the Pope to abolish the office of *comisario general* in the colonial branches of the religious orders by claiming that these superiors contributed to the frequent disputes and disorders of the regulars.[5] Its next move, the transfer of second instance jurisdiction from these superiors to the diocesan courts, might have been equally successful but for an audacious clause included in

---

[1] A.G.I., Ind. Gen. 73, Expedientes sobre breves de secularización, 1790–4.

[2] R.A.H., Col. Mata Linares 76, Respuesta Fiscal Council, 24 Nov. 1796. The *cédula* (issued in 1797?) is mentioned in A.G.I., Mexico 1140, Acuerdo Council, 11 Feb. 1803.

[3] See above, pp. 32–38, and below, pp. 115–23.

[4] For material on these briefs and complaints from the colonial authorities, see A.G.I., Mexico 2545, Consultas Council, 14 Sept. 1805 and 24 July 1806; Mexico 1150, Carta acordada to Archbishop of Mexico, 28 June 1808; Mexico 2646, 2649, expedientes from 1806 to 1825.

[5] R.A.H., Col. Mata Linares 76, Informe si son útiles los comisarios generales en el Perú y Nueva España, 1796. A.G.I., Mexico 2544, Consulta, 23 July 1801, summarizing the various expedientes dating from 1771.

the draft brief submitted to the Pope in 1802: 'The bishops are to pass all these sentences to the King and Council of the Indies for final approval.'[1] The Spanish Ambassador in Rome reported that the draft had proved totally unacceptable to the Pope, who had called it a 'blot on the honour of the Papacy' and had declared that he could no more sanction secular review of ecclesiastical cases in this form than he could in the form of the *pase regio*.[2] Although royal archivists searched in vain for any shred of evidence that previous pontiffs might have conceded this authority, the problem was resolved in typically regalist fashion. By equating this clause with the *pase regio*, a long-established custom that had not been openly resisted, the Pope, so argued the Council, gave his tacit consent, although he could not publicly endorse the practice.[3] With this absurd argument, the king dispensed with the brief and simply instructed the bishops by royal authority to hear these appeals and submit their decisions to the Council.[4]

The Crown had good reasons for trying to confine all ecclesiastical cases in America to the diocesan courts, for these courts were subject to such close supervision from the State that the much disputed boundaries between royal and ecclesiastical jurisdiction were often indiscernable. The personnel of the ecclesiastical courts were of fundamental importance, and their selection was brought increasingly under royal control. The Habsburg law code had already prohibited ecclesiastics from representing laymen either in secular or ecclesiastical courts[5] and specified that all scribes and notaries should be registered with the royal tribunals and should also be laymen (except in reserved cases dealing with matters of conscience), so that they could be prosecuted by the civil authorities for malpractice.[6] The *provisores*, who exercised the bishops' ordinary judicial authority, and the diocesan *visitadores*, who exercised

---

[1] A.G.I., Ind. Gen. 2995, Preces for papal brief prepared by Fiscal Council of the Indies, 9 Feb. 1802.

[2] *Ibid.*, Antonio de Vargas y Laguna, Spanish Minister to the Holy See, to Antonio de Ceballos, 10 Sept. 1802.

[3] *Ibid.*, Consulta Council, 23 Feb. 1805.

[4] *Ibid.*, R.C. circular to all archbishops and bishops of the Indies, 6 Oct. 1805.

[5] *Recop. Indias*, ley 1, título 12, Libro 1.

[6] *Ibid.*, ley 37, título 8, Libro 5.

F

their delegated jurisdiction, were originally appointed solely by the bishops in each diocese, but the *Junta del Nuevo Código*, commissioned to revise the 1681 colonial law code, decided that they too should be subject to the approval of the vice-patron, who was to ensure that they had the 'proper qualifications'.[1]

The precise extent to which the Crown regulated judicial procedure in the diocesan courts is not certain, despite various laws stipulating court costs and suitable punishments for different offences.[2] A royal *fiscal* expressed the official policy thus:

> It is necessary that the ecclesiastical courts follow the civil judicial system even in spiritual cases, because the King has the responsibility to ensure that all litigation concerning his ecclesiastical as well as his lay subjects should proceed fairly and efficiently.[3]

The records of proceedings in the colonial Mexican courts of law indicate that both the secular and ecclesiastical cases followed essentially the same pattern, but the similarities may have been due to the fact that both canon and Spanish civil law have the same origins in Roman law, rather than to any royal mandates. But, according to the same *fiscal*, if there was any practice in the ecclesiastical courts that conflicted with Spanish civil procedure, this was only because the king generously permitted it out of deference to the Holy See.[4]

The ecclesiastical courts were dependent upon the secular authorities for the execution of most sentences which were not strictly spiritual penances: although the Church claimed authority to administer some forms of temporal punishment in addition to penance,[5] the diocesan courts were not equipped with either the personnel or the means to do more than serve summonses and keep a few prisoners under minimum security.[6]

---

[1] A.G.I., Ind. Gen. 1653, Junta del Nuevo Código, 13 Sept. 1784; Ind. Gen. 2883, R.C. circular, 4 Aug. 1790, promulgating the new law.

[2] *Recop. Indias*, leyes 12 and 47, título 7, Libro 1; ley 32; título 8, Libro 5. See also J. de Solórzano Pereira, *op. cit.*, Libro 4, cap. 7, nos. 10–13; and cap. 8, nos. 40–4.

[3] B.N., 10653, Respuesta Fiscal, Council of the Indies, 16 Aug. 1774.

[4] *Ibid.*

[5] G. de Villarroel, *Gobierno eclesiástico pacífico*, Part II, quest. 18, art. 1.

[6] Ecclesiastical magistrates often had to entrust dangerous criminals to royal prisons. See, for example, A.G.I., Mexico 2617, Archbishop Rubio y Salinas to Viceroy Cruíllas, 12 Jan. 1763, complaining that a determined child could escape from the diocesan jail.

This secular assistance, or *auxilio real*,[1] was supposed to be rendered automatically at the request of the ecclesiastical judge, but the royal officials often refused to carry out an order for arrest or deportation without consulting the evidence and deciding for themselves if the warrant or sentence was justified. In 1795, for example, Viceroy Branciforte, who had been requested to deport two Franciscans, decided to undertake his own *proceso informativo*, suspecting that the two friars had actually plotted to return to Spain before their ten-year mission term was completed.[2] When the Franciscan *Comisario General* protested that this action infringed his jurisdiction, the Council supported the viceroy's right to withhold *auxilio real* until the *sala del crimen* investigated the validity of the charges.[3] In another case in Mexico, two constables were punished for arresting someone by order of an ecclesiastical judge without 'previous investigation of the case'.[4]

The king's efforts in 1802 to gain papal approval of his right to review ecclesiastical cases, although unsuccessful, were actually superfluous. For centuries the judicial decisions of both the regular superiors and the diocesan courts had been subject to royal review through appeals to the Council of the Indies and to the local *audiencias*. The appeals to the king or his Council were not established in the colonial law code but seemed rather to be accepted as a procedure emanating logically from the king's position as royal patron, which to the majority of the colonial clergy meant also the supreme magistrate in the ecclesiastical judicial system. Thus when an ecclesiastic petitioned the king for a reprieve or reversal of his sentence, his action was not considered a renunciation of his ecclesiastical *fuero*, nor was the king's intervention considered a violation of immunity.

Certainly not all ecclesiastics under trial by their superiors sought a hearing in the Council of the Indies, but the ease with which this protection was gained is illustrated by the number and variety of petitions received by the Crown. Both regulars

---

[1] *Recop. Indias*, ley 11, título 10, Libro 1.

[2] A.G.I., Mexico 2675, Expediente instruído por el Alcalde del Crimen . . ., 1795.

[3] A.G.I., Mexico 2542, Consulta Council, 4 July 1796.

[4] A.G.I., Mexico 2631, Decree Sala del crimen, 20 Oct. 1781.

and seculars from every religious order and from every diocese in New Spain sought and obtained 'royal protection' either for release from a diocesan prison, for a case to be heard by the Crown instead of an ecclesiastical court, for the remission of a sentence already pronounced, or for the raising of a writ of excommunication.[1] All these questions were deemed within the jurisdiction of the Council of the Indies, which not only replaced the Roman congregations, but also assumed powers beyond those of an ordinary appellate court, whether ecclesiastical or secular, which normally would not have intervened in a case while the first-instance tribunal was still conducting proceedings.

There were, of course, occasions on which the Council rejected an appeal, although its decisions were not based on any discernible criterion. For example, it turned down a petition from a prebendary in Durango to quash a sentence imposed by his bishop (he had been fined for neglecting his duties) on the grounds that 'there are tribunals in the Indies which have full authority to decide this case', and the appellant was instructed to seek redress through an appeal either to the metropolitan court or to the *audiencia* of his district.[2] Yet this same argument would have served equally well to reject the majority of petitions that were in fact accepted.

The ecclesiastical appellants could not be entirely blamed for seeking intervention from the State, since their superiors were so often willing to relinquish their judicial authority to the king. A Bethlemite friar in Mexico who had requested aid from the viceroy—rather than subject his order to the 'public scandal of a formal appeal to the *audiencia*'—in order to force the order's *visitador* to hear his defence, had no intention of renouncing his *fuero* but only sought the opportunity of a fair trial.[3] Yet he was compelled to present his defence to the king, because the

---

[1] See A.G.I., Mexico 2669, Instancia de D. Antonio Escalante implorando a S.M. se le haga justicia, 27 March 1790; and Guadalajara 568, Representación de parte de José Sánchez de Lara a S.M., 5 Oct. 1784. The series Mexico 1691–1761, 'Expedientes de cartas diarias e instancias', 1760–1800, contains a great number of similar petitions.

[2] A.G.I., Guadalajara 545, Consulta Council, 5 Dec. 1803.

[3] A.G.I., Mexico 2646, Petition from Fr Joseph de San Ignacio to the viceroy, 10 Nov. 1794.

visitador abruptly sent the whole case on his own initiative to Madrid for 'His Majesty to pronounce a verdict'.[1]

Nor was it surprising that an ecclesiastic should look to the Crown for a reprieve when in so many cases the ecclesiastical superiors were only an instrument for the execution of a verdict dictated solely by a royal minister or council. The Franciscan Provincial of Jalisco, sentenced by the Council of the Indies to indefinite loss of active and passive voice in the province for negligence in the performance of his duties,[2] naturally by-passed the *Comisario General*, his direct superior, who had only communicated the decision to him, and appealed directly to the Council for a reduction of his sentence.[3] The ecclesiastical authorities had virtually no intervention in the case, for even the evidence against the defendant had been gathered and forwarded by the viceroy of New Spain.[4]

The only recorded attempt of an ecclesiastical superior to curtail these appeals was an edict issued by the Franciscan *Comisario General* in Spain to the Provincial of Quito in 1772, prohibiting the friars from either appealing to the Crown or informing it of any judicial questions within the order. As soon as this alarming document came to the king's attention, he sent out a circular *cédula* to the *audiencias* and viceroys to confiscate all copies of the edict in their districts.[5] But the king's anxiety was apparently uncalled for, at least outside Quito. In Guadalajara the various provincials replied to the *audiencia* that they had never received the edict,[6] and when instructed to reassure all their subjects, in any case, that they could and should seek royal protection, answered that even the statutes their provinces were ruled by expressly permitted recourse to the Crown.[7]

---

[1] *Ibid.*, Copy of Decree of Visitador, enclosed with petition from Fr Ignacio to the king, 30 Nov. 1794.

[2] A.G.I., Guadalajara 358, Consulta Council, 28 March 1794.

[3] *Ibid.*, Fr Vicente Pau to the Council, 8 Jan. 1795.

[4] *Ibid.*, Viceroy Revillagigedo to the king, 29 July 1793.

[5] A.G.I., Guadalajara 341, R.C. circular, 22 Feb. 1775.

[6] *Ibid.*, Provincials of Zacatecas and Jalisco to the Audiencia, 14 July 1775; Guardián Colegio de Propaganda Fide to the Audiencia, 27 July 1775.

[7] *Ibid.*, Audiencia to the king, 12 July 1776.

2. THE 'RECURSO DE FUERZA'

The commonest apparatus for royal review and one of the State's most effective arms in the struggle for supremacy over the Church was the peculiar institution called the *recurso de fuerza*, by which a person who considered himself aggrieved by an act or sentence of an ecclesiastical magistrate could find redress in a secular tribunal, usually the local *audiencia*.

Although the regalists attempted to hallow the *recurso* by discovering its origins in the Castilian medieval law code or in the Visigothic Councils of Toledo[1]—one jurist even found reference to it in the Old Testament[2]—the practice was not established in Spain until the reign of Charles V and was undoubtedly imported from France, whose legal historians generally date its appearance there from the mid-fifteenth century.[3] There was only a brief time lag between the formal regulation of the *recurso* in Spain[4] and its introduction into the new colonies in the Indies,[5] where the institution flourished even more vigorously than in the mother country. In Spain, the Crown had to contend with papal attempts to curtail this infringement of ecclesiastical jurisdiction in the form of briefs revoking the decisions of the *audiencias*, strongly worded letters to the Crown, and obstructive censures delivered by papal nuncios against both the appellants and the magistrates who accepted the *recursos*.[6] In America, on the other hand, the prelates managed only feeble protests against the excessive use of the *recurso de fuerza* without questioning the premise of State supremacy on which the institution rested.[7]

[1] J. Covarrubias, *Máximas sobre recursos de fuerza y protección* . . . (Madrid, 1785), título 6, máx. 3; Conde de la Cañada, *Observaciones prácticas sobre los recursos de fuerza* . . . (Madrid, 1793), Part I, cap. I, no. 4. The latter was governor and the former an *abogado* of the Council of Castile. Both works constitute a definition of late Bourbon policy towards this institution.

[2] Biblioteca del Palacio, Col. Ayala 19, Breve instrucción sobre retención de bulas, 1768, by Fiscal Pedro Salcedo (reference to Jeremiah, 21).

[3] R. Génestal, *Les origines de l'appel comme d'abus* (Paris, 1951), p. 9.

[4] J. Maldonado, 'Los recursos de fuerza en España', *Anuario de Historia del Derecho Español*, xxiv (1954), p. 292, quoting a royal *cédula* of 7 July 1542.

[5] According to *Recop. Indias*, ley 134, título 15, Libro 2, the *recurso* was already in use in the Indies by 1559.

[6] See R. de Hinojosa, *Los despachos de la diplomacia pontificia en España* (Madrid, 1896), p. 355; and J. Maldonado, *op. cit.*, pp. 295–8.

[7] G. de Villarroel, *Gobierno eclesiástico pacífico*, Part 2, quest. 12, art. 5, no. 96.

The theoretical justification of these *recursos* was based on the familiar image of the king as father to his subjects, the guardian of justice to whom all could appeal for the restitution of their rights and protection against injury (*fuerza* originally meant injury or harm).[1] The *recurso* was not supposed to be an appeal but a complaint lodged by a party to any litigation in an ecclesiastical court who had no recourse in an ordinary appeal.[2] There were three types of *fuerza* or abuse that could not be rectified through the ordinary channels: illegal procedure in trying a case; failure to grant a legitimate appeal; and, finally, lack of jurisdiction altogether. The *audiencia*, upon receiving the *recurso*, requested all the pertinent documents from the ecclesiastical judge, ordering him to suspend proceedings for the duration of the appeal,[3] and on the basis of these documents decided whether or not an abuse existed. In the first type of *fuerza* (*en el modo de conocer y procedor*), the ecclesiastical judge could be obliged to adhere to lawful forensic procedure; in the second type, *en no otorgar apelación*, he could be ordered to suspend the execution of his sentence and grant an appeal to the higher ecclesiastical court; and in the third type, *fuerza en conocer*, the audiencia could declare him incompetent to hear the case at all and turn it over to the appropriate secular court.[4]

Originally intended to protect ecclesiastics from oppression at the hands of their superiors, the *recurso* actually afforded them almost unlimited opportunity to obstruct the course of justice and, often, to elude punishment altogether. The Spanish legal system, with its complicated apparatus of written depositions, notification, and multiple series of charges and defences interspersed with extracts and summaries, seemed designed to prolong litigation indefinitely under normal circumstances; when extraordinary appeals were introduced, chances of

---

[1] F. Salgado de Somoza, *De regia protectione* ... (1626), Part I, cap. I, prael. 5; and Conde de la Cañada, *op. cit.*, Part I, cap. 10, no. 8.

[2] J. Covarrubias, *op. cit.*, título 6, máx. 7 and 8; título 24, máx. 15.

[3] *Recop. Indias*, ley 10, título 10, Libro I.

[4] For descriptions of the various types of *recursos*, see J. Covarrubias, *op. cit.*, títulos 8, 10 and 12; and Conde de la Cañada, *op. cit.*, Part I, caps. 2–9.

See also, A.H.N., Códices 724, R.C. to Archbishop of Santo Domingo, 2 April 1604; and Códices 689, R.C. to Bishop of Quito, 15 June 1573, in reply to protests against particular uses of the *recurso*.

reaching a verdict were indeed remote. One trial of a Carmelite friar in Mexico, charged with misusing his commission as executor of a will, was delayed by *recursos* and appeals for over twenty-five years[1] and never received a final verdict even when the Crown was called upon to intervene. The Council had to deliberate in its ponderous fashion each new petition the friar submitted,[2] and the case ended only with the death of this persistent appelant.

If, as royal ministers and colonial officials so often alleged, the standard of discipline in the American clergy was woefully lax, *recursos de fuerza* and the other extraordinary appeals were partly to blame. They may not have caused the disturbances and crimes that plagued both the civil and ecclesiastical authorities, but they undeniably impeded efforts to remedy the problem. In the majority of cases, the *audiencias* and the Council accepted the appeals without any desire to protect a delinquent from his just punishment but, as long as a defendant was permitted to challenge any measure unfavourable to him, it was impossible for the ecclesiastical magistrates to deal with him effectively.

Recursos de fuerza and other appeals for secular intervention certainly exacerbated the disorders and disputes of the regular clergy. A typical example was the upheavals within the order of San Hipólito Mártir which, like those in most colonial orders, had their origin in an internal struggle for power. One dispute began in 1787 with accusations of embezzlement, illegal holding of office for twenty years, and the usual charges of oppression and tyranny against the order's general.[3] When the archbishop, delegated by the pope to take cognizance of the order's judicial questions, refused to hear these complaints, the accusers presented a *recurso de fuerza en el modo de conocer y proceder* to the *audiencia* and wrote to the king complaining that the archbishop was in league with the general and his supporters,

[1] A.G.I., Mexico 2644, Testimonio de autos de los recursos de fuerza que ha interpuesto Fr Antonio de San Alberto . . ., 1762–90.

[2] *Ibid.*, Real Congregación del Apóstol Santiago (on behalf of Fr Antonio) to the king, 27 Oct. 1788; Fr Antonio to the king, 26 Jan. 1789, 4 Nov. 1789 and 26 Jan. 1790.

[3] A.G.I., Mexico 2540, Representación del Prior del Convento del Espíritu Santo to the archbishop, 16 June 1787.

who were able to buy favour from influential people, including the *oidores*, with funds embezzled from the order's patrimony.[1]

Precisely the same pattern was followed after new superiors from the opposing faction were elected a year later, but this time with the ex-general and his secretary in the role of victims. Accusations were made and ignored, a *recurso* was presented to the *audiencia*, the accusers were arrested by their superiors,[2] and complaints made to the Crown which produced decrees almost identical to those sent the previous year, ordering the viceroy and archbishop to 'relieve the innocent from the oppressions suffered at the hands of their adversaries'.[3] By the time the second round of *recursos* appeared, the civil authorities in Mexico realized that the complaints were merely a subterfuge to avoid submitting to the authority of the incumbent superiors, and that monastic obedience, so essential to the restoration of peace and discipline within the order, was being destroyed by the protection obtained from the State.[4] Despite the royal decrees, both the *audiencia* and the viceroy decided to reject the *recursos* and other appeals and, with the archbishop's concurrence, the viceroy informed the king that to permit new ones would only encourage further dissension.[5] Unconvinced, the Council continued to order them to investigate the complaints,[6] and the dispute apparently continued even after the ex-general and his secretary obtained briefs of secularization from the pope permitting them to leave the order.[7]

The Crown's opposition to ecclesiastical appeals to the papal nuncio in Spain was expressed in terms that could be applied with greater validity to the *recurso de fuerza*: they were condemned for 'delaying the administration of justice, undermining the authority of the prelates, and enabling delinquents

---

[1] *Ibid.*, Representación del Prior to the king, 4 Nov. 1787.

[2] *Ibid.*, Testimonio del expediente formado por real orden . . . en 5 cuadernos, 1787-9.

[3] *Ibid.*, R.O.'s to archbishop and viceroy, 14 June 1788; and R.C.'s to the same, 19 April 1789, with identical phrasing.

[4] *Ibid.*, Auto Audiencia, 30 July 1789; Respuesta Fiscal to the viceroy, 17 Nov. 1789.

[5] *Ibid.*, archbishop to the viceroy, 13 Nov. 1789; viceroy to the king, 14 Dec. 1789.

[6] *Ibid.*, archbishop to Council, 30 Dec. 1791, acknowledging receipt of R.C., 6 Sept. 1791.

[7] *Ibid.*, Pase dado al breve pontificio de 8 May 1790.

to escape punishment';[1] and, although the Crown would never have admitted that interference from its own courts was as harmful to ecclesiastical discipline as interference from the papal nuncio, it gave tacit recognition to the *recurso*'s shortcomings and the problems it created by prohibiting its use whenever royal interests were at stake. This prohibition was made, for example, in patronage cases.[2] Since the king claimed jurisdiction over them in any event, it would have been illogical to permit *recursos* from one of his representatives to another. Not only would the vice-patrons' exclusive authority be usurped by the *audiencias*, but also any appeal, whether ordinary or extraordinary, would defeat the Crown's intention of using summary judgements for the speedy resolution of patronage problems. This prohibition did not stop the parties from presenting *recursos de fuerza* in patronage cases, which could frustrate the course of justice even if they were eventually rejected. For example, a delinquent curate in Yucatán, whose bishop and vice-patron sought to deprive him of his benefice, was able to postpone the final verdict for years, since each time he presented a *recurso*, the proceedings had to be suspended until the *audiencia*'s decision that the *recurso* was illegal reached Mérida.[3]

In the *visitas* of the religious orders, so essential to Caroline ecclesiastical policy, the Crown vacillated between the desire to achieve the reform of regular discipline, for which the unrestricted authority of the *visitadores* was necessary, and a reluctance to relinquish royal control over their actions. Solórzano Pereira had written that it was preferable for the regulars to endure any injustice during a *visita* rather than disrupt it with *recursos*,[4] but other regalists thought that the king could not ignore a plea for protection from any of his vassals, no matter what the circumstances were.[5] Charles III

---

[1] S. Sánchez, ed., *Colección de todas las pragmáticas, cédulas, provisiones circulares, autos acordados, bandos y otras providencias publicadas en el actual reinado del señor Don Carlos IV* (4 vols., Madrid, 1794–1805), iv, 466–76, R.O. circular, 26 Nov. 1767, reissued 28 Aug. 1804.

[2] *Recop. Indias*, ley 39, título 6, Libro 1.

[3] A.G.I., Mexico 3064, Testimonio de autos contra el cura de Umán, Bishop of Yucatán to the king, 20 Sept. 1783.

[4] J. de Solórzano Pereira, *op. cit.*, Libro 4, cap. 26, no. 21; see also *Nueva Recopilación de las leyes de Castilla* (1567), ley 40, título 5, Libro 2.

[5] J. Covarrubias, *op. cit.*, título 24, máx. 44 and 48; título 27, máx. 1–10.

decided to sidestep the issue by limiting the judicial sphere of the *visitas*: he prohibited the *visitadores* from conducting trials of individual regulars and subjected their general reform measures to the supervision of the viceroys,[1] whose intervention would be extra-judicial and therefore presumably less disruptive than the cumbersome procedure that the *audiencias* were obliged to follow.

This system was often ignored in Peru, where the viceroy complained that the *visitas* of the orders of St Augustine and San Juan de Diós were constantly delayed by *recursos*.[2] In Mexico most of the appeals and petitions were handled by the viceroys, although this method did not necessarily ensure the rapid and satisfactory conclusion of the *visitas*.[3] When the *audiencia* did accept *recursos* and pronounced in favour of the appellants, the *visitadores* were often able to convince the king that the persecution the friars alleged was nothing more than efforts to reform their unlicenced behaviour, and they were able to persuade him to overrule the *audiencia*'s decisions in the interests of monastic discipline.[4] But the delays from both the *recursos* in Mexico and the subsequent petitions to Madrid nevertheless obstructed the course of the *visitas*.[5]

Even when *recursos* were not prohibited for reasons of state, the *autos de fuerza* were by no means automatically in favour of the appellant, especially when his plea opposed the dictates of public order and the proper administration of justice. A prebendary of Michoacán, on trial for concubinage, tried every extraordinary appeal available to a recalcitrant ecclesiastic, including recusation of his judges, four *recursos* to the *audiencia* of Mexico, and a request for *real amparo* from the viceroy,[6]

---

[1] A.G.I., Ind. Gen. 3040, Instrucción real para visitadores-reformadores, 26 May 1771.

[2] M. de Amat y Junient, *op. cit.*, pp. 95–8.

[3] See, e.g., the problems that faced successive viceroys with the *visita* and other internal disputes of the Bethlemites, from 1771 to 1804, in A.G.I., Mexico 2750 and 2751, and above, pp. 43–5.

[4] B.N., 3535, Expediente sobre los recursos de fuerza interpuestos por los Agonizantes (Order of San Camilo Lelis) . . ., 1777.

[5] A.G.I., Mexico 2537, Consultas Council, 9 March 1779 and 28 May 1784, concerning the *visita* of the Agonizantes.

[6] A.G.I., Mexico 2635, Viceroy Bucareli to the Bishop of Michoacán, 17 Feb. 1779.

all of which were rejected. The judicial evidence and independent reports from residents in Michoacán indicated that he was in fact guilty of the crime with which he was charged; the examples of unjust treatment he cited, such as being held in custody during the trial,[1] were false and, in any case, would have been normal practice in criminal cases in both secular and ecclesiastical courts. When he escaped to Madrid 'to cast myself at the feet of Your Majesty and seek royal protection from the vile vengeance I am suffering',[2] he was immediately sent under military escort to Cadiz and placed on the first ship back to Veracruz, to be restored to the custody and jurisdiction of his prelate.[3]

But occasionally the *audiencias* came into conflict with the Crown's general policies on ecclesiastical questions when, preoccupied with strict adherence to the law, they upheld the jurisdiction of the ecclesiastical magistrate. According to royal law, for example, a *recurso de fuerza* was inadmissible if the appellant could obtain redress of his grievance through the normal channels of his own *fuero*. When a Carmelite friar in Mexico presented a *recurso* in 1788 against a sentence pronounced by his provincial,[4] the *audiencia* rejected it on the grounds that the provincial had committed none of the three varieties of *fuerza*—he had neither refused to grant an ordinary appeal, conducted the case illegally, nor exceeded his jurisdiction in trying it—and told the friar to appeal the sentence to the higher ecclesiastical judge, who was the Carmelite General in Rome.[5] The legalistic *oidores* failed to realize that their recommendation, though in accordance with the letter of the law, was in direct opposition to the Crown's policy of isolating the American Church from Rome. The Council of the Indies was probably indifferent to the friar's complaints of oppression, but it hastened to forestall his appeal to Rome by placing him under the viceroy's protection and ordering the

[1] A.G.I., Mexico 2635, Representación de Josef de Villanueva a S.M., 1781.

[2] A.G.I., Mexico 1152, Representación from Villanueva to the king via José de Gálvez, 11 Oct. 1782.

[3] *Ibid.*, R.C. to Cabildo sedevacante Michoacán, 19 June 1783.

[4] A.G.I., Mexico 2644, Recurso de fuerza to Audiencia, 13 Sept. 1787.

[5] *Ibid.*, Auto de fuerza, 3 Oct. 1788 (the bull of 1573 did not apply to religious orders that had generals in Rome).

audiencia to make a thorough investigation of the injustices he complained of.[1] The Council also reminded the *oidores* gently that the king's representatives should always be careful to help royal subjects avoid the 'unnecessary expense and hardship of an appeal to Rome'.[2]

The conflict in royal policy between the necessity of maintaining ecclesiastical discipline and that of supervising the ecclesiastical judicial system was especially marked in the use of the *real provisión de fuerza*, a short-cut method of extending royal protection to subjects living in areas remote from the *audiencias*. Each provincial centre of government could oblige the ecclesiastical courts in the district to cease proceedings immediately without the inevitably long delay of communicating with the *audiencia* and waiting for its decision.[3] The *provisión* was not supposed to be in lieu of a *recurso de fuerza* but an interim measure to check abuses against a possibly innocent party until he could communicate with the *audiencia*. The Crown was well aware of the possibility of unjustified petitions which could result in delaying a deserved sentence, but the governors had no discretionary powers in the release of the *provisión* regardless of the circumstances, since a fraudulent *recurso* had the ultimate remedy in the *audiencia*, which could declare in favour of the ecclesiastical magistrate.[4]

The ecclesiastical hierarchy, generally opposed to secular supervision in inverse proportion to the rank of the official who exercised it (the intervention of royal ministers, for example, was rarely, if ever, challenged), was bound to resent this interference from local officials, while at the same time accepting the principle of judicial review by the *audiencias*. In 1781 the Governor of Durango issued a *real provisión de fuerza* on behalf of a priest, supposedly suffering severe persecution from the diocesan *provisor*, and insisted that the *provisor* not only send all the pertinent documents to the *Audiencia* of Guadalajara, but

---

[1] *Ibid.*, R.C.'s to Audiencia, viceroy, and the Carmelite provincial, 8 June 1789.

[2] *Ibid.*, R.C. to the Audiencia, 8 June 1789.

[3] *Recop. Indias*, ley 136, título 15, Libro 2.

[4] See, A.H.N., Códices 706, R.C. to Governor of Venezuela, 27 Aug. 1747; and A.G.I., Mexico 3070A, R.C. to Governor of Havana, 25 Nov. 1755 (copy), reprimanding them for refusing to issue a *real provisión de fuerza*.

also immediately release the priest from prison, absolve him from excommunication, and restore his confiscated property.[1] The *provisor* responded by excommunicating the *asesor general* for having suggested this measure and by threatening the governor with the same unless he revoked the offensive decree,[2] although he eventually forwarded the documents to the *audiencia*.[3] His objection was to the clause demanding that he quash the sentence pronounced against the priest; for, as he argued, even the *audiencia*, which had the exclusive right to declare an ecclesiastical sentence invalid, would not do so before it had studied the evidence.[4]

The use of the provincial *provisión* for a *recurso de protección* was even more open to controversy, because appeal could be made against any form of procedure, not necessarily judicial. Faced with demands to interfere with anything from severe physical violence down to a merely disagreeable command from an ecclesiastical superior, the local royal officials often had to make the difficult choice between failing to exercise this cherished royal prerogative and fostering rebellion or bad conduct in an ecclesiastical subject. In one case in Yucatán the governor was requested to protect a Franciscan friar against future persecution by ordering his superiors to permit him to reside in a monastery of another order.[5] The Franciscan provincial objected to the order on the reasonable grounds that one could not appeal a non-existent abuse,[6] and the governor's legal advisers agreed that both the petition and the *real provisión* were illegal,[7] but the governor still felt obliged to 'alleviate the almost [*sic*] evident sufferings of this unfortunate vassal'.[8] The Council of the Indies, approving of the governor's

[1] A.G.I., Guadalajara 568, Real provisión de fuerza intimada por el Governador de Durango al Provisor, 26 Aug. 1781.

[2] *Ibid.*, Auto del Provisor, 17 Sept. 1781.

[3] *Ibid.*, Provisor to Audiencia, 13 Oct. 1781.

[4] *Ibid.*, Auto Provisor, 17 Sept. 1781.

[5] A.G.I., Mexico 3070A, Recurso de protección on behalf of Fr Gabriel Rodríguez Arfián to Governor Gálvez, 13 Oct. 1790; and Oficio Governor to the provincial, 13 Oct. 1790.

[6] *Ibid.*, provincial to governor, 13 Oct. 1790.

[7] *Ibid.*, Dictamen Auditor de Guerra, 16 Oct. 1790; Dictamen Asesor de Intendencia, 21 Oct. 1790.

[8] *Ibid.*, governor to the king, 8 March 1791.

decision to intervene on the friar's behalf, rebuked the advisers for their 'lack of zeal in defending the *regalía* of royal protection' and expressed concern that His Majesty's vassals should not be deprived of their rights simply because they lived far from an *audiencia*.[1] The fact that the friar had never expressed any intention of making a *recurso de fuerza* to the *audiencia*, and the fact that he could not even allege oppression at the time of his petition, were legal technicalities considered irrelevant to the larger question of royal control over the ecclesiastical judiciary.

Although the Holy See consistently condemned the *recurso de fuerza* from its inception and provided canonical censures against its use as late as the twentieth century,[2] the contrast between its attitude and that of the ecclesiastical hierarchy in Spain and the Indies was almost complete. Several works written by Spanish ecclesiastics in defence of this institution were placed on the Roman *Index*.[3] In addition, while the popes issued the annual bull, *In Coena Domini*, listing secular violations of ecclesiastical jurisdiction, of which the *recurso de fuerza* was deemed the most blatant,[4] a noted Spanish American canonist and prelate asserted that the same bull conceded the right to make these *recursos*.[5] Although many bishops might have merely tolerated these appeals, believing that protest would not have remedied the abuse in any case, most were too imbued with regalism even to question its legality. A *provisor* of Durango, who demonstrated the most determined resistance to an unfavourable *auto de fuerza*, still acknowledged 'the justice and necessity of this privilege', although he felt that, if abused, the *recurso* could be a serious impediment to the administration of justice.[6]

---

[1] A.G.I., Mexico 3005, Consulta Council, 13 April 1792.

[2] *Codex Juris Canonici*, cc. 2333 and 2334.

[3] e.g., Enrique Henríquez, a Jesuit, whose *De clavibus romani pontificis* (Salamanca, 1619) one of the first Spanish apologias of the *recurso*, was placed on the *Index* in the early seventeenth century, according to V. de la Fuente, *Historia eclesiástica de España* (6 vols., Madrid, 1873-5), v, 442-3. The work of another Spanish cleric, F. Salgado de Somoza, *De regia protectione*, was placed on the *Index* in 1628, according to A. de Egaña, *op. cit.*, p. 131.

[4] Paragraph 16 of the papal bull 'In Coena Domini', issued annually on Holy Thursday from the time of Boniface VIII. See J. López, *Historia legal de la bula llamada In Coena Domini* (Madrid, 1768, written in 1688), pp. 106-12, for a Spanish translation of the version of Pope Clement X.

[5] G. de Villarroel, *Gobierno eclesiástico pacífico*, Part 2, quest. 12, art. 5, no. 96.

[6] A.G.I., Guadalajara 568, Provisor of Durango to governor, 15 Sept. 1781.

A few ecclesiastical judges, such as Bishop Pedro Tamarón y Romeral of Durango, sought to punish those ecclesiastics who, 'knowing that their case is hopeless in their own courts, seek aid from the secular judges in order to suppress the truth and escape punishment for their crimes'.[1] These appeals were made technically at the risk of excommunication, since canon law forbade ecclesiastics to renounce their own *fuero*,[2] a legal concept that neither the secular authorities nor the ecclesiastical appellants were willing to accept. Bishop Tamarón, having already warned his subjects of this risk, applied the appropriate censure to three of his canons who signed a petition to the Governor of Durango requesting him to exhort the bishop to cease proceedings against them.[3] The Council *fiscal* considered this action prejudicial to royal authority on two counts: first, ecclesiastics were not to be denied their right to seek royal protection; and second, the bishop had cited the bull *In Coena Domini* as the authority for the censures, and this bull had long since been denied the royal *exequatur* and formally denounced to the pope as an encroachment on the Crown's sovereignty.[4] Bishop Tamarón was to be reprimanded for his illegal action and reminded that the bull had no legal force either in Spain or in the Indies. But twenty years later, despite a general *cédula* condemning the bull,[5] the Bishop of Oaxaca applied it in similar circumstances to excommunicate a priest who had sought protection from the viceroy.[6]

There is no evidence that these censures were actually used against ecclesiastics who made formal *recursos de fuerza* to an *audiencia* and, even if they had, royal law provided a remedy for this type of 'abuse' also. Secular control of the ecclesiastical judicial system was not limited to the criminal and civil cases

[1] P. Tamarón y Romeral, *Demostración del vastísimo obispado de la Nueva Vizcaya 1765*, edited by Vito Alessio Robles (Mexico, 1937), 'Instrucción a los vicarios eclesiásticos', pp. 399–400.

[2] 'In Coena Domini', paragraph 16.

[3] A.G.I., Ind. Gen. 350, Expediente sobre la Bula de la Cena en Indias, 1768.

[4] *Ibid.*, Respuesta Fiscal, 17 March 1768.

[5] *Ibid.*, R.C. circular to all secular and regular prelates in the Indies, 2 Dec. 1768.

[6] A.G.I., Mexico 2666, Revisión de la causa seguida a D. José Paz y Mendoza, 17 Sept. 1787; and Mexico 2637, Paz y Mendoza to Ventura de Taranco, 2 Sept. 1788.

of the *fuero externo* but extended over the strictly spiritual *fuero* of conscience as well. A writ of excommunication, whether against an ecclesiastic or a layman, could be appealed in a *recurso de fuerza* and, if the *audiencia* judged that the ecclesiastical magistrate had committed *fuerza* in issuing it, the writ was declared invalid.[1]

The excommunication of royal judges who usurped, or who were alleged to have usurped, ecclesiastical authority was the Church's principal weapon in the jurisdictional disputes that occurred so frequently in the Indies. Royal law prohibited this use of ecclesiastical censures, and the Crown repeatedly banned the papal bull on which they were based,[2] but the *recurso de fuerza* provided the most effective defence. In addition, it gave the secular judiciary the decisive voice in defining the boundary between ecclesiastical and secular jurisdiction: the majority of *competencias* were referred to the *audiencias* for resolution through *recursos de fuerza*, and, if the *audiencia* decided that the excommunicated royal judge had not exceeded his authority (for example, in summoning a priest to give testimony before him or in extracting a fugitive criminal from a church), then the ecclesiastical court was obliged to absolve him and relinquish all jurisdiction in his favour.[3] Royal magistrates still feared the 'dishonour and scandal' attached to a public notice of excommunication,[4] but the efficacy of canonical censures as a political weapon against secular supremacy was destroyed by the *recurso de fuerza*.

Once the *audiencia* had promulgated an *auto de fuerza* unfavourable to the ecclesiastical magistrate, there was little he could do. The *audiencia* could confiscate his property and even deport him to Spain if he refused to obey the *auto*, since a

[1] *Recop. Indias*, leyes 9 and 10, título 10, Libro 1.

[2] A.G.I., Ind. Gen. 350, Expediente sobre la Bula de la Cena . . ., 1768, summarizing previous *cédulas* and the cases in which they were ignored; and R.C. circular, 2 Dec. 1768.

[3] See, e.g., A.G.I., Mexico 3068, Bishop of Yucatán to the king, 24 May 1786, and Audiencia to the king, 26 Oct. 1787, concerning a *competencia* with the *alcalde ordinario* of Mérida; Guadalajara 534, Consulta Council, 6 April 1804, and 27 Jan. 1807, concerning a *competencia* between the Bishop of Sonora and a local *subdelegado*.

[4] See, A.G.I., Mexico 2617, Oidor Domingo Valcárcel to Julián de Arriaga, 22 April 1763, concerning his excommunication by the Archbishop of Mexico.

G

refusal was equivalent to sedition.[1] There is no record of such drastic action in this period, although one ecclesiastical judge gained a sharp rebuke from the Crown and a rejection of his application for promotion,[2] because he had defied an *auto* issued by the *Audiencia* of Guadalajara. He first claimed falsely that he had executed the *auto*'s provisions, although the royal notary in Durango certified that he had not.[3] Then he used the formula 'I obey but do not execute', informing the *oidores* that they had to be either very malicious or very ignorant to have made a decision so contrary to both canon and royal law.[4] Next he appealed the *auto*, basing his petition on a copy of the *audiencia*'s proceedings he had obtained by bribing the *receptor*.[5] He finally submitted, but only after three more years of similar subterfuges: in this period even a determined prelate lacked the power to defy royal authority indefinitely.

The *audiencia* was curiously unassertive in the face of this energetic resistance and was accused by the Council of the Indies of a 'singular disregard for one of His Majesty's most precious prerogatives' in neglecting to enforce their decree with the severe measures provided by royal law for ecclesiastical magistrates 'who abuse their authority with such unexampled persistence'.[6]

Royal policy concerning appeals of *autos de fuerza* was weighted against the ecclesiastical magistrate. Theoretically final, the *auto* was open to appeal in practice only if it favoured ecclesiastical jurisdiction.[7] There were rare instances, such as the reform *visitas* of the religious orders, when the ecclesiastical magistrates could gain a favourable hearing from the Council, but only because it was in the Crown's interest to support their authority in the particular cases. Usually they were compelled to submit to secular review of their proceedings and denied

---

[1] *Recop. Indias*, ley 143, título 15, Libro 2. See also Real Decreto, 14 Nov. 1745, in J. Covarrubias, *op. cit.*, appendix, pp. 297–9.

[2] A.G.I., Mexico 2534, Consulta Council, 1 Oct. 1787, with undated real resolución.

[3] A.G.I., Guadalajara 568, Certificate Notario publico, Durango, 5 Feb. 1782.

[4] *Ibid.*, Oficio Provisor to Audiencia, 4 April 1782.

[5] *Ibid.*, Respuesta Fiscal Audiencia, 2 Jan. 1783, requesting punishment for the *Receptor*.

[6] A.G.I., Guadalajara 244, Consulta Council, 12 May 1787.

[7] J. Covarrubias, *op. cit.*, título 31.

the right to protest a decision that these proceedings were abusive;[1] yet the records contain many appeals from the contending parties—both royal judges and ecclesiastical defendants—who were successful in gaining a reversal of an *auto de fuerza* that had upheld the sentences and jurisdiction of the ecclesiastical court.[2]

The Crown resorted to these methods of supervising the ecclesiastical judicial system because, despite the various indirect checks on ecclesiastical immunity such as patronage prerogatives and executive intervention, the clergy were still subject to the judicial jurisdiction of their own magistrates. Only in the later years of the eighteenth century did the State attempt a direct attack against this ancient privilege of the *fuero*, an attack in which the machinery of judicial review was applied in a new context. Although theoretically a means to provide royal protection for ecclesiastics suffering abuses from their superiors, the *recurso de fuerza* could also be extended to deprive an ecclesiastic of immunity against his will. This procedure, originally used to curtail ecclesiastical jurisdiction over laymen, required little modification for use in *competencias* over ecclesiastical delinquents, when the Crown decided to place them under the direct jurisdiction of the secular courts.[3]

---

[1] *Recop. Castilla*, ley 35, título 5, Libro 2; *Recop. Indias*, ley 10, título 10, Libro 1; and R.C. circular (copy), 15 Nov. 1758, in A.G.I., Ind. Gen. 3027.

[2] See, e.g., A.G.I., Mexico 2531, Consulta Council, 25 Feb. 1761, overruling an *auto de fuerza* at the petition of the ecclesiastical defendant; and Mexico 2631, Acuerdo Council, 30 Oct. 1786, overruling an *auto* at the petition of a royal justice. *Legajos* Mexico 2609, 2630, 2644, 2647 contain other examples from this period.

[3] See Ch. VIII, sect. 2.

PART II

The Crisis of Royal Policy

CHAPTER IV

The Caroline Programme of Ecclesiastical Reform

THE PRIVILEGE of ecclesiastical immunity claimed by all ordained ecclesiastics remained technically inviolate in the Spanish colonies despite the different indirect methods the Crown had created to control the clergy. Extra-judicial investigations, patronage jurisdiction, and royal review of ecclesiastical judicial decisions, all encroached upon this privilege in varying degrees, but the Crown had never imposed any direct limitation on ecclesiastical *fuero*.

Sanctioned by law,[1] this exclusive immunity was also honoured in practice. Jurisdictional disputes between ecclesiastical and royal judges were frequent but, arising solely over subsidiary questions, they demonstrate that the fundamental principle of immunity was commonly regarded as an unalterable element in Spanish colonial jurisprudence. Royal jurists sought, for example, to refute the Church's extension of ecclesiastical *fuero* to its dependants (*familiares*),[2] arguing that only ordained ecclesiastics could enjoy this privilege. (A typical *competencia* over this question arose in Mexico in 1781, when an *alcalde del crimen*, insisting on his right to 'proceed against a lay defendant in a temporal [as opposed to spiritual] case', arrested a bailiff of the archdiocesan court on a criminal charge.[3])

There were often disputes over the identity and status of an ecclesiastical offender who had been apprehended in secular

---

[1] *Recop. Indias*, ley 73, título 14, Libro 1.

[2] G. de Villarroel, *Gobierno eclesiástico pacífico*, Part 1, quest. 2, art. 3, nos. 39–43, asserting that notaries, bailiffs and other 'servants' of the Church, though laymen, were subject to ecclesiastical jurisdiction.

[3] A.G.I., Mexico 2631, Alcalde del Crimen, Josef de Urízar, to Provisor, 15 Oct. 1781.

dress,[1] or over the summoning of an ecclesiastic to give testimony before a royal magistrate.[2] The common feature of all these disputes was the respect paid by the royal judges to the basic concept of immunity in their attempts to prove in each instance that they had not violated this privilege. The same attitude is revealed in the elaborate, though not always convincing, theories devised by regalist authors to justify the State's extra-judicial control of the clergy.[3]

In many cases the Madrid government even supported the Church's position in the borderline areas of conflict.[4] Yet, in the last decades of the eighteenth century, the Crown suddenly reversed its traditional policy towards ecclesiastical immunity and subjected the clergy to the direct judicial jurisdiction of the royal courts in civil and criminal cases.[5]

This attack on ecclesiastical immunity cannot be studied in isolation, since it was only one aspect of a general programme of ecclesiastical reform initiated during the reign of Charles III, which in turn rested on a totally new concept of the relationship between Church and State formulated by Charles's regalist ministers. The Crown's traditional policy towards the privileges and authority of the Church was a product of the Habsburg view that Church and State were equal and mutually dependent partners, a view often expressed in the medieval image of the two swords, spiritual and temporal.[6] Within this framework of interdependence, secular and ecclesiastical authority were entwined in a complex relationship which produced many minor conflicts between the representatives of

---

[1] See, e.g., A.G.I., Mexico 2614, Expediente sobre el proceso por incontinencia . . ., 1766–7.

[2] A.G.I., Guadalajara 310, Bishop of Guadalajara to the king, 14 Oct. 1778; and Mexico 3068, Bishop of Yucatán to the king, 24 May 1786.

[3] For regalist theories on executive intervention, see above, pp. 39–42.

[4] See A.H.N., Códices 689, R.C. to Bishop of Cartagena, 19 March 1757, concerning ecclesiastical *fuero* for *familiares*; and Guadalajara 344, R.C. to Audiencia, 4 Feb. 1781, concerning ecclesiastical witnesses.

[5] See Ch. VII, on ecclesiastical *fuero* in civil cases, and Ch. VIII, on ecclesiastical *fuero* in criminal cases.

[6] This image appears frequently in G. Castillo de Bobadilla, *Política para corregidores y señores de vasallos en tiempo de paz y de guerra y para prelados en lo espiritual y temporal entre legos* (2 vols., Madrid, 1775, first published in 1574), i, Libro 2, caps. 15, 16, a standard work of Spanish jurisprudence, often quoted by both canonists and royal jurists in this period.

Church and State, precisely because the boundary between their areas of jurisdiction was so vaguely defined.[1] But the close identification of interests precluded any fundamental antagonism: by furthering the aims of one, the other gained equally. The balance of authority was weighted in favour of the State, which claimed the right to act as final judge in these conflicts, but equality was preserved in practice because the king, who considered himself the head of both Church and State in the Indies, was generally an impartial arbitrator, as quick to reprimand royal officials as he was the ecclesiastical authorities for overstepping the limits of their respective jurisdictions. Similarly, although the Crown claimed the right to supervise the Church's administration (even in certain spiritual matters) and the conduct of its ministers, the Church in turn was permitted to intervene in many temporal matters, and its authority was supported by the power of the State. Ecclesiastical institutions in the Indies were limited in independence but not in strength.

The fundamental nature of this system remained unaltered throughout the Habsburg period of colonial history and survived well into the eighteenth century, until Charles III, whose reign marked the appearance of so many innovations in other areas of administration, formed a new ecclesiastical policy that was to upset the traditional equilibrium between ecclesiastical and secular authority.

The ecclesiastical policy pursued by Charles III was a hybrid, combining traditional elements from the Habsburg system with purely Caroline innovations, but all having the same end: the expansion of royal power at the expense of that of the Church. The Habsburgs had already transformed the original *patronato* concept into a convenient variation called the *vicariato*[2] and had used their authority as 'vicars general' to replace papal with royal intervention in many areas of ecclesiastical administration, with particular success in the Indies.

[1] For comments on this problem and the need for a more clearly defined boundary, see *Instrucciones que los virreyes*, i, Advertimientos del Marqués de Montesclaros a S.M., 1607, pp. 129–35; Instrucción del Conde de Revillagigedo I, 1754, pp. 360–70; and *Memorias de los virreyes que han gobernado el Perú* (5 vols., Lima, 1859), iv, Manso de Velasco to Amat y Junient, 1756, pp. 6–8.

[2] For a discussion of the *vicariato* concept, see above, pp. 28–30.

Charles III employed this same concept, infused with supporting Gallicanist and divine right theories from foreign authors,[1]
to consolidate and improve upon the gains made by his predecessors. He reduced papal intervention in the Indies still
further and strengthened royal control over the colonial
Church[2] at the same time that he applied in Spain certain
prerogatives that were already in use in the Indies, such as the
royal *exequatur*, which gave the Crown veto power over papal
legislation and judicial decisions.[3]

But if the Church under the traditional *patronato* and *vicariato*
concepts had been permitted, indeed encouraged, to flourish
within the boundaries of the national State, the Caroline policy
was aimed at reducing all ecclesiastical power, not merely that
of the pope. While reaffirming and extending royal control over
ecclesiastical institutions from above, Charles III also proposed
to limit or even to abolish many of them. The contractual concept of the Habsburgs had no place in the Caroline system,
for Charles III, unlike his predecessors, was not prepared to
support the power and authority of the clergy in his realms,
even if he could succeed in creating a national Church completely independent from Rome and subordinate to the State.[4]

The application of the new policy was to have a profound
effect on ecclesiastical institutions in New Spain but, since the
initiative lay entirely with the Madrid government, its origins
must be sought in currents of political thought, conditions, and
events in Spain which influenced the Crown to repudiate a
system that had functioned for centuries to the apparent benefit
of both Church and State. The key to this new policy is the
relationship between ecclesiastical power and privilege and

---

[1] Z. van Espen, *Jus ecclesiasticum universum* (Louvain, 1700); J. von Hontheim
(pseud., Justinus Febronius), *De statu ecclesiae et legitima potestate Romani Pontificis*
(Boulogne, 1763); and C. Fleury, *Institution au droit ecclésiastique* (2 vols., Paris,
1676), were the three most widely quoted authors.

[2] Chs. I–III contain material on Caroline innovations in the traditional methods
of royal control.

[3] Decreed in 1761, suspended, and reinstated in 1768 in response to the publication of the papal *Monitorio de Parma*, excommunicating the Bourbon Duke of
Parma. See P. Rodríguez de Campomanes, *Juicio imparcial sobre las letras en forma
de breve que ha publicado la Curia Romana* (Madrid, 1768).

[4] See W. E. Shiels, *King and Church: the rise and fall of the Patronato Real* (Chicago,
1961), Chapter 6, entitled 'Perversion of the *Patronato*'.

the two overriding goals of Charles III and his ministers, to which all other questions were subordinated: the first political, the extension of royal absolutism; the second economic, the development of Spain's (and the colonies') material prosperity.[1] With these primary aims in view, the Caroline policy-makers, principally the two *fiscales* of the Council of Castile, Pedro Rodríguez de Campomanes (Count of Campomanes), and José de Moñino (Count of Floridablanca), formed a corollary programme of ecclesiastical reform which sought to limit or abolish any ecclesiastical institution that would interfere with their realization.

The desire to see Spain recover its former position of dominance, or at least one of importance among the other European nations, was a recurrent theme in Spanish literature, both official and unofficial, from almost the beginning of the eighteenth century,[2] and this desire was strengthened by the humiliating defeat suffered at the hands of the English in the Seven Year Wars, which Spain entered shortly after Charles III's accession to the throne (1759). This defeat, though disastrous to Spanish pride, was also a valuable lesson, for it demonstrated that Spain could not re-emerge as a strong international power without the development of its internal strength, for which—and Charles's ministers were sufficiently clear-sighted to realize this—a rejuvenation of the stagnant national and colonial economy was the main prerequisite.

The reasons for Spain's economic decadence were numerous, but one of the major obstacles to prosperity, according to Charles's ministers, was the immense material wealth the Church had been permitted to accumulate over the centuries. They considered ecclesiastical mortmain harmful to both society and the State: it contributed to the poverty of laymen, depriving them of property and the opportunity to apply their industry for personal gain, and increased their share of the burden of taxation; while at the same time it reduced the Crown's

---

[1] See L. Sánchez Agesta, *El pensamiento político del despotismo ilustrado* (Madrid, 1953), particularly pp. 99–106 and 115–37.

[2] Though the theme of Spain's decadence appeared in the previous century (in the poetry of Quevedo, for example), Feijóo (1726) was perhaps the first to combine it with practical suggestions for reform: see M. Colmeiro, *Biblioteca de los economistas españoles de los siglos XVI, XVII y XVIII* (Madrid, 1861).

revenues.[1] Charles's most prolific and influential economist, Campomanes, asserted that merely to discourage further acquisitions by the Church would not remedy the fundamental problem; rather, he proposed that all property in mortmain be expropriated and the clergy be left with an 'adequate sustenance' from tithes, first fruits, and parochial fees.[2]

Reappraising the Church's role in Spanish society, Charles's ministers relied on a classical principle of Spanish jurisprudence, that of the 'common good' (*el buen común*), but also employed a utilitarian criterion that was new to Spanish political philosophy. This criterion was applied to ecclesiastical institutions and the clergy as well as to the property owned by the Church. It was argued that the number of people dedicated to the priesthood and the religious life should correspond to the spiritual needs of the people and that, since there were many more ecclesiastics in Spain than were necessary or useful, their number should be reduced,[3] along with that of other unproductive members of society, such as beggars and idle *hidalgos*, all of whom hindered the nation's economic development.[4]

The centralization of power in the hands of the Crown (both for its own sake and to enable the Crown to speed economic recovery) was the second major preoccupation of the Caroline reformers, who believed that the clergy's power and influence, as well as the number of ecclesiastics, had to be reduced in order to achieve this goal. They were, for example, opposed to the clergy's predominance in education. University 'curricula clouded with superstition', which they believed had stultified cultural and technical progress in Spain centuries behind the level achieved in the rest of Europe,[5] were only one reason for

---

[1] P. Rodríguez Campomanes, *Tratado de la regalía de amortización* (Madrid, 1765), pp. 17–20; 'Instrucción reservada a la Junta de Estado', 8 July 1787, art. 24, in *Obras originales del Conde de Floridablanca*, p. 216.

[2] Campomanes, *Tratado de la regalía de amortización*, pp. 22, 105.

[3] A.H.N., Consejos 494, Respuesta Fiscal Moñino, 12 April 1767; J. Covarrubias, *op. cit.*, título 24, máx. 9

[4] *Cartas político-económicas al Conde de Lerena* (Madrid, 1878), pp. 20–1. Written in the 1780's, the letters have been attributed variously to Campomanes, the Count of Cabarrús, León de Arroyal, and José María Urquijo.

[5] A.H.N., Consejos 494, Respuesta Fiscal Campomanes, 16 July 1767. See also, F. de Cabarrús, *Cartas sobre los obstáculos que la naturaleza, la opinión y las leyes oponen a la felicidad pública* (written in 1792 to Jovellanos, published in Vitoria, 1808),

their opposition: they were also, or perhaps mainly, interested in extending royal control over education so that it could serve the interests of the State. The expulsion in 1767 of the Jesuits, who had been especially influential in higher education, provided an opportunity to make certain reforms in the universities, such as the introduction of more directly useful subjects, like botany, physics and modern languages. The Jesuits were not responsible for Spain's intellectual backwardness—indeed, they were often more progressive than the other educationists—but, no longer present, they were ideal scapegoats, and, more important, their firm support of ecclesiastical, particularly papal, authority was in opposition to the regalist principles held by the majority of royal ministers. It was necessary, according to the Crown, to 'enlighten those who lack solid principles . . . on the true limits between Church and State'.[1] Thus university studies were not only revised but also placed under the direct supervision of the State, in the form of a royal censor who was to ensure that they did not challenge the Crown's prerogatives nor conflict with royal policies.[2]

Education was only one aspect of national life dominated by the clergy that Charles III sought to bring under royal control. The *cofradías*, or religious confraternities established with lay membership under diocesan authority, were another. The clergy, it was argued, could easily organize the *cofradías* into centres of opposition to royal policies, and their considerable wealth, usually in the form of capital loaned out to merchants and landowners, provided the Church with still another means of dominating economic affairs.[3]

But the main source of the clergy's power, and consequently the main target of the Caroline reforms, was the Church's

[1] R.O. to the Count of Aranda, signed by Manuel de Roda, 19 Nov. 1768, published in P. Rodríguez de Campomanes, *Colección de las alegaciones fiscales del Excmo. Sr. Conde de Campomanes* (4 vols., Madrid, 1841), ii, 71–2.

[2] *Documentos históricos mexicanos* (2 vols., B.M.), ii, no. 16, Real provisión para preservar las regalías de la corona, 6 Sept. 1770.

[3] A.H.N., Estado 6438, Minuta de un informe reservado . . ., Antonio Ventura de Figueroa to Roda, 1774.

pp. 124–9, recommending the complete secularization of education, from primary to university level.

judicial jurisdiction. In addition to adjudicating spiritual matters of conscience, the ordinary diocesan courts had exclusive jurisdiction over a number of offences, such as bigamy and sexual perversions (*crímenes nefandos*),[1] and also had the right to intervene in any criminal case in which the accused had sought asylum in a church, monastery, or other ecclesiastical property. This privilege of asylum did not exempt an offender from prosecution or punishment, but it did entitle him to the protection of the ecclesiastical magistrates, who saw to it that he was given a fair trial and that he received no penalty involving bloodshed or loss of life or limb.[2] The diocesan courts also had jurisdiction over a variety of civil suits, mainly divorce proceedings, almost all types of probate, and any litigation involving ecclesiastical property.[3]

Such extensive judicial jurisdiction was naturally unacceptable to any king who aspired to absolute rule. The Habsburg kings had supported this jurisdiction (though they had sought to place it under royal supervision, since they regarded the Church's judiciary as an auxiliary to the secular courts) but Charles III looked upon it as a powerful rival which should be checked.

Another major limitation on the State's judicial authority and one of the most serious challenges to royal absolutism was the personal immunity of the clergy. Royal ministers found the idea of an autonomous state-within-a-state, particularly when it was composed of such a large and influential segment of society, as intolerable as the specific acts which they believed inevitably resulted from this autonomy. Society had no protection from the crimes and vices of the clergy, who were exempt from any direct control by the State and, consequently, from any effective restraint.[4] But crimes against society were not considered the only or even the most serious problem caused by ecclesiastical immunity. Considering themselves free from any obligation of allegiance owed by all vassals to the king, as

---

[1] For a list of crimes under ecclesiastical jurisdiction, see G. Castillo de Bobadilla, *op. cit.*, ii, 600–15.

[2] *Ibid.*, 471–2; *Recop. Indias*, leyes 2 and 3, título 5, Libro 1.

[3] G. Castillo de Bobadilla, *op. cit.*, ii, 615–25. See also below, Ch. VII.

[4] See below, Ch. V for a more detailed discussion of regalist arguments against ecclesiastical immunity.

well as from royal authority, the clergy, it was argued, were encouraged to criticize the government, undermine royal prerogatives with 'false doctrines' on the supremacy of ecclesiastical authority, and even to organize active opposition to royal policies, utilizing their influence over the masses.[1]

Perhaps as important as the specific arguments against ecclesiastical immunity was a new attitude towards privilege in general. Campomanes's statement that 'all privileges are odious' expressed an opinion commonly held by reform-minded officials in the period,[2] most of whom had achieved their position through ability and effort rather than through family connections and who had no ties with the privileged classes. But this new attitude was in direct opposition to the traditional structure of the Spanish State, based on a multiplicity of *fueros* and exemptions enjoyed by every group and class able to obtain them from the Crown. Not only the clergy, but also members of the universities, the *consulados*, the Inquisition, the army, and the military orders, among others, claimed the right to be governed by special sets of regulations and to be tried by their own fellows rather than by the ordinary royal judges.[3] The right of *fuero* was the most coveted of all privileges, having the social advantage of prestige and the practical one of ensuring a more favourable hearing, but it was only beneficial to the individual, in the opinion of Charles's ministers, who argued in favour of curtailing or abolishing special *fueros* in the interests of the 'common good' and the fair administration of justice.

The Crown's advisers, then, had a variety of empirical arguments against the Church's jurisdiction over laymen and the closely related privilege of ecclesiastical immunity. But Charles III was not as absolute in his rule as, for instance, his cousin on the French throne, and the ecclesiastical privileges which he proposed to limit or suppress were viewed by the

---

[1] A.H.N., Estado 6438, Minuta de un informe reservado . . ., Ventura de Figueroa, 1774. See also below, Ch. VI.

[2] Campomanes, *Colección de las alegaciones fiscales*, i, 158. See also *Cartas político-económicas*, pp. 214–18, condemning *mayorazgos* and the privileges of the nobility and the military orders.

[3] For a discussion of this multiplication of *fueros* and the problems they created, see Revillagigedo, *Instrucción reservada*, pp. 22–7.

vast majority of his subjects—not only the uneducated masses—
as sacred and inalienable rights. Considering the drastic nature
of the proposed reforms and also the legalistic mentality of the
Spanish, exemplified in the sixteenth-century debates over the
Crown's just title to the Indies, it is only natural that regalist
authors in this period should have devoted so much effort to
devising theories that would justify their attacks on ecclesiastical jurisdiction.[1]

These authors—again mainly the seemingly inexhaustible
Campomanes and his colleague in the *fiscalía* of the Council of
Castile, Floridablanca—sought to end the centuries-old debate
on the limits between secular and ecclesiastical authority by
arguing that the Church's only inherent right was to regulate
the purely spiritual questions of dogma, liturgy, and the sacraments, and that its original function of administering spiritual
penance for sins had developed illegally into a massive judicial
system rivalling that of the State.[2] Unclear in their writings
over whether this system had developed with or without the
consent of the temporal monarch,[3] the regalists were convinced
that it was an encroachment on his lawful authority which he
could and should eliminate. Since by their definition all contentious and coercive authority was intrinsically temporal in
nature, the Church's jurisdiction over laymen had to be reduced
to the *fuero interno* of conscience: its cognizance of civil suits
and crimes, its bailiffs, prisons, and administration of temporal
penalties, such as fines and flogging, were merely usurpations
of the State's exclusive functions.[4]

---

[1] An early expression of these theories was the 'Respuesta' made to the Council
of Castile in 1708, by Melchor de Macanaz, a minister of Philip V, compiling the
Crown's grievances against papal and episcopal authority, but it did not gain
official acceptance until Charles III's reign, when it first appeared in print in
Semanario erudito, edited by Antonio Valladares (34 vols., Madrid, 1787–91), ix,
as part of an 'Explicación jurídica e histórica que hizo el Real Consejo de
Castilla . . .'

[2] A.H.N., Consejos 494, Respuesta Fiscal Moñino, 12 April 1767; Respuesta
Fiscal Campomanes, 16 July 1767.

[3] In the same work, *Juicio imparcial*, pp. 4, 65, Campomanes calls this jurisdiction
both an abuse and a concession from the king.

[4] See Campomanes's prologue to J. López, *Historia legal de la bula llamada In
Coena Domini* (Madrid, 1768). This work is an earlier attack on ecclesiastical
jurisdiction written in 1688 and published by Campomanes in support of his
policies. See also Biblioteca del Palacio, Col. Ayala 62, Principios sobre la esencia,

Ecclesiastical immunity was condemned as intrinsically illegal by the same token, since, according to the regalists, civil litigation involving ecclesiastics and offences committed by them were also purely temporal questions. They rejected the conservative canonist view that immunity was a divine institution established by God through the Holy Scriptures,[1] as well as the more moderate claim that it was an irrevocable law of the Church.[2] According to Charles's ministers, immunity was only a concession granted by the first Christian emperors of Rome in order to protect the dignity of the ecclesiastical state from the turbulence of litigation. Succeeding Christian princes had confirmed the privilege for the same reason but, if other considerations in favour of limiting or rescinding it were to outweigh the reason for preserving immunity, then the king had the right to do so, 'despite the theories propounded by the ultra-montanists that it is an inalienable right'.[3]

Starting with the reign of Charles III and continuing until the end of Spanish rule in the Indies, the Crown issued a series of decrees reducing ecclesiastical jurisdiction, for the pragmatic reasons previously outlined, but utilizing regalist theories on the purely spiritual nature of the Church's authority. Since the Church was considered incapable of imposing punishments commensurate with 'public sins', crimes formerly prosecuted by the diocesan courts were to be placed under the jurisdiction of the secular judges, except for the administration of penance.[4] The privilege of asylum, though not abolished, was greatly restricted: it was limited to minor offences with penalties that

[1] F. Suárez, *Defensio fidei*, Book 4, Chapters 2 and 9.
[2] R. Bellarmino, *De controversiis christianae fidei* (Milan, 1586), Book I, 'De clericis'.
[3] A.H.N., Consejos 494, Respuesta Fiscal Moñino, 12 April 1767; Respuesta Fiscal Campomanes, 16 July 1767. See also Campomanes, *Juicio imparcial*, section 10, dealing with the personal immunity of the clergy.
[4] See *Novísima Recopilación de las leyes de España* (Madrid, 1805), ley 10, título 8, Libro 1, from R.C., 19 Nov. 1771, concerning 'public sins' in general. A.G.I., Mexico 2619, R.C. to Archbishop of Mexico, 14 Oct. 1770; and Nuevo Código, ley 15, título 7, Libro 1, concerning *crímenes nefandos*. A.G.N., Bandos y ordenanzas 15, R.C. circular, 10 August 1788, inserted in viceregal Bando of 17 Jan. 1789, concerning bigamy.

---

distinción y límites de las potestades espiritual y temporal, unnamed Fiscal of the Council of Castile, 1784.

H

canon law did not forbid; the number of churches that could offer asylum was reduced; and, finally, the intervention of the ecclesiastical judges in the cases that qualified for local immunity was made virtually nominal.[1]

The boundary between secular and ecclesiastical authority in civil suits was also redefined. All property was declared temporal in nature, so that the secular courts were to take cognizance of all litigation over ecclesiastical property, even if it was destined for a spiritual use.[2] Jurisdiction over cases of mixed *fuero* (*mixti fori*)—divorce for example—was divided: the diocesan judge was to decide the actual separation of a married couple, and the royal judge any questions involving property, such as the restitution of dowries.[3]

The same distinction between spiritual and temporal questions provided a useful legal basis for the Crown's offensive against the clergy's personal immunity, which was gradually reduced in most civil and criminal cases,[4] and a large category of ecclesiastics—those in minor orders—was deprived of the privilege altogether.[5] The Caroline ministers asserted that these judicial reforms were designed to restore the balance between secular and ecclesiastical authority, which 'through false piety, self-interest and ignorance' had for centuries been weighted in favour of the latter.[6] But what these ministers actually proposed was to upset the balance in the opposite direction: they sought to eliminate the Church's jurisdiction over temporal matters— that is, over the civil and criminal cases of laymen and ecclesiastics—without in turn relinquishing the Crown's intervention in purely spiritual matters through such prerogatives as the royal *exequatur* and royal review of ecclesiastical sentences of excommunication.

Charles's ecclesiastical policy, sketched here in outline, formed only one part of a general programme of reform that

---

[1] See A.G.I., Ind. Gen. 3025, R.C. circular, 2 Nov. 1773; and Ind. Gen. 2995, R.C. circular, 15 March 1787.

[2] See below, Ch. VII.

[3] A.G.I., Mexico 2636, R.C. circular, 20 March 1787.

[4] See Chs. VII and VIII.

[5] *Novís. Recop. España*, ley 13, título 10, Libro 1, from Real Decreto, 26 July 1771.

[6] Campomanes, *Colección de las alegaciones*, ii, 71–2, R.O. to the Count of Aranda, signed by Manuel de Roda, 19 Nov. 1768. See also, *Cartas político-económicas*, pp. 179, 192–3.

was to result in a rearrangement of the various components of the State, in response to the new (to Spain, at least) pragmatic and utilitarian criteria employed by the Crown. The institutions and groups considered valuable in promoting the material prosperity and the security of the State—for example, the army, the merchants, and the mine-owners—were encouraged and their *fueros* and privileges increased.[1] Campomanes's censure against 'all privileges' applied, in fact, only to those components of the State that were no longer considered 'useful': the nobility, the *gremios*, the *mesta*, and the Inquisition, among them. Their activities were to be discouraged and their privileges curtailed.[2]

The Church in particular was assigned a much less important role in the Spanish State than under the Habsburgs. Philip II deployed his armies and his financial resources as much in defence of the Catholic faith as in pursuit of imperial unity; but Charles III, without abandoning the ideal of religious orthodoxy, was to subordinate this ideal to secular considerations and to evaluate the Church and the clergy in terms of their contribution to economic progress and the maintenance of the empire. This secular criterion is illustrated in Campomanes's attitude towards charity: without disregarding its spiritual value to the donor, he emphasized the material value to the recipient and society and suggested that the State supervise almsgiving and other forms of charity dispensed by the Church, in order to ensure that they actually reduce poverty instead of merely fostering idleness and beggary.[3]

Willing to support some aspects of ecclesiastical intervention in the life of the nation, as long as they were both useful and amenable to royal control, the Crown relied increasingly on

[1] See L. McAlister, *The 'Fuero Militar' in New Spain 1764-1800* (Gainesville, 1957); and W. Howe, *The Mining Guild of New Spain and its Tribunal General 1770-1821* (Cambridge, Mass., 1949), Chapter 4, on *fuero* in mining disputes.

[2] Campomanes, *Discurso sobre la educación popular de los artesanos y su fomento* (Madrid, 1775), p. 225, concerning the privileges of the *gremios*; R. Herr, *The Eighteenth-Century Revolution in Spain* (Princeton, 1958), pp. 115–16, on the *mesta*; and A.H.N., Códices 730, R.C. circular, 29 Feb. 1760; Nuevo Código, leyes 6 and 17, título 10, Libro 1, curtailing the *fuero* of the Inquisition.

[3] Campomanes, *Apéndice a la educación popular* (4 vols., Madrid, 1775-7), volume ii contains a comprehensive programme for combating idleness and unnecessary poverty.

secular institutions and laymen to perform many of the Church's traditional functions. One of the most striking illustrations of this new policy was the changing character of the frontier area of northern New Spain, an area administered almost exclusively by the regular missionaries from the first explorations until the reform *visita* of José de Gálvez (1765–71). A number of factors —the expulsion of the Jesuits, who had held many of the missions, the need to strengthen the defences of the viceroyalty's northern border, and the desire to increase the yield of royal revenues, among them—influenced a decision to replace the friars with secular clergy, who would be assigned only spiritual duties, and to give the army and civil officials, previously few in number, the exclusive responsibility for defending and administering the region.[1] The programme was only partially successful. Not enough secular priests were willing or able to subsist in these sparsely settled areas, and the army, despite reinforcements, was even less capable of fending off or civilizing the barbarous tribes than the friars had been.[2] Nevertheless, the fact that the programme was undertaken reveals that the Madrid government no longer looked upon the clergy as the best support of Crown and empire.

This attitude is perhaps the key to the change in relations between Church and State discernible in the reign of Charles III. The close collaboration between Church and State that had been such a notable feature of the Habsburg period was abandoned by Charles, for he and his ministers believed that the interests of the two no longer coincided, but were, if not actually antagonistic, at least divergent. Thus, since the Church and its ministers could no longer be regarded as wholly reliable and effective instruments of royal policy, even if subjected to extensive supervision from the State, their immense power and influence over the thoughts and actions of the Crown's lay subjects had to be reduced.

A number of authors have condemned the Caroline ecclesiastical policy as an attempt to destroy the Church and the

[1] See H. Priestley, *José de Gálvez, Visitador General of New Spain, 1765–71* (Berkeley, 1916), pp. 213, 250–85.

[2] This was the conclusion reached in the Informe sobre las misiones, 31 Dec. 1793, written under the direction of Viceroy Revillagigedo, in A.G.I., Mexico 1142.

Catholic religion[1] and have sought to reconcile this charge with the generally accepted piety of Charles III by suggesting that the policy was imposed on a naïve king by his ministers, several of whom were 'high officials in Masonic lodges'.[2] There can be little doubt that the architects of the reform programme in general were the progressive ministers and *fiscales*, such as Campomanes, Floridablanca, and Manuel de Roda, rather than Charles himself. There is even evidence to suggest that they exaggerated the dangers and harmful effects of the clergy's activities in order to gain his approval of a more drastic policy than he might otherwise have been prepared to follow.[3] Charles was apparently easily influenced, especially by any appeal to his notorious puritanism and vanity. Roda, for example, was able to persuade him to administer severe reprimands to prelates who protested against royal decrees—even though Charles had originally decided to ignore the protests—by convincing him that these critics either were 'libertines' (*'calaveras'*) or had failed to display the proper 'spirit of veneration and humility when addressing the Vice-God on earth [i.e., the king]'.[4]

Yet, even though this new policy may not have been Charles's creation, no convincing evidence has so far appeared to support a theory that the policy was pursued independently of an either unwitting or protesting monarch, any more than to support an allegation of anti-clericalism against his ministers. It is obvious that the Caroline reform programme was based on pragmatic rather than ideological considerations. Royal ministers viewed ecclesiastical immunity and power as obstacles to economic progress and checks on royal absolutism, as they did those of other traditionally privileged groups. The reform

---

[1] See J. García Gutiérrez, *La persecución religiosa en México desde el punto de vista jurídico* (Mexico, n.d.), p. 9; M. Cuevas, *op. cit.*, iv, 388, 400–2.

[2] M. Menéndez y Pelayo, *Historia de los heterodoxos españoles* (6 vols., Madrid, 1946), vi, 37; M. Giménez Fernández, *El Concilio IV Provincial Mejicano*, pp. 17–26, asserts that the influence of the royal confessor, Padre Eleta, whom the ministers were able to manipulate, was decisive.

[3] See, e.g., A.G.I., Ind. Gen. 3041, Respuesta Fiscal Campomanes, 26 June 1768, asserting that all the religious orders in the Indies had been 'infected' by the Jesuits with disloyal doctrines.

[4] A.H.N., Estado 6438, Roda to Ventura de Figueroa, 12 Aug. 1774, quoting his conversation with the king concerning complaints addressed to the Crown by the Archbishop of Toledo and the Bishops of Plasencia and Teruel.

programme set the pattern for subsequent and more drastic
attacks on the Church and clerical privilege, and the emphasis
on utilitarian criteria, temporal authority, and material values
undoubtedly helped to prepare the way for the emergence of
the unequivocally secular State in the liberal revolution of the
early nineteenth century. But the motives and influences were
fundamentally different. Official impatience with the clergy's
'factious meddling' in civil government and with their resistance to change was not concealed,[1] but exasperation cannot be
equated with a basic antipathy to religion or the Church.
Campomanes, for instance, expressed indignation in a confidential letter to Roda that certain bishops had waited until
after publication to attack a book he had submitted for their
examination several weeks in advance.[2] However, he in no way
questioned their right to object to clauses they believed theologically unsound and in fact was willing to give prior authorization
to any deletions or changes they should consider necessary.[3]

The Caroline ministers were heavily influenced by the French
philosophes and other exponents of the rational enlightenment,[4]
but if they applied rationalist criteria to dogma as well as to
temporal phenomena, they were careful to keep their heterodox
ideas concealed. To declare openly against the Christian faith
would, in any case, have defeated their purpose by alienating
both the king and the vast majority of the population, who
were strictly orthodox. They confined themselves to attacks on
papal authority and the power of the national Church, but
even in these attacks, though they relied for their arguments
on foreign canonists whose works had been condemned by the
Roman Holy Office,[5] they were far more cautious in practice
than the theories they admired and copied. Despite their
arguments in favour of abolishing ecclesiastical immunity
completely, they chose a half-way procedure involving joint

---

[1] A.H.N., Estado 6438, Minuta de un informe . . ., 1774, by Ventura de
Figueroa.

[2] His *Juicio imparcial*, attacking the *Monitorio de Parma*.

[3] Campomanes, *Colección de las alegaciones*, ii, 57–60, Campomanes to Roda,
18 Oct. 1768.

[4] See L. Sánchez Agesta, *op. cit.*, pp. 157–9, 166–75.

[5] Fleury, Van Espen, and Febronius were all placed on the Roman but not
on the Spanish *Index*, according to M. Góngora, *op. cit.*, pp. 113, 124.

prosecution by the ecclesiastical and secular judges, a procedure which had originated in France in the sixteenth century[1] but which had already been replaced there by exclusive secular jurisdiction by the time Spain adopted it.

This hiatus between precept and practice was a general characteristic of the Caroline reform programme. Many of the original proposals of its authors suffered dilution when translated into concrete legislation, mainly for two reasons: the influence of conservative advisers to the Crown, and the necessity of reconciling theories on what was desirable with the reality of what was possible in the context of existing institutions and attitudes.

Charles's ecclesiastical policy was to face almost as much opposition from within the government as it did from the ecclesiastical hierarchy. The bishops' reactions were only natural. If many myopic prelates agreed or actively co-operated with the *vicariato* aspect of royal policy, believing that they could increase their own authority at the expense of papal supremacy and the autonomy of the religious orders,[2] they could not be expected to support any attacks on their own authority and privileges. One anonymous ecclesiastic asserted that the regalists had deliberately deceived the Spanish bishops, holding out the promise of greater episcopal power as a lure for their co-operation, while at the same time intending to destroy that power completely.[3]

The majority of Spanish prelates approved of the expulsion of the Jesuits,[4] yet the same five bishops who were members of the extraordinary council that had built up a case against the Jesuits and recommended this measure condemned a regalist work by Campomanes. They did not condemn the main thesis, which sought to prove that the popes had no jurisdiction over temporal sovereigns—'a just cause', in the opinion of the bishops—but the author's supporting arguments against the Church's contentious jurisdiction and ecclesiastical

---

[1] C. Fleury, *op. cit.*, ii, cap. 15, part 1.

[2] See above, pp. 35–6 and 62–4.

[3] Biblioteca del Palacio, Col. Ayala 26, Informe sobre el libro de Justino Febronio acerca del estado de la iglesia y legítima potestad del Papa, (n.d., late eighteenth century).

[4] R. Herr, *op. cit.*, p. 23.

immunity.[1] Cardinal Lorenzana of Toledo, who as Archbishop of Mexico had organized the extremely regalist Fourth Mexican Provincial Council in 1771,[2] shortly afterwards became one of the most outspoken critics of the Caroline ecclesiastical programme. The programme's most drastic aspects had only been formulated and not yet put into practice but, referring only to those measures already applied, Lorenzana warned the king that his reforms were 'Protestant heresies'.[3] Lorenzana's protests were not unique. The Bishops of Cuenca, Teruel, and Plasencia were among those who summoned the courage to protest openly against the subjection of ecclesiastical property to royal taxes and the curtailment of ecclesiastical jurisdiction and *fuero*.[4]

These protests received a favourable hearing from certain members of the administration who did not welcome the innovations contained in Charles III's ecclesiastical policy and gained the epithet of 'inmunistas y curialistas' from their opponents.[5] This faction, represented in general by the collegiate bodies, the Councils of Castile and of the Indies (conservative both in structure and mentality), was aligned against a smaller but more energetic group of individual ministers and *fiscales* who advocated drastic reforms. The latter group sometimes accused its opponents of ignorance of royal law or negligence in defending the Crown's lawful sovereignty against the encroaching power of the Roman Curia and the excessive pretensions of the national clergy.[6] But the conflict could also produce more serious allegations, like those contained in a vehement attack made by one of the royal *fiscales* against the higher courts of justice: the councils and *audiencias* in both

---

[1] Campomanes, *Colección de las alegaciones*, ii, 53, Bishop of Tarazona to Manuel de Roda, 2 Oct. 1768, spokesman for the four other members, the Archbishops of Zaragoza and Burgos and the Bishops of Orihuela and Albarracín.

[2] See above, pp. 32–5.

[3] A.H.N., Estado 6438, Lorenzana to the king, 20 July 1774.

[4] *Ibid.*, referred to in Minuta de informe . . ., 1774, Ventura de Figueroa, and in *Novis. Recop. España*, leyes 5 and 10, título 8, Libro 1. See also, A.H.N., Consejos 494, Bishop of Cuenca to the king, 23 May 1766.

[5] A.H.N., Estado 6438, Roda to Ventura de Figueroa, 12 Aug. 1774.

[6] See Biblioteca del Palacio, Col. Ayala 4, Dictamen de D. Manuel Pablo Salcedo, Fiscal, 1765; and A.G.I., Ind. Gen. 2994, Informe a S.M., 11 Nov. 1781, signed by Campomanes, Santiago de Espinosa, and José García Rodríguez.

Spain and the Indies. According to the *fiscal*, the hidden enemies of progress were a 'false and fanatic sense of piety' and the 'insidious influence' of the Jesuits, which persisted longer after their expulsion from Spain.[1] It was no mystery that reform legislation was being sabotaged, he declared, when those responsible for its promulgation and interpretation (councillors and *oidores*) had been educated by 'sworn enemies of the Crown': before their expulsion, the Jesuits had controlled the *colegios mayores* and succeeded in filling all the higher judicial offices with persons indoctrinated with ultra-montanist ideas concerning ecclesiastical jurisdiction and privilege.[2] But despite evidence that at least a few councillors subscribed to 'curialist' rather than regalist interpretations of ecclesiastical authority,[3] the more likely explanation is that the majority of councillors opposed the new legislation because of a general reluctance to accept any change in the *status quo*.

The progressives achieved a significant victory with the creation of a special *junta* in 1776, which was commissioned to revise the seventeenth-century colonial law code, the *Recopilación de las leyes de Indias*.[4] Composed of a small number of ministers and more radical councillors,[5] the *Junta del Nuevo Código* was to be the principal agent for the Caroline ecclesiastical programme in the Indies, and the product of its sessions, Book One of a *Nuevo Código de las leyes de Indias*,[6] the concrete expression of Caroline ecclesiastical policy. Rather than a simple revision of the old code, this was a revolutionary body of law, which superseded the *Recopilación* on virtually all ecclesiastical questions with various reform *cédulas* of Charles III or entirely new laws created by the *Junta*.

---

[1] A.G.I., Ind. Gen. 2995, Dictamen del Fiscal (unnamed), 27 Oct. 1783, commissioned by José de Gálvez.   [2] *Ibid.*, Dictamen del Fiscal, 27 Oct. 1783.

[3] See, e.g., A.G.I., Mexico 2617, Voto particular, in Consulta Council of the Indies, 14 Nov. 1763; Ind. Gen. 3027, Voto particular, 5 Jan. 1796.

[4] A.G.I., Ind. Gen. 1653, Reales decretos, 9 May 1776 and 7 Sept. 1780.

[5] Whether by chance or by design, those from the Council of the Indies— Manuel Lanz de Casafonda, the Count of Tepa, and Juan González Bustillo— were the ones who took the most regalist position on ecclesiastical issues that came before the Council: see, e.g., the dissenting *votos particulares* in A.G.I., Mexico 2632, 6 Sept. 1781, and Ind. Gen. 2995, 18 April 1788.

[6] A.G.I., Mexico 1159, Borradores del Nuevo Código de las leyes de Indias, 1790.

The *Nuevo Código* is especially relevant to a study of relations between Church and State in New Spain, for, not only were the new laws applied there with particular vigour,[1] but almost all of the important innovations were based on conflicts arising in Mexico that had been referred to Madrid for resolution.[2] In addition, the Count of Tepa, who as Antonio de Viana had served as *oidor* for many years in Mexico, drew on his knowledge of conditions in the viceroyalty to persuade his colleagues in the *Junta* to accept his more extreme views on reform.[3]

The formation of the *Nuevo Código* did not represent the total defeat of the conservatives. Even after the first and only book had been completed and had obtained royal confirmation in 1792, the Crown decided to order its publication, not as a whole, but by individual laws, and only as the specific topics they referred to arose in the colonies and were submitted to the king for his decision by the Council of the Indies.[4] Thus the introduction of reforms in the Indies was made dependent on a body that was inimical to the new law code on two counts: the revolutionary nature of many of its laws and the fact that it had been formed by an independent *junta* without any supervision from the Council.[5]

The Crown's decision against the publication of the new code in its entirety was influenced by the second factor that caused modifications in the original programme formulated by Campomanes and his colleagues: the necessity of reconciling theories with the dictates of prudence and caution. Charles III, although in agreement with his more radical ministers over the need for drastic reforms, disagreed over the questions of timing and method. He preferred, whenever possible, to enlist the aid of the Holy See in curtailing the power and privileges of the Spanish clergy, even when he considered his own authority sufficient;[6] and he emphasized the need to choose the 'appro-

---

[1] See below, Chs. VII and VIII.
[2] A.G.I., Ind. Gen. 1653, Acuerdos de la Junta para la corrección de las leyes de Indias, 1776–90.
[3] *Ibid.*, 4 Sept. 1782 and 17 March 1784.
[4] *Ibid.*, Real decreto, 25 March 1792.
[5] *Ibid.*, Consulta Council of the Indies, 26 April 1794, proposing that the code be submitted to the Council for revision.
[6] 'Instrucción reservada a la Junta de Estado', 8 July 1787, arts. 5–7.

priate occasions' for reform, to introduce the changes gradually, and to treat the clergy with 'much gentleness' in order to avoid opposition.[1] Both he and his successor, Charles IV, heeded the counsel of prudence, particularly in the delicate question of ecclesiastical reform. Deference to tradition and to attitudes that had been formed by centuries of 'ignorant fanaticism and deeply rooted superstition that equate any limitation of clerical privilege with heresy',[2] and the clergy's immense influence over public opinion both in Spain and the colonies,[3] were considerations that restrained the Crown from pursuing more extreme policies as much as any opposition from its conservative advisers.

Many aspects of the comprehensive and radical programme of reform originally outlined by Charles III's ministers were modified or ignored altogether, and the programme also lost impetus with the death of that monarch and the disintegration of his cabinet. But a sufficient number of its essential points were introduced into colonial law to produce tangible effects in New Spain. A rearrangement of the various components of the State, with a strong emphasis on the army and the relegation of the clergy to a less prominent role, has already been noted. The programme was also to affect the traditional social structure and judicial system of the colonies. Charles's ministers were influenced by the desire to strengthen the political and economic foundations of the State, without any egalitarian aims, but, in curtailing the *fueros* and exemptions of the different privileged groups and subordinating all the Crown's subjects to the supreme judicial authority of the State, they attacked the essential support of a rigid social system. One historian has described the effect of these reforms as the 'gradual erosion of a social structure based on estates, corporations, and judicial inequality and outlines at least of a new system based on economic class', clearly discernible by the end of the colonial period.[4]

---

[1] 'Instrucción reservada', 8 July 1787, arts. 12–14, 23, 24.

[2] R.A.H., Col. Mata Linares 76, Respuesta Fiscal, Council of the Indies, 1804; see also A.H.N., Estado 6438, Minuta de informe . . ., 1774, Ventura de Figueroa.

[3] 'Instrucción reservada', 8 July 1787, arts. 30, 86.

[4] L. McAlister, 'Social Structure and Social Change in New Spain', *H.A.H.R.*, xliii (1963), p. 370.

Charles's new ecclesiastical policy, particularly the measures curtailing the personal immunity of the clergy, had a profound effect on relations between Church and State in New Spain. But before dealing with the introduction of these measures and their consequences, it will be necessary to analyse the particular conditions and events in this period that helped both to stimulate and justify the Crown's decision to reverse its long-standing policy towards ecclesiastical privilege. Despite the many arguments in favour of centralizing judicial authority and checking the clergy's power, conservative opposition and the inertia of tradition could easily have prevented the application of the proposed reforms, if the advocates of reform had not been able to produce concrete evidence that supported (or at least seemed to support) their contention that the welfare of society and the security of the State demanded the abolition of ecclesiastical immunity.

CHAPTER V

Ecclesiastical Discipline
and Judicial Reform

THE DECISION to subject the clergy to the direct judicial authority of the State, primarily motivated by a desire to strengthen royal absolutism, was also influenced by arguments that the preservation of ecclesiastical immunity was incompatible with the Crown's responsibility to maintain public order and to ensure the effective administration of justice. Starting with the premise that the clergy were subject to the same temptations as the rest of mankind, the advocates of judicial reform went on to argue that the existing apparatus for restraining and correcting ecclesiastical malefactors was totally inadequate and actually encouraged immorality and crime among the clergy.[1]

The fundamental weakness of the existing system, as diagnosed by the reformers, was its almost exclusive reliance on the jurisdiction of the Church, whose coercive authority was limited to spiritual penances and certain mildly corrective measures, such as reclusion or fasting.[2] The severe temporal punishments that all but the most insignificant offences demanded were 'repugnant to the spirit of mercy and gentleness of the canons'.[3] However, this canonical limitation was not considered the only nor even the main deficiency in the Church's administration of justice. The clergy, it was argued, were not

---

[1] Biblioteca del Palacio, Col. Ayala 39, Disertación sobre lo que ordena la Instrucción de Corregidores acerca de la jurisdicción de los clérigos, anonymous, n.d. (internal evidence suggests that it was written by a royal official between 1772 and 1780); A.G.I., Ind. Gen. 1653, Junta del Nuevo Código, 12 Nov. 1783.

[2] A.H.N., Consejos 494, Respuesta Fiscal Moñino, 12 April 1767; Respuesta Fiscal Campomanes, 16 July 1767.

[3] A.G.I., Mexico 1159, Nuevo Código, ley 12, título 9, Libro 1.

deterred by any fear of punishment, as laymen were, because the ecclesiastical judges, either through negligence or a misguided sense of loyalty to their own class, usually failed to impose even those penalties within their capacity, and in some cases failed to prosecute the offender at all.[1] The ecclesiastical courts were likened to the ancient Senate of Rome: harsh in dealing out justice to others but always lenient with their own members.[2]

Objections to ecclesiastical immunity were not confined to the policy-makers in Madrid. Many colonial officials shared the view that the clergy's exemption from secular jurisdiction often meant their exemption from punishment as well.[3] In some cases it is impossible to determine whether or not the complaints were justified. Allegations that an ecclesiastical delinquent was being shielded from his just punishment could obviously be valid only if the person was in fact guilty, and the evidence presented in the ecclesiastical court often contradicted the evidence gathered by the secular authorities.

A case referred to the Crown from Yucatán in 1767 illustrates this problem. According to an investigation commissioned by the governor, the curate of an outlying Indian village was oppressing his parishioners with physical mistreatment, forced labour, and extortion of parochial fees.[4] But a preliminary inquest and formal trial carried out shortly later by the diocesan judge concluded that these accusations were false and that the villagers, far from being oppressed, were 'so arrogant and disobedient that a new conquest is necessary'.[5] The diocesan *provisor* therefore acquitted the priest, but the governor, convinced that the defendant was guilty, complained to the king and warned him that these abuses of justice would continue

---

[1] A.G.I., Ind. Gen. 3027, Respuesta Fiscal de Nueva España, Council of the Indies, 23 May 1791; Respuesta Fiscal del Perú, 20 Aug. 1791.

[2] *Ibid.*, Pedimento Fiscal del Crimen Mexico, 11 July 1799.

[3] See M. de Amat y Junient, *op. cit.* (1776), pp. 9–11; A.G.I., Mexico 3053, Governor of Yucatán to Julián de Arriaga, 18 Oct. 1767; Mexico 2629, Bucareli to the King, 27 Oct. 1775; Estado 20, Revillagigedo to Antonio Porlier, 27 Sept. 1790.

[4] A.G.I., Mexico 3053, Sumaria información, commissioned by the governor, June 1767.

[5] *Ibid.*, Autos formados, by order of the provisor, July 1767; and Pedimento Promotor Fiscal, 1 Aug. 1767.

unchecked unless the civil courts were given greater authority over the clergy.[1]

The underlying rivalry between the two jurisdictions helps to explain the conflicting versions in this and similar cases.[2] Each magistrate was primarily interested in extending or defending the limits of his jurisdiction (evidence against the defendant would provide the secular magistrate with an excuse to intervene in ecclesiastical jurisdiction, while evidence of his innocence would justify a rebuff of secular intervention) and was able to obtain the appropriate evidence by a careful selection of witnesses and questions for the inquiry. If, as was often the case, the only witnesses were Indians or *castas*, they were easily induced to give different versions of events according to which court they were in.

There were, however, other cases in which the evidence against an ecclesiastical defendant was irrefutable. The case of a Capuchin friar who entered Mexico illegally in 1737 and was arrested ten years later by the civil authorities on a charge of concubinage certainly lent plausibility to the charge that ecclesiastical superiors were inclined to overlook the misdeeds of their subordinates. First the local Capuchin superior, in supporting the defendant's claim to ecclesiastical immunity, admitted that he knew of the friar's illegal entry, his concealed identity, and the offence with which he was charged. Then the diocesan court, to which he was turned over for trial, acquitted him, despite the incontrovertible evidence of two acknowledged children and the testimony of his accomplice, and it also failed to execute its own decree ordering his deportation to Spain for illegal entry. The friar was arrested again in 1766 on the same charge, and this time the royal judges decided to deport him themselves. They demanded an explanation from the diocesan court for its previous negligence, but no record existed of why the friar had been permitted to remain in Mexico or even why he had been acquitted.[3]

[1] *Ibid.*, Governor of Yucatán to Julián de Arriaga, 18 Oct. 1767.

[2] See, e.g., A.G.I., Mexico 3072, Testimonio de autos contra Fr José Perdomo, 1792; and Ind. Gen. 3027, Testimonio de autos contra el cura interino de Petatlán, 1797.

[3] A.G.I., Mexico 2614, Testimonio de los autos criminales fhos. por incontinencia contra Fr Francisco de la Zerda, 1747–68.

Royal officials usually attributed these abuses of justice to a conscious desire on the part of the ecclesiastical superiors to protect the offender,[1] but in the majority of cases the superiors were more negligent or incompetent than indulgent. The diocesan *Provisor* of Oaxaca, for example, ignored complaints for several years about an apostate Spanish friar who created public disturbances in every village he visited in the diocese. Yet once the viceroy issued a warrant for the friar's arrest, the *provisor*, far from seeking to establish his innocence, had him detained immediately and turned him over to the civil authorities for deportation.[2]

The bishops attending the Fourth Mexican Provincial Council in 1771 acknowledged this problem and, reminding the ecclesiastical judges that 'the purpose of the Holy Mother Church in defending the clergy's personal immunity is not to hide their crimes nor to permit their status to become a licence for sin', exhorted them to be more diligent in indicting ecclesiastics even for minor offences.[3] The judges were also instructed not to release those accused of serious crimes on bail, for they tended to disappear and escape punishment.

The Spanish Crown had long recognized the deficiencies, both inherent and accidental, in the Church's administration of justice and had devised the complex system of royal control over the clergy in order to overcome these deficiencies. But this system of indirect control had obvious shortcomings also. The inefficient and confusing method of removing beneficiaries demonstrated the limitations of indirect intervention: if the vice-patron was convinced that a beneficiary was a threat to public order or otherwise unsatisfactory, but the bishop did not agree, he was powerless to remedy the situation. The right to make an extra-judicial inquiry into the conduct of a delinquent ecclesiastic was equally meaningless if the ecclesiastical judge chose to ignore the results of the inquiry.

Even the receipt of specific instructions from the Crown had little effect when the prelate was either negligent or obstructive.

[1] See A.G.I., Mexico 3072, Governor of Yucatán to the king, 18 May 1792; and Ind. Gen. 3027, Respuesta Fiscal del crimen, 5 Oct. 1798.

[2] A.G.I., Mexico 1476, Testimonio de lo conducente del religioso carmelita, 1791–4, cuaderno 1; Mexico 2646, Testimonio de lo conducente . . ., cuaderno 2.

[3] *CIVM*, canon 5, título 22, Libro 3.

A bishop might seek to evade an order for punishment by trying to convince the king that the accused was really innocent or that the gravity of his offence had been exaggerated.[1] In other cases the prelates admitted that the charges were true but then proceeded to give reasons why they could not carry out the order: 'the delicate nature of the crime', and the fear of scandal were common excuses for not prosecuting an offender, particularly if the charge involved any form of sexual misconduct.[2]

Other forms of intervention, less dependent on the will of the ecclesiastical superiors, were effective in individual cases but impracticable as a general rule. Expulsion was an efficient means of removing a delinquent ecclesiastic from the scene, and during the early years of colonization missionaries were shipped back to Spain for relatively minor offences.[3] But the gradual increase in both the number of ecclesiastics in the Indies and the proportion of Creole to peninsular ecclesiastics limited the application of this punishment to exceptional cases. The same limitation applied to the *vicariato* prerogative, which enabled the king, as the head of the American Church, to prosecute and sentence ecclesiastical delinquents himself. Neither the Minister nor the Council of the Indies, his immediate representatives, could intervene in every case that arose in this vast overseas empire: the size of the territory and the difficulties of communication with the peninsula made it necessary to delegate the main task of supervising ecclesiastical discipline to the colonial authorities who, unlike the royal vicar, could not ignore the restrictions imposed on secular jurisdiction by ecclesiastical immunity.

The traditional methods of indirect intervention were by no means a total failure, but neither were they wholly reliable,

---

[1] A.G.I., Mexico 3051, Provisor of Yucatán to the king, 5 Sept. 1763, in which he first asserts that the defendant is innocent and then admits he committed the offence but claims that he was justified in doing so. See also Guadalajara 315, Bishop of Guadalajara to Antonio Caballero, 16 April 1802.

[2] See A.G.I., Mexico 3167, Bishop of Yucatán to the king, 16 June 1750; and Guadalajara 315, Bishop of Guadalajara to Antonio Caballero, 20 Oct. 1803 (not the same case referred to in preceding note), employing almost identical phrases in two cases concerning adultery.

[3] See, e.g., various royal *cédulas* of the 1550's ordering the expulsion of friars from Mexico, in *Documentos inéditos ó muy raros*, xv, 126–32.

I

since their effectiveness depended in large measure on the co-operation and efficiency of the ecclesiastical superiors, who might be either unable or unwilling to correct their subordinates. However, the shortcomings of indirect intervention were inherent in a judicial system that had functioned throughout the colonial period without stimulating a decision to implement it with more stringent measures. The canonical prohibition against penalties involving death, bloodshed, or mutilation had appeared centuries earlier in ecclesiastical law[1] and had been noted by royal jurists long before the publication of the Habsburg colonial law code in 1681.[2] In fact, the Crown had sought a special dispensation from the pope in the sixteenth century so that ecclesiastical members of the Council of the Indies could 'hear and vote in' criminal cases that involved the death sentence.[3] Yet only in the later Bourbon period did this canonical limitation serve as a pretext to curtail the Church's judicial jurisdiction over both laymen and the clergy.[4] Perhaps previous monarchs had been indifferent to the dangers of preserving ecclesiastical immunity, but the explanation given by the Caroline reformers was that the inadequacies of the traditional system were only beginning to reveal themselves during this period in the form of a serious breakdown of ecclesiastical discipline.[5]

The question of ecclesiastical discipline in the Spanish colonies has been dealt with in a number of works, mainly of a polemical nature. Some authors describe a complete degeneration of morals among the clergy, both secular and regular: crimes of violence, extortion from the poor, gambling, drunkenness, and almost every other vice known to mankind.[6] There is

---

[1] See, e.g., Concilio IV Toledo (633 a.d.), canon 31, in J. Tejada y Ramiro, *op. cit.*, ii, 286–7.

[2] G. Castillo de Bobadilla, *op. cit.*, ii, 514–17; J. de Solórzano Pereira, *op. cit.*, Libro 4, cap. 7, no. 65.

[3] A.H.N., Códices 718, R.C. to the Spanish Ambassador in Rome, 13 Nov. 1535.

[4] See A.G.I., Mexico 2619, R.C. to the Archbishop of Mexico, 14 Oct. 1770, using the same argument for curtailing ecclesiastical jurisdiction over laymen.

[5] A.G.I., Ind. Gen. 3041, Respuesta Fiscal Campomanes, 26 June 1768; Consulta Extraordinary Council, 3 July 1768.

[6] Among the more responsible but still vituperative works are: G. García, Introduction to volume xv of *Documentos inéditos ó muy raros*; E. Portes Gil, *La labor sediciosa del clero mexicano* (Madrid, 1935); and Alfonso Toro, *La iglesia y el estado en México* (Mexico, 1927).

a comparable degree of bias in the whitewashed descriptions of a universally selfless clergy who sacrificed all worldly comforts, and often their lives as well, to bring Christianity to the New World and to save the downtrodden Indians from their European and Creole oppressors; in the biographies of saintly bishops who, without exception, lived in extreme poverty in order to distribute their livings to the poor.[1]

Both descriptions, though exaggerated, are in a sense equally valid, since they are based on a reality which underwent considerable transformation during the course of the colonial period. There was a gradual decline from the truly dedicated zeal of the early missionaries until, by the middle of the eighteenth century, there were distinct signs of a widespread breakdown of ecclesiastical discipline. This is not to say that no blemishes existed in the early period or that the later decadence was universal, but merely that there was a swing of the pendulum.

Evidence of this general breakdown comes from a variety of contemporary sources. An early and, to the Crown, convincing source was a series of reports describing the deplorable state of the religious orders in New Spain. These reports, submitted to the king in 1768 by two prelates, Archbishop Lorenzana of Mexico and Bishop Fabián y Fuero of Puebla, have already been mentioned in connection with the two reform projects they stimulated: the provincial councils and the *visitas* of the religious orders.[2] Both prelates alleged that the disorders and immorality of the regular clergy had reached scandalous proportions: with few exceptions (the entire order of Descalzed Carmelites and individual members of other communities), the friars created public disturbances with their internal feuding and used their religious habits as a cloak for a clandestine existence of vice and crime; or, what was worse, they lived openly as laymen in their own houses, engaging in commercial activities in order to support their concubines and illegitimate offspring.[3]

[1] See, e.g., V. Andrade, *Noticias biográficas sobre los ilustrísimos prelados de Sonora, de Sinaloa y de Durango* (Mexico, 1899); J. Dávila Garibi, *La obra civilizadora de los misioneros de la Nueva Galicia* (Guadalajara, 1919); and J. García Gutiérrez, *Apuntes para la historia del origen y desenvolvimiento del Regio Patronato Indiano hasta 1857* (Mexico, 1941).　　　　　　　　　　　　　　[2] See above, pp. 32–8.
[3] A.G.I., Ind. Gen. 3041, Respuesta Fiscal Campomanes, 26 June 1768, quotes

Lorenzana and Fabián y Fuero were not disinterested witnesses. Both were energetic opponents of the privileges and immunities enjoyed by the religious orders, and the purpose of their reports was to persuade the Crown that, since the regular superiors failed to maintain discipline, the only remedy was to transfer a large part of their authority to the secular prelates. As further proof of this thesis, Lorenzana soon sent in another report on the widespread practice in New Spain of expelling friars from the religious orders if they repeatedly misbehaved.[1] If these friars were incorrigible, he argued, they should be imprisoned indefinitely rather than released to infect society with their depraved habits. But he was convinced that the friars were rarely incorrigible: their superiors were simply unable to control them, and he gave the example of several recently expelled Augustinians and *Agonizantes* whom he had been able to send back to their communities completely reformed after six months of corrective treatment in the diocesan prison. Lorenzana claimed that if delinquent regulars were subjected to the jurisdiction of the bishops, who in any case were burdened with the task of correcting them once they had been expelled, then both the expulsions and the repeated offences that caused them could be prevented.[2]

Yet, even though these allegations suited their particular ends, the evidence produced by Lorenzana, Fabián y Fuero, and other bishops who made similar allegations in this period[3] cannot be dismissed as pure propaganda. A certain decadence of monastic rule was apparent to other, less interested observers. The damning description of the regular clergy in Peru, contained in the report made to the Crown in 1749 by the naval

[1] A.G.I., Ind. Gen. 2993, Archbishop Lorenzana to the king, 26 June 1768.
[2] *Ibid.*; see also Mexico 2622, Relación del estado material y formal de la iglesia de la Puebla de los Angeles, Fabián y Fuero, 2 Dec. 1772.
[3] A.G.I., Ind. Gen. 3041, Respuesta Fiscal Campomanes, 26 June 1768, also mentions similar letters from the Archbishops of Manila and Guatemala. B.N., 5806, Extracto compendioso de las actas del *CIVM*, 1771, contains frequent references made by other Mexican bishops to the disorders and scandalous behaviour of the regular clergy.

letters from Archbishop Lorenzana and Bishop Fabián y Fuero to the king's confessor, dated 25 and 29 March 1768. See also Biblioteca Pública de Toledo, Col. Borbón-Lorenzana, vol. 178, nos. 3 and 4, Escrito del Arzobispo de Mexico, 16 April 1768, and Relación enviada por el Obispo de Puebla, 21 April 1768.

officers Jorge Juan and Antonio de Ulloa, can be considered fairly impartial, since the authors did not spare the civil authorities either and made a point of exempting the Jesuits from most of the charges brought against the other orders.[1] The regular superiors themselves acknowledged the fact that monastic institutions in the Indies were in a deplorable state,[2] and the reports of the reform *visitadores* in the latter part of the eighteenth century, as well as the volumes of records on which the reports were based, corroborate this view.[3]

Many colonial bishops implied that moral laxity and unruly behaviour were problems exclusive to the regular clergy. Their reluctance to condemn the secular clergy with equal severity is understandable, since such condemnation would have indicated incompetence or negligence on the part of the secular prelates and would have tended to invalidate their claim that the solution to the disciplinary problems of the friars lay in subjecting these to diocesan supervision. But many of the excesses of which they accused the regulars were also evident among the secular clergy.[4] In fact, Archbishop Lorenzana's successor, Alonso Núñez de Haro y Peralta, had to establish a special *Colegio de Instrucción y Corrección* in the former Jesuit College at Tepozotlán in order to cope with the large number of 'unruly and vicious clerics' in the archdiocese.[5]

An *expediente* originating from Oaxaca in the same period also helps to balance the picture, for it reveals serious defects in the administration of justice in that diocese. An investigation carried out jointly by the Archbishop of Mexico and the viceroy in 1775 by order of the Crown produced substantial evidence to support earlier allegations made to Madrid that the Bishop of Oaxaca was in large part to blame for the extremely

---

[1] J. Juan and A. de Ulloa, *Noticias secretas de América* (1749; 2 vols., Madrid, 1918), ii, 41, 85, 195, 207–15.
[2] See, e.g., A.G.I., Ind. Gen. 63, Franciscan Comisario General to Pedro García Mayoral, 27 March 1772.
[3] See the sources cited above on p. 37, note 1.
[4] See J. Juan and A. de Ulloa, *op. cit.*, ii, 170, 177–8; and H. Villarroel, *Mexico por dentro y por fuera*, p. 8.
[5] A.G.I., Mexico 2627, Núñez de Haro to Ventura de Taranco, 26 Feb. 1779. See also A. Núñez de Haro y Peralta, *Constituciones que formó para el mejor régimen y govierno del Real Colegio Seminario de Instrucción voluntaria y corrección para el clero secular* (Mexico, 1774).

low standard of discipline among the secular clergy under his jurisdiction.[1] Well-intentioned, but lenient and ingenuous, the bishop had relied almost exclusively on the judgement of his venal private secretary, who accepted bribes from delinquent and immoral clerics in return for his protection and who also suppressed evidence of the widespread graft and corruption in the collection of tithes, from which he benefited.[2]

The majority of contemporary observers agreed that the colonial clergy in this period were in drastic need of reform, although some objected to the sweeping condemnations and exaggerated tone of many accounts, which implied that any person who became ordained or took religious vows was 'automatically destined to become a blot on society'.[3] The existence of the problem was rarely contested, but opinion diverged widely over its fundamental causes. There were actually a variety of reasons for the decline in standards of discipline, apart from the inevitable loss of missionary fervour after the main work of conversion had been completed. A lack of religious vocation was common to both branches of the clergy. People entered religious orders and became ordained for the wrong reasons: some did so to gain social status for themselves and their families and also to avoid the dishonourable necessity of earning a living;[4] and many took minor orders merely to qualify for an inherited private benefice or for ecclesiastical privileges, mainly immunity from taxation and from secular jurisdiction.[5] It was also a common practice among wealthy Creoles to force younger offspring to enter convents and monasteries so that the family fortune would not be dissipated

---

[1] A.G.I., Mexico 2628, Representación de Juan de Aponte y Francisco Díaz Inguanzo a S.M., 19 Oct. 1769.

[2] A.G.I., Mexico 2629, Testimonio del proceso informativo hecho por orden del virrey y del arzobispo de Mexico, 26 Sept. 1775.

[3] B.N., 5806, Extracto compendioso . . ., by Dr Ríos, delegate of the Bishop of Michoacán, commenting on the session of 5 July 1771.

[4] J. Juan and A. de Ulloa, op. cit., ii, 205; Mexican Political Pamphlets (B.M.), vii, no. 76, 'Carta de los frailes liberales que apetecen la reforma' (early nineteenth century). See also J. Fernández de Lizardi, El periquillo sarniento (first published in 1816; 3rd ed., Mexico, 1961), an essay in the form of a picaresque novel on social evils in colonial Mexico, pp. 63–8.

[5] Biblioteca del Palacio, Col. Ayala 39, Disertación sobre lo que ordena la Instrucción de corregidores.

in dowries and multiple legacies.[1] It is also possible, as the reformers alleged, that a belief in their freedom from punishment encouraged wrongdoing. Viceroy Revillagigedo asserted that this belief was shared by all those who enjoyed privileged *fueros*—not only the clergy—with the result that they all 'commit excesses they would not dare to if they knew that the ordinary royal judge could correct them'.[2]

The problem of excessive numbers was also cited frequently by both the ecclesiastical and civil authorities. The religious orders accepted more novices than their incomes could support, so that, although many friars abandoned the cloister because they were unwilling to follow the strict monastic life, many others did so out of necessity, and were reduced to begging alms or resorting to less honest means of support—at the least they were a burden to the productive members of society.[3] Of the secular clergy it was estimated that at the end of the century only one-fifth held benefices under royal patronage.[4] Some of the rest held private benefices with varying stipends, but the majority, described by a fellow member of the clergy as 'idle vagabonds who serve only to fill the ecclesiastical courts and prisons',[5] had no fixed income at all. However, one bishop maintained that the solution was not to reduce the number of clerics but to distribute them more evenly. The clergy, he said, were concentrated in the large cities of the viceroyalty while benefices in the outlying areas remained vacant, a situation that had two harmful consequences: on the one hand, unemployment with its attendant evils of idleness, theft and other excesses; and, on the other, the degeneration of morals among the few priests in the outlying areas due to their isolation.[6]

The ecclesiastical superiors must take a large share of the

[1] A.H.N., Consejos 20683, Respuesta Fiscal, Testamentaría de Da. Eugenia Calzado y Terreros, 1786.
[2] Revillagigedo, *Instrucción reservada*, p. 27.
[3] M. de Amat y Junient, *op. cit.*, pp. 99–100.
[4] B.N., 12009, Representación del Obispo y Cabildo de Michoacán a S.M., 11 Dec. 1799.
[5] B.N., 12054, Reflexiones sobre el Tomo Regio, 1771, Dr Antonio Ríos, Canon of Michoacán.
[6] A.G.I., Mexico 2383, Carta pastoral, Bishop-elect Abad y Queipo of Michoacán, 7 March 1811.

blame for this breakdown of ecclesiastical discipline. A number of cases have already been cited as evidence that many prelates failed to correct the offences committed by their subordinates, even when they were brought to their attention. There are also indications that this negligence actually encouraged further wrongdoing. The records of two murder cases in Mexico, one in 1772 and the other in 1790, reveal that each crime was the culmination of a series of violent physical assaults committed by the defendants (one a cleric and the other a friar) whom the ecclesiastical judges had failed to punish.[1]

These two cases were, of course, extreme examples, but the same applies to less serious offences. One viceroy complained that the regular superiors encouraged apostasy by permitting newly professed or disorderly friars to wander at liberty outside the cloister, and he enclosed a report on a Franciscan who had been arrested four times for different crimes he had committed while disguised as a layman. Each time the civil authorities had turned him over to the provincial, assuming that steps would be taken to prevent a recurrence and, when an explanation was finally demanded on the last occasion, the provincial's only excuse was that he had permitted the friar to leave his monastery in order to collect the considerable fortune he had amassed during a previous apostasy, because the monastery was badly in debt.[2]

The various methods of indirect royal control over the clergy were supposed to ensure the maintenance of discipline even if the ecclesiastical superiors were unable or unwilling to do so, but, aside from their limitations as methods of control, they actually contributed to the problem. The system contained an inherent fallacy: it left the ultimate responsibility for ecclesiastical discipline in the hands of the prelates but deprived them of the necessary authority to control their subordinates effectively.

The bishops certainly did not have a free hand either in choosing, removing, or governing the ecclesiastics under their

---

[1] A.G.I., Ind. Gen. 64, Testimonio de los antecedentes de la causa seguida contra el Pe. Luis Palacios, 1772; Mexico 2646, Autos seguidos por el Pe. Provincial de la Merced contra Fr Jacinto de Miranda, 1780-9.

[2] A.G.I., Guadalajara 358, Revillagigedo to the king, 29 July 1793.

jurisdiction. The problems presented by the State's control over ecclesiastical appointments, which also tended to produce beneficiaries who were not necessarily the most worthy and able ecclesiastics but the most co-operative,[1] were apparent even in the early years of the empire. The first Bishop of Mexico, Fray Juan de Zumárraga, complained to Charles V in 1540 that he was forced to accept ecclesiastical appointees sent from Spain, without any opportunity to determine their character, and stated his intention of shipping back those who had proved to be greedy or immoral if they did not reform.[2]

In contrast with this vigorous stand, the bishops in eighteenth-century Mexico accepted a much more comprehensive system of secular intervention, which the Crown had developed and refined during the intervening years, and which undermined their authority to a much greater degree than the basic patronage prerogative. Some bishops in this period even encouraged further encroachments on their jurisdiction, confessing their inability to cope with delinquent subordinates and appealing to the State to solve their disciplinary problems for them.[3] Those who sought to chastise an offender on their own authority were often hampered rather than aided by the secular authorities, for royal review of ecclesiastical cases almost invariably worked in favour of the defendant.[4] But even when secular intervention did not actually protect an ecclesiastical offender, by dividing authority and affording so many possibilities for obstruction, it interfered with the administration of justice and encouraged delinquency among those whom it was actually supposed to control.

The Spanish government was certainly aware of the deterioration of ecclesiastical discipline. The allegations from the colonial authorities, both prelates and civil officials, supported by voluminous evidence from judicial records, convinced Charles III that the 'immorality and laxity [relajación] of a large

---

[1] See above, pp. 16–18.
[2] M. Cuevas, op. cit., ii, 113–14, quoting from Bishop Zumárraga to Charles V, 17 April 1540.
[3] See, e.g., A.G.I., Guadalajara 545, Bishop of Durango to the king, 2 June 1771; and Mexico 2637, Bishop of Michoacán to Ventura de Taranco, 17 June 1788.
[4] See above, Ch. III, sect. 2, on the recurso de fuerza.

part of the American clergy is, unfortunately, too certain'.[1] But the two general projects for reforming the colonial clergy—the provincial councils and the *visitas* of the religious orders—suffering from the same shortcomings that impaired the effectiveness of other forms of indirect control, were a resounding failure.

Faced with the fundamental inadequacy of the existing system, the Crown had two choices: to refrain altogether from intervening in ecclesiastical administration or to impose a system of direct control over the clergy. But, given the hostile attitude towards ecclesiastical privilege prevalent among royal ministers in this period and the Crown's general policy of strengthening royal power, as well as the substantial evidence that the ecclesiastical superiors were not able to cope with their subordinates, the first choice was clearly out of the question. The Crown's decision to subject the clergy to the direct judicial jurisdiction of the State was, then, both politically expedient and, in the opinion of the royal ministers, absolutely necessary in order to protect society from ecclesiastical malefactors. However, there is no evidence that this new method of control succeeded in checking the disintegration of ecclesiastical discipline, which, if anything, increased as the colonial period drew to a close, especially among the regular clergy. Between 1798 and 1800 alone, more than 150 regulars (out of an estimated total of 3,000)[2] petitioned the Roman Curia for release from their monastic vows,[3] and the large number of insurgents from both branches of the clergy in the independence period certainly indicates a widespread refusal to submit to the authority of either the Church or the State.[4]

---

[1] 'Instrucción reservada a la Junta de Estado', 8 July 1787, art. 87, in *Obras originales del Conde de Floridablanca*.

[2] F. Navarro y Noriega, *Memoria sobre la población del reino de Nueva España*, appendix 'Estado de la población . . .', gives the figure 3,112 for the number of regulars in 1810.

[3] A.G.I., Mexico 1140, 1150 and 2651. Expedientes sobre pases para breves de secularización, 1800–4. For contemporary comments on this acceleration, see Mexico 2696, Archbishop of Mexico to His Holiness, 25 Nov. 1803 (copy); and Representación a S.M. del Prior del convento de San Juan de Dios, 16 Jan. 1811.

[4] See below, Ch. IX, and Appendix, 'Ecclesiastical participants in the Mexican independence movement 1808–20'.

Perhaps the breakdown of ecclesiastical discipline was merely a symptom of a general breakdown in the colonial social order, which culminated in the war for independence, and which the whole Caroline programme of reform, by changing traditional institutions and creating new tensions, did more to hasten than to retard.

CHAPTER VI

The Clergy and State Security

I. SUSPICIONS OF ECCLESIASTICAL DISLOYALTY

THE CONCERN expressed by Charles III for the moral standards of the clergy and for the fair administration of justice was doubtlessly sincere but, if there was one consideration outweighing all others in prompting the shift in royal policy on ecclesiastical immunity, it was a more personal concern for the security of his own crown. The theory that the clergy's exemption from secular authority constituted a potential danger to the security of the State had already been expressed by several seventeenth-century regalists, who had pointed out that the clergy might be encouraged to indulge in criticism of the government and even more serious acts of subversion, from which a layman would be deterred by fear of the severe penalties prescribed in royal law.[1] Though mainly interested in subordinating ecclesiastical institutions to royal control, rather than eliminating them entirely, these early regalists had argued that the king's responsibility to protect himself and his subjects from harm required that he abolish the clergy's personal immunity in cases of crimes against the State.[2]

Yet, despite instances of ecclesiastical participation in open rebellion against the State, such as the *comunero* movement in the early sixteenth century and the War of the Spanish Succession (during which a number of Spanish ecclesiastics had actively supported the Austrian cause against Philip V), the Spanish kings had chosen to ignore these arguments until the

---

[1] See B.N., 4175, Discurso acerca de la inmunidad eclesiástica en el Perú, Juan Luis López, 1684, cap. 7.

[2] J. López, *Discurso jurídico*, cap. 11; and P. Frasso, *De regio patronatu Indiarum*, Libro 1, caps. 44, 46–8.

latter part of the eighteenth century. The general ideology of the Enlightenment, prevalent in ministerial circles during that period, worked in favour of curtailing ecclesiastical privilege,[1] but other more immediate and dramatic forces proved decisive. The focal point of this shift in royal policy was the early years of the reign of Charles III, and the catalyst a brief but repercussive incident in 1766 which seemed to prove that the clergy was capable, not merely of lending support to an opposition movement, but of actually organizing and leading such a movement.

In March 1766 an ostensibly spontaneous uprising occurred in Madrid and spread rapidly to other cities in Castile.[2] A scarcity of wheat and other food, a rise in taxes and in prices, hostility to the many foreign-born ministers in Charles's government—these and other underlying causes of discontent were reinforced by an unpopular decree prohibiting the traditional Spanish cape and wide-brimmed hat (which supposedly enabled criminals to conceal their identity), which actually provoked the riot.[3] In Madrid the crowds reached the palace gates and clamoured for the removal of the Minister of Finance, the Marquis of Squillace, an Italian and the author of the decree. The impression produced on Charles III, who possessed firm ideas on absolute monarchy, must have been extremely painful, for he was forced to take refuge in the royal palace at Aranjuez, revoke the decree, and dismiss a minister in whom he had complete confidence.[4]

The question of ecclesiastical complicity in the incident has been disputed by various authors, who seem to agree only that the uprising was planned by some influential group of conspirators who were dissatisfied with the Crown's policies.[5] Both the nobility and the clergy had cause to fear the loss of their privileged positions, especially in the economic sphere:

[1] See above, Ch. IV.
[2] A. Ferrer del Río, *op. cit.*, ii, Chapters 1 and 2. For an eye-witness account of the *motín* in Madrid, see Conde de Fernán Núñez, *Vida de Carlos III* (2 vols., Madrid, 1848), i, 197–205.   [3] See R. Herr, *op. cit.*, pp. 20–1.
[4] Fernán Núñez, *op. cit.*, i, 147, 185–6 and 205, stresses Charles's extreme reluctance ever to part with any ministers or servants.
[5] See *ibid.*, i, 202. C. Egúia Ruiz, *Los Jesuítas y el motín de Esquilache* (Madrid, 1947), rules out Jesuit complicity; while A. Ferrer del Río, *op. cit.*, ii, 129–44, among others, suggests the contrary.

Charles's agricultural reforms were already threatening the income of the landed aristocracy, and the tax exemptions traditionally enjoyed by all property in ecclesiastical mortmain had been curtailed.[1] The presence of ecclesiastics among the rioters, the appearance of provocative pamphlets from ecclesiastical printing presses, and the intercepted correspondence of the papal nuncio have been offered as evidence of clerical complicity,[2] in the absence of more conclusive proof, owing to the disappearance of the documents gathered by the extraordinary Council appointed to investigate the uprising. Whatever the truth of the matter, Charles III and his ministers chose to believe that certain members of the clergy were, if not the sole instigators, at least involved in the plot.[3]

It has been argued that certain royal ministers had already been planning various anti-clerical measures, for which the *motín de Esquilache* was simply a convenient pretext.[4] Proof of this allegation is again inconclusive, because of the missing documents of the extraordinary Council, but there is little doubt that an atmosphere propitious for these measures already existed. From the beginning of Charles's reign, for example, increasingly outspoken attacks against the Church and her ministers, expressed in articles in the *Gaceta de Madrid* or official documents, were noted,[5] and the tone of these attacks was considerably more hostile than that of earlier regalist works, in which the authors had generally favoured supporting ecclesiastical institutions and the clergy, as long as they remained under royal control.[6]

There were other factors besides complicity in the *motín de Esquilache* which may have influenced Charles to view the clergy,

[1] See A.H.N., Códices 687, R.C., 29 June 1760, ordering the payment of taxes on all ecclesiastical property acquired since the Papal Concordat of 1737.

[2] V. Rodríguez Casado, *La política y los políticos en el reinado de Carlos III* (Madrid, 1962), pp. 133–40.

[3] M. Dánvila y Collado, *El poder civil en España* (6 vols., Madrid, 1885–7), iv, 14–15.

[4] M. Menéndez y Pelayo, *op. cit.*, vi, 37; M. Cuevas, *op. cit.*, iv, 402.

[5] A.H.N., Consejos 494, Bishop Carvajal y Lancaster of Cuenca to the king, 23 May 1766. See also, J. F. de Isla, *Cartas inéditas del Padre Isla* (Madrid, 1957), pp. 244, 249–51.

[6] Compare, for example, Campomanes, *Juicio imparcial*, a bitter attack on the pope and the clergy in general, with Solórzano Pereira, *Política indiana*, Libro 4 (on ecclesiastical questions).

and especially the Jesuits, which such suspicion and alarm that he was prepared to reverse the Crown's traditional policy of upholding ecclesiastical privileges. Several Spanish Jesuits had written works that were considered politically dangerous, asserting that it was morally justifiable in certain circumstances to disobey and even to kill a ruler.[1] Although these works had been published over a century before, the Jesuits' 'unhealthy doctrines' were often cited as justification for their expulsion from Spain and the king's subsequent insistence on the extinction of the order.[2] Some critics even maintained that the Jesuits had put these ideas on regicide into practice and had actually organized every plot against the life of a legitimate monarch from Henry IV of France to João Manuel of Portugal (1758).[3]

The Jesuits were also accused of seeking to manipulate and even to supplant the civil government, especially in the Crown's colonial possessions in America and the Philippines.[4] In the mission territory of Paraguay, what had originally been rights granted to the Jesuit missionaries by the Crown, such as arming the Indians and training them to fight, had in a new context become grounds for suspicion. Royal ministers were convinced —although the evidence is far from conclusive—that the Jesuits had organized the armed resistance to the transfer of territory from Paraguay to Brazil that had been agreed upon in a 1750 treaty with Portugal,[5] an act that to already suspicious

[1] J. de Mariana, De rege et regis institutione (Toledo, 1599); and F. Suárez, De legibus ac de deo legislatore (Coimbra, 1612), Lib. 3, cap. 10. See also G. Lewy, Constitutionalism and Statecraft during the Golden Age of Spain (Geneva, 1960), Chapters 5 and 9, for a discussion of Mariana's views on regicide and their influence.

[2] See, e.g., Archivo diocesano de Toledo, Sala 4, no. 127, Carta Pastoral, Cardinal Lorenzana of Toledo, 7 Oct. 1773, referring to both the expulsion and the extinction.

[3] See Papeles tocantes a la iglesia espanola 1625–1790 (B.M.), no. 33, Carta Pastoral, Archbishop of Manila, 27 Dec. 1770; and Consulta, Council of Castile, 1 July 1768, on the suppression of Jesuit studies, quoted in L. Sánchez Agesta op. cit., pp. 110–13.

[4] A.G.I., Ind. Gen., 3041, Consulta Extraordinary Council, 3 July 1768: (referring to the Society of Jesus) 'aquel incesante manejo sordo con que se apoderaba de los ánimos y los gobiernos'.

[5] G. Kratz, El tratado hispano-portugués de límites de 1750 y sus consecuencias (Rome, 1954), pp. 45–72 and Chapter 3, discusses this charge and asserts that the missionaries sought only to postpone the execution of the treaty.

minds might seem the prelude to an independence movement.[1]
The *motín de Esquilache* and the other subversive acts with
which the Jesuits were charged were not the only evidence
produced to convince Charles that the clergy were capable of
using their influence against his throne. The case of the
Bishop of Cuenca, Isidro de Carvajal y Lancaster, if discussed
by historians at all, has been offered only as an indication of
clerical discontent with royal policies during this period,[2] but
the interpretation given by the Council of Castile was that the
bishop's actions were part of a general ecclesiastical conspiracy
to incite the masses against the king under the guise of religious
zeal and defence of the Church. In April 1766, barely a month
after the *motín*, Carvajal wrote to the royal confessor, Padre
Eleta, warning him of his grave responsibility for his own and
the king's soul, because of recent royal enactments which
constituted a 'persecution of the Church'.[3] Instructed by the
king to clarify this allegation, he replied with a passionate but
respectful enumeration of all the offences against the Church—
such as the subjection of ecclesiastical property to taxation and
the exile of the Spanish Inquisitor-General—that had been
committed in the royal name, 'in spite of the fact that everyone
recognizes Your Majesty's personal piety'.[4]

The royal *fiscales*, Campomanes and Moñino, after studying
the voluminous documentation on this case gathered by the
Council, including reports from other bishops and from local
royal officials, papal bulls, and royal decrees, concluded that
Carvajal's accusations, totally unfounded, had been made with
the sinister purpose of discrediting the king and his ministers
and of 'igniting the fire of sedition in these turbulent times'.[5]
The fact that Carvajal had written his first letter shortly after
the *motín* was, to the *fiscales*, conclusive proof that he was in
league with its leaders. As further proof of the bishop's treasonous intentions, Moñino asserted that the contents of both letters

---

[1] See Fernán Núñez, *op. cit.*, i, 209–10.
[2] V. Rodríguez Casado, *op. cit.*, pp. 122–6.
[3] A.H.N., Consejos 494, Carvajal to Padre Eleta, 15 April 1766.
[4] *Ibid.*, Carvajal to the king, 23 May 1766.
[5] *Ibid.*, Respuesta Fiscal Moñino, 12 April 1767; see also Respuesta Fiscal
Campomanes, 16 July 1767.

had been revealed in Spain, indicating in his opinion that they had been publicized in foreign courts as well and, on the basis of this assumption, he charged Carvajal with being in league with foreign enemies of the Crown.

The illogical arguments of both *fiscales'* denunciations, based mainly on conjecture, reveal the obsession with conspiracy prevalent at that time. The official acts that resulted from the Crown's shift in ecclesiastical policy after the *motín de Esquilache* are understandable only in the light of this atmosphere of suspicion and hysteria within the government, an atmosphere in which words and actions that would have been ignored or dismissed as innocuous at other times were considered evidence of disaffection with the regime, if not outright treason. The official witch hunt for conspirators and dangerous doctrines was epitomized by the reaction to the Bishop of Cuenca's complaints, which were considerably milder than some of those addressed by prelates to previous monarchs. A Spanish bishop was, in any case, automatically 'of His Majesty's Council' and thus had the right to offer complaints and advice to his king. But on the basis of Carvajal's complaints, the *fiscales* were able to convince the Crown that the bishop had conspired with the Jesuits and possibly others to overthrow the government.[1] He was called before a plenary session of the Council of Castile to receive a public reprimand, exiled permanently from Court, and threatened with prosecution if he repeated his allegations.[2] Such severity was considered necessary as a public example to any other ecclesiastics who might contemplate similar criticism, and all his fellow bishops received a written warning from the Council as well.[3]

Obsession with ecclesiastical conspiracy also reached the American colonies. At this stage—in the 1760's—official apprehension was due to circumstances in Spain rather than to any spate of disloyal activities in the colonies. In debating whether to send to America a *cédula* that had been promulgated in Spain in 1766, warning ecclesiastics to refrain from 'declaiming

---

[1] A.H.N., Consejos 494, Memorial ajustado de los fiscales, Campomanes and Moñino, summarizing the entire *expediente* and their charges, 1767.

[2] *Ibid.*, Consulta Council of Castile, 28 Sept. 1767.

[3] *Ibid.*, Carta acordada to all bishops and archbishops in Spain, 22 Oct. 1767.

K

or murmuring' against the government,[1] the Council of the Indies admitted that there was little fear of the clergy's rebelling in the colonies, because the royal officials there, unlike those in Spain, were authorized 'to take the most severe disciplinary action' against disorderly ecclesiastics. The Council decided that the *cédula* was unnecessary and perhaps even harmful: to its knowledge no American ecclesiastic had criticized the government, and the *cédula* might well provoke discussion on the situation in Spain that had occasioned its promulgation.[2]

Despite this reassurance, the government was so obsessed with the idea of danger to the security of the State that officials found evidence of disloyalty everywhere. Prelates who defied the prohibition against the papal bull *In Coena Domini* (which prescribed excommunication against royal judges who interfered with ecclesiastical jurisdiction) had previously been considered lacking in docility, if their actions had been noticed at all, but now they were charged with wilful subversion. The *fiscal* of the Council of the Indies, in discussing recent examples in America of the bull's use to justify canonical censures, claimed that any act tending to defraud a royal prerogative, in this case the *exequatur*, weakened the regime and was a direct prelude to rebellion. He then qualified the Council's earlier statement on the tranquillity of the Indies: 'Although they have been the most peaceful of our dominions since their discovery, it is never wise to assume that they are entirely safe from the danger of rebellion'.[3]

Mexican historians have noted the increase of inquisitorial activity at the end of the eighteenth century as a result of the impact of the French Revolution and its doctrines and of the incipient movement for independence within Mexico itself.[4] Yet there also existed an earlier flurry of activity immediately after the expulsion of the Jesuits, which was directed especially

---

[1] R.C., Council of Castile, 18 Sept. 1766, made into ley 7, título 8, Libro 1, *Novís. Recop. España.*

[2] A.G.I., Ind. Gen. 350, Consulta Council, 30 Jan. 1767.

[3] *Ibid.*, Respuesta Fiscal, 17 Aug. 1768.

[4] L. Alamán, *Historia de México* (5 vols., Mexico, 1883–5), i, 344–5. See also *Precursores ideológicos de la guerra de independencia* (vols. 13 and 21 of Publicaciones del Archivo General de la Nación, Mexico, 1929 and 1932).

against the clergy. The lethargy and incompetence that had overcome the Inquisition by this time had considerably reduced its effectiveness against heresy and witchcraft,[1] but it was propelled into activity by the secular authorities in Mexico and Madrid, who wished to employ the Inquisition as a purely political arm of the State to combat treason rather than to combat crimes against the faith.

Viceroy Croix and *Visitador* Gálvez were convinced that members of the clergy were largely responsible for popular protests against the expulsion of the Jesuits, and theirs was the main force behind the government's and the Inquisition's repressive measures against the offenders. The expulsion was the occasion of a number of disturbances, particularly in the mining centres to the north of the capital, such as San Luis Potosí, where a mob had seized the Jesuit fathers and refused to permit them to be escorted into exile.[2] Gálvez led a military expedition to this area to restore peace and expelled some of the secular clergy who he believed had incited some of the rioters. He also obtained from a Minorite friar a confession of the authorship of the seditious pamphlets circulated in the area urging defiance to the order of expulsion, and he sent the culprit to prison in Mexico.[3]

The royal officials did not feel that the Inquisition was doing its part in combating the danger. When a certain priest was denounced in 1767 for saying that it was not a moral offence to wish for the king's death, the Mexican Holy Office, instead of arresting him immediately, first consulted the Supreme Council of the Inquisition in Madrid. But before the Council's instructions could be carried out, the impatient viceroy had already arrested the priest himself and imprisoned him in a military fortress.[4] The Inquisition was jolted out of its lethargy

[1] M. Pérez-Marchand, *Dos etapas ideológicas del siglo XVIII en México* (Mexico, 1945), pp. 39–44. The author notes the general decadence of the Inquisition without referring specifically to these two periods of increased activity.

[2] C. de Croix (Marqués de Croix), *Cartas*, pp. 22–3, letter to his brother in Lille, 24 Dec. 1767.

[3] For material on this expedition, see R.A.H., Legajos de Jesuítas 100, Causas criminales formadas sobre los motines suscitados . . ., 1768; and H. I. Priestley, *José de Gálvez*, pp. 215–25.

[4] A.H.N., Inquisición 2286-A, Mexican Holy Office to Consejo Supremo, 27 July 1768.

after an incident which, according to the Mexican authorities, indicated a suspicious lack of loyalty on its part. After the expulsion, an avalanche of anonymous letters, pamphlets, and satirical verses appeared condemning the measure and accusing Gálvez, Croix, and the king (who was termed the 'miserable *caudillo* of the devilish troops' in one poem)[1] of planning to destroy the Catholic religion. A letter sent to the Holy Office and signed by the 'poor Christians of Puebla' warned that the people were arming themselves to kill all the 'heretics' in the government and to defend the Church against their attacks.[2]

Archbishop Lorenzana and the Bishop of Puebla, Fabián y Fuero, were favoured targets of these anonymous pamphleteers.[3] They were attacked for their sycophantic and theologically questionable pastoral letters in which they applauded the expulsion as a divine judgement against the 'impious and fanatical Jesuits'[4] and exhorted the faithful to render unquestioning obedience to the king, who had been 'commissioned by God to guard his subjects from influences dangerous to their faith'.[5] Both prelates seconded Croix's demand that the Holy Office seek out and punish the authors of the libellous tracts written against them, but the Inquisitors committed the blunder of following royal orders too literally: they refused to publish an edict banning this literature because, they said, the Pragmatic Sanction of 1767 decreeing the expulsion had prohibited any comment for or against the measure.[6]

Lorenzana, Croix, and Gálvez complained to the king, who informed the Holy Office, through the Supreme Council in Madrid, of his extreme displeasure at their indifference and inaction.[7] Given this mild warning, the Inquisitors promptly

[1] A.H.N., Inquisición 2287, Anonymous poem beginning 'Arma, arma, guerra, guerra . . .', in trial of Pedro Joseph Velarde, 1767.

[2] *Ibid.*, Anonymous letter to the Inquisition, April 1768.

[3] A.H.N., Inquisición 2286-B, contains many of these pamphlets and poems, e.g., a couplet directed against Lorenzana (whose first name was Francisco), denounced to the Inquisition in December 1767: 'La iglesia está viuda sin manto ni toca/ porque la gobierna Paquita la loca.'

[4] Archivo diocesano de Toledo, sala 4, no. 125, Carta pastoral, Lorenzana, 12 Oct. 1767.

[5] R.A.H., Col. Jesuítas 28, Carta pastoral, Fabián y Fuero, 28 Oct. 1767.

[6] A.H.N., Inquisición 2286-B, Mexican Holy Office to Consejo Supremo, 26 July 1768, justifying their refusal.

[7] *Ibid.*, Consejo Supremo to Holy Office, 12 June 1768.

issued an edict prohibiting any writings that in any way detracted from the 'justification, piety and religion of His Majesty or his prudent ministers', under pain of excommunication,[1] and also began a frantic search for any suspicious actions or literature on their own initiative.

Their new-found zeal was directed mainly against subversive ideas that the clergy might disseminate through the confessional or in conversation.[2] Confessors who assured penitents that disloyal thoughts against the government were not even a venial sin were considered an especially dangerous influence: one priest even told a layman to disregard the censures imposed by the Inquisition's edict, because it had been published only to please the king.[3] These reports alarmed the Supreme Council in Madrid, which recommended a new edict ordering everyone to denounce confessors who advised them against their duties as Christians and loyal subjects of the king, but the Mexican Holy Office thought that voluntary denunciations would be sufficiently effective.[4]

Despite their vigorous efforts, the authorities were able to uncover even less evidence of sedition in Mexico than in Spain. The ecclesiastical hierarchy in the main declared itself in support of the expulsion, and the riots in the North, which may have been due to economic and social grievances in any case,[5] were actually put down with the aid of the local clergy.[6] The cases in Mexico were the inevitable examples of resentment against the government's particular measures or of imprudent interest in intellectual innovations that might occur in any period, rather than indications of an organized plot.

But more important than the cases themselves were the

---

[1] *Ibid.*, Edict Holy Office, 15 July 1768.
[2] *Ibid.*, Mexican Holy Office to Consejo Supremo, 26 July 1768.
[3] A.H.N., Inquisición 2286-A, Mexican Holy Office to Consejo Supremo, 27 Sept. 1768.
[4] *Ibid.*, Consejo Supremo to Manuel de Roda, 12 April 1769.
[5] A.G.I., Estado 34, Informe (unsigned), August 1773, alleging that Gálvez purposely confused the issue of the expulsion with that of several unpopular decrees. See also A.G.N., Reales cédulas 91, R.C.'s, 6, 9, 18 and 21 Feb. and 3 March 1767, all referring to riots in Guanajuato, Pachuca, and Pátzcuaro before the expulsion, caused by unpopular decrees.
[6] See R.A.H., Legajos de Jesuítas 100, Informe del Alcalde Mayor de Apatzingán, 1767; and H. I. Priestley, *op. cit.*, p. 215.

government's genuine belief that danger did exist and its eagerness to support this belief with even the most scanty evidence. One priest, for example, was prosecuted for merely 'discussing', not recommending, a work promising English support for independence in return for free trade.[1] In Oaxaca, two canons who denounced the other members of the chapter and Bishop Miguel Álvarez de Abreu for a variety of offences, mentioned vaguely that certain statements had been made against the king.[2] Their accusations might have been ignored in any other period as a spiteful manœuvre in one of the frequent capitular feuds. But the Crown seized upon this particular item and ordered the viceroy to make a thorough investigation.[3]

In fact two investigations were made, because the Crown was not satisfied with Viceroy Croix's conclusion that there was nothing to the denunciation. His successor, Bucareli, reported that one canon had said during the recent Seven Years War: 'We would be better off with the English than with the *gachupines.*' Another had said that the king had expelled the Jesuits in order to take over their property. But both canons had been reprimanded for these remarks, and the allegations against the bishop that he had opposed the expulsion of the Jesuits and fomented rebellion were completely groundless.[4] Since the bishop and both canons had died by the time the report was submitted, the Council took no further action.

This atmosphere of suspicion naturally put the clergy on the defensive. The prelates who denounced the Jesuits so eagerly and even requested the pope to suppress the order[5] were perhaps not moved entirely by sincere antipathy or a wish to join the anti-Jesuit campaign as a means of currying royal favour. Another possible explanation is their anxiety to dissociate themselves from any taint of disloyalty. As Fabián y

---

[1] A.H.N., Inquisición 2286-A, Holy Office to Consejo Supremo, 29 Aug. 1768. The work was entitled, 'Protección de la nación inglesa a la América oprimida'.
[2] A.G.I., Mexico 2628, Representación de Juan de Aponte y Francisco Díaz Inguanzo, canónigos de la merced, 19 Oct. 1769.
[3] *Ibid.*, R.C. to Viceroy Croix, 27 Jan. 1770.
[4] *Ibid.*, Informe Bucareli to the king, 27 Oct. 1775.
[5] Biblioteca pública de Toledo, Col. Borbón-Lorenzana, vol. 178, no. 14, Representación de los padres del Concilio a Su Santidad, 24 Oct. 1771 (copy).

Fuero lectured his fellow members of the Provincial Council in 1771: 'We must demonstrate our loyalty to His Majesty with even greater fervour now' because of the treacherous acts of one section of the ecclesiastical community, i.e., the Jesuits.[1] The necessity of impressing upon the clergy their duties as loyal subjects of the king and of suppressing any theories to the contrary received much attention during this period. Charles, ignoring the recommendation of the Council of the Indies, sent a *cédula* already issued in Spain to America, warning ecclesiastics against criticizing the government.[2] The Council had thought the measure unnecessary, but the king wished to inform the clergy in all his dominions that their ecclesiastical status did not exempt them from the responsibility of showing respect and veneration for the Crown.[3] Subsequently, the ministerial *junta* that Charles appointed to revise the colonial law code changed the old law concerning the 'oath of fidelity' to the Crown that American prelates were required to swear when they took possession of a bishopric.[4] The oath was now to be entitled 'oath of obedience and submission' and to include in its preamble the phrase: 'All my vassals, without excepting the ecclesiastical prelates, are equally obliged by divine and natural law to comply with the duties inherent in vassalage', in order to banish the opinions that challenged the supremacy of secular authority.[5]

The emphasis placed on theories of ecclesiastical vassalage and immunity at this time was demonstrated by the government's reaction to a thesis accepted by the University of Valladolid in 1770, defending the clergy's total exemption from secular authority.[6] The Royal College of Lawyers in Madrid, to which the thesis was referred by the Council of Castile, reported that the general body of canon law taught in the law faculties, on which the thesis was based, contained

[1] B.N., 5806, Extracto compendioso de las actas . . ., 16 Oct. 1771.
[2] A.G.N., Reales cédulas 92, R.C. 17 March 1768.
[3] A.G.I., Ind. Gen. 350, Real resolución to Consulta, 30 Jan. 1768.
[4] *Recop. Indias*, ley 1, título 7, Libro 1.
[5] A.G.I., Ind. Gen. 1653, Juntas del Nuevo Código, 4 Feb. and 11 March 1782.
[6] *Documentos históricos mexicanos* (B.M.), ii, no. 16, Tesis defendida por el Br. Miguel de Ochoa, 31 Jan. 1770, in Real provisión para preservar las regalías de la corona . . ., Madrid, 1770.

many canons that conflicted with Spanish law. Their wide-spread acceptance among the clergy was dangerous to public tranquillity, having led to 'certain unhappy events we have witnessed in our times' (i.e., the *motín de Esquilache*), and the College thought it would be opportune to warn the clergy that the king possessed coercive authority to enforce their obedience to his laws, regardless of what certain 'apocryphal' canons might hold.[1]

The measures taken by the Crown as a result of this thesis were a serious blow to academic freedom. Both the Dean of the Valladolid law faculty and the author of the thesis were dismissed from their posts, the university was instructed to arrange for new theses vindicating royal prerogatives, and the post of royal censor, who was to examine all theses before their acceptance, was established for each university in Spain, in order to defend royal authority from any dangerous doctrines.[2]

2. 'lèse-majesté' and ecclesiastical 'fuero'

The most famous consequence of the shift in royal policy in this period was the expulsion of the Jesuits from all the royal dominions in Spain and America, for 'very serious causes relative to my obligation to maintain subordination, tranquillity, and justice in my kingdom and other urgent, just, and necessary causes', which the king did not choose to divulge.[3] This measure, which followed similar decrees expelling the Jesuits from Portugal in 1759 and from France in 1764, was not an isolated and arbitrary act of reprisal, but part of a systematic plan to strengthen the State against any threat to its security and any possible opposition to royal policies.

Another measure that formed part of this general plan was the expulsion of all foreign ecclesiastics from the Indies, decreed several months after the expulsion of the Jesuits in 1767. The reasons for this sudden insistence on the laxly enforced laws of the colonial law code forbidding foreigners to travel to the

---

[1] *Ibid.*, Dictamen del Real Colegio de Abogados, 8 June 1770.
[2] *Ibid.*, Real provisión para preservar las regalías de la corona . . ., 6 Sept. 1770. See also R. Herr, *op. cit.*, pp. 24–5.
[3] *Decretos reales tocantes a la iglesia* (B.M.), no. 20, Pragmatic Sanction, 2 April 1767, inserted in R.C., 5 April 1767. See also above, pp. 51–2.

Indies were stated clearly in the *cédula*'s opening paragraph: the king was forced to act because of the 'serious disadvantages caused by the presence of these foreign ecclesiastics, devoid of any loyalty to the nation and possessing sympathies contrary to the security of my dominions in the Indies . . .'[1] This order was not based on any evidence either that there had been a notable increase in the numbers of foreign clergy residing in the colonies or that their behaviour had been suspicious.[2] It was a purely precautionary measure designed to eliminate a possible threat to the external security of the State.

The expulsion of particularly untrustworthy elements within the clergy, such as foreign ecclesiastics and Jesuits, was only a partial solution to the problem of protecting the State against potentially or actively dangerous ecclesiastics. The Jesuits, with their suspect ideas, enormous influence over public opinion, and powerful organization, were the epitome of all the dangers and obstructions feared from ecclesiastics in general. It was neither feasible nor desirable to expel the entire clergy but, as long as they were immune from civil prosecution, they remained a potential threat. Regalist arguments justifying the abolition of ecclesiastical immunity in cases of sedition or any other crime against the State were already in existence and required only the proper circumstance, now provided by the *motín de Esquilache*, to induce the Crown to translate them into law. Soon after the *motín* in 1766, the Council of Castile issued a *cédula* that would enable the civil authorities to proceed against any ecclesiastics who had been implicated in the uprising: all privileged *fueros* 'of any class whatsoever' were suspended in cases of riot, rebellion, or any form of public disorder, which were placed under ordinary civil jurisdiction.[3] In another *cédula* this jurisdiction was extended to cover any ecclesiastics who advocated doctrines against or criticized the king, the royal family, or members of the government.[4]

At the time of their promulgation, these laws were not applied to the fullest extent that their wording implied. A

---

[1] A.G.I., Mexico 3053, R.C. circular, 17 Oct. 1767.
[2] See above, pp. 52–3.
[3] *Novís. Recop. España*, ley 4, título 11, Libro 12, from R.C., 7 Aug. 1766.
[4] *Ibid.*, ley 7, título 8, Libro 1, from R.C., 18 Sept. 1766.

number of prominent ecclesiastics were arrested in Madrid and other Castilian cities shortly after the *motín*, but they were sent into exile without a formal trial.[1] The Bishop of Cuenca, who was accused of libel with seditious intent, was only given a public reprimand before the Council of Castile and exiled from Court, although the *Fiscal* Campomanes had called for his prosecution as an 'enemy of the State', so that the public should not think that episcopal consecration gave one *'carte blanche* to libel the King'.[2]

The existence of these laws, however, was fully as important as their enforcement. Along with the other measures taken to safeguard public order, such as the prohibition of printing presses on or near ecclesiastical property (subversive pamphlets appearing during the *motín* had been attributed to the Jesuits[3]), they reveal the deep distrust with which the government came to view the clergy in this period. But more important, these *cédulas*, which represented the first official attack on ecclesiastical *fuero*, were a public statement of the Crown's new policy of direct judicial control of the clergy. Even if Charles III chose not to apply them fully when they were first promulgated (his successor, Charles IV, did not hesitate to use them later during the period following the French Revolution),[4] they remained in force as a warning to any ecclesiastics who might be tempted to foment discord or disrupt public order that their privilege of immunity was no longer sacrosanct.

A *cédula* directed against expelled Jesuits who returned from exile was another direct curtailment of ecclesiastical immunity. Arrest, civil prosecution, and severe penalties—the death sentence for a lay brother and life imprisonment for an ordained priest—were prescribed for Jesuits who re-entered Spanish territory, even if they had become secular priests or had entered other religious orders after the expulsion.[5] Despite its ominous

---

[1] See V. Rodríguez Casado, *op. cit.*, pp. 162–7; and *Cartas inéditas del Padre Isla*, pp. 368–72.

[2] A.H.N., Consejos 494, Respuesta Fiscal Campomanes, 16 July 1767.

[3] M. Dánvila y Collado, *op. cit.*, iv, 14.

[4] See, e.g., A.H.N., Consejos 51560, Causa reservada por cartas y papeles recogidos a D. Juan Gómez Pacheco, cura párroco del Escorial . . ., 1797–8. Consejos 8925 contains a similar case dated 1796.

[5] A.G.N., Bandos y ordenanzas 7, R.C. Council of the Indies, 11 Nov. 1767 (from R.C., Council of Castile, 22 Oct. 1767).

wording, this *cédula* also seems to have been issued as a warning and a deterrent without the intention of strict application. Returning Jesuits were arrested and prosecuted in violation of their immunity, but they were merely sent back to Italy rather than sentenced to death or imprisonment.[1] The decrees issued shortly after the *motín de Esquilache*, though indicating a radical departure from the traditional royal policy of controlling the clergy through extra-judicial means, had in fact little tangible effect on judicial practice in the Indies. The *cédulas* abolishing all privileged *fueros* in cases of riot, sedition, and subversion[2] were worded in such general terms that the colonial authorities never agreed on whether or not they included ecclesiastical *fuero*,[3] and the decree curtailing the immunity of fugitive Jesuits, though enforced in the Indies,[4] applied only to a particular and relatively small section of the clergy. However, a case that arose in Mexico in the 1760's established a clear precedent for secular prosecution of treasonous ecclesiastics and, more important, formed the basis for a new law that applied unequivocally to the entire clergy in the Indies. This pivotal case concerning an Italian friar accused of spying, who before the *motín de Esquilache* and the expulsion of the Jesuits was dealt with by the old method of deportation,[5] and then deprived of his *fuero* when re-arrested after these events, reveals most clearly the source and nature of the change in royal policy towards ecclesiastical immunity and thus deserves a detailed analysis.

In October 1762, while Havana was under British occupation, Viceroy Cruíllas of New Spain and other royal officials received letters from Havana informing them of the departure for Campeche of a certain Fray Juan Annovacio, an Italian

[1] See R.A.H., Legajos de Jesuítas 89, for trials of expelled Jesuits who returned to Spain, 1768–91.
[2] The R.C., 18 Sept. 1766, was sent to Mexico by R.O., 23 Sept. 1766, A.G.N., Bandos y ordenanzas 6. Another more emphatic law, a Real Pragmática of 1774, made into ley 5, título 11, Libro 12, *Novís. Recop. España*, was at least known in Mexico.
[3] See A.G.N., Obispos y arzobispos 3, Bishop of Oaxaca to viceroy, 8 Jan. 1811; and Dictamen Junta de Seguridad, 18 Jan. 1811.
[4] See A.G.I., Mexico 1152, Petition from Thomás de Rubalcava, 27 June 1779; and Ind. Gen. 563, Real resolución, 31 Aug. 1786, concerning a case in Buenos Aires. [5] See above, pp. 57–9, for a discussion of the deportation case.

Servite from Venice, who had been on very friendly terms with the British commander, Lord Albemarle, and warning them that the trip was a reconnaissance mission in preparation for an invasion.[1] Annovacio was arrested soon after his arrival and transported under military escort to the royal prison in Mexico, where he was held *incommunicado* for questioning.[2] When the viceroy was satisfied that a full testimony had been given, he informed the archbishop of his decision to deport the friar to Spain.[3] The ensuing controversy between the archbishop and the civil authorities over whether the measures ordered by the viceroy had violated the friar's immunity, during which the two *oidores* who had questioned the suspect and the royal *escribano* who had assisted were excommunicated, was finally resolved by a *recurso de fuerza* to the *audiencia*, which declared that the archbishop 'hace fuerza en conocer' and ordered him to revoke the censures.[4] As soon as this issue was settled, the viceroy proceeded with his plan to send the friar to Cadiz, where he was detained in the prison of the *Casa de Contratación* to await the king's decision on his fate.

Despite the archbishop's violent reaction to what he termed a 'previously unheard of attack on the sacred privileges of the clergy',[5] the procedure followed with Annovacio was the accepted method of dealing with ecclesiastics charged with *lèse-majesté*. During the revolt of the *comuneros* in the sixteenth century, ecclesiastical rebels were exiled and their property confiscated,[6] and in the beginning of the eighteenth century certain friars in the employ of the Habsburgs during the War of the Spanish Succession, who had been sent to foment rebellion in the Indies, were questioned by the civil authorities and

---

[1] A.G.I., Mexico 2617, Padre Joseph Butler, Rector of the Jesuit College in Havana, to Joseph Crespo, Governor of Campeche, 14 Oct. 1762. Other unsigned letters to the viceroy and the Governor of Veracruz were dated 19–23 Oct. 1762.

[2] *Ibid.*, Testimonio de los autos instruídos sobre el arresto . . ., 1762.

[3] *Ibid.*, Cruíllas to Rubio y Salinas, 30 Dec. 1762.

[4] *Ibid.*, Auto de fuerza, 7 May 1763.

[5] *Ibid.*, Rubio y Salinas to Cruíllas, 30 Dec. 1762.

[6] R. B. Merriman, *The Rise of the Spanish Empire in the Old World and the New* (4 vols., New York, 1918–34), iii, 121, writes of the one exception, the Bishop of Zamora, who was executed after killing his jailor in an attempt to escape from prison.

shipped back to Spain.[1] In fact, the archbishop had not objected to the viceroy's decision to deport the friar, but only to the fact that it had been made without consulting him and without the intervention of the ecclesiastical judges in the friar's interrogation.

Annovacio's case, and especially the archbishop's peremptory censures against high-ranking royal magistrates, produced a flood of *dictámenes* and petitions from jurists both in Mexico and Madrid on the subject of ecclesiastical immunity, in which the effectiveness of this traditional, extra-judicial method of punishing crimes against the State was called into question.[2] Although their immediate purpose was to demonstrate that the viceroy and his subordinates had not violated the friar's *fuero* and that therefore the canonical censures were unjustified, the jurists, with few exceptions,[3] then proceeded to argue in favour of revoking the privilege in cases of espionage and to request that the king establish a general rule that would avoid similar clashes of jurisdiction in the future by placing these crimes under the exclusive authority of the secular magistrates.[4]

They used the special circumstances of this case to argue that in time of war the claims of ecclesiastical immunity conflicted with the duty of the State to protect itself from the enemy. After the capture of Havana by the British in August 1762, the panic-stricken officials in New Spain believed that an attack on the viceroyalty was both imminent and likely to succeed, and it was in the midst of frantic attempts to strengthen defences along the Gulf Coast that Viceroy Cruíllas had received the warnings from Havana concerning Annovacio's proposed mission of espionage. Considering the evidence against the friar, Cruíllas thought he had acted with restraint in not formally prosecuting and sentencing 'this cunning explorer' to a severe

---

[1] See A.H.N., Códices 722, R.C. circular, 5 March 1703, ordering the deportation of these friars.

[2] A.G.I., Mexico 2617, Respuestas Fiscal Velarde, Mexico, 13 Jan., 5 March and 25 June 1763; Escrito Oidor Valcárcel to the Audienca, 13 Jan. 1763; Dictamen reservado (unsigned) 'Tratadillo por la regalía', 1763; Respuesta Fiscal de Nueva España (Madrid) 22 Sept., 1763.

[3] *Ibid.*, the Fiscal del Perú favoured preserving the privilege in his Respuesta, 19 Sept. 1763, and two councillors in a Voto particular, 24 Nov. 1763, agreed with him.

[4] See also *ibid.*, Cruíllas to Arriaga, 12 April 1763.

penalty.[1] For the past two years Annovacio had been travelling around the Caribbean, interspersing trips to the most strategic Spanish ports with visits to the British island of Jamaica[2] and, even without the reports from Havana that Annovacio had been in daily contact with the British officers there, from whom he had received many gifts, the Mexican officials felt that the passport signed by 'Albemarle' stating that Annovacio had his permission to go to Campeche 'in my service'[3] was sufficient proof of his intentions.

The opponents of ecclesiastical immunity asserted that if, instead of arresting and questioning Annovacio on the spot, the royal officials had waited for the ecclesiastical judges to act, he might have escaped to Havana with his mission accomplished. Certainly, if they had turned him over to the ecclesiastical authorities immediately and waited for the results of their inquiry, as the archbishop had proposed, the delay in receiving vital information might have meant the difference between safety and a successful British invasion.[4] One jurist argued that the claims of ecclesiastical immunity were nothing but a blessing to any enemy, who could take advantage of Spain's notorious respect for the clergy:

The English will have a grand laugh, for now they have discovered a foolproof way to vanquish us. They need only look for ecclesiastics, real or imposters, and we will have to surrender the kingdom out of veneration for the Church. . . . Would it not be better to hang ourselves from the start, than attempt to wage war under these conditions?[5]

The specific dispute over violation of immunity had been settled in Mexico by the *audiencia*'s *auto de fuerza*, but the larger issue raised by the royal jurists, of whether immunity should be rescinded, remained unresolved. Despite the recommenda-

---

[1] A.G.I., Mexico 2617, Cruíllas to Arriaga, 12 April 1763.

[2] *Ibid.*, Cuaderno de los instrumentos . . ., 1762: passports, licences to preach in different Caribbean dioceses, etc.

[3] *Ibid.*, Free conduct pass (in English), 14 Oct. 1762, signed 'Albemarle'.

[4] *Ibid.*, Defensa Valcárcel to the Audiencia, 13 Jan. 1763; Respuesta Fiscal Velarde to the Audiencia, 5 March 1763; and Cruíllas to the king, 24 Aug. 1763.

[5] *Ibid.*, 'Tratadillo por la regalía', sent by Cruíllas to Arriaga, 12 April 1763.

tions of the *fiscal* for New Spain and several ministers, the Council of the Indies and the king decided not to prosecute Annovacio for 'this horrendous crime of *lèse-majesté*',[1] but to place him in the custody of the Bishop of Cadiz and then, when his identity had been established conclusively, turn him over to the Servite superiors in Italy.[2] In 1765 the same *fiscal* for New Spain addressed a new *dictamen* directly to the king, urging him to issue a general law abolishing ecclesiastical *fuero* in cases involving the security of the State,[3] but his lengthy and detailed argument had no more effect than his first *respuesta*, that is, until Annovacio's case was brought up again and the issue re-examined in the light of the events of 1766 and 1767: the *motín de Esquilache*, the case of the Bishop of Cuenca and other examples of alleged ecclesiastical subversion, and the expulsion of the Jesuits.

In 1768 Annovacio, now serving as a soldier in a Spanish regiment stationed in Madrid, was arrested for the second time.[4] The file on his previous arrest was re-opened, and the Council noticed an item of evidence previously overlooked, namely, Annovacio's contacts with Jesuits in several of the Caribbean ports he had visited, which in the light of subsequent occurrences were considered extremely sinister.

The Council commissioned an official to re-examine the friar in what was an undisguised attempt to establish a Jesuit plot to turn the American colonies over to the English; for now that the Society had been expelled, it was very convenient to find new reasons to justify that measure and to support Charles III's demand to the pope to have the order suppressed. The questions were designed to show that Annovacio had been recruited by the Jesuits in Europe to carry secret letters to and between Caribbean ports, and that the English had invaded Havana with the aid of the Jesuits.[5] No one bothered to question why, if Annovacio was supposed to be in the service

---

[1] A.G.I., Mexico 2616, Voto particular, three councillors, 10 Nov. 1764.

[2] *Ibid.*, R.C.'s to Bishop of Cadiz, 24 Dec. 1764 and 7 May 1765.

[3] Bib. del Palacio, Col. Ayala 4, Dictamen de D. Manuel Pablo Salcedo en apoyo del que dió como Fiscal, 1765.

[4] A.G.I., Mexico 2616, Informe Alcalde de Corte, 7 Sept. 1768.

[5] *Ibid.*, Declaración tomada al Padre Annovacio por Pedro Ávila y Soto, 22–7 July 1769.

of the Jesuits, the Rector of the Jesuit College in Havana had warned the Mexican officials of his intended trip to Campeche.[1] Realizing that his inquisitors were more interested in defaming the Society than in establishing his own guilt, the friar obliged them by implicating the Jesuits in his confession, which in most instances even conflicted with the testimony he had given in Mexico.

Although he was now known to be a 'spy for the fathers of the Company'[2] (no longer a British spy), the Council of the Indies maintained that Annovacio could not be prosecuted, but should be turned over to the ecclesiastical judges, and some councillors argued that he could not even be questioned by the royal authorities without permission from his religious superior.[3] But the king agreed with the *fiscal* that Annovacio had forfeited his right to immunity by committing this heinous crime, and he was sentenced to life imprisonment.[4] There was no new evidence that made the crime any more serious than in 1764, for his second testimony incriminated only the Jesuits. The only change was in the attitude of the government, which had come to regard ecclesiastical immunity as a dispensable concession rather than a sacred right to be enjoyed under any circumstances.

The atmosphere of suspicion and fear resulting from the *motín de Esquilache* and other internal circumstances on the one hand, and from the Seven Years War with England on the other, inevitably diminished with time. The Crown, however, did not forget the lesson learned from these events and incorporated the new policy towards ecclesiastical immunity into the revised colonial law code, with the case of the Italian Servite friar as a precedent:[5] 'The cognizance of crimes of *lèse-majesté* committed by ecclesiastics in riots, uprisings, sedition or other similar cases corresponds to our royal courts.' Ecclesiastical judges were not to interfere but rather to send the cases immediately to the secular judges as soon as the summary

---

[1] See above, p. 140, note 1.

[2] A.G.I., Mexico 2616, Consulta Council of the Indies, 20 Dec. 1769.

[3] *Ibid.*, Voto particular, in Consulta of 8 April 1769.

[4] *Ibid.*, Respuesta Fiscales, 21 Feb. 1769, and Real resolución to Consulta, 20 Dec. 1769.

[5] A.G.I., Ind. Gen. 1653, Junta del Nuevo Código, 31 Jan. 1785.

indictment or any other proceedings indicated that the crime was of this nature.[1]

Even after the crisis in royal policy, expulsion was still the accepted procedure for ecclesiastics who were only a possible threat to security and whose actions were not necessarily suspicious in themselves: in 1769, for example, another Italian priest, arrested in Porto Bello, was eventually shipped back to Italy after careful investigation had established that he was guilty of no more than illegal entry and had not shown 'undue interest in the fortifications and defences of the port'.[2] But when the time came that the monarchy and empire were truly threatened seriously—by discontented Creoles from both the clergy and the laity, determined to end Spanish rule in America by force—the legal foundation for direct civil prosecution of subversive and rebellious ecclesiastics had already been laid and was available for use in attempting to suppress the Mexican independence movement.[3]

[1] A.G.I., Mexico 1159, Nuevo Código, ley 13, título 12, Libro 1.
[2] A.G.I., Ind. Gen. 2993, Consultas Council of the Indies, 25 June and 19 Aug. 1768 and 15 Sept. 1769.
[3] See below, Ch. IX.

L

PART III

Direct Control of the Clergy

CHAPTER VII

Ecclesiastical Immunity in Civil Suits

I. CONCEPTS OF 'FUERO' IN CIVIL SUITS

THE first direct restriction of the personal *fuero* of ecclesiastics that seriously affected the whole mass of the colonial clergy was in the area of civil litigation. Although this immunity was confirmed in general by Charles IV in the *Nuevo Código de las leyes de Indias*, the new law code also contained several important exceptions, in addition to the first formal proclamation by law of the Crown's incontestable authority to limit any ecclesiastical privilege at will.[1]

Regalists and canonists had long disputed the origin and nature of ecclesiastical immunity, a dispute that culminated finally in the triumph of the regalists, who had asserted that the privilege was a concession of previous temporal sovereigns, rather than an institution of divine origin, and could therefore be rescinded by their successors whenever the safety of the royal realms or the welfare of their subjects required this measure.

Although they agreed upon the king's right to abolish ecclesiastical *fuero*, the regalists had varying opinions about the expediency of doing so. The Royal College of Lawyers of Madrid thought that these privileges, though originating in secular law, had been granted as a contract in return for the innumerable benefits and honours God and the Church had bestowed upon Spain, which would be jeopardized if the king revoked his part of the agreement.[2] At the other extreme,

---

[1] A.G.I., Mexico 1159, Nuevo Código, leyes 10–12, título 9, and ley 13, título 12, Libro 1.

[2] *Documentos históricos mexicanos* (B.M.), ii, no. 16, Dictamen del Real Colegio de Abogados de Madrid, 8 June 1770.

certain authors argued that the welfare of society and the State demanded that all ecclesiastical privileges be abolished.[1] The late Bourbon ecclesiastical policy for the colonies, exemplified in the *Nuevo Código*, was a compromise between these two extremes. The king declared his right to rescind entirely this 'concession of our glorious progenitors', but chose to deprive the clergy of their immunity only in certain categories (in reality the most important) and to confirm it in the remaining 'as a demonstration of the honour which their high status as ministers of the altar deserves'.[2]

Before the Caroline attack on ecclesiastical privileges, there was no ostensible conflict between royal legislation and canon law over immunity in civil suits, for the legal formula *actor sequitur forum rei*, which meant that the plaintiff was obliged to sue in the *fuero* of the defendant, was common to both.[3] With several exceptions this rule was the established practice in the law courts of both Spain and the Indies. Thus an ecclesiastical plaintiff, whether a religious order, a particular convent, or an individual cleric, who wished to sue a layman for the collection of a debt or to file a claim for the adjudication of boundary disputes, title to land, water rights and other civil questions, did so in the appropriate secular tribunal.[4] Similarly laymen who had a claim against an ecclesiastic—often parishioners who complained that the local curate had overcharged them for parochial duties, such as baptisms and burials—filed suit before the diocesan magistrate.[5]

---

[1] Bib. del Palacio, Col. Ayala 4, Dictamen de Manuel Pablo Salcedo, 1765.

[2] A.G.I., Mexico 1159, Nuevo Código, ley 11, título 9, Libro 1.

[3] C. Rodríguez-Arango Díaz, *El fuero civil y criminal de los clérigos en el derecho canónico* (Rome, 1957), pp. 152–3. See also A.H.N., Códices 756, Consulta Council of the Indies, 18 May 1767.

[4] See, e.g., A.H.N., Consejos 20675, Convento de Santa Clara con Joseph Gómez de Cervantes, 1768; and A.G.I., Mexico 2534, La Provincia de Carmelitas descalzos con el Conde de la Cortina, 1797. Guadalajara 315, Estado de los negocios civiles pendientes en la Real Audiencia de Guadalajara, 1805, lists many civil suits brought by ecclesiastics against laymen.

[5] See, e.g., A.G.N., Clero regular y secular 5, Los naturales del pueblo de Malacatepec con su cura sobre aranceles, 1774–8. Vols. 30, 67, 83, 153 and 204 of the same section contain similar suits. For suits over payment of debts, see, e.g., Clero regular y secular 32, D. Manuel Argumedo con el Br. Francisco de Araujo sobre deuda, 1775; and Obras pías 6, D. Manuel de los Ríos con el Convento de Bethlemitas, 1786–7.

Though filing suit in the *fuero* of the defendant was the general rule, there were a number of important exceptions. Ecclesiastical defendants had been deprived of their *fuero* in certain questions that directly concerned the Crown even before the promulgation of the *Nuevo Código* laws. The extensive jurisdiction the Spanish kings claimed by virtue of the *patronato* concession was a significant limitation of ecclesiastical immunity, since all litigation concerning benefices held under royal patronage and many other matters related to the administration of the Church in the Indies were decided by the king and his vice-patrons rather than by the ecclesiastical judges, even if the defendant or all parties concerned were ecclesiastics.[1] In addition, members of the clergy who held public office under the Crown, such as viceroys and *oidores*, were not exempt because of their ecclesiastical status from judicial inquiries into the performance of their duties, but were obliged, like any layman holding such an office, to undergo *visitas* and *residencias* carried out by royal judges,[2] since the Crown claimed inherent jurisdiction over any litigation to which it was a party.[3]

The balance of exceptions to the general rule in civil suits was, however, overwhelmingly in favour of ecclesiastical litigants. Since the majority of civil suits concerned some form of property, whether capital or real estate, the question of personal *fuero* was often involved with, and largely subordinated to, that of *inmunidad real*, or the immunity of ecclesiastical property from secular authority. Real immunity originally meant only exemption from taxation and the inalienability of property in mortmain, but as a corollary the Church had developed certain claims to exclusive jurisdiction over all judicial matters concerning ecclesiastical property,[4] through

---

[1] See above, pp. 20–3, on patronage suits.

[2] *Recop. Indias*, ley 37, título 34, Libro 2. See J. Mariluz Urquijo, *Ensayo sobre los juicios de residencia indianos* (Seville, 1952), pp. 91–2, on *residencias* of ecclesiastical viceroys in the seventeenth century; and *Mexican Political Pamphlets* (B.M.), i, no. 4, Pesquisa secreta hecha en la residencia del Arzobispo-virrey Juan Antonio Vizarrón, 1734–40.

[3] See *Siete Partidas*, ley 23, título 6, Partida 1; and J. de Hevia Bolaños, *Curia Philipica*, Part 1, párr. 5, no. 22.

[4] P. Rodríguez Campomanes, *Tratado de la regalía de amortización*, Chapter 1, especially pp. 3–25.

which, in Mexico, it came to control a large share of all civil litigation.

This judicial dominance of the ecclesiastical courts, to the exclusion of royal magistrates, was by no means unchallenged. The growth of *competencias* and the increase in complaints from colonial royal officials, reaching a peak in the mid-eighteenth century, coincided with the Crown's emerging policy of limiting ecclesiastical power and privileges and finally stimulated the creation of a series of new regulations, which went further than restoring the balance of jurisdiction and gave a decided advantage to both secular judges and lay litigants.

In order to analyse the development of this new legislation, it will be necessary first to describe the previous practice and the causes of friction between the two jurisdictions. As in all cases of *mixti fori*, boundaries between the two were ill-defined and tended to vary according to the zeal and forcefulness of the particular officials. A prominent seventeenth-century Spanish jurist, after giving the theoretical arguments on behalf of each jurisdiction, admitted that there was no generally accepted rule in Spain for cases concerning ecclesiastical property, and that the same type of suit was often filed either in a diocesan or royal court without any discernible criteria governing the choice.[1]

The most obvious source of ecclesiastical property was tithes, which were levied on all agricultural and livestock products.[2] In the beginning of the colonial period judicial jurisdiction over tithes belonged to the royal courts, since all ecclesiastical tithes in the Indies had been donated to the Spanish Crown by Pope Alexander VI in 1501[3] and, although they had been re-donated in turn to the Church (except for a small portion, called the *reales novenos*, reserved by the Crown), they were still considered royal property.[4] Thus the *audiencias* and the Council of the Indies, rather than the ecclesiastical courts, adjudicated disputes concerning the collection and payment of tithes, such

---

[1] J. de Hevia Bolaños, *op. cit.*, Part 1, párr. 5, no. 13.
[2] *Recop. Indias*, leyes 2–5 and 12, título 16, Libro 1.
[3] Papal bull, 'Eximiae devotionis', in F. J. Hernáez, *op. cit.*, i, 20–1.
[4] See J. de Solórzano Pereira, *op. cit.*, Libro 4, cap. 1, nos. 23 and 30–2.

as the protracted suit between the Jesuits and the various bishoprics in America over the former's claim to exemption from tithes, even though the Jesuits argued that the Church had exclusive jurisdiction over the case, which they wished to refer to Rome.[1] The Crown ignored this argument and confirmed royal jurisdiction over all tithe litigation in the Indies. But in 1672, when a decision was reached in the Council of the Indies in favour of the bishoprics, its sentence was implemented with a royal *cédula* that in effect was to deprive the local royal courts of all cognizance in suits concerning the collection and distribution of tithes, even those paid by laymen.[2] Each diocese was authorized to appoint two canons as *jueces hacedores*, who were to enforce the sentence against the Jesuits and who eventually assumed complete judicial control over these matters,[3] reverting to the original system practised in Castile, where the Crown had never held title to ecclesiastical tithes.[4]

The *jueces hacedores* had extremely wide powers: they could order the imprisonment of anyone, layman or ecclesiastic, who defaulted in payment of his tithes, and they could also issue canonical censures against tithe collectors who embezzled funds and those who failed to denounce graft or default in payment, as well as against the offenders themselves.[5] Acting as judge, party, and prosecutor in the same case, these judges often proceeded with determined harshness against many laymen, and fellow clerics as well, confiscating the property of collectors whose accounts revealed a shortage, calculating tithes on crop yields that were higher than what was actually

---

[1] J. de Solórzano Pereira, *op. cit.*, Libro 4, cap. 1, nos. 24–5.

[2] R.C., 1672, quoted in R.C., 21 Dec. 1766, which gave the final decision against the Jesuits, in *Decretos reales tocantes a la iglesia* (B.M.), no. 19. See also W. Borah, 'Tithe Collection in the Bishopric of Oaxaca, 1601–1867', *H.A.H.R.*, xxix (1949), p. 505.

[3] See A.G.I., Mexico 2622, 'Práctica y ejercicio de la Real jurisdicción en las materias diezmales de ambas Américas', by José Lebrón y Cuervo, abogado de la Real Audiencia de Mexico (n.d., sent to the Council of the Indies in 1771).

[4] See J. Sempere y Guarinos, *Historia de las rentas eclesiásticas de España* (Madrid, 1822), pp. 110–11.

[5] *CIVM*, canon 2, título 15, Libro 3. See also B.N. 12054, Representación del Dr Ríos, Doctoral de Valladolid, sobre la jurisdicción de los jueces hacedores, 6 June 1778.

produced, and excommunicating defaulters who could not pay the entire amount of their assessed tithes.[1]

These extensive judicial powers, so open to abuse, were not seriously challenged until after the *visita* of José de Gálvez, who crowned his efforts at fiscal reform with the *Ordenanza de Intendentes* of 1786, which, among other innovations, placed the collection of tithes under the direct supervision of the treasury officials and drastically limited the judicial jurisdiction of the *jueces hacedores*.[2] They were to have only a minority vote in a new *Junta de Diezmos*, which would have jurisdiction over all administrators and collectors, while their jurisdiction over suits concerning payment of tithes was to be regarded as merely delegated from the Crown, so that they could no longer use ecclesiastical prisons or canonical censures, and their decisions could be appealed to the higher royal courts.[3]

This judicial reform in the system of tithe collection was, however, extremely short-lived, for Charles III soon succumbed to protests from Mexican prelates and suspended execution of the pertinent articles of the *Ordenanza*.[4] The royal courts had never lost control over major tithe cases, such as exemption from payment or division of the product of tithes, even when both parties were ecclesiastics, and they continued to decide these disputes until the end of the colonial period.[5] But in suits over collection, the king was willing to confirm ecclesiastical jurisdiction over his lay subjects, in violation of their *fuero* as defendants.[6] Mexican prelates had argued that tithes, being

[1] See A.G.I., Mexico 2628, Representación de Juan de Aponte y Francisco Díaz Inguanzo a S.M., 6 January 1770; and Mexico 2629, Informe del Pbro. Manuel Márquez, 17 June 1769, concerning these abuses in the diocese of Oaxaca. Cases of confiscation of property and canonical censures in the dioceses of Mexico and Michoacán are cited in B.N., 12054, Representación del Dr. Ríos, 6 June 1778.

[2] F. de Fonseca and C. de Urrutia, *Historia general de Real Hacienda, escrita por . . . orden del virrey conde de Revillagigedo . . .* (6 vols., Mexico, 1845-53), iii, 248-9, 'Real ordenanza para el establecimiento e instrucción de intendentes de exército y provincia en el reino de Nueva España', 4 Dec. 1786, articles 168-208.

[3] *Ibid.*, arts. 173, 176.

[4] R.C. reservada, 23 March 1788, in Fonseca and Urrutia, *op. cit.*, iii, 260.

[5] See A.G.I., Guadalajara 245, Consulta Council, 3 Sept. 1796, concerning a suit between the dioceses of Guadalajara and Durango; and Guadalajara 534, Consulta, 12 Feb. 1801, concerning a suit between the diocese of Durango and the members of the military in the Provincias Internas.

[6] A.G.N., Bandos y ordenanzas 19, R.C., 20 July 1797.

the property of the Church, were subject to *inmunidad real* and could not be placed under secular jurisdiction, but their more pragmatic argument that the *jueces hacedores* (who, as canons, derived their income from tithes) would enforce payment more rigorously and efficiently than the treasury officials, who were burdened with so many other tasks,[1] probably had more effect on a king as preoccupied with fiscal matters as Charles III.

2. CIVIL SUITS OVER TESTAMENTS

Equal to tithes as a source of the Church's wealth in Mexico were the numerous legacies which testators made for the benefit of their souls, to be used for periodical masses, the maintenance of a monastery, dowries for orphaned girls, and other 'pious works'.[2] The combination of a zealous confessor and the near prospect of death usually overcame the resistance of any moribund penitent, who was often willing to disinherit his family in order to ensure the salvation of his own soul. As the Madrid government noted: 'It is well known that His Majesty's subjects in the Indies are excessively pious, so that there is scarcely a testament which does not contain a legacy for pious works.'[3] But excessive piety was not the only reason for these legacies. Since no taxes were paid on ecclesiastical property, which was also inalienable, many families established *capellanías* (or chantries)[4] as a tax-free trust fund for a male heir, who had only to take holy orders to qualify for the benefice, and sometimes the heir had only to pay a priest to fulfil the spiritual functions of the endowment while he used the rest

---

[1] B.N., 13224, Petition to the king from the Archbishop and Chapter of Mexico and the Bishop and Chapter of Michoacán (n.d., but from internal evidence, 1795).

[2] A. von Humboldt, *Ensayo político sobre el reino de la Nueva España* (5 vols., Mexico, 1941), iii, 167, calculated the annual income from tithes in New Spain for the end of the eighteenth century at 2.4 million *pesos*. The income from investments of ecclesiastical property (derived mainly from legacies and donations) was approximately 2.2 million *pesos* a year (calculated on the usual 5 per cent interest rate): see M. Abad y Queipo, *Colección de los escritos más importantes que en diferentes épocas dirigió al govierno* (Mexico, 1813), pp. 95–112, 'Escrito presentado a D. Manuel Sixto Espinosa del Consejo de Estado . . .', 1805.

[3] A.G.I., Ind. Gen. 2994, Informe, three Ministers of the Council of Castile to the king, 11 Nov. 1781.

[4] A *capellanía* was a private ecclesiastical benefice with the obligation to perform stipulated spiritual duties, usually masses for the soul of the deceased benefactor.

of the income from the chantry for his own support.[1] Since the ecclesiastical courts handled almost all suits concerning wills that contained pious legacies, in addition to those cases involving ecclesiastical testators or heirs, the Church exercised a very substantial judicial control over the inheritance of property.

Litigation over testaments was perhaps the most disputed of all the cases of *mixti fori* because of the complex combination of factors that determined jurisdiction: the spiritual or temporal nature of the property involved and the *fuero* of both the testator and the heir all had to be taken into consideration. Royal judges claimed exclusive jurisdiction over all these cases, basing their claim on royal laws that stated that the *Juez de bienes de difuntos*, or royal Judge of Testaments (an office held by *oidores* in rotation), had cognizance over all litigation concerning the distribution of legacies and intestate property.[2] But in practice the diocesan Judges of Testaments, Chantries and Pious Works (*Jueces de testamentos, capellanías y obras pías*) ignored the clause prohibiting them to 'interfere' in these cases, countering with an arsenal of legal theories appropriate to every situation. When the testator was an ecclesiastic with a lay heir, they used the old concept of *fuero pasivo*, which meant that the testament acquired the *fuero* of the testator, even though he naturally had no part in the litigation himself.[3] When the situation was reversed, they emphasized the personal immunity of the heir who, they argued, was entitled to litigate in his own ecclesiastical *fuero*. In the case of pious legacies, the property was said to acquire *inmunidad real* through its spiritual designation, and the ecclesiastical judge was considered executor *a jure* of the legacies.[4]

Thus lay litigants were at a disadvantage no matter what the circumstances of the case. When an ecclesiastic was designated

---

[1] For material on *capellanías de sangre*, see B.N., 12054, Memorial del Arzobispo de Mexico sobre capellanías fundadas en favor de parientes . . ., 26 Sept. 1776.

[2] *Recop. Indias*, leyes 3, 7 and 8, título 32, Libro 2. See also *Mexican Political Pamphlets* (B.M.), i, no. 5, Instrucción dada por el Juez de bienes de difuntos a los governadores, alcaldes mayores y demás justicias locales . . ., Mexico, 1763.

[3] See, e.g., A.G.I., Guadalajara 332, Respuesta Defensor de obras pías (diocese of Durango), 11 May 1764.

[4] See A.G.I., Mexico 2632, Bishop of Michoacán to Audiencia of Mexico, 2 Dec. 1761; and J. de Hevia Bolaños, *op. cit.*, Part i, párr. 5, no. 40.

executor of an estate of which the testator and the heir were laymen (which was frequently the case), any suit brought against him for negligence or fraud in conveying the property had to be brought before the diocesan court, the defendant's *fuero*, in accordance with the standard practice in civil suits.[1] Yet this rule was usually disregarded when the defendant was a lay debtor or executor of an estate that had been left to the Church or to an individual ecclesiastic, in which case the defendant was cited in the *fuero* of the plaintiff, who was either the heir or the administrator of a pious foundation, and his property could be confiscated by the diocesan judge.[2]

The absence of clearly defined rules in royal legislation had worked to the advantage of ecclesiastical judges in all areas of jurisdiction in the seventeenth century, the apogee of the Church's power in the Indies. Both the central authority of the Crown and local administration were considerably weaker and less effective in this century than in the ones preceding and following it. The incompetence of the later Habsburgs and the majority of their ministers is well known; on the lower levels of administration, the increasing sale of public offices produced officials who were more interested in enlarging private patrimonies than in defending royal authority and the Crown's prerogatives.[3] The energetic and efficient colonial clergy filled the resultant vacuum, taking over many judicial and administrative functions formerly reserved to the servants of the Crown, even when specific royal laws forbidding this practice existed. These encroachments might have been prevented by an equally vigorous secular government, but since that did not exist, the Church had an almost unobstructed path to domination in economic and judicial matters.

Not all royal judges permitted the ecclesiastical courts to

---

[1] See, e.g., A.G.I., Mexico 2644, Informe del Juez de testamentos, capellanías y obras pías, Michoacán, 1 April 1787.

[2] See, e.g., A.G.I., Guadalajara 358, Testimonio de la testamentaría de doña Eugenia Ludgarda Zavalza, 1751–68; and A.H.N., Códices 715, R.C. circular, 24 Feb. 1638, ordering royal probate judges to check this practice, common throughout the Indies.

[3] See J. H. Parry, *The Sale of Public Office in the Spanish Indies under the Hapsburgs* (Ibero-Americana: 37, Berkeley, 1953), especially pp. 48–63, 69–73, who concludes that this practice forced many officials to embezzle or extort funds in order to repay loans for the purchase of their offices.

monopolize testament litigation without a challenge, and these challenges increased towards the middle of the eighteenth century as the invigorating effect of the strong, centralized rule of the new Bourbon dynasty filtered down to local administration. The majority of *competencias* were focused upon jurisdiction over probate cases (which included the inventory of estates as well as the publication of wills), since most secular judges agreed that, once a will had been declared valid, the conveyance of the property to either ecclesiastical heirs or pious works came under the jurisdiction of the Church. The source of these disputes was the welter of legal concepts and conflicting laws, which were extremely bewildering even to the most competent jurists. The responsibility for the disputes, as was often the case, lay with the Madrid government, which had failed to provide a general rule of procedure, so that the local authorities naturally relied upon particular legislation, often inconsistent, to resolve their doubts.

The ecclesiastical judges naturally claimed universal validity for the laws that favoured their jurisdiction, the most frequently cited law being a royal *cédula* of 1698 to the Bishop of Caracas, which authorized the diocesan courts to handle probate cases that involved ecclesiastical testators and heirs or legacies made to pious works.[1] But the royal judges were able to cite another *cédula* (1662) to the *Audiencia* of Guadalajara, which confirmed royal jurisdiction over all probate cases.[2] Established practice offered no reliable guide in these disputes: in a *competencia* that arose in Durango in 1764 concerning probate of a will in which a priest bequeathed his estate to pious works,[3] both the diocesan judge and the governor were able to produce precedents from their files proving that similar cases had been handled in both courts in the past. The Durango *competencia* was settled by the *Audiencia* of Guadalajara, using the 1662 *cédula* as a basis for the decision, in favour of the royal courts,[4] but the Bishop of Durango appealed to the king to reverse this

---

[1] A.G.I., Guadalajara 332, R.C., 7 June 1698 (copy).

[2] A.H.N., Códices 687, R.C., 18 June 1662.

[3] A.G.I., Guadalajara 332, Testimonio de la testamentaría de Joseph de Arzapalo, presbítero, 1764-7.

[4] *Ibid.*, Auto de fuerza, Audiencia of Guadalajara, 17 July 1764.

decision and to issue a general law that would make the 1698 *cédula* applicable in all districts.[1]

But this and the other *competencias* that inevitably arose over testament litigation received attention from the Council of the Indies only when the petitions from prelates and royal officials for a general law became too numerous and too insistent to ignore. The first appeals, which came from the Bishop of Popoyán and the Dean of the *sede vacante* Chapter of Panama, were dismissed with a reprimand declaring that the Council had not been established to waste time with 'frivolous matters that could be easily resolved by consulting any standard work of jurisprudence'.[2] But the number and tenor of the petitions indicate that the matter was far from frivolous. The next appeal came from the Governor of Cuba, who pointed out the harmful effect of these jurisdictional disputes on all the litigants, especially the beneficiaries of wills, who often had to wait years before receiving their legacies.[3] The Bishop of Durango's petition for a general law was the next to be received, followed shortly after by similar appeals from the *Audiencia* of Mexico and the Bishop of Michoacán, based on a *competencia* almost identical to the one in Durango.[4] The *audiencia*, though favouring the 1662 *cédula*, had agreed with the bishop that impartial royal adjudication was necessary, since the established practice in the diocese of Michoacán had conformed with the other *cédula* of 1698.

Both the ecclesiastical and the royal authorities appear to have been interested primarily in ending these disputes that were so detrimental to all parties, but they understandably sought to influence the king to confirm their own jurisdictions. Royal judges pointed out that the jurisdictional sphere of the royal courts was seriously limited by ecclesiastical intervention in these cases, which enabled the diocesan courts to control the

---

[1] *Ibid.*, Bishop of Durango to the king, 12 March 1765.

[2] A.G.I., Mexico 2632, R.C. to Bishop of Popoyán, 6 Aug. 1766, in Expediente sobre testamentarías . . ., 1781. The R.C. to the Dean of Panama, 7 Nov. 1766, had similar wording.

[3] *Ibid.*, Governor of Cuba to the king, 13 April 1761.

[4] *Ibid.*, Audiencia of Mexico to the king, 2 Dec. 1768; Bishop of Michoacán to the king, 23 Dec. 1768.

inheritance of property.[1] The prelates, on the other hand, argued that the royal magistrates were so occupied with other matters that probate cases dragged on for years in their courts, a delay that would cause great harm to the soul of any testator who made legacies to pious works, since his soul would remain that much longer in purgatory if the legacies were not distributed immediately.[2]

The arguments of the ecclesiastical judges apparently held greater weight with the Council of the Indies: it ordered the Cuban and Mexican officials to follow the 1698 *cédula*, which favoured ecclesiastical jurisdiction,[3] and also recommended this procedure to the king in 1781, when the councillors were finally prodded into forming a universally applicable rule for the entire Indies.[4] This recommendation, however, was totally unacceptable to the king, who ordered the Council to deliberate the point again and gave it a clear indication of the decision he expected by sending a report from 'other ministers with whom I am well satisfied' for the Council's consideration.[5]

Written by three members of the Council of Castile, the report accused the Council of the Indies of ignorance of colonial law, as indicated by its original *cédula* of 1698, and indifference to royal prerogatives. The decision to extend this practice to all the colonies was an 'abominable negligence of its duty to protect royal jurisdiction from ecclesiastical encroachment'.[6] The *cédulas* sent to Mexico and Cuba had already encouraged ecclesiastical judges in other areas, where previous practice had favoured the secular courts, to usurp the authority of the secular judges, as demonstrated by a recent case in Puebla.[7]

A reversal of the trend towards ecclesiastical judicial dominance in the Indies required not only a change of dynasty and

---

[1] A.G.I., Mexico 2632, Governor of Cuba to the king, 13 April 1761.

[2] *Ibid.*, Bishop of Michoacán to the king, 23 Dec. 1768. See also Bishop of Durango to the king, 12 March 1765, in Guadalajara 332.

[3] *Ibid.*, R.C. to Governor and Bishop of Havana, 29 Sept. 1763; R.C. to Audiencia of Mexico and Bishop of Michoacán, 28 June 1769.

[4] *Ibid.*, Consulta Council, 6 Sept. 1781.

[5] *Ibid.*, Real resolución to Consulta of 6 Sept. 1781.

[6] A.G.I., Ind. Gen. 2994, Informe a S.M., 11 Nov. 1781, signed by Conde de Campomanes, Santiago de Espinosa and José García Rodríguez. An unsigned copy of the *Informe* sent to the Council is in Mexico 2632.

[7] A.G.I., Mexico 2632, Audiencia of Mexico to the king, 23 Nov. 1780.

the appointment of progressive and capable royal ministers, but also a vigorous effort to impose the new royal policy on the conservative Council, which insisted upon maintaining the *status quo* or even extending ecclesiastical jurisdiction. Advancing much further than the *fiscales* for the Council of the Indies, who had suggested only that secular judges be given cognizance over probate cases,[1] the three ministers proposed to eliminate ecclesiastical intervention in all suits concerning testaments, thereby restoring to laymen their right to litigate in their own *fuero*, of which they had been unjustly deprived for so long.[2] Although the result would be a corresponding loss of *fuero* on the part of ecclesiastical litigants, the ministers justified their proposal by separating the question of *fuero*, or personal immunity, from that of real immunity and producing a theory that was to affect the Church's claims and privileges for the rest of the colonial period: the concept of the temporal nature of all property, regardless of its function or owner, and the corollary right of the temporal sovereign to regulate its ownership, use and transfer, to the exclusion of all other particular jurisdictions.[3]

This concept of the intrinsically temporal nature of property was new in Spanish jurisprudence, which had always distinguished between property destined for a spiritual use and ordinary property.[4] Only several months before the ministers' report was written, the *fiscales* of the Council of the Indies, in suggesting that all probate cases be placed under royal jurisdiction, had used the empirical argument that royal judges could better ensure the conveyance of legacies to the heirs, without mentioning any juridical concept concerning the nature of property or the Crown's inherent right to control it.[5] The Council, pointing out that this new concept had not previously existed in either peninsular or colonial law, protested the

---

[1] *Ibid.*, Respuesta Fiscales, 18 May 1781.

[2] A.G.I., Ind. Gen. 2994, Informe a S.M., 11 Nov. 1781.

[3] *Ibid.* See also P. Rodríguez de Campomanes, *Tratado de la regalía de amortización*, Chapter 1, on which most of the *Informe* is based.

[4] See, e.g., A.G.I., Mexico 2661, R.C. to Archbishop of Mexico and Bishop of Puebla, 11 July 1767, concerning ecclesiastical jurisdiction over '*bienes espiritualizados*'.

[5] A.G.I., Mexico 2632, Respuesta Fiscales, 18 May 1781.

M

injustice of the accusation that it had shown ignorance of or indifference to the Crown's prerogatives,[1] but it took the very strong hint the king had given and followed the recommendations contained in the ministers' report. In 1784 a circular *cédula* was issued ordering all testament cases to be heard in royal courts and adding that wills were to be considered public instruments entirely subject to royal laws and jurisdiction.[2] The king expressed his satisfaction with the 'zeal and care the Council has shown in protecting the *regalías* of my Crown in the Indies'.[3]

In the absence of fuller documentation on civil suits in Mexico, especially from diocesan archives, it is difficult to determine to what extent the law was actually applied. There is evidence that its application depended in large part on the status and attitude of the litigants: ecclesiastical executors and heirs often ignored the law and continued to file for probate and bring suits for the conveyance of legacies in the diocesan courts,[4] while layman were more likely to take advantage of the law, which enabled them to litigate in their own *fuero*.[5]

If all the parties in a suit were clerics, or laymen who for some reason chose to litigate in the diocesan courts, the royal judge had no means of even ascertaining the suit's existence. A particularly zealous royal judge or *fiscal* might learn extra-officially of a particular case that was illegally being heard in the diocesan court and present a *recurso de fuerza* to the *audiencia* in order to have the case turned over to the royal court,[6] but the *recurso* was obviously not a general remedy, since it applied

---

[1] A.G.I., Mexico 2632, Consulta Council, 30 Jan. 1784.

[2] R.C. circular, 27 April 1784, in E. Ventura Beleña, *Recopilación sumaria de todos los autos acordados de la Real Audiencia y Sala del Crimen de esta Nueva España* (2 vols., Mexico, 1787), i, 340.

[3] A.G.I., Mexico 2632, Real resolución to Consulta Council of 30 Jan. 1784.

[4] See A.G.I., Guadalajara 358, Testimonio de la testamentaría de Felipe Narciso de Silva, 1788–96; and A.G.N., Clero regular y secular 61, Testamentaría del Br. don Juan Manuel Primo, 1793.

[5] See A.H.N., Consejos 20691, Los herederos de Ramón Mateo con Manuel Lucero, presbítero, albacea . . ., 1791–4. A.G.I., Guadalajara 315, Estado de negocios civiles . . ., 1800–5, contains a number of suits heard in the *audiencia* involving ecclesiastical testators and heirs and legacies to pious works.

[6] See A.G.I., Mexico 3068, Audiencia of Mexico to the king, 26 Nov. 1786, concerning a case in the diocese of Yucatán; and Guadalajara 358, Recurso de fuerza, presented by the Fiscal de lo Civil, 18 Oct. 1790.

only to the one case and could not ensure that other litigants would not ignore the law in the future. There was, in fact, nothing to prevent the ecclesiastical judges from successfully violating the new law indefinitely.

3. CIVIL SUITS OVER ECCLESIASTICAL INVESTMENTS

Having eliminated ecclesiastical control over probate litigation, at least in theory if not entirely in practice, the government turned to the more serious but less legally tangled problem of judicial jurisdiction over ecclesiastical property once it had been transferred to the Church by legacy (or in some cases by simple gift during the donor's lifetime). The Crown's eventual resolution of this issue in favour of royal jurisdiction was one of the most important pieces of legislation produced during the Caroline reform period, affecting not only the judicial but also the economic sphere of life in Mexico.

Perhaps the most serious limitation of the *fuero* of laymen in favour of ecclesiastics was in suits concerning chantries and pious works. As soon as gifts and legacies for pious works or chantries were turned over to the Church, the ecclesiastical authorities, rather than administer the funds themselves, loaned the capital to an individual or corporation, usually with some form of real estate as security, in return for a fixed annual income (almost invariably 5 per cent interest) to be paid to the chaplain, monastery, or other religious foundation.[1]

The importance to the Mexican economy of ecclesiastical property, estimated by some authors at over half the total wealth of the country at the end of the eighteenth century,[2] was even greater than its actual size would indicate. The Church did not own particularly large amounts of real estate, although individual members of the secular clergy and several religious orders—notably the Jesuits before their expulsion, the Dominicans and, to a lesser extent, the Augustinians—had acquired

---

[1] See A.G.N., Cofradías y archicofradías 12, Reconocimiento y obligación de 4000 pesos y sus réditos otorgados por el Lic. don Ignacio de Iglesias, sobre su hacienda Agangueo . . ., 1786, a typical contract for a *censo*, as these mortgages were called.

[2] L. Alamán, *Historia de México*, i, 99, probably the first author to publish this estimate.

considerable holdings despite royal laws prohibiting the sale of land to ecclesiastics.[1] Most of the Church's vast wealth was in liquid assets. Manuel Abad y Queipo, Judge of Testaments, Chantries, and Pious Works in the diocese of Michoacán, and thus a reliable source, gave the figure of 44.5 million *pesos* as the total value of ecclesiastical property at the beginning of the nineteenth century, of which only three million at the most were in land.[2] But if the Church did not hold immense *haciendas* by direct title, the greater part of the real estate owned by laymen was mortgaged for ecclesiastical loans. In 1793 the Intendant of Puebla wrote that the *hacendados* in his district were 'nothing more than contributors to mortmain at 5 per cent annual interest on ecclesiastical mortgages, which comprise all or almost all the total value of their estates'.[3]

The shortage of currency in Mexico, due mainly to the excess of imports over exports, made the Church indispensable as the main source of working capital for mercantile enterprises and mining operations as well as for agricultural development. The extent of the economy's dependence on ecclesiastical capital became apparent by the protests against the Crown's order in 1804 for the alienation of all real estate and capital belonging to chantries and pious works, which was to be deposited in the Royal Treasury at 3 per cent annual interest[4] in order to redeem the huge amount of *vales reales*, or promissory notes, the improvident Charles IV had issued. It was only natural that the clergy should object to a two-fifths reduction in their income, but it was the merchants, miners, and *hacendados* who made the most anguished protests, predicting that business would collapse, mines cease to operate, and economic activity in general come to a standstill if ecclesiastical capital were withdrawn from circulation.[5]

---

[1] See F. Chevalier, *La formation des grands domaines au Mexique* (Paris, 1952), pp. 309–29, on the growth of estates belonging to the religious orders.

[2] M. Abad y Queipo, *op. cit.*, pp. 95–112, 'Escrito presentado a D. Manuel Sixto Espinosa del Consejo de Estado . . .', 1805.

[3] A.G.I., Mexico 1885, Manuel de Flon to Pedro de Acuña, 1 Feb. 1793.

[4] *Mexican Political Pamphlets* (B.M.) iii, no. 38, Real Instrucción para la enagenación de bienes de obras pías en America, 26 Dec. 1804, incorporating a royal decree issued in Spain, 19 Sept. 1798.

[5] B.N., 19709, no. 34, Memorial de los hacenderos de Mexico sobre la venta de bienes y fincas de obras pías, November 1805; Manuel Abad y Queipo, *op. cit.*,

Thus, even if the Church owned no more than half of the capital in Mexico, the immense power held by ecclesiastical magistrates, who were in effect the country's only bankers and who, in addition, claimed judicial jurisdiction over these funds, is evident.

Any claim for the payment of the interest, for the redemption of the principal, or any other litigation concerning these investments was brought before the diocesan Judge of Testaments, Chantries, and Pious Works, so that, although the plaintiff might be an individual chaplain or monastery, he was often the Defender of Pious Works from the court itself, which in any case had the decided advantage of being judge and interested party in the same suit.[1]

As in probate cases, the question of this jurisdiction was confused by an apparent contradiction in royal legislation, in this instance within the *Recopilación* itself. One law prohibited secular judges from interfering with the collection of interest on chantries and pious works,[2] while another declared that ecclesiastical judges had no jurisdiction over laymen and could not attach or confiscate their property.[3] Aided by this contradiction and by the same lack of strong civil administration noted in the section on testaments, the ecclesiastical judges gradually gained exclusive control over these suits. In fact, by the middle of the eighteenth century, they had succeeded in dominating civil litigation so completely that royal officials complained that their courts might as well not exist. The Governor of Yucatán wrote in 1758: 'Since all the houses and property of this province have liens from pious foundations and most of the *vecinos* of substance are involved in these transactions, there is nothing left for the royal magistrates to do.'[4] Both he and the Governor of Cuba, who made a similar

---

[1] See A.G.N., Obras pías 2, Autos sobre réditos caídos de la obra pía de dotar huérfanas . . ., 1763-4.

[2] *Recop. Indias*, ley 15, título 10, Libro 1.

[3] *Ibid.*, ley 12, título 10, Libro 1.

[4] A.G.I., Mexico 3072, Governor of Yucatán to the king, 14 June 1758.

---

pp. 66-94, 'Representación a nombre de los labradores y comerciantes de Valladolid de Michoacán', 1805. A similar *Memorial* written on behalf of the *Cuerpo de Minería* by the *Corregidor* of Querétaro, Miguel Domínguez, is cited in F. Osores, *op. cit.*, ii, 184.

complaint in 1767,[1] suggested that the Crown prohibit this encroachment on royal jurisdiction.

Yet the Crown appears to have been unaware of the extent of the Church's judicial control until a dispute in Yucatán in the 1750's and the Council's resolution of it led to a series of petitions and complaints from many other districts. The royal judge had attempted to prevent the diocesan court from confiscating a layman's property for default in payment of the interest due on a chantry investment, claiming secular *fuero* for the defendant, and had been excommunicated for interfering in what the Bishop of Yucatán regarded as the Church's exclusive jurisdiction. The result of the *competencia* was a royal *cédula* issued in 1757, declaring the censure illegal and forbidding ecclesiastical judges to proceed against laymen for the collection of these annuities,[2] and another even more explicit *cédula* in 1760, ordering the execution of the first, which the governor had suspended because of the bishop's determined opposition.[3]

It became apparent that this almost exclusive jurisdiction over property suits was not limited to Yucatán. Similar disputes arose shortly afterwards in other areas when royal officials seized the opportunity that these *cédulas* ostensibly provided to force the issue with the ecclesiastical judges in their districts and regain what they considered their legitimate authority. In Puebla, the *alcalde mayor* refused a request from the ecclesiastical judge for *auxilio real* to attach the property of a layman for arrears in the interest due on a chantry. He informed the judge that the two *cédulas* sent to Yucatán had deprived the ecclesiastical courts of cognizance in these cases, and he ordered the plaintiff to file the claim in the royal court. But the *Audiencia* of Mexico cautiously upheld the jurisdiction of the ecclesiastical judge and consulted the Crown concerning a rule for future cases.[4]

Attempts to apply these two *cédulas* in Mexico and Cuba were equally unsuccessful. As in Puebla, the ecclesiastical

---

[1] A.H.N., Códices 698, Governor of Cuba to the king, 22 Jan. 1767, quoted in R.C., 1 March 1768.

[2] A.G.I., Mexico 3072, R.C. to Governor of Yucatán, 9 Aug. 1757.

[3] *Ibid.*, R.C. to Governor of Yucatán, 2 April 1760.

[4] A.H.N., Códices 756, Consulta Council of the Indies, 18 May 1767.

judges naturally refused to accept the validity of a law, promulgated in another area, which would deprive them of
judicial control over the Church's main source of income.
They appealed to the king to revoke the two *cédulas*, or at least
to declare that they applied only to Yucatán.[1]

The Council *fiscales* were shocked to learn that this 'gross
abuse and corruption of the law, which the prelates call
hallowed practice and immemorial custom' was so widespread.[2]
They had thought that Yucatán was a scandalous exception,
but found instead that its governor and magistrates were not
the only ones guilty of abandoning their authority to the
Church. Yet, despite these violations of the legal formula that
the plaintiff should follow the defendant's *fuero*, the term 'gross
abuse' applied to the practice in New Spain was an exaggeration. By recommending that the pertinent law of the *Recopilación* be revoked throughout the Indies, the *fiscales* tacitly
admitted that the ecclesiastical judges had, at the most, taken
advantage of a legislative contradiction rather than usurped
royal jurisdiction.

But the conservative Council had no intention of revoking
the old law. It confirmed ecclesiastical jurisdiction over these
cases in *cédulas* to Cuba, Mexico and Puebla,[3] and rejected
later requests for a change in the old law from royal judges
in Oaxaca, Santa Domingo, Bogotá, Guatemala, and Cumaná.[4]
As in testament cases, the intervention of ministers more regalist
and reform-minded than the councillors was necessary to bring
about a general curtailment of the Church's judicial dominance
in this area of litigation. This time it was the members of the
Junta del Nuevo Código: after studying the numerous petitions
in the Council's files, the *junta* formed a new law placing all

---

[1] A.H.N., Códices 756, Consulta Council of the Indies, 18 May 1767, summarizing a protest from the Archbishop of Mexico; Códices 698, R.C. to the Bishop of
Havana, 1 March 1768.

[2] A.H.N., Códices 756, Respuesta Fiscales, inserted in Consulta Council, 18
May 1767.

[3] A.G.I., Mexico, 2661, R.C. to Bishop of Puebla, Archbishop and Audiencia
of Mexico, 11 July 1767; A.H.N., Códices 698, R.C. to Bishop of Havana and
Governor of Cuba, 1 March 1768.

[4] A.G.I., Mexico 2661, Consulta Council, 26 Aug. 1776, concerning Oaxaca;
Ind. Gen. 2995, Consulta Council, 18 April 1788, summarizing the other *expedientes*, all from the 1770's.

suits concerning payment of the capital and income belonging to chantries and pious works under the jurisdiction of the royal judges,[1] which was promulgated throughout the Indies in 1789.[2]

The similarity between this law and the 1784 *cédula* concerning testament cases extended to their application. Here too, the diocesan courts appear to have continued to hear suits involving only ecclesiastical parties (e.g., a cleric who held a loan from a pious foundation),[3] but more often defaulters were sued in the royal courts in accordance with the new law,[4] since the majority of debtors were laymen and could now legally ignore a citation from the ecclesiastical judge in any case.

In 1801 the Crown added still another law to fill the remaining loop-hole by which the ecclesiastical courts had still retained a certain amount of judicial authority over property suits—the administration of the capital belonging to chantries and pious works after it had been donated or conveyed to the Church by the executors. Several *audiencias* had sought to extend the 1784 and 1789 laws to cover suits concerning the distribution of this capital and had even taken upon themselves the actual investment of pious legacies. When the ecclesiastical judges protested that their functions were being usurped,[5] the Crown not only commended the *audiencias* for their initiative, but also ordered all royal courts in the Indies to follow suit, to the 'positive and total exclusion of the ecclesiastical courts'.[6]

The Crown's choice of this time to correct 'abuses' which, by the admission of the secular authorities, had been in existence for at least a century and a half, was due to several

---

[1] A.G.I., Ind. Gen. 1653, Juntas del Nuevo Código, 19 June 1782, 28 May and 2 June 1783.

[2] A.G.I., Ind. Gen. 2995, R.C. circular, 22 March 1789.

[3] A.G.N. Capellanías 1, Autos sobre réditos caídos de la capellanía de D. Francisco Mondragón, 1799.

[4] A.G.N., Cofradías y archicofradías 16, Autos sobre que D. José Adalid exhiba 4,000 pesos de la capellanía . . ., 1808; A.G.I., Mexico 2672, Petición de D. Juan Francisco Avellafuerte sobre 2,500 pesos de censos y réditos, 29 Nov. 1794.

[5] A.G.I., Mexico 2647, Archbishop of Mexico to the king, 26 Sept. 1798. Mexico 1140, R.C. circular, 20 Nov. 1801, mentions similar complaints from the Archbishop of Lima.

[6] A.G.I., Mexico 1140, R.C. circular, 20 Nov. 1801.

reasons. In the first place, ecclesiastical judges, by a number of arbitrary and harsh acts against lay debtors, had drawn the government's attention to their judicial control and convinced many royal officials that this control was extremely harmful to the colonies' economy.[1] In Yucatán the bishop had imprisoned laymen, confiscated their property and excommunicated several people, including royal officials.[2] From Cumaná the king received complaints that the diocesan judge had foreclosed a mortgage on a layman's *hacienda* for the sum of twenty *pesos* that he owed in back interest, and the *Audiencia* of Santo Domingo furnished other examples of ecclesiastical tyranny over the liberty and property of the Crown's lay subjects.[3]

It is likely, however, that the economic ills were due to more fundamental causes than the loss of *fuero* on the part of lay defendants. In 1793, several years after the new law had been promulgated, the Intendant of Puebla wrote that ecclesiastical mortgages in his region were still being foreclosed and estates frequently auctioned off, presumably, by this time, under the orders of the secular judges. The reason was that the *haciendas* were overburdened and could not produce sufficient income to meet interest payments.[4] Thus if the ecclesiastical authorities were at fault it was for making unsound investments.

The main reason for the new law was that at this time the king and his most influential ministers looked upon the Church's extensive jurisdiction as a challenge to royal absolutism and its vast wealth as a barrier to the economic development of both Spain and the colonies. The same abuses had undoubtedly existed for years and, as the Council had pointed out in its first *consulta*, these could be corrected without revoking the law of the *Recopilación*.[5] But, influenced by utilitarian theories on economic progress and the role of the Church in society,[6] the Crown foresaw beneficial results from abolishing the traditional system entirely.

These laws eliminating ecclesiastical judicial intervention

[1] A.G.I., Ind. Gen. 2995, Consulta Council, 18 April 1788.
[2] A.G.I., Mexico 3072, R.C., 2 April 1760.
[3] A.G.I., Ind. Gen. 2995, Consulta, 18 April 1788.
[4] A.G.I., Mexico 1885, Manuel de Flon to Pedro de Acuña, 1 Feb. 1793.
[5] A.H.N., Códices 756, Consulta Council, 18 May 1767.
[6] See above, pp. 91–2 and 99.

were only part of a larger programme to curtail the Church's economic exemptions and control of property. The king's concern for his subjects' *fuero* was secondary to his concern for the health of the Royal Exchequer, and a case in the late 1790's illustrates this predominance of economic over judicial considerations. When a *competencia* arose over the probate of the estate of a prominent Mexican merchant, who had left all his considerable fortune to a religious order, and was referred to the Council of the Indies,[1] the *fiscal* passed quickly over the question of jurisdiction to concentrate on the testament itself. The testator had left his entire estate to his confessor's order, which was illegal, and disinherited his rightful heirs; but a more important point, the *fiscal* declared, was that this type of legacy disrupted the economy by transferring so much property into mortmain and defrauded the Royal Exchequer through the loss of death duties.[2]

The Crown had long attempted to discourage the passage of property into mortmain, but without much success. Ecclesiastical ingenuity together with the great piety of the Mexican faithful had made a mockery of the sixteenth-century law which declared that original land grants were to be made under the condition that the property should not be sold or otherwise transferred to the Church.[3] The periodic prohibitions against bequeathing property to one's confessor or disinheriting lay heirs in favour of the Church were equally fruitless.[4] But if the Crown was not able to prevent the Church's accumulation of land and capital, it could regain control over the use of these assets by reasserting royal jurisdiction over all property, regardless of the owner. In addition, both Charles III and Charles IV sought to discourage this accumulation indirectly, first by eliminating the Church's tax exemptions,[5] and then by adding

---

[1] A.G.I., Mexico 2648, Expediente sobre la testamentaría de D. Joseph de Lanzagorta, 1785–1800.

[2] *Ibid.*, Respuesta Fiscal, 26 May 1786.

[3] *Recop. Indias*, ley 10, título 12, Libro 4. F. Chevalier, *op. cit.*, pp. 303–9, gives evidence that the law was ignored from the time of its promulgation.

[4] A.G.I., Mexico 2648, R.C.'s, 20 June 1766, 18 Aug. 1775 and 13 Feb. 1783, which, according to the Council Fiscal, Respuesta, 20 May 1786, had been consistently violated.

[5] A.G.N., Bandos y ordenanzas 7, R.C., 17 Dec. 1770, from R.C. for Spain, 29 June 1760.

an extraordinary 'amortization' tax of 15 per cent to be levied upon all property that passed into mortmain.[1] The final step in the colonial period was the direct attack on mortmain itself in the 1804 order to alienate all property belonging to chantries and pious works.[2]

To the ecclesiastics themselves, the loss of their personal *fuero* in these cases was infinitely more painful than a curtailment of their economic influence or even a heavy burden of taxes. Although the king had confirmed their immunity in civil cases in general, this concession was meaningless if the most important and common suits were excepted, and ecclesiastical immunity reduced in reality to nothing more than the realm of purely spiritual questions. When the Archbishop of Mexico protested to the king in 1766 that royal magistrates sought to impose the new practice in his diocese, he did not mention the immunity of ecclesiastical property but complained instead that the law was a serious violation of the clergy's personal immunity. Since most clerics were supported from chantries and the religious orders derived much of their income from pious works, the vast majority of the clergy, he declared, would be forced to relinquish their own *fuero* and sue for payment in secular courts.[3]

At the end of the century, as if anticipating the Crown's plan to alienate property in mortmain, the Bishop and Chapter of Michoacán claimed that they had submitted without question to the curtailment of their real immunity and would even willingly sacrifice all the Church's property if the Crown needed it, but they objected vigorously to the loss of their *fuero* and pleaded with the king to restore their former privileged status.[4] For, in their view, the privilege of personal immunity was what set the clergy apart from laymen: it was the '*Magna Carta* of the liberties and venerated status of each individual ecclesiastic'. The right to be judged by magistrates of their own

[1] A.G.I., Mexico 1143, R.C., 2 Nov. 1796, from R.C. for Spain, 24 Aug. 1795.
[2] *Mexican Political Pamphlets* (B.M.), iii, no. 38, 'Real Instrucción para la enagenación de bienes de obras pías en América', 26 Dec. 1804.
[3] A.H.N., Códices 756, Archbishop of Mexico to the king, 29 May 1766, quoted in Consulta Council, 18 May 1767.
[4] B.N., 12009, Representación del Obispo y Cabildo de Michoacán, 11 Dec. 1799.

state and class was, in fact, one of the concessions most coveted by the king's subjects. Nobles, academics, merchants, miners, and the military all enjoyed this vestige of medieval jurisprudence, the right of *fuero*, and the fact that the Crown was actually increasing the privileges of some groups at this time[1] undoubtedly added to the clergy's resentment.

But the clergy's protests were not directed only, or even mainly, against their loss of *fuero* in civil suits. This innovation had been accepted with surprising meekness (perhaps because it was difficult to enforce strictly), but it was only the beginning. As late as 1794 Viceroy Revillagigedo could write:

Despite the gradual reduction in ecclesiastical jurisdiction, most seriously limited by the recent declaration that secular courts hear cases concerning chantries and pious works, it still remains the most important of the privileged *fueros* in the kingdom.[2]

By the end of the century, however, the Crown's ecclesiastical reform programme had culminated in a vigorous attack on the 'most precious of our immunities'[3]—the exemption from prosecution by the State in criminal cases—and the clergy was not prepared to surrender this last bastion of privilege without a struggle.

---

[1] See L. McAlister, *The 'Fuero Militar' in New Spain 1764-1800*; and W. Howe, *The Mining Guild of New Spain*, Chapter 4, on *fuero* in mining disputes.

[2] Revillagigedo, *Instrucción reservada* (30 June 1794), p. 21.

[3] B.N., 12009, Representación del Obispo y Cabildo de Michoacán, 11 Dec. 1799.

CHAPTER VIII

Ecclesiastical Immunity
in Criminal Cases

I. JOINT PROSECUTION OF ECCLESIASTICAL CRIMINALS

THE colonial clergy's exemption from criminal prosecution by the State survived intact until the last decade of the eighteenth century. The curtailment of ecclesiastical *fuero* had been one of the major points in the Caroline programme of reform outlined in the early years of Charles III's reign, but not until 1795 did the Crown promulgate a general law, already prepared by the *Junta del Nuevo Código* in 1783, authorizing royal judges in the Indies to intervene directly in the prosecution of serious crimes committed by ecclesiastics.[1]

Royal ministers and colonial officials sought to justify this attack on the clergy's most cherished privilege with the same arguments that had been used to persuade Charles III to review the Crown's traditional policy of relying solely on indirect methods to control the clergy: the deficiencies in the Church's administration of justice and the consequent inadequacy of these indirect methods, which depended ultimately on the ecclesiastical judiciary.[2] Since the Church was unable to impose penalties sufficiently severe to 'satisfy public vengeance and curb the perverse inclinations' of ecclesiastical malefactors, it was argued once again, the Crown could ensure the proper administration of justice only by subjecting the clergy to direct royal prosecution in criminal cases.[3] The new law was also to serve as a deterrent to crime. The ecclesiastical

---

[1] A.G.I., Ind. Gen. 3027, R.C. circular, 25 Oct. 1795, promulgating ley 71, título 15, Libro 1, of the Nuevo Código.

[2] See above, Ch. V, for a discussion of these arguments.

[3] A.G.I., Mexico 1159, Nuevo Código, ley 12, título 9, Libro 1. See also Ind. Gen. 3027, Respuestas fiscales, Council of the Indies, 9 Dec. 1788 and 2 March 1789.

judges not only were unable to impose effective penalties but also seemed unwilling even to bring their delinquent subordinates to trial, 'leaving the public', according to the Crown, 'with the justified fear that the deed will be repeated'.[1]

Yet these objections to ecclesiastical immunity were equally valid throughout the colonial period, and it is surprising that the Crown waited so long to provide a remedy, especially in view of the fact that the inevitable result (if we are to believe the royal jurists) of the Church's inadequate administration of justice—a degeneration of ecclesiastical discipline endangering the morals, property, and even the lives of His Majesty's lay subjects—had already been noted decades before the law's appearance. It is not suggested that these arguments were fictions invented by royal ministers and officials, only that they cannot be considered an explanation for the Crown's choice of this particular time (the 1790's) to curtail the colonial clergy's criminal *fuero*. They served as a justification for the creation and the application of the new law, but the introduction of this direct method of control into the colonies hinged on the outcome of a struggle within the Madrid government between those who advocated and those who opposed drastic changes in the old order—a struggle that affected almost every aspect of the Caroline reform programme.[2] Like the reform programme in general, the shift in royal policy towards ecclesiastical immunity was not a product of unanimous thought among the Crown's advisers but the creation of a small group of energetic ministers, and it is likely that, despite the myriad arguments offered by these reformers, both the new policy and the legislation it produced would have been relegated to oblivion if the colonial authorities themselves had not forced the Crown's hand by applying the new method on their own authority when a suitable opportunity presented itself.

The alignment of factions over this particular issue began in 1774 in connection with a murder case that was to create a precedent for secular intervention in all subsequent cases of serious crimes in both Spain and the Indies. In March of that year, the Council of Castile received a letter from the *Alcalde*

---

[1] A.G.I., Ind. Gen. 3027, R.C., 25 Oct. 1795.
[2] See Ch. IV on the genesis and vicissitudes of the reform programme.

Mayor of Sanlúcar de Barrameda reporting that he was holding in custody for the ecclesiastical court a Carmelite friar who had murdered a young girl and requesting instructions on what further action, if any, he should take to ensure that this unprovoked attack should receive its just punishment.[1] The *fiscal* and some of the Council members felt that the case provided a suitable opportunity for decreeing the total abolition of immunity in criminal cases,[2] while another group supported the Church's position (voiced by the Carmelite provincial and the Archbishop of Seville) that long tradition and existing legislation, which gave the ecclesiastical court sole jurisdiction over the case, must be honoured.[3] The result of this conflict was the formation of a compromise system called 'association of judges' that formed the basis for future colonial as well as peninsular legislation. The trial was divided into three main sections: the preliminary investigation and substantiation of the case were to be carried out jointly by the ecclesiastical and royal magistrates; the diocesan court was then to proceed independently to pronounce the canonical sentence of degradation, defrock the defendant, and deliver him to the secular court; the secular authorities would then be free to impose and execute the appropriate sentence.[4]

Although clearly a definite limitation of immunity, this procedure was far from the total offensive on the privilege that the more radical ministers had proposed. Joint prosecution was the only innovation, for the secular court was to sentence the defendant only after he had been defrocked, a procedure long established in canon law by which an ecclesiastic was formally deprived of his status and privileges.[5] This compromise method was considered more suitable to 'pious Spain' than the complete elimination of immunity (as practised in France, for example) and praised as a 'most prudent' means of reconciling the need

[1] A.G.I., Ind. Gen. 1654, Council of Castile to Alcalde Mayor, 15 March 1774, in reply to his report of 7 March.

[2] *Ibid.*, Respuesta Fiscal Campomanes, 12 March 1774.

[3] R.A.H., Col. Mata Linares 76, Carmelite provincial to Council, 8 March 1774; and Carta acordada to Archbishop of Seville, 14 April 1774.

[4] B.N., 3534, Instrucción para el seguimiento de la causa . . ., 14 April 1774, written by Fiscales Pedro Rodríguez de Campomanes and Juan de Alvinar.

[5] See *Decretales* (Pope Gregory IX), Book II, part 1, canon 10.

for deterring ecclesiastical criminals with the traditional Spanish respect for the canons of the Church.[1]

There is further evidence that the Crown's conservative advisers had a powerful voice in royal decisions, aided by the king's consideration for public opinion and deeply rooted traditions. Rather than confirm the death penalty recommended by the Council in the case of the Carmelite friar, Charles III ordered that the defendant be imprisoned for life in an overseas *presidio*,[2] and in two subsequent murder cases he intervened before the conclusion of the trial and either prescribed a term of imprisonment or decided to turn the case over to the ecclesiastical authorities for sentencing.[3]

In 1783 the *Junta del Nuevo Código* created a new law for the Indies incorporating the procedure of joint prosecution created by the Council of Castile,[4] but the Madrid government made no attempt to transfer this innovation to the colonies until more than a decade later, after local magistrates had already applied the new system on their own initiative and demonstrated its relevance to conditions in the Indies. In two unconnected but almost identical cases involving the apparently premeditated murder of a friar by another member of his religious order— one in Guatemala in 1788 and the other in Mexico in 1790— the colonial courts decided that the 1774 Sanlúcar case, of which they had obtained extra-official information, was a valid precedent and ordered the ecclesiastical and royal judges to follow the procedure outlined in the Council of Castile's *Instrucción*.[5]

In neither case did the colonial courts question the legal basis for their actions. The Mexican *sala del crimen* merely consulted the Crown on the subsidiary point of whether, in view of the distance from Madrid, the final sentence it imposed could be submitted to the viceroy for confirmation rather than to the king.[6] The *Audiencia* of Guatemala (which had no separate

---

[1] A.G.I., Ind. Gen. 3027, Voto particular, Council of the Indies, 5 Jan. 1796.

[2] R.A.H., Col. Mata Linares 76, R.O. to Council of Castile, 6 Nov. 1784.

[3] See summaries of the trials of Gómez Mesía de León, 1776–9, and Fr Francisco Ramírez, 1784–7, in A.G.I., Ind. Gen. 3027.

[4] A.G.I., Ind. Gen. 1653, Junta del Nuevo Código, 12 Nov. 1783.

[5] A.G.I., Ind. Gen. 3027, Auto Audiencia de Guatemala, 9 May 1788; and Auto Sala del Crimen (Mexico), 27 Sept. 1790.

[6] *Ibid.*, Sala del Crimen to the king, 30 Sept. 1790.

sala del crimen) did not even notify the king, who learned of the case only through the archbishop's letter protesting about these 'innovations'.[1]

The Council of the Indies was prepared to accept the *fait accompli* in these two cases and approved the actions taken in Guatemala and Mexico, but the promulgation of a universal law for direct secular intervention in criminal cases was delayed by the same conflict that had characterized the debate over ecclesiastical *fuero* in civil suits. The Council rejected the *fiscales*' recommendation to provide for a similar procedure in all future cases, declaring that 'for the moment' there was no need for a general law.[2]

However, a case arising in Guadalajara in 1794 provided the reformers with further ammunition for their arguments, which this time convinced the Council. The case involved an offence much less serious than murder (though with apparently equal scandal to the community)—the seduction of a young girl from a prominent Creole family—but it contained several aggravating circumstances that indicated the need for a universal rule. First, the initial failure of the ecclesiastical superiors to punish the offender (a Franciscan friar) until after repeated orders from the viceroy, and their mild sentence of reclusion, from which the friar had escaped to continue 'illicit communication with his accomplice', seemed to demonstrate beyond doubt that the ecclesiastical superiors were unable to control their subordinates.[3] And second, the viceroy's decision to take only the administrative measures of a *proceso informativo* and deportation supported the earlier contention of the Council *fiscales* that colonial officials would not ordinarily exercise direct judicial intervention without a general authorization in advance.[4]

On the Council's recommendation, the king approved the viceroy's extra-judicial measures in this case but ordered him and all other royal officials in the Indies, along with all ecclesiastical judges, to proceed in accordance with the new

---

[1] *Ibid.*, Archbishop of Guatemala to the king, 2 June 1788.
[2] *Ibid.*, Consulta Council, 17 March 1792.
[3] *Ibid.*, Viceroy Branciforte to the king, 30 April 1795.
[4] *Ibid.*, Consulta Council, 19 Sept. 1795.

N

method of association of judges in all similar cases in the future.[1]

This general *cédula*, rather than the 1790 murder case, was the decisive factor in a general offensive against ecclesiastical immunity in Mexico. In 1791 the *sala del crimen* had expressed satisfaction that its actions in this 'rare, extraordinary and unprecedented case' had met with royal approval[2] but had made no attempt to use this approval as a basis for transforming the traditional practice of ecclesiastical immunity. Even the *Nuevo Código*, unofficial copies of which were available in Mexico, had no practical effect: the *fiscal del crimen* cited several of its laws to support his point in a dispute with the Archbishop of Mexico over the 1790 case,[3] but he was aware that without official promulgation the *Código* had no legal force. The 1795 *cédula*, however, was interpreted as a mandate for direct secular intervention in a wide variety of cases and was the signal for a vigorous attack on the last and most important stronghold of ecclesiastical immunity in Mexico.

The *sala del crimen* lost little time in launching this attack. The *cédula* reached Mexico in May 1796,[4] and in October of the same year the *fiscal* was recommending the joint prosecution of a priest from the diocese of Puebla for the 'atrocious' crime of defying royal jurisdiction.[5] By the end of the century, the royal courts had initiated proceedings against at least fifteen ecclesiastical defendants in the majority of the viceroyalty's dioceses: Mexico, six persons, accused of murder, conspiracy, theft, 'incorrigibility', and defiance of royal jurisdiction; Puebla, four, all accused of defying royal jurisdiction; Michoacán, two, accused of theft and defying royal jurisdiction; Oaxaca, two, accused of adultery and rape; Yucatán, one, charged with being an accessory to murder.[6]

---

[1] A.G.I., Ind. Gen. 3027, R.C. circular, 25 Oct. 1795, promulgating ley 71, título 15, Libro 1, of the Nuevo Código.

[2] *Ibid.*, Sala del Crimen to the king, 26 Nov. 1791.

[3] B.N., 20265, Recurso de fuerza, Fiscal del Crimen, 11 June 1793.

[4] A.G.I., Ind. Gen. 3027, Audiencia of Mexico to Council, 3 May 1796.

[5] B.N., 12009, Dictamen Fiscal del Crimen, 23 Oct. 1796.

[6] *Ibid.*, Causas y alegatos de inmunidad, 1800; A.G.I., Ind. Gen. 3027, Expedientes reunídos sobre delitos escandalosos y homicidios perpetrados por eclesiásticos, 1788–1800.

As might be expected, this widespread attack on ecclesiastical immunity met with strong opposition from the Mexican hierarchy. After recovering from a brief period of shock at the 'horrifying spectacle' of the first murder case in 1790[1] and realizing that this case was not to be an exception but a precedent for further encroachments on their jurisdiction, the ecclesiastical judges began to resist the application of the new law and to defend the clergy's immunity with increasing determinaton. According to the Mexican prelates, this resistance was not based on dogmatic opposition to the law itself, though a few highly conservative canonists challenged its basic legality, but on the way in which the *fiscal* and the *sala del crimen* sought to apply it. They accepted, at least in theory, the king's right to curtail immunity in exceptional or 'atrocious' crimes, but they alleged that, 'contrary to Your Majesty's intentions', the law was being used by 'impious enemies of the Church as a means of persecuting the clergy'.[2]

Their main dispute with the royal courts concerned the type of case in which the new procedure was applicable. Since the law stated that a joint trial was to be held only for 'atrocious' crimes,[3] but without specifying which crimes belonged in that category, both sides felt free to interpret the term according to their divergent interests, aided by two apparently contradictory royal decrees. The ecclesiastical judges asserted that only crimes incurring the death penalty (e.g., murder) could be considered atrocious, and they were able to cite in their favour a recent royal *cédula* of the Council of Castile which had declared that manslaughter was not sufficiently serious to deprive an ecclesiastic of his *fuero*.[4] But the *fiscal*'s broader definition, which also included crimes that carried the less severe penalty of imprisonment, was supported by another royal *cédula* in which the Crown applied the term atrocious to the relatively minor offence of seduction 'without violence or deceit'.[5]

---

[1] A.G.I., Ind. Gen. 3027, Archbishop of Mexico to the king, 30 Sept. 1790.

[2] See, e.g., *ibid.*, Bishop of Puebla to the king, 30 Oct. 1799.

[3] Nuevo Código, ley 71, título 15, Libro 1.

[4] A.G.I., Ind. Gen. 3027, R.C. Council of Castile to Real Chancillería de Granada, 27 Feb. 1787 (copy).

[5] *Ibid.*, R.C. circular, 25 Oct. 1795.

The degree of resistance from the prelates in each case was usually in inverse proportion to the gravity of the crime. Thus in the first murder case the ecclesiastical court readily consented to a joint trial and agreed with the *fiscal*'s declaration that the accused 'obviously deserves the death sentence',[1] because even preliminary inquiries had revealed that the murderer's attack was totally unprovoked, the knife wound he inflicted of necessity fatal, and his guilt established both by his own confession and by the testimony of several eye-witnesses.[2] The one case of conspiracy in this period, which arose in 1794, was also characterized by harmonious relations throughout the joint trial,[3] for the ecclesiastical hierarchy considered *lèse-majesté* 'even more execrable and villainous than murder'.[4]

The conflicts arose when the *fiscal* applied the term 'atrocious' to such offences as petty theft (30 *pesos* and two watches) and adultery,[5] neither of which posed any considerable threat to society or the State, and asserted that these offences justified joint prosecution. A cleric's resistance to arrest by a royal justice was also an atrocious crime in the *fiscal*'s opinion, but the ecclesiastical judge rejected the demand for a joint trial, explaining that, since the offence was little more than a youthful misadventure for which 'not even the *Fiscal* could remotely consider recommending the death penalty', the ecclesiastical court was perfectly capable of dealing with the accused without the aid of the secular authorities.[6]

The crime described as 'defiance of royal jurisdiction' by the *fiscal* produced the sharpest divergence of opinion, especially in view of the fact that the ecclesiastical authorities denied the

[1] A.G.I., Ind. Gen. 3027, Pedimento Fiscal del Crimen, 26 Sept. 1790.
[2] *Ibid.*, Proceso informativo, conducted by an Alcalde del Crimen, 23 Sept. 1790; and Testimonio de autos seguidos . . ., by the archdiocesan Provisor, 24 Sept. 1790.
[3] For details on this case, which involved several lay defendants and one priest, see below, pp. 204–5.
[4] R.A.H., Col. Mata Linares 76, Cathedral Chapter of Puebla to the king, 18 Nov. 1800.
[5] See A.G.I., Ind. Gen. 3027, Causa seguida por robos a los reos Agustín Frajeiro y Luis Marulanda, 1797–9; and Causa formada a instancia de D. Pedro de la Vega, ultrajado en su honor . . ., 1797–1800.
[6] *Ibid.*, Bishop of Puebla to Intendant, 4 Sept. 1799.

existence of any crime at all in the three cases that arose in this period. The circumstances of all three were almost identical: a dispute over the punishment of a lay delinquent between the local royal justice and the curate of an Indian village in each instance degenerated from verbal insults into an undignified physical scuffle witnessed by the villagers.[1] These personal squabbles, in which each party used his judicial authority to gain advantage over his rival for power and influence within the particular *pueblo*, were a common feature of local administration in Mexico and often led to the intervention of the higher courts of Church and State, both equally determined to protect their respective jurisdictions from encroachment. But, whereas previously the royal officials had been forced to rely on indirect methods of counteracting clerical power (power often wielded in the form of canonical censures),[2] the new law provided them with a much more effective means of retaliation.

Whether justified or not, the *fiscal* was convinced that the local curates, encouraged by their bishops, were intentionally intimidating the justices in order to gain complete control of their areas. Their insults to the justices were so frequent, he alleged, that he feared 'no one will be found to take the office of royal justice', and he was determined to make an example of these cases in order to teach the other curates that they could no longer 'reign over their petty domains like independent lords'.[3] But the Bishop of Puebla, in whose diocese two of the incidents occurred, had conducted his own investigations and was equally convinced that the fault lay with the 'arrogant and tyrannical justices, who interfered with the clergy's attempts to defend public morality'.[4] He admitted that the accused in one case had exceeded the limits of 'priestly mildness' by thrashing the *teniente de justicia* with a whip and locking him in

[1] *Ibid.*, Testimonio de Rafael Ramos, teniente de justicia de Quimixtlán, 1799; Sumaria hecha por el Subdelegado de San Juan de los Llanos, 1799; and Queja contra el cura interino de Petatlán, 1797.

[2] For material on these local rivalries, see A.G.I., Guadalajara 242, Audiencia to the king, 11 Dec. 1778; Mexico 2538, Consulta Council, 30 March 1786; and Mexico 3072, Governor Lucas de Gálvez of Yucatán to the king, 27 April 1792.

[3] B.N., 12009, Recurso de fuerza, Fiscal del Crimen, 11 July 1799; A.G.I., Ind. Gen. 3027, Pedimentos Fiscales, 26 April 1797 and 9 May 1799.

[4] A.G.I., Ind. Gen. 3027, Bishop of Puebla to the king, 30 Oct. 1799.

his own jail, but this had been done in self defence and with 'due provocation'.[1]

The ecclesiastical authorities disagreed not only with the *sala*'s interpretation of what circumstances justified the new law but also with the *sala*'s manner of applying it. Just as the term 'atrocious' was open to conflicting interpretations, the phrase 'association of judges' was the source of dispute over the operation of the new procedure. Ideally both judges were to share authority equally, but in practice each claimed that his jurisdiction was exclusive and that the 'associate' was no more than an assistant whose function was merely to ensure that the trial was conducted fairly. The disputes were usually expressed in terms of priorities and precedence—that is, whether an ecclesiastical offender automatically lost his immunity when he committed a serious crime (the intervention of the ecclesiastical judge being a generous concession from the king)[2], or whether he retained it until the diocesan court reduced him to lay status by the ceremony of degradation.[3] But the fundamental cause of the conflict was that each side suspected the other of bad faith: the *fiscal* believed that the diocesan judges sought to protect their fellow ecclesiastics from punishment regardless of the circumstances, while the latter believed that the *fiscal* was determined to obtain a conviction whether the defendant was actually guilty or not.

The first two cases tried after the promulgation of the new law convinced both parties that their suspicions were well founded. In one case, involving a local jurisdictional dispute in Michoacán, the evidence gathered by the associate judges exonerated the defendant completely;[4] in the other, involving a murder committed in Mexico, the judges admitted a plea of insanity which, if proven, would exempt the accused from criminal liability and thus almost certainly result in acquittal.[5] (Spanish criminal law, alongside a number of barbarous practices, followed the principle of diminished responsibility,

---

[1] B.N., 12009, Defensa Bishop of Puebla to the Audiencia, Aug. 1799.

[2] See B.N., 20265, Recurso de fuerza, 11 June 1793.

[3] See A.G.I., Ind. Gen. 3027, Archbishop of Mexico to the king, 30 May 1794.

[4] *Ibid.*, Testimonio de autos seguidos por el Intendente y discreto Provisor de Valladolid, 1798.

[5] *Ibid.*, Autos de los jueces asociados en el proceso por asesinato . . ., 1795.

which could result from insanity, temporary loss of reason and even the influence of alcohol.) After studying the records of both joint trials, the *fiscal* concluded that the equal intervention of the ecclesiastical judges, naturally disposed to favour the defendants and able to influence the inquiries accordingly, was a serious obstacle to the proper administration of justice. The defendants' custody in the diocesan prisons, to which the royal judges had no access without the consent and presence of their ecclesiastical associates, was considered another obstacle, a particularly frustrating one in the Mexican murder case, since the *fiscal* felt certain that a re-examination of the defendant in the royal prisons would reveal that his plea of insanity was nothing but a hoax. The *fiscal* therefore recommended the transfer of the defendants to the royal prisons and a retrial in both cases in which the royal judge would conduct all proceedings independently, except for the examination of the defendant and any ecclesiastical witnesses.[1]

It is impossible to determine how large a part sincere belief in the defendant's guilt—as opposed to interest in curtailing ecclesiastical immunity—played in the *fiscal*'s anxiety to obtain a conviction in these and other similar cases. Nor are the motives of the ecclesiastical judges completely clear. They believed (or professed to believe) that the accused were either innocent or not criminally liable and on that basis refused to comply with the *fiscal*'s recommendations, condemning them as proof that he and the *sala* persecuted the person, not the crime, for the sake of aggrandizing secular jurisdiction,[2] but in defending the rights of the accused they were also defending their own jurisdiction. Whatever its underlying causes, this pattern of conflict established in the first trials was repeated in all subsequent cases, with the *fiscal* and the *sala del crimen* pressing for convictions, and the diocesan judges resisting this pressure, sometimes refusing even to agree to a joint indictment.

2. THE FAILURE OF REFORM

If the purpose of the new system was to ensure the efficient administration of justice, then it must be judged a total failure:

[1] A.G.I., Ind. Gen. 3027, Respuesta Fiscal, 5 Oct. 1798; R.A.H., Col. Mata Linares 76, Respuesta Fiscal, 27 Sept. 1799.

not one of the fifteen ecclesiastics indicted in this period was ever sentenced and, with one exception, no case even reached the stage of degradation proceedings. The energy and initiative of the *fiscal del crimen* in finding suitable (and sometimes not so suitable) opportunities to apply the new law were not in themselves enough, for the clergy had not been deprived of their *fuero* completely. The procedure of joint prosecution had been designed specifically as a compromise method, in which the Crown had retained elements of the traditional practice so that the ecclesiastical judge would have no excuse to delay the trial with jurisdictional disputes and thus prevent the 'satisfaction of public vengeance'.[1] But precisely because it was a compromise procedure, its success depended upon the co-operation of both jurisdictions and, by refusing to co-operate, the ecclesiastical judges could effectively frustrate the royal judges' attempts to apply the new system.

In two instances the system itself was not at fault. There were no jurisdictional disputes and, if the full judicial process— secular imposition of the death penalty after degradation— was not concluded, this was owing to external circumstances. In one case, involving a conspiracy, the king intervened directly before the end of the trial and ordered the defendants to be deported to a *presidio* in Africa;[2] in the other case, involving the murder of Governor Lucas de Gálvez of Yucatán, the defendants (including a priest charged with complicity in the crime) were acquitted after an eight-year trial, when the real murderer suddenly confessed.[3]

But in every other case arising in this period the new procedure revealed shortcomings more serious than those of the traditional indirect methods of royal control. Preventing the

---

[1] A.G.I., Ind. Gen. 3027, Auto Council of Castile, 15 March 1774; and Respuesta Fiscal Council of the Indies, 23 Sept. 1795.

[2] A.G.I., Estado 39, R.C. to viceroy, 27 March 1800.

[3] A.G.I., Mexico 1476, Testimonio del expediente sobre el homicidio perpetrado en Mérida de Yucatán . . ., 1792–1800. See also E. Ancona, *Historia de Yucatán desde la época más remota hasta nuestros días* (3 vols., Mérida, 1878–9), ii, 493–500.

---

[2] A.G.I., Ind. Gen. 3027, Respuesta Promotor Fiscal to Provisor Mexico, 21 June 1799. See also Bishop of Puebla to the king, 30 Oct. 1799.

application of the new law required much less effort than obstructing an executive order for deportation or an *auto de fuerza*; the prelates had only to apply the strategy of passive resistance. Since the royal judges could not legally prosecute a defendant on their own, the prelates, by refusing to appoint an associate judge (or sometimes failing even to answer requests for their appointment),[1] could forestall the trial indefinitely. In some cases they acceded initially to a joint trial and then withdrew at a later stage in the proceedings, an equally effective tactic that could completely immobilize the secular court.[2]

The *sala del crimen*'s most frustrating experience of this strategy occurred in the first murder case that began in 1790. The joint trial proceeded harmoniously until the stage of defrocking, without which the royal court could not impose the death penalty. The *sala* petitioned the ecclesiastical court for the defendant's degradation in 1791 but, despite the archbishop's repeated assurances that he would do everything to facilitate the prompt dispatch of the case,[3] its conclusion was still pending the diocesan court's sentence of degradation in 1800.

In authorizing the viceroy to confirm the final sentence pronounced by the *sala* instead of requiring the Crown's approval, the Council of the Indies had warned that any delay would frustrate the course of justice by 'giving time for compassion to develop',[4] which turned out to be an accurate prediction. By the time the archbishop was ready to hear the case for degradation, the defence attorney had discovered the extenuating circumstance that the crime had been committed while the accused was under the influence of alcohol (three litres of *mezcal*, to be exact).[5] By diminishing the defendant's responsibility, this *excepción*, if proven, would change the verdict to

---

[1] See, e.g., A.G.I., Ind. Gen. 3027, Bishop of Puebla to Intendant, 4 Sept. 1799, replying to the fourth reminder in 18 months.
[2] See, e.g., *ibid.*, Provisor Mexico to Sala del Crimen, 28 June 1799.
[3] A.G.I., Mexico 2542, Archbishop of Mexico to viceroy, 9 Nov. 1791, 18 May 1792 and 11 Feb. 1793.
[4] A.G.I., Ind. Gen. 3027, Consulta Council, 13 April 1791.
[5] A.G.I., Mexico 2646, Defence plea presented in the archdiocesan court, 15 Feb. 1792.

manslaughter, preclude the death penalty, and therefore justify a refusal to defrock the defendant.[1] Whether or not the archbishop, as the *sala del crimen* alleged, deliberately obstructed the course of the trial with the 'intention of protecting this vile criminal from his just punishment, which is the death sentence',[2] the end result was the same. The disputes, interpolations, and additional proceedings arising from this new defence plea caused enough delays to dampen even the zeal of the *fiscal*, who decided that the impasse could be ended only by changing his original recommendation for a death sentence to one for ten years' imprisonment, thus sparing the ecclesiastical authorities the unpleasant necessity of deciding whether or not to send an ordained priest to the gallows, a spectacle never before witnessed in Mexico.[3] But this effort at compromise failed to provoke any action from the diocesan court.[4] Even though the accused had already spent eight years in irons in an underground cell in the royal prison,[5] the ecclesiastical judges apparently preferred to keep him there indefinitely rather than relinquish formal jurisdiction over him by pronouncing degradation.

As it became increasingly apparent that the ecclesiastical hierarchy were not prepared to accept even the partial loss of their jurisdiction without a struggle, the *fiscal* decided that only more vigorous and direct action on the part of the royal judges could overcome this resistance, which he considered a malicious defiance of royal authority. The direct action he recommended was the immediate arrest of any ecclesiastic who committed an 'atrocious' crime: faced with this *fait accompli*, the ecclesiastical judges would be forced to participate in a joint trial, and royal custody of the accused would also prevent them from protecting him once proceedings had started.[6] Acting promptly on this

---

[1] A.G.I., Mexico 2646, Auto de prueba, Archbishop of Mexico, 29 May 1793.

[2] A.G.I., Ind. Gen. 3027, Sala del Crimen to the king, 31 May 1794.

[3] *Ibid.*, Respuesta Fiscal del Crimen, 30 April 1798.

[4] A.G.I., Mexico 2542, Viceroy Berenguer de Marquina to Antonio de Caballero, 10 June 1800.

[5] A.G.I., Mexico 2646, Certificate of the Alguacil del Corte to the Sala, 8 Nov. 1798. See also Mexico 2542, Fr Jacinto de Miranda to Godoy, 28 March 1796, giving a pathetic description of his sufferings, claiming that his cell, with neither daylight nor a bed, was covered with slime and overrun with rats.

[6] A.G.I., Ind. Gen. 3027, Respuesta Fiscal, 10 April 1799.

recommendation, the *sala* in April 1799 ordered the Intendant of Puebla to arrest a certain priest accused of offending royal jurisdiction and then notify the bishop that the priest was being held pending a joint trial.[1]

But this measure did not have the effect envisaged by the *fiscal*. The bishop was not to be so easily intimidated and, instead of appointing an associate judge, he threatened the intendant with immediate excommunication if he did not release the priest.[2] In addition, this flagrant violation of the privilege of the canon (which protected ecclesiastics from any physical violence), a violation that had no sanction in the new law, directly stimulated a flood of ecclesiastical protests against the new law and the *sala*'s application of it.

According to the Mexican hierarchy, the *sala*'s attempts to impose the new procedure of joint prosecution in unwarranted cases, although contrary to the letter and spirit of the law, could 'generously be excused as errors of judgement arising from an excessive zeal' in executing the king's orders, but this deliberate violation of the privilege of the canon was 'incontrovertible proof of its bad faith and perfidious intentions'.[3] These intentions, in the hierarchy's opinion, were not merely to destroy every vestige of ecclesiastical privilege but also to reduce the clergy to a status inferior to the laity.[4] Even laymen above the plebeian class were never detained in the noisome public prisons with common criminals, as the priest had been, but always given house arrest.[5] In addition, the intendant, by publicizing the deed—dragging his prisoner through the streets at midday, accompanied by a great display of troops, drums and trumpets—had obviously intended, they asserted, to disgrace the clergy as a whole and demonstrate to the masses that ecclesiastics were not worthy of any consideration. This act was a 'mortal blow to the twin edifices of reverence and

[1] A.G.I., Ind. Gen. 3027, Sala del Crimen to Intendant of Puebla, 20 April 1799.
[2] *Ibid.*, Bishop of Puebla to Intendant, 30 April 1799.
[3] R.A.H., Col. Mata Linares 76, Cathedral Chapter of Puebla to the king, 18 Nov. 1799.
[4] *Ibid.*, Cathedral Chapter of Mexico to the king, 28 Nov. 1799.
[5] The *audiencia* also used this argument to protest the *sala*'s actions, B.N., 12009, Audiencia of Mexico to the king, 30 Oct. 1799.

respect for the clergy which the Catholic Kings of Spain had constructed over the centuries'.[1]

If the *sala*'s attempts to transform the traditional practice of immunity in New Spain were unsuccessful, the responsibility for this failure lay as much with the lack of co-operation from fellow royal officials as with the opposition from the ecclesiastical superiors. The *fiscal* and the *alcaldes del crimen*, who had taken the initiative in introducing the new procedure in 1790, were also the only active force in the application of the general *cédula* of 1795. The lower royal magistrates—intendants, *subdelegados* and municipal judges—continued to acknowledge the Church's exclusive jurisdiction over delinquent ecclesiastics, as if the *cédula* had never been promulgated, so that even the most diligent effort on the part of the *fiscal* and the *sala* could not impose the practice of direct royal prosecution throughout the viceroyalty.

Opportunities to apply the new procedure were limited to cases which the *sala* learned of unofficially or which were referred to it via the viceroy. One case came to the *fiscal*'s attention purely by accident, when the parents of an apostate priest, who had sought the aid of the secular authorities in locating their son, reported that he had been found. Investigation revealed that a local *subdelegado* had arrested the priest and charged him with both adultery and armed resistance to arrest but had turned him over to the diocesan authorities as soon as the culprit had revealed his ecclesiastical status.[2]

Since there was no machinery by which the *sala* exercised control over the lower courts except through formal appeals and, since the local judiciary made no attempt to initiate proceedings on its own, the application of the general *cédula* was confined almost exclusively to the areas immediately surrounding the viceregal capital—the Intendancies of Mexico, Puebla and Michoacán—where extra-judicial information on suitable cases was most accessible to the *sala*. This divergence in practice between the populous centre and the outlying areas

---

[1] A.G.I., Ind. Gen. 3027, Bishop of Puebla to the king, 30 Oct. 1799. See also B.N., 12009, Bishop and Chapter of Michoacán to the king, 11 Dec. 1799.

[2] A.G.I., Ind. Gen. 3027, Testimonio de diligencias seguidas por motivo del arresto del Br Manuel Aguilar del Pozo, 21 Sept. 1796.

was not due to the ignorance of the local officials. The *cédula* had been sent to all bishops and intendants in the Indies,[1] and the authorities as far away as Chihuahua even had copies of the *Nuevo Código*, as well as the officially promulgated law.[2] Nor did the local officials lack suitable opportunities. They made no effort to prosecute ecclesiastics for offences, such as interference with royal jurisdiction, that the *fiscal del crimen* (rightly or wrongly) had qualified as atrocious crimes, but continued to handle these and other problems of ecclesiastical discipline by the old methods of executive, or extra-judicial, intervention.[3]

Even when the *sala* took the initiative, the local magistrates did not give their full co-operation. They often failed to arrest the accused and made only desultory efforts to have an associate judge appointed.[4] This apathy was particularly surprising in the cases involving local rivalries between the two jurisdictions. The same *subdelegados* and intendants who complained that the curates intimidated the royal justices in their efforts to gain complete control in their parochial bailiwicks[5] failed to take advantage of this potentially effective weapon of direct prosecution which the new law provided. The *fiscal's* allegation that they were afraid to provoke a serious clash with the clergy[6] is a possible explanation. The Intendant of Oaxaca, for example, ordered by the *sala* to prosecute one of the canons of the cathedral chapter on the charge of adultery (the suggestion for the joint trial had come from the outraged husband), refused outright, protesting that his 'participation in this

---

[1] See, e.g., *ibid.*, Intendant of Oaxaca to the Council, 21 June 1796, and Intendant of Michoacán to the Council, 29 May 1796, acknowledging the *cédula*'s receipt.

[2] A.G.I., Guadalajara 569, Comandante General de las Provincias Internas to Antonio de Llaguno, 30 April 1795.

[3] See, for example, A.G.I., Guadalajara 534, Audiencia to the Council, 16 Nov. 1802; and Guadalajara 315, Expediente contra el cura de Chapala por ultrajes en la persona del Teniente de justicia . . ., 1802.

[4] A.G.I., Ind. Gen. 3027, Intendant of Puebla to Sala del Crimen, 26 June 1799, informing the *sala* that the bishop had failed to answer its order for a joint trial, issued on 16 Feb. 1798.

[5] *Ibid.*, Intendant of Puebla to Sala del Crimen, 27 Jan. 1799. See also Subdelegado de Huatusco to the viceroy, 9 Feb. 1799.

[6] *Ibid.*, Respuesta Fiscal del Crimen, 2 June 1799.

odious case would shatter the harmonious relations I have preserved with the clergy in my district'.[1]

Another explanation is the inertia of tradition which, along with a reluctance to clash with vested interests, had caused a discrepancy between precept and practice in many other questions—an enduring feature of colonial administration in Mexico since the conquest. An example of this inertia was a case that arose in the viceregal capital in 1797. A month after the incident—a stabbing in the central *Alameda*—had become public knowledge, the *sala* learned that one of its own constables and the *corregidor* had immediately turned the case over to the archdiocesan *provisor* 'to take the appropriate action against the aggressor, who enjoys ecclesiastical *fuero*'.[2] Supported by the full authority of the *sala del crimen*, located literally a stone's throw from the site of the crime, these officials had no reason to fear a collision with the ecclesiastical authorities and must have relinquished custody of the offender (in violation of the *sala*'s specific instructions concerning all crimes of violence committed by a member of the clergy) through force of habit, a 'gross negligence of duty' for which they were reprimanded and fined.[3]

If the *sala*'s attempts to apply the new law were hindered by lack of co-operation from the lower magistrates, they were completely frustrated by the highest appellate court, the *audiencia*. In theory the impasse caused by the refusal of the ecclesiastical judges to participate in a joint trial was merely temporary, for the ultimate decision in any *competencia* between the two jurisdictions lay with the royal *audiencias* through the institution of the *recurso de fuerza*.

As a means of depriving ecclesiastical judges of their jurisdiction over a defendant, the *recurso* was originally applied in cases involving local immunity. When the Crown, in accordance with the general Caroline policy of curtailing ecclesiastical judicial authority, placed limitations on this privilege of asylum in the mid-eighteenth century,[4] the colonial *fiscales* were

---

[1] A.G.I., Ind. Gen. 3027, Intendant of Oaxaca to Branciforte, 22 Sept. 1797.

[2] *Ibid.*, Corregidor of Mexico, Mariano Fagoaga, to Provisor, 26 Dec. 1797.

[3] *Ibid.*, Auto Sala del Crimen, 1 Feb. 1798.

[4] See A.G.I., Ind. Gen. 3025, Expediente general sobre inmunidad de los reos que se refugian al sagrado, 1764–87 (entire *legajo*).

instructed to ensure the execution of these laws by presenting a *recurso de fuerza en conocer*, whenever the ecclesiastical courts interfered with the prosecution of a delinquent whose claim to local immunity was unjustified.[1] This procedure required little modification for use in disputes arising from the curtailment of personal immunity: whenever the ecclesiastical judge made a formal refusal to appoint an associate judge or to continue a joint trial, the *fiscal del crimen* immediately presented a *recurso de fuerza en el modo de conocer*.[2] Though an annoying delay, the *recurso* was considered an infallible means of countering ecclesiastical resistance to the new law's enforcement for, once the *audiencia* had declared that the ecclesiastical judge 'hace fuerza en el modo', he had no choice but to take part in a joint trial until its conclusion.

But instead of supporting the *fiscal*'s allegations that the ecclesiastical judges were abusing their authority, the *audiencia* declared in each case that they were acting completely within their rights. Usually the *oidores* declared unequivocally that the new law was inapplicable because the particular crime was not 'atrocious';[3] but even when they upheld a plea for a joint trial in two of the cases, they condemned the *sala*'s attempts to gain custody of the accused and to deny the ecclesiastical judge equal jurisdiction.[4] The *fiscal* and *sala* had assumed that the *audiencia* would at the very least resolve these *competencias* in their favour, if not act as unqualified supporters of royal jurisdiction by issuing a general order for the prompt appointment of associate judges in all future cases without possibility of refusal on any grounds.[5] They found instead that the *audiencia* was as strongly opposed as the clergy to their attacks on ecclesiastical immunity and was the firm ally of the hierarchy in protesting the *sala*'s 'scandalous' actions to the king.[6]

[1] *Ibid.*, R.C. circular, 4 Oct. 1770. For a description of the three types of *recurso de fuerza*, see above, p. 70.

[2] The various *recursos de fuerza* presented by the *fiscal*, some combining several cases, are in A.G.I., Ind. Gen. 3027, 22 March 1798, 27 June 1799, 17 Sept. 1799 and 15 Oct. 1799; and B.N., 12009, 11 July 1799.

[3] A.G.I., Ind. Gen. 3027, Autos de fuerza, 27 Nov. 1799, 22 Dec. 1799; B.N. 12009, Autos de fuerza, 3 Jan. 1800 and 16 Feb. 1800.

[4] *Ibid.*, Auto de fuerza, 19 Aug. 1799; R.A.H., Col. Mata Linares 76, Auto medio, 16 Oct. 1799.

[5] *Ibid.*, Petition to the Audiencia, 11 July 1799.

Thus the conflict between progressives and conservatives, which had characterized the formation and promulgation of the new law, became an equally prominent feature of its application in New Spain, resulting in fierce verbal battles between the *fiscal* and the *oidores* during the *recurso* hearings and accusations to the Crown of professional misconduct that rivalled in bitterness any of the exchanges between the royal and ecclesiastical judges. The *sala* and *fiscal* actually reserved their most scathing criticisms for the *oidores*, whose lack of zeal in defending royal prerogatives they considered infinitely more culpable than the inevitable opposition from the clergy, and whom they accused of applying 'ultra-montanist doctrines' in a deliberate attempt to sabotage the Crown's progressive legislation.[1]

The *audiencia*, on the other hand, argued that it had merely upheld reason and fairness. The *fiscal*, it contended, in addition to distorting the texts of canons, royal laws and standard works of jurisprudence in order to support his arguments, had purposely exaggerated the gravity of the offences committed: he had applied the term 'sedition' in one case because a crowd had flocked to the scene of a scuffle between a curate and the royal justice, yet anyone with experience of conditions in New Spain, they explained, knew that in the villages the smallest incident immediately produced a gathering of curious Indians. Finally, the 'public and scandalous' arrest of a priest by royal troops acting on the *sala*'s orders was such an affront to the Church and its ministers, and so unnecessary an act, that the motives of the *alcaldes* must be suspect.[2]

The *audiencia* merely hinted that the *sala* and *fiscal* acted for more sinister motives than a sense of duty, but the ecclesiastical hierarchy were more outspoken. If ultra-montanism (as applied by the *audiencia*) was the enemy of progress and reform, the Freemasons and the French *philosophes*, with whose 'pernicious doctrines . . . a few unfortunate officials have been

---

[1] A.G.I., Mexico 2647, Fiscal del Crimen to the king, 26 Sept. 1799; R.A.H., Col. Mata Linares 76, Sala del Crimen to the king, 23 Aug. 1799.

[2] B.N., 12009, Audiencia to the king, 30 Oct. 1799.

---

[6] B.N., 12009, Audiencia to the king, 30 Oct. 1799.

contaminated', were to blame for the *sala*'s actions, according to the hierarchy.[1]

The person singled out as the primary exponent in Mexico of a deliberate plan to destroy the Church was the *fiscal del crimen*, Ambrosio de Sagarzurrieta. There was nothing in his background to explain his vigorous opposition to ecclesiastical immunity (which was undeniable, even if his motives were not those ascribed to him by the hierarchy). The one feature that distinguished him from his colleagues—his ordination as priest and appointment to ecclesiastical benefices before he became a civil servant[2]—should, if anything, have made him more sympathetic to clerical privilege. Rather than harbouring any particular animosity towards the clergy, it is more likely that he was simply ambitious, and a record of zeal in defending royal prerogatives could be extremely helpful for promotion within the service.[3] He was certainly one of the most energetic and conscientious officials in Mexico during this period and was praised in a confidential report made in 1809 for his 'great integrity and zeal in the service of the Crown', in contrast with the apathy and self-interest of his fellow members of the judiciary.[4]

The *audiencia*'s failure to uphold royal jurisdiction in these *competencias* left the *fiscal* and *sala del crimen* only one possible source of support—the king. They did not appeal the unfavourable *autos de fuerza*; that would merely eliminate the obstacles in these particular cases, and they were sure that the ecclesiastical courts would only find new loopholes through which the law could be evaded. Instead they petitioned the king to replace this law with a new one that would authorize the royal courts to prosecute delinquent ecclesiastics without any intervention from the diocesan courts.[5]

[1] R.A.H., Col. Mata Linares 76, Cathedral Chapter of Mexico to the king, 28 Nov. 1799.

[2] A.G.I., Guadalajara 243, Relación de méritos y servicios del Dr D. Ambrosio de Sagarzurrieta, 1786.

[3] See the various *consultas* concerning candidates for promotion, 1780–90, in A.G.I., Ind. Gen. 563.

[4] A.H.N., Consejos 58, Advertencias útiles para la conservación tranquila y permanente del Reyno de Nueva España, Juan Jabat to the Junta Central, 10 Jan. 1809.

[5] R.A.H., Col. Mata Linares 76, Fiscal del Crimen to the king, 25 Oct. 1800; A.G.I., Ind. Gen. 3027, Sala del Crimen to the king, 29 Oct. 1800.

O

The argument that the clergy's immunity was equivalent to freedom from any punishment and thus encouraged crime, an argument first produced by Charles III's ministers to persuade him to review the Crown's traditional ecclesiastical policy and then resurrected when the promulgation of the *Nuevo Código* law on joint prosecution was being discussed, now made its appearance in the third round of the struggle for judicial reform. But in seeking to convince Charles IV that it was necessary to eliminate ecclesiastical *fuero* entirely, the Mexican *fiscal* and *sala del crimen* advanced this argument further: they asserted that the immunity enjoyed by the clergy in Mexico had resulted in an alarming rise in the incidence of 'atrocious' crimes committed by ecclesiastics out of all proportion to the ecclesiastical population of the viceroyalty.[1] And this rise had accelerated drastically, according to the *fiscal*, after the successes gained by the diocesan courts in the recent *recursos de fuerza*, which had served to embolden ecclesiastical delinquents.[2]

As proof of their allegation, the *fiscal* and *sala* submitted the records of all the cases that had arisen in New Spain in the decade 1790–9, starting with the first murder case of 1790 (no documentation was sent on the alleged crime wave of 1799–1800). Their diligent search had produced fifteen ecclesiastics charged with 'atrocious' crimes (ranging from *lèse-majesté* down to petty theft) during that decade, out of an estimated total of 8,000 ecclesiastics in the entire viceroyalty.[3] Even if not all the defendants were in fact guilty (charges against one, as accessory to Governor Gálvez's murder, were dropped in 1800), the record is not enviable; but neither does it necessarily prove that the ecclesiastical crime rate had increased. No statistics were given for previous periods, but the colonial records show that delinquent ecclesiastics were by no means an exclusive feature of the late eighteenth century.[4]

[1] R.A.H., Col. Mata Linares 76, Sala del Crimen to the king, 23 Aug. 1799; A.G.I., Mexico 2647, Fiscal del Crimen to the king, 26 Sept. 1799.

[2] R.A.H., Col. Mata Linares 76, Fiscal del Crimen to the king, 25 Oct. 1800.

[3] A.G.I., Guadalajara 323-A, Estadística de Nueva España (n.d., beginning of the nineteenth century), a revised version of the 1793 census.

[4] Sample *legajos* from the series A.G.I., Contratación 4038–4377, Registro de naos de generales de Nueva España, 1556–1784, reveal that ecclesiastical criminals had been deported to Spain under *partida de registro* from the beginning of this period.

As for a disproportionate number of crimes committed by the clergy in comparison to laymen, the evidence actually leads to the opposite conclusion: in one year, (1793) for example, the *Tribunal de la Acordada* convicted 181 laymen for the crimes of murder and manslaughter (*homicidio* and *muerte*) alone,[1] and this total excludes cases arising outside the central area of the viceroyalty, where the *Acordada* functioned, as well as the cases handled by the *sala del crimen* and the municipal magistrates.

Though the *fiscal* and *sala* failed to prove that the Mexican clergy were any more prone to crime (or any less clever in escaping detection) than laymen, the records they submitted did support their plea for a revision of the law by demonstrating that the 1795 *cédula* was virtually unenforceable. They decided to suspend their attack on ecclesiastical *fuero* pending the king's decision, since the hierarchy's opposition, backed by the *audiencia*'s authority, could frustrate any attempts to prosecute new cases, as well as prevent the conclusion of the trials already started.[2] After the recent unfavourable decisions in the *recursos de fuerza*, the *fiscal*, rather than risk any further 'insults' from the *audiencia*, had merely urged the prelates to punish the offenders. The prelates' consistent failure to take even independent action in these cases was conclusive proof, in his opinion, that they were determined to protect their fellow ecclesiastics and that ecclesiastical immunity was incompatible with the maintenance of public order.[3]

At the same time the prelates were barraging the Crown with vehement arguments in favour of restoring their jurisdiction to its formerly exclusive status, suggesting that the king was unaware of the 'sinister plot' to destroy the Church hatched by some of his ministers and carried out by officials in Mexico.[4] These sentiments were unanimous and widespread, indicating that the entire clergy—not only in Puebla, Mexico, and Michoacán,[5] the areas of the *sala*'s intensive attack, but also

---

[1] A.G.I., Mexico 1476, Plan que demuestra las operaciones del Real Tribunal de la Acordada, 1793, sent by Revillagigedo to Pedro de Acuña, 31 March 1794.

[2] R.A.H., Col. Mata Linares 76, Sala del Crimen to the king, 3 Dec. 1800.

[3] *Ibid.*, Fiscal del Crimen to the king, 25 Oct. 1800 and 27 Dec. 1801.

[4] A.G.I., Ind. Gen. 3027, Bishop of Puebla to the king, 30 Oct. 1799.

[5] See also, R.A.H., Col. Mata Linares 76, Archbishop of Mexico to the king, 26 Sept. 1799; Cathedral Chapter of Puebla to the king, 18 Nov. 1799; Cathedral

in dioceses in which no cases had occurred, such as Durango[1]—
felt themselves in danger, if not of annihilation, as they hinted,
at least of losing that privileged and honoured status within
society that they had enjoyed since the beginning of the
colonial period.

Deluged by these opposing petitions, the king ordered a re-
appraisal of the system. Actually a revised general rule had
supposedly been under study since 1796, when the Council
fiscal recommended the same change his successor was to
recommend in 1802: the total exclusion of ecclesiastical jurisdiction from criminal trials.[2] No amount of firmness on the
part of the royal judges, it was argued, could succeed against
the 'guile and craft' of the ecclesiastical judges, and this
privilege of immunity—'merely a licence for vice and crime'—
could no longer be tolerated 'in our enlightened age'.[3]

But although the question was submitted to the king in
1803,[4] his final decision, if he made one at all, was never
communicated to the colonial authorities.[5] The compromise
procedure of association of judges was clearly unworkable:
as a half-way measure, it succeeded only in alienating the
clergy and frustrating the royal judges without ensuring the
efficient administration of justice. Yet despite these shortcomings it was to persist well into the next century, until the
extraordinary circumstances of a civil war forced the Mexican
viceroy to review the case against ecclesiastical immunity and
reject the counsel of caution in the face of 'deeply rooted superstition and ignorant fanaticism'[6] that had probably restrained
the king from abolishing the privilege altogether.

[1] R.A.H., Col. Mata Linares 76, Bishop and Chapter of Durango to the king,
2 Dec. 1799.

[2] A.G.I., Ind. Gen. 3027, Respuesta Fiscal de Nueva España (Council of the
Indies), 19 Sept. 1796.

[3] R.A.H., Col. Mata Linares 76, Respuesta Fiscal de Nueva España, 29 April
1802.   [4] *Ibid.*, Consulta Council, 13 Jan. 1803.

[5] B.N., 20245, Respuesta Promotor Fiscal, Mexico, 10 Sept. 1811, quotes as the
last official pronouncement on this issue known in Mexico, a R.O. sent to the
Audiencia of Seville, 19 Nov. 1799, ordering that all cases of 'atrocious' crimes be
sent to the king, pending a new *Instrucción*, to be formed by the Council of Castile.

[6] R.A.H., Col. Mata Linares 76, Respuesta Fiscal del Perú, 1804.

Chapter of Mexico to the king, 28 Nov. 1799; and B.N., 12009, Bishop and
Chapter of Michoacán to the king, 11 Dec. 1799.

CHAPTER IX

Ecclesiastical Immunity
during the Independence Period

I. SEDITIOUS CLERGY AND THE CURTAILMENT
OF IMMUNITY

THE problem of secular control of the clergy reached its crucial stage in New Spain during the war for independence. The development of the Crown's ecclesiastical policy towards a system of direct judicial control had halted short of eliminating immunity entirely in a confusing compromise that proved unacceptable to both the secular authorities and the clergy. The Spanish government, its attention diverted by more pressing matters in Europe (first the threat of a French invasion and then the invasion itself), had postponed the final decision on this question, but the viceregal government was forced by equally critical events within Mexico to reconsider the problem and to provide a solution on its own initiative.

The Mexican independence movement progressed through various stages,[1] beginning with the period of the precursors from the mid-1790's to 1808 during which general intellectual ferment and political dissatisfaction developed into a specific desire for independence among a small group of leading Creoles. The abdication of Charles IV and Napoleon's invasion of Spain provided a pretext for the colony's peaceful separation, a project which the Creoles hoped to carry out with the aid of Viceroy José de Iturrigaray.[2] But this possibility ended in

---

[1] L. Alamán, *Historia de México*, is one of the most valuable sources for the independence period, containing a detailed record of the years 1808–25 based on original documents and eye-witness accounts (including his own), many of which are no longer available.

[2] A.G.I., Mexico 1662, Relación sucinta y razonada de los hechos antecedentes que precedieron a la separación del virrey, D. José de Iturrigaray, November 1808, prepared by the *Audiencia* of Mexico.

September 1808 when a strongly loyalist faction of peninsular Spaniards deposed Iturrigaray and inadvertently initiated a new phase in the independence movement. The Creoles became convinced that they could achieve their objective only by force—a conviction that strengthened as the new government resorted to increasingly repressive measures to stifle disloyal activities—and their steadily growing opposition to Spanish rule now took the form of concrete plans for its violent overthrow. Finally, on 16 September 1810, the movement entered its third phase—armed rebellion. A village curate in Michoacán, Miguel Hidalgo y Costilla, 'set off a spark in the small town of Dolores that ignited the whole kingdom with the speed of a wind-borne plague'.[1]

The government's ability to defend itself against this independence movement, in all its phases, was directly related to the question of ecclesiastical immunity. The total subordination of the clergy to the State's coercive authority, previously advocated as a means of ensuring their co-operation in furthering the interests of the Crown, became in this period a question of whether or not the Crown would survive at all in the colony. No longer merely a potential threat to the security of the State, a significant proportion of the Mexican clergy conspired and took up arms against the government and confirmed the fears expressed decades previously, during the crisis of royal policy provoked by the *motín de Esquilache*.[2]

In the absence of official records of the insurgent forces, it is difficult to arrive at even an approximate figure for the number of ecclesiastics who aligned themselves with the independence cause. From government documents and personal accounts of the period, a partial list has been formed of 401 individuals (244 seculars and 157 regulars) who were recorded as having taken an active part,[3] representing only those who were included in official reports as captured in battle or convicted of subversion, and those mentioned in the memoirs and

---

[1] A.G.I., Mexico 1664, Informe de la Audiencia, 18 Nov. 1813, párr. 42. The report is an account from the royalist point of view of the rebellion's origin and progress. The most complete biography of Hidalgo, though confessedly eulogistic, is L. Castillo Ledón, *Hidalgo, la vida del héroe* (2 vols., Mexico, 1948–9).

[2] See above, Ch. VI.

[3] See Appendix.

correspondence of fellow insurgents;[1] the list fails to include, for example, the many who must have escaped detection while collaborating with the rebels, or who fought in the rebel forces but were too obscure for mention.

The clergy's contribution to the independence movement was far greater than the numbers involved: even if the entire clergy had joined the rebel forces, their number, estimated at slightly over one-tenth of 1 per cent (0.12%) of the total population,[2] could not have been decisive as far as military strength was concerned. But they were the leaders, both military and political, and their choice of allegiance was often decisive in determining that of large sectors of the population. Entire villages either remained loyal or joined the insurrection according to the dictates of the parish priest, and many curates followed Hidalgo's famous example, 'pronouncing' for the revolution and leading their parishioners as a contribution to the rebel troops.[3]

Ecclesiastics were associated with all the major developments in the independence movement, from the first scheme discovered in Mexico for separation from Spain in 1794 to the various conspiracies that preceded and followed the Dolores uprising.[4] Creole clerics helped to direct the course of the rebellion, to lead the ideological warfare against the royalists conducted through the medium of the insurgent press (mainly in the newspapers, *Despertador americano*, *Correo americano del Sur*, *Ilustrador americano*, and *Semanario patriótico americano*, all edited by ecclesiastics)[5] and to define the confused and amorphous

---

[1] C. M. Bustamante, *Cuadro histórico de la revolución mexicana* (6 vols., Mexico, 1843–6), is a particularly useful source, since the author was in communication with the rebels from the beginning of the war, which he joined openly in 1812.

[2] F. Navarro y Noriega, *Memoria sobre la población de Nueva España*, appendix, 'Estado de la población . . ., 1810', gives the total population as 6,122,354 and the number of secular and regular clergy as 7,341.

[3] Some of them are mentioned in A.G.I., Mexico 1321, Viceroy Venegas to Minister of War, 27 Jan. and 12 March 1811; and A.G.N., Operaciones de Guerra 1013, Bishop-elect of Michoacán, Manuel Abad y Queipo, to Venegas, 20 Sept. 1812.

[4] For trials of the ecclesiastical conspirators, see A.G.N., Infidencias 23, nos. 1 and 5 (Valladolid de Michoacán, 1809); Infidencias 172 (Mexico, 1811); Infidencias 10 and 11 (Oaxaca, 1811); Infidencias 58, 63 and 85 (Valladolid, 1813); and Infidencias 92 (Zacatecas, 1814).

[5] These and other insurgent newspapers published from 1810–14 are reproduced in *D.H.M.*, iii and iv.

political aspirations of the revolution in manifestoes and constitutional decrees.[1] Perhaps the most curious and typically Mexican phenomenon was the ecclesiastical *cabecilla* or military officer. Creole clerics in other colonies, like Deán Funes in the Río de la Plata,[2] played an active political role but did not ordinarily lead troops in battle. Hidalgo and his successor, José María Morelos (another village curate from Michoacán)[3] were the most famous soldier-priests, but there were many other ecclesiastics—Mariano Matamoros, José Navarrete, Pablo Delgado, José Izquierdo, Fray Luis de Herrera, to name a few—who attained high rank among the insurgent forces and often displayed considerable military talents, particularly in guerrilla warfare.

Without full documentation, the clergy's contribution to the rebellion can best be judged by the opinions of contemporary witnesses. In 1812 a Mexican *oidor* reported his impression of the war in terms similar to those used by other royal officials and private observers:

No one can deny that the ecclesiastics were the principal authors of this rebellion, which they now foment and sustain, not only with their plans and pernicious influence but also with arms; for one can count by the hundreds the generals, brigadiers, colonels, and other officers of their state in the numerous bands of the traitors, and there is scarcely a military action of any importance in which priests are not leading the enemy.[4]

The Mexican clergy's support of the insurrection was by no means unanimous. The bishops and canons were almost exclusively loyal to the régime with a few exceptions: the canons José San Martín and Francisco de Velasco, were both active revolutionaries; several others were convicted of espionage or

[1] See, e.g., 'Plan de paz y plan de guerra', 1812, by Dr José María Cos, published in C. M. Bustamante, *Cuadro histórico*, i, 389–400; A.G.I., Mexico 1482, Proclamación para un Congreso Constitucional, 11 Sept. 1813, José María Morelos.
[2] R. Levene, *A History of Argentina*, trans. by W. S. Robertson (Chapel Hill, 1937), pp. 226–7.
[3] A. Teja Zabre, *Vida de Morelos* (Mexico, 1959), is a balanced account of Morelos's role in the movement, based largely on original sources.
[4] A.G.I., Mexico 1664, Pedro de la Puente to Regency Council, 15 Dec. 1812. See also Mexico 1321, Venegas to Minister of War, 12 March 1811.

conspiracy; and a few canons in Mexico and Valladolid formed part of the subversive group called *Los Guadalupes*, which supplied the rebels with information, money, and arms.[1] But the large number of ecclesiastics who either remained neutral or opposed the insurrection with pastoral letters, sermons, money, and even with military service in the royalist forces[2] could not erase the fact that the viceregal government was faced with a large-scale rebellion initiated by a priest and sustained to a great extent by Creole members of the lower clergy.

The task of suppressing this revolution was, in the opinion of the viceregal government, incompatible with the preservation of ecclesiastical immunity. The defenders of this immunity continued to use the orthodox canonist argument, employed in previous controversies, that the coercive power of the Church was sufficient to maintain ecclesiastical discipline without any interference from the secular arm.[3] But if this argument had seemed invalid to the secular authorities before, it was now totally contradicted by the indisputable evidence of the insurrection.

The inability of the ecclesiastical superiors to control their subordinates effectively, already apparent in the comparative tranquillity and order of the colonial period, became accentuated in the chaotic conditions of a civil war. There was no lack of effort: both before and during the rebellion the Mexican hierarchy employed the entire weight of their influence and authority to control seditious ecclesiastics, as well as to help to stifle the independence movement in general, but the means at their disposal proved totally inadequate. Pastoral exhortations had little if any effect. The Bishop of Puebla, for example, who had convoked the clerics of his diocese to sign an oath of allegiance to the government in 1810,[4] was forced to confess two years later that many of these same priests had joined the

[1] A.G.I. Mexico 1480, Certificaciones que acreditan la complicidad de varios individuos . . ., 31 May 1813, sent by Viceroy Calleja to the Minister of War.

[2] For an example of the curious phenomenon of two opposing forces headed by ecclesiastics, see the report of a skirmish near Guadalajara, in A.G.I., Mexico 1482, 'El mentor de la Nueva Galicia' (royalist newspaper), 12 July 1813.

[3] A.H.N., Consejos 21212, Pedimento Promotor Fiscal, Dr Medrano, 21 Aug. 1811.

[4] *Gaceta del gobierno de Mexico* (Mexico, 1810–21), 30 Oct. 1810, Acta del Obispo y clero de Puebla, 27 Oct. 1810.

rebel forces.[1] Decrees of excommunication may have deterred some vacillating ecclesiastics (and laymen), but those already committed to the rebel cause ignored these censures and some even published refutations of their validity.[2] The prelates were willing to take more direct action, but the ecclesiastical courts lacked sufficient personnel to detect and arrest suspected subversives, much less to apprehend active revolutionaries.

The regular superiors were presumably in a better position to curtail sedition among their subordinates who lived within the confines of the monasteries but, despite viceregal orders to keep the friars under close surveillance,[3] regulars suspected of treason and even those being held in custody continually escaped to join the rebellion. And in 1811 a large-scale plot to take over the capital was organized—complete even to an arsenal of firearms and explosives—within the main Augustinian monastery itself and might easily have remained undetected if one of the friars had not denounced his fellow conspirators the night before the proposed coup.[4]

The Inquisition played an even less important part in controlling seditious and rebellious ecclesiastics than the prelates. As an organ for suppressing heresy it had declined since the beginning of the eighteenth century, and its ability to impose political orthodoxy on either the laity or the clergy was hardly more impressive. During the pre-revolutionary period from 1795 to 1810 the inquisitors, spurred by the government, were active in prosecuting suspected advocates of republicanism and freedom of conscience, among other dangerous new doctrines,[5] but after the outbreak of the rebellion their only contributions to the royalist cause were an edict excommunicating Hidalgo and his followers—an edict issued only after several prelates

---

[1] J. Hernández y Dávalos, ed., *Colección de documentos para la historia de la guerra de independencia de México* (6 vols., Mexico, 1877–82), iv, 272, Edict Bishop of Puebla, 10 July 1812.

[2] Hidalgo, for example, in his Manifiesto, 15 Dec. 1810, published in G. García and C. Pereyra, *Documentos inéditos ó muy raros*, ix, 44–9. See also *D.H.M.*, iii, 'Despertador americano', 3 Jan. 1811; and iv, 'Correo americano del Sur', 29 May 1813.

[3] G. García and C. Pereyra, *Documentos inéditos ó muy raros*, ix, 233–8, Venegas to Padre Guardián de San Fernando, 12 Aug. 1811.

[4] See A.H.N., Consejos 21212, Causa seguida a los padres agustinos, 1811.

[5] See *Precursores ideológicos de la guerra de independencia* (Mexico, 1929).

had taken the lead[1]—and the use of their secret dungeons for the custody of particularly dangerous prisoners. The suppression of the Inquisition by order of the Spanish *Cortes* in the years 1812–14 was the final blow to its prestige and effectiveness. Although reinstated after the return of Ferdinand VII, its activities were by then considered totally irrelevant to the task of suppressing the rebellion. The Mexican Holy Office tried the insurgent leader Morelos for heresy in 1815,[2] but it is clear from the records that this intervention was gratuitous and tolerated by the viceroy only on the condition that it should not delay the military trial, the outcome of which was already a foregone conclusion.[3]

The viceregal government could not, and did not, rely to any extent on the well-meaning but futile efforts of the hierarchy and the Inquisition to help preserve Spanish rule over the colony. The apprehension, prosecution, and punishment of treasonous ecclesiastics were almost solely civil and military functions, in which the intervention of the ecclesiastical magistrates became increasingly insignificant as the rebellion gained in intensity and duration. The suppression of conspiracies and other forms of subversion was the responsibility of the civil authorities, while the punishment of ecclesiastics who engaged in open rebellion was almost exclusively the task of the royalist army officers. The inevitable emphasis on the latter function, as the independence movement was transformed into a widespread civil war, resulted in the elimination, not only of ecclesiastical immunity, but also of the basic legal rights traditionally enjoyed by both the laity and the clergy.

The clergy's exclusive immunity in criminal cases had already been curtailed by the *Nuevo Código* law prescribing the association of ecclesiastical and royal judges for the prosecution of 'atrocious' crimes.[4] In theory this same procedure of joint

---

[1] The edicts of Abad y Queipo of Valladolid, 24 Sept. 1810, and the Archbishop of Mexico, 11 Oct. 1810, preceded the Inquisition's edict of 13 Oct. 1810, *Gaceta del gobierno*, 28 Sept. and 19 Oct. 1810.

[2] The heresy proceedings against Morelos, Nov. 1815, are published in G. García and C. Pereyra, *Documentos inéditos ó muy raros*, xii, 59–119.

[3] G. García and C. Pereyra, *Documentos inéditos ó muy raros*, xii, 69, Calleja to Mexican Inquisitor General, 23 Nov. 1815.

[4] A.G.I., Ind. Gen. 3027, R.C., 25 Oct. 1795, promulgating ley 71, título 9, Libro 1, of the Nuevo Código de las leyes de Indias.

prosecution was followed in all civilian trials of subversive ecclesiastics (as distinct from military trials of insurgents, which will be dealt with separately) during the entire independence period, since the more pertinent *Nuevo Código* law, which declared that ecclesiastics forfeited all immunity in cases of *lèse-majesté*,[1] was never formally promulgated in the Indies. But the supposedly equal jurisdiction of the ecclesiastical judges was reduced in these trials to a purely nominal intervention, and the partial loss of *fuero* became total in everything but name.

The reduction of ecclesiastical intervention was a rapid process. The first treason case, which began in 1794, already revealed a modification of the system followed in trials of other serious crimes, such as murder and theft. In these trials the balance of jurisdiction, if anything, was weighted in favour of the ecclesiastical courts, for (despite opposition from the *fiscal del crimen*) they not only participated equally in all the proceedings but also retained custody of the defendant.[2] But in the 1794 conspiracy trial, the ecclesiastical judge, though present throughout most of the proceedings, intervened actively only when the defendant or an ecclesiastical witness was questioned and when the evidence was summed up for the benefit of the *sala del crimen*.[3]

By the time the next ecclesiastical subversive was tried in 1808, the process was almost complete: joint prosecution had become a secular trial in which the ecclesiastical judge merely ratified the findings of his associate,[4] presumably to satisfy the diocesan court that the accused had received a fair trial. He was called in only after the suspect had been arrested and charged by the secular authorities, and he had no part either in directing the course of the hearings, or in determining the verdict or the sentence imposed upon him: both were decided

[1] A.G.I., Mexico 1159, Nuevo Código, ley 13, título 12, Libro 1.

[2] With the one exception of the Carmelite friar charged with murder in 1790 and held in the royal prison. See above, Ch. VIII for a discussion of this and other trials of atrocious crimes from 1790 to 1799.

[3] A.G.I., Estado 22, Testimonio de autos en la causa de Juan Guerrero y cómplices, 1794; and A.G.N., Infidencias 29 and 139, the same, from 1795–1800.

[4] A.G.I., Mexico 1662, Razón del proceso contra Fr Melchor de Talamantes, 1808.

exclusively by the secular court and confirmed by the viceroy.[1] In fact the presence of the ecclesiastical judge as passive observer during the examination of the defendant was often the only feature to distinguish the trials of ecclesiastics charged with sedition from those of laymen.[2]

In contrast with the prosecution of crimes against society, in which the prelates disputed every aspect of the proceedings, these trials for crimes against the State were almost completely free from jurisdictional disputes. Instead of protesting that the crime was not serious enough to deprive the accused of his exclusive immunity, or insisting that the secular judge was merely an auxiliary to his ecclesiastical associate, the bishops readily assented to a joint trial without always knowing what specific crime had been committed or even the identity of the accused[3] and accepted the subordinate role assigned to their delegates, apparently without a murmur. The first ecclesiastic prosecuted for conspiracy in 1794, in complaining to the Crown that his immunity had been violated by the almost exclusively secular trial and his long detention in the royal prison, was less indignant at the royal judges' illegal assumption of authority than at the 'indolence and indifference' with which the ecclesiastical court had treated its own jurisdiction and the 'sacred privilege of the *fuero*'.[4]

The 'indifference' shown by the archdiocesan court of Mexico in this case—a precedent which was to be followed in all future treason trials throughout the viceroyalty—seems surprising in view of the vigorous protests the archbishop and his fellow prelates made when their jurisdiction was threatened with the slightest encroachment in other types of criminal cases. The explanation for this inconsistency lies in the nature of the crime: the hierarchy never challenged the curtailment of immunity in cases of *lèse-majesté* because they considered this

[1] *Ibid.*; see also A.H.N., Consejos 21081, Causa seguida a Fr Miguel Zugasti, 1809.

[2] Compare, for example, the trials of Manuel Peimbert (layman) and Manuel Palacios (priest), both charged with sedition in 1809, in A.H.N., Consejos, 21203.

[3] A.G.I., Estado 22, Trial of Juan Guerrero y cómplices, 1794. See also A.G.N., Operaciones de guerra 1012, Venegas to Abad y Queipo, 17 Sept. 1810, requesting the appointment of an associate judge for a conspiracy in Querétaro; and Abad y Queipo to Venegas, 27 Sept. 1810.

[4] A.G.I., Estado 39, Juan de Vara to Antonio de Llaguno, 27 Aug. 1796.

crime 'the most atrocious of all crimes', as serious a threat to religion and the Church as it was to the State.[1] Nor did they believe that their interests would be served by quibbling over the finer points of judicial procedure. Sharing with the secular authorities a 'common desire to suppress this dangerous ferment of sedition', as one royal magistrate explained,[2] they were willing to co-operate fully, even if this involved accepting serious encroachments on their jurisdiction.[3] There were disputes, but they had nothing to do with jurisdiction; they involved the outcome of a particular trial (i.e., whether or not an ecclesiastical defendant should suffer the death penalty)[4] rather than the manner in which it was conducted.

In addition to the almost total restriction of *fuero*, ecclesiastics accused of treason (and laymen as well) suffered a gradual loss of the normal legal safeguards to which all Spanish subjects had been entitled under the traditional judicial system. The peninsular faction which deposed Viceroy Iturrigaray in 1808 initiated a vigorous policy designed to stifle any incipient separatist activities and 'to calm public unrest': curfews were imposed, public gatherings prohibited, and many Creoles detained on charges of suspicious behaviour or conversations.[5] But perhaps the most important innovation was the creation in June 1809 of a *Junta consultiva*, an extraordinary tribunal which replaced the ordinary royal courts for the prosecution of all cases of *infidencia*, or treason.

This tribunal, soon renamed *Junta de seguridad y buen orden*,[6] had two advantages over the ordinary courts as an instrument for suppressing subversion—select membership and simplified procedure. It was feared that the ordinary royal courts would be lenient with traitors: they had already incurred the Crown's

[1] R.A.H., Col. Mata Linares 76, Archbishop of Mexico to the king, 26 Sept. 1799.

[2] A.G.I., Estado 22, Alcalde del Crimen to Branciforte, 1 Oct. 1794.

[3] See, e.g., A.G.N., Obispos y arzobispos 3, Bishop of Oaxaca to Venegas, 3 Jan. 1811.

[4] See below, pp. 213–14, 221–2.

[5] A.G.I., Mexico 1662, Audiencia to Junta Central, 24 Sept. 1808; and A.H.N., Consejos 21081, Gabriel de Yermo (leader of the coup) to Junta Central, 12 Nov. 1808.

[6] See A.G.I., Mexico 1662, Real acuerdo, 26 June 1809; and A.G.N., Infidencias 128, no. 19, Bando interim Viceroy (Archbishop of Mexico), 21 Sept. 1809.

displeasure for being overly scrupulous in observing due process of law in previous treason trials,[1] and some of the Creole magistrates were suspected of sympathizing, perhaps even collaborating, with the rebels.[2] But by creating a special court with membership limited to a few peninsular magistrates, specially selected for their pronounced loyalty to the metropolis,[3] the government could ensure both the zealous detection of any subversive activities and the harsh punishment of the offenders.

The second advantage of the *Junta* was its ability to dispatch cases quickly. It was felt that the crime of treason 'by its urgent and delicate nature demands brevity'[4] and, in order to avoid any delay in punishing the offenders, the *Junta* simplified the cumbersome and time-consuming judicial procedure of the ordinary royal courts to the point that their trials were later condemned by the Council of the Indies as lacking even the formalities of a preliminary inquest.[5] Indictment and verdict were barely separated by a brief examination of the defendant, possibly the testimony of one or two witnesses for the prosecution, and a summing up by the *fiscal*.[6] The accused were denied any defence or opportunity to appeal, since these formalities were considered 'inconsistent with the *Junta*'s primary objective, which is a prompt conviction'.[7]

The first conspiracy trial in the 1790's had lasted six years, mainly because of the many extensions requested by the defence counsel. In contrast, the *Junta de seguridad* was able to dispatch most of its cases within a few weeks, relying on the

[1] A.G.I., Estado 22, R.O., 19 Jan. 1795; Guadalajara 247, Real resolución, 15 March 1803.

[2] For reports on the loyalties of various Creole magistrates (e.g., *Alcalde del Crimen* Jacobo de Villarrutia), see A.G.I., Mexico 1661, Audiencia to Junta Central, 12 Nov. 1808; Mexico 1474, Venegas to Secretary of Gracia y Justicia, 10 Nov. 1810; Mexico 1487, Calleja to Minister of Ultramar, 6 April 1815.

[3] Miguel Bataller, President of the *Junta* from 1810, was rewarded for his 'unswerving loyalty and zeal' with promotion from *oidor* to Regent of the Audiencia, A.G.I., Mexico 1665, Consulta Council, 1 March 1820.

[4] A.G.I., Mexico 1662, Real acuerdo, 26 June 1809.

[5] A.G.I., Mexico 1147, Consulta Council of the Indies, 18 May 1818.

[6] See, e.g., A.G.I., Mexico 1476, Trial of Fr Pedro Rivera and Fr Manuel Suárez, 1811; and A.G.N., Infidencias 99, no. 5, Trial of Tiburcio Valderas and Alexo Norzagaray (both clerics), 1811.

[7] A.G.I., Mexico 1473, Exposición que hicieron los tres fiscales, 26 June 1809.

principle that a verdict of guilty could be reached 'as soon as the mere fact of the crime is established'.[1] The efficiency of the *Junta*'s procedure, as well as its zeal in detecting subversion, can be judged by comparing the number of ordinary criminal cases handled by the *sala del crimen* in the years 1810–12, which were 9,080, with those prosecuted by the *Junta* in the same period, which were five times as many.[2]

This cursory method of conducting trials could result in serious injustices, since there was no effort to make further investigation of contradictory evidence or testimonies which extenuated the guilt of the accused. One village curate was denounced for refusing to participate in a ceremony of allegiance to Ferdinand VII. His plausible explanation, that he had only refused permission to use the parish church on a particular day, Good Friday, because it would have been irreverent, was disregarded and the defendant speedily convicted of *lèse-majesté*, in spite of the *fiscal*'s recommendation that further witnesses be called to corroborate the denouncer's testimony.[3] In another case, a Creole friar was charged with 'seditious utterances'. Even his denouncers admitted that he was habitually drunk and noted for his imprudent but harmless chatter, but he was declared guilty of 'high treason' on the assumption that any ecclesiastic who gossiped about revolution, when his thoughts should have been on the Christian ideal of peace, was obviously an active conspirator.[4] Both defendants, who were deported to Spain for punishment, may have been guilty of treason; the point is that the evidence produced in their trials was far from conclusive. There were, on the other hand, defendants acquitted for lack of evidence who turned around and joined the rebel forces as soon as they were released,[5] but more often an ecclesiastic whose guilt lacked even the minimum proof required by the *Junta de seguridad* was simply left in prison at the discretion of the viceroy.[6]

---

[1] A.G.I., Mexico 1473, Exposición que hicieron los tres fiscales, 26 June 1809.
[2] Informe, Sala del Crimen, 8 Feb. 1813, published in *Gaceta del gobierno*, 11 March 1813.   [3] A.H.N., Consejos 21203, Trial of Manuel Palacios, 1809.
[4] A.H.N., Consejos 21081, Trial of Fr Miguel Zugasti, 1809.
[5] A.G.N., Operaciones de Guerra 1011, Archbishop of Mexico to Venegas, 5 Jan. 1811; and Operaciones de Guerra 1012, Archbishop to Venegas, 22 Jan. 1811.

The system of an extraordinary tribunal, with its simplified procedure of summary trials, was extended to most portions of the viceroyalty after the rebellion started in September 1810: another main *Junta de seguridad* was created in Guadalajara, and subsidiary *juntas* in the provincial centres, whose proceedings were subject to review by those in the *audiencia* capitals.[1] The establishment of these special courts, though resulting in the loss of certain legal safeguards, had no effect on the privilege of ecclesiastical *fuero*, since a representative of the diocesan court was permanently attached to the *Junta de seguridad* and automatically joined one of the royal magistrates whenever an ecclesiastic was brought to trial.[2] There were several exceptions to this rule outside the capital—newly formed local *Juntas* seeking to exclude the ecclesiastical judges entirely from the trials[3]—but it was the viceroy's policy to uphold the system of joint prosecution whenever these attempts to modify it were brought to his attention.[4]

2. REBELLION AND THE TOTAL ABOLITION OF ECCLESIASTICAL IMMUNITY

The modified system of joint prosecution, which retained little more than the appearance of equal jurisdiction as a concession to ecclesiastical immunity, functioned smoothly and effectively as long as the government had the task of controlling an increasingly restless but still non-violent independence movement. Rather than punishment, the government's objective in the pre-revolutionary period was to 'rid these provinces of disturbing and dangerous elements',[5] so that ecclesiastics, and

---

[1] See, e.g., A.G.N., Infidencias 10 and 11, no. 4, Trial of lay and ecclesiastical members of a conspiracy in Oaxaca, 1811, conducted by the Oaxacan *Junta* and submitted to the Mexican *Junta* for confirmation.

[2] A.G.N., Operaciones de guerra 1011, Archbishop of Mexico to Venegas, 5 Jan. 1811, complying with the *Junta*'s request to appoint a permanent delegate.

[3] See A.G.N., Historia 411, Sumaria contra Fr Bernardino de la Sma. Trinidad, 1811 (Oaxaca); and Infidencias 165, Juez eclesiástico de Veracruz, Ignacio López de Luna, to Venegas, 14 Dec. 1811.

[4] A.G.N., Obispos y arzobispos 3, Dictamen Junta de seguridad, 18 Jan. 1811.

[5] A.H.N., Consejos 21203, Distamen Fiscal, 14 June 1809.

---

[6] See, e.g., A.G.N., Infidencias 172, nos. 55–6, Trial of Fr Francisco Antelo, 1811.

P

laymen, convicted of treason were simply deported to Spain[1] (or, in the first conspiracy trial, to an overseas *presidio*).[2] Although the direct prosecution by secular judges and the judicial sentence of exile were innovations, the final result did not differ from the extra-judicial method of deportation by which royal officials had controlled unruly or delinquent ecclesiastics since the beginning of the colonial period. Even when the crime, supported by incontrovertible (in the opinion of the court) proof, was serious enough to merit the death penalty, the Mexican authorities were not yet prepared to impose capital punishment on an ecclesiastic in Mexico, where the clergy were 'so universally venerated',[3] but preferred the more prudent solution of sending the convict to Spain with the record of his trial, so that the Spanish government could take the responsibility of deciding his fate.[4]

But as soon as the growing political discontent was expressed in open rebellion, the traditional method of dealing with delinquent ecclesiastics was no longer considered adequate. Not only was it impracticable to ship large numbers of rebels to Spain (itself involved in a bitter struggle against foreign conquest), but also the government felt that it could no longer afford to be lenient: the enormity of the crime of rebellion and the grave danger threatening the colonial régime demanded the imposition of the death penalty on all insurgents, whatever their status, as retribution for the bloodshed, destruction of property, and social and political chaos they had caused.[5] The immunity of the ecclesiastical insurgents could not be considered an impediment. On the contrary, royal officials were convinced that so many members of the clergy had joined the rebellion precisely because their privileged status encouraged them to believe that they had nothing to fear. And since the

---

[1] A.G.I., Mexico 1474, Lista de los reos de estado que se remiten con sus causas, 12 Feb. 1810.

[2] A.G.I., Estado 39, R.C. to viceroy, 27 March 1800.

[3] A.G.I., Mexico 1662, Pedro Catani (Regent Audiencia) to Junta Central, 15 July 1809.

[4] See *ibid.*, Trial of Fr Melchor de Talamantes, 1808; A.H.N., Consejos 21081, Trial of Fr Miguel Zugasti, 1809 (though both he and Talamantes died in Veracruz awaiting deportation); and Consejos 21203, Trial of Manuel Palacios, 1809.

[5] A.G.I., Mexico 1321, Venegas to Calleja, 13 April 1811.

clergy contributed such decisive support to the rebellion, the royalists believed that one of the most vital steps for its suppression was a public declaration that 'these monsters neither deserve immunity nor will be spared any consideration because of it'.[1]

This public declaration appeared in the form of a viceregal *bando*, dated 25 June 1812, which abolished the last vestiges of *fuero* and the privilege of the canon in one blow by authorizing the royalist military commanders to try all ecclesiastical insurgents without any intervention from the ecclesiastical courts and to execute them without prior degradation.[2]

Viceroy Francisco Xavier de Venegas had postponed this measure as long as possible in deference to public opinion, explaining that 'one of the major conflicts facing me is the choice of a policy capable of restraining them [ecclesiastical insurgents] in such a way that will not scandalize, offend, or produce dangerous consequences'.[3] But by the middle of 1812, events had forced the government to the conclusion that it had no choice: its existence was in serious jeopardy from an increasingly successful rebellion that was, in the opinion of the royalists, almost solely the handiwork of ecclesiastics'.[4] Apparently extinguished in 1811 after the capture of its original leaders, the rebellion rapidly recovered strength, and by 1813 a large part of the vice-royalty's territory was in rebel hands, except the major cities—isolated pockets of royalism able to communicate with each other only by infrequent and extremely hazardous military convoys.[5]

Believing that this rebellion would disintegrate without the clergy's leadership (which may or may not have been an optimistic view), the government also became convinced that so long as any concession was made to the immunity of ecclesiastical insurgents they could neither be punished effectively nor deterred from joining the rebellion in the first place.

[1] A.G.I., Mexico 1664, Pedro de la Puente to Regency Council, 15 Dec. 1812. See also *ibid.*, Informe Audiencia of Mexico, 18 Nov. 1813, párr. 42.
[2] Bando, 25 June 1812, párr. 7 and 10, in *Gaceta del gobierno*, 30 June 1812.
[3] A.G.I., Mexico 1321, Venegas to Minister of War, 27 Jan. 1811.
[4] A.G.I., Mexico 2571, Carta pastoral, Bishop-elect of Michoacán, 26 Sept. 1812.
[5] See A.G.I., Mexico 1664, Informe Audiencia of Mexico, 18 Nov. 1813, describing conditions in the viceroyalty.

Moreover, without the threat of execution, they were not spurred to seek the *indultos*, or amnesties, offered to all rebels who abandoned the movement voluntarily; or, if they did obtain an *indulto*, they simply took up arms again when it suited them. One priest was able to repeat this stratagem three times during the course of the war.[1] The policy of leniency followed in the early treason cases had also backfired, for some of the ecclesiastics had been released or permitted to return from exile only to join the rebellion at the first opportunity.[2]

But although it became apparent to the royalists that the only way of 'restraining' these insurgents was to execute any rebel priest they could capture, it became equally apparent that the intervention of the ecclesiastical courts, which had presented no problem in the pre-revolutionary trials of seditious ecclesiastics, could be an insurmountable obstacle as soon as the question of capital punishment arose. The privilege of the *fuero* had already been reduced to a nominal status, but the privilege of the canon, which required the degradation of an ecclesiastic by his bishop before he could be put to death, had so far remained intact, and not all the bishops were prepared to treat this last vestige of immunity as a mere formality also.

The various aspects of this conflict are best illustrated in the case of the ecclesiastical insurgents, Hidalgo among them, captured at Norias de Baján, Coahuila, in March 1811.[3] Hidalgo was taken along with the other leaders—Ignacio Allende, Juan Aldama, Mariano Abasolo, and Mariano Jiménez —to Chihuahua, the capital of the Provincias Internas, where they were all tried by a court martial and, with the exception of Abasolo who was granted a reprieve, condemned to death.[4]

The intervention of ecclesiastical jurisdiction in Hidalgo's

---

[1] A.G.N., Infidencias 160, nos. 65–80, Proceso formado al cura de Nopala, José Manuel Correa, 1817. See also Operaciones de Guerra 1013, Abad y Queipo (Bishop-elect of Michoacán) to Venegas, 20 Sept. 1812, mentioning other examples.

[2] A.G.I., Mexico 1482, Declaración de Fr Manuel Gutiérrez Solano, mentioning Fr Vicente de Santa María, involved in the 1809 Valladolid conspiracy; and Los Guadalupes to Morelos, 15 Dec. 1813, mentioning Manuel Palacios, convicted of subversion in 1809.

[3] *D.H.M.*, vi, 95–8, Relación de los individuos aprehendidos en Norias de Baján, 21 March 1811.

[4] The records of the trials of Hidalgo and his companions are published in J. Hernández y Dávalos, *op. cit.*, i, 7–76.

trial resulted in a slight delay, for he was not executed until more than a month after his co-defendants. But this delay was due only to technical difficulties. The associate ecclesiastical judge appointed by the Bishop of Durango had no part in the trial other than to examine the records of the hearings, and he co-operated readily by pronouncing the charges 'well proven'.[1] But when requested to defrock Hidalgo, he demurred on the ground that only a consecrated bishop could perform this ceremony. The bishop was consulted and authorized, in fact ordered, his delegate to pronounce the sentence of degradation and reduce Hidalgo to lay status[2] (an impressive ceremony which involved stripping the culprit of his priestly robes and symbolically erasing the signs of his status, such as the clerical tonsure). With the removal of this obstacle, the death penalty was carried out on 1 August 1811, less than a month after the formal petition for degradation had been made.[3]

The ten other ecclesiastics captured with Hidalgo, four regulars and six secular priests, were sent to Durango for their trial. The *Comandante General* of the Provincias Internas had fore-seen that, while the degradation of Hidalgo—who was after all the leader of the rebellion with the rank of *generalísimo*—would be virtually automatic, it would be more difficult to secure the same sentence against those lesser figures, most of whom were no more than chaplains, and for that reason had decided that they should be prosecuted in the diocesan see.[4]

His fears were justified. Although six of the prisoners were promptly condemned to death (the other four were eventually exiled),[5] the bishop insisted upon exercising his independent judgement in the degradation trial and refused to agree with the military court's verdict or its sentence. He distinguished between the enormous and freely confessed guilt of Hidalgo and the less serious crime of these ecclesiastics who, according

---

[1] J. Hernández y Daválos, *op. cit.*, i, 22, Dr Francisco Fernández Valentín to Asesor Rafael Bracho, 14 June 1811.

[2] *Ibid.*, i, 44–5, Bishop Gabriel Olivares to Fernández Valentín, 18 July 1811.

[3] *Ibid.*, i, 31–4, Dictamen Asesor Rafael Bracho, 3 July 1811; p. 35, Auto Comandante General Nemesio Salcedo, 4 July 1811.

[4] *D.H.M.*, vi, 101–2, Nemesio Salcedo to interim Governor of Coahuila, 28 March 1811.

[5] See, e.g., A.G.N., Infidencias 160, no. 145, Trial of José Francisco Olmedo, 1811–13. See also below, pp. 220–1.

to the evidence provided, had not borne arms but only administered the sacraments to the rebel troops.[1] The governor
threatened to execute them even without degradation, if the
bishop would not yield; but it was only after the governor
received the *bando* of 25 June 1812 a year later, declaring
degradation unnecessary, and the bishop had conveniently
died, that the death penalty was finally carried out.[2]

In publishing the *bando*, the viceroy's intention was to
eliminate any obstacles to a swift and effective suppression of
the rebellion and to impose a uniform method of dealing with
all insurgents, regardless of their status. Ecclesiastical *fuero* was
abolished completely, since all captured insurgents were subjected to exclusive military jurisdiction—to be sentenced 'with
the brevity of the ordinance' rather than the formalities of
civil judicial procedure.[3] In areas under military control even
cases of subversion, as well as rebellion, were tried by courts
martial. In Jalapa, for example, which already had a civilian
Junta de seguridad, a 'council of war' was created in 1812, which
prosecuted a Creole canon on the charge of spying for the
insurgents, in spite of interference from the old *Junta* and the
local ecclesiastical judge on the grounds that the accused had
not been captured in battle and thus was not legally subject
to military jurisdiction.[4]

This clause of the *bando* was neither a startling innovation nor
a radical departure from existing royal legislation. Although
never published in the Indies and therefore technically without
legal force, a law of the Caroline *Nuevo Código* had already provided for the abolition of ecclesiastical *fuero* in favour of military
jurisdiction in the event of armed rebellion.[5] In practice, this

---

[1] Official records of the trial are not available, but material referring to it and
to the controversy between the bishop and governor is contained in A.H.N.,
Consejos 21215, Expediente promovido con motivo de haber hallado en Durango
un pasquín revolucionario por haber condenado a muerte a seis clérigos . . .,
1812, and confirms the versions given by C. M. Bustamente, *Cuadro histórico*, ii,
277–8; and L. Alamán, *op. cit.*, ii, 157.

[2] A.H.N., Consejos 21215, Governor of Durango, Bernardo Bonavía, to Nemesio
Salcedo, 20 July 1812, informing him that the six had been executed on 17 July.

[3] Bando, 25 June 1812, párr. 2, *Gaceta del gobierno*, 30 June 1812.

[4] A.G.I., Mexico 1477, Testimonio del expediente de la creación de la Comisión
militar ejecutiva, 1812.

[5] A.G.I., Mexico 1159, note on ley 13, título 12, Libro 1, of the Nuevo Código.

jurisdiction had already replaced the civil courts in many areas occupied by royalist troops, and ecclesiastics charged with subversion, as well as captured rebels, had been tried by military courts and sentenced by royalist commanders without any delegate from the diocesan court.[1] The *bando* merely made this practice uniform throughout the viceroyalty.

Thus the main innovation contained in the *bando* was the formal abolition of the privilege of the canon, a privilege that even the ultra-regalist authors of the *Nuevo Código* had not dared challenge. In the first years of the war, the royalist military officers had spared the lives of ecclesiastical insurgents because of their privileged status: after the battle of Aculco (November 1810), for example, all the rebel lay officers were executed after a summary court-martial, and the rank and file *quintados* (one in five shot),[2] but the two captured priests, although guilty of the same crime, were sentenced to imprisonment instead.[3] And even when the military courts did impose the death penalty on an ecclesiastic, they still respected the privilege of the canon, recommending that the prisoner be defrocked before his sentence was carried out.[4]

However, this concession to ecclesiastical privilege was extremely onerous to the royalist commanders and became more so as the rebellion increased in scope and intensity. Only a few months after the Dolores uprising one commander had complained to the viceroy of the 'extraordinary difficulties' presented by the ecclesiastical rebels, whom he could not execute 'without a multitude of formulas and legal procedures for which I have neither the time nor the personnel to spare'.[5] But although Viceroy Venegas had instructed at least one officer (General Félix María Calleja) in early 1811 to execute

[1] See, e.g., A.G.N., Infidencias 99, nos 9–11, Trial of Fr Luis Oroñoz, (San Luis Potosí), 1811; Infidencias 134, no. 17, José de la Cruz to Venegas (Michoacán), 24 Nov. 1810; and B.N., 3650, Trial of Hermenegildo Montes (Michoacán), 1811, a subversive.

[2] A.G.N., Infidencias 5, Trials of prisoners captured in battle of Aculco, 1810.

[3] A.G.N., Infidencias 99, no. 3, Trial of Dr José Abad y Cuadra, 1811; Infidencias 114, nos 1–4, Trial of Dr José Gastañeta, 1811.

[4] See, e.g., A.G.N., Historia 412, no. 1, Trial of Fr Juan Salazar, 1811 (Monclova), in addition to the trials of Hidalgo and the other ecclesiastics captured with him.

[5] A.G.N., Infidencias 134, no. 42, José de la Cruz to Venegas, 31 Dec. 1810.

all rebels as soon as captured 'especially if they are clerics or friars' (presumably more culpable than lay rebels),[1] it seems that the officers were not prepared to take this drastic step without a specific authorization from the viceroy in each case or a public statement of official government policy.[2] Thus many of them were encumbered in their campaigns by ecclesiastical prisoners or forced to detach troops they could ill afford to spare to escort the prisoners to the nearest diocesan see for trial[3] (with the risk of escape *en route*);[4] and even then there was no guarantee that further time and trouble would not be wasted in unsuccessful attempts to secure the rebels' degradation.

Shortly before the *bando*'s publication several officers had apparently become sufficiently exasperated to dispense with these formalities required by law and to order the summary execution of captured insurgent priests without even benefit of trial.[5] The viceregal *bando*, in ordering this same practice to be followed as a general rule, not only sanctioned these acts but also provided an answer to the inquiries from more cautious officers, some of whom hastened to execute the undefrocked ecclesiastics in their custody, whose lives had been spared for over a year after they had been condemned to death.[6]

A few ecclesiastical superiors sought to protect their subjects from execution by refusing to defrock them,[7] but none protested against either the *bando* itself or the extreme violations

[1] J. Hernández y Dávalos, *op. cit.*, ii, 408, Venegas to Calleja, 22 Feb. 1811.

[2] A.G.N., Historia 409, no. 6, Expediente formado en el Real Acuerdo acerca de si el virrey puede o no mandar a los comandantes de división . . ., 1812.

[3] See, e.g., dispatches from royalist officers published in the *Gaceta del Gobierno*, 26 Feb. 1811, 9 June 1812, 25 June 1812 and 11 July 1812.

[4] The justification given for the one recorded execution of an ecclesiastic (Fr Luis de Herrera) without degradation before 1812: Col. Joaquín Arredondo to Venegas, 17 April 1811, *Gaceta del gobierno*, 10 May 1811.

[5] Three recorded cases: José Guadalupe Salto, executed in Valladolid; and José Luis Tirado and an unidentified cleric, both executed in Tenancingo, *Gaceta del gobierno*, 11 June and 20 June 1812.

[6] Fr Juan de Salazar, condemned to death in May 1811, was executed in Monclova at approximately the same time as the six ecclesiastics in Durango (July 1812), according to A. Villaseñor y Villaseñor, *Biografías de los héroes y caudillos de la Independencia* (2 vols., Mexico, 1910), i, 164.

[7] A.H.N., Consejos 21215, Governor of Durango to Nemesio Salcedo, 20 July 1812, reporting that the *sede vacante* chapter had also refused to defrock the six. See also below, pp. 221–2, for a similar case in Mexico.

of immunity it authorized. One bishop, on learning extra-officially of a curate's execution, merely asked the viceroy to confirm this information so that he might know whether or not to declare the benefice vacant and appoint an interim curate.[1] The Bishop-elect of Michoacán published a pastoral letter in defence of the *bando*, calling it a 'just, beneficial and necessary' measure, and arguing that degradation was, in any case, only a ceremony without any legal effect.[2] But he was alone in his public approval. A few bishops expressed privately the view that an ecclesiastic automatically forfeited his immunity by committing the enormous crime of rebellion, 'so alien to the priestly character'.[3] Others regarded the execution of an un-defrocked priest as a deplorable violation of immunity but one that should be overlooked for the sake of their own reputations: the clergy were already so suspect, they argued, that any protests would risk the charge of disloyalty and sympathy with the revolution.[4] As one ecclesiastical jurist prudently suggested, the best method under the circumstances of preserving immunity was not to become involved in the rebellion.[5]

The rebels and even members of the royalist clergy condemned the hierarchy's failure to defend immunity and the interests of the Church.[6] But, aside from their reluctance to jeopardize their own position with futile protests, the bishops believed that the Church could not survive without the maintenance of order and civil obedience, so that the struggle against revolution was synonymous with the defence of religion,[7]

---

[1] A.G.N., Operaciones de guerra 1011, Archbishop-elect of Mexico to Viceroy Calleja, 2 July 1814.

[2] A.G.I., Mexico 2571, Carta pastoral, 26 Sept. 1812.

[3] A.H.N., Consejos 21212, Dictamen Bishop of Puebla, 25 Aug. 1811; and Dictamen Bishop of Oaxaca, 10 Sept. 1811.

[4] *Ibid.*, Dictámenes Bishops of Nuevo León and Guadalajara, 19 Aug. and 29 Aug. 1811.

[5] A.G.N., Historia 409, Respuesta Promotor Fiscal, Archdiocese of Mexico, 11 July 1812.

[6] A.G.I., Ind. Gen. 110, Proclama del Dr Cos (against Abad y Queipo), 27 March 1811; *D.H.M.*, iv, 'Sud', 25 Jan. 1813; and C. M. Bustamante, *Cuadro histórico*, ii, 156. A 'Representación que hace el clero mexicano al Venerable Deán y Cabildo', 6 July 1812, published in *D.H.M.*, iii, 'Semanario patriótico americano', 26 July 1812, was signed by royalist clerics as well as rebel sympathizers.

[7] A.G.N., Operaciones de guerra 1013, Bishop of Oaxaca to Venegas, 19 Nov. 1810; and Abad y Queipo to Venegas, 23 Nov. 1812.

a cause in which the temporary abolition of ecclesiastical privileges seemed a relatively minor sacrifice.

The *bando* of 1812 was not directed solely against ecclesiastical immunity, but was the expression of a general policy of 'sangra y fuego' that the royalists had developed in answer to the increasing danger to their own lives and property.[1] By far the most legally questionable aspect of this official policy, as outlined in the *bando*, was the blanket authorization to put to death all prisoners without any judicial proceedings whatsoever. The minimum safeguards of a summary court martial and confirmation of the sentence by the viceroy, established in one paragraph, were made illusory by another, which permitted the officers to carry out executions immediately and at their own discretion if circumstances so demanded.[2] Thus the application of the *bando* varied, as did the rigour of reprisals in general, according to the whim of the individual officers. Some were extremely severe. Brigadier José de la Cruz, commander of the Guadalajara district, was criticized by the *audiencia* for his methods, which 'varied only between the scaffold and the firing squad'.[3] And the Creole Colonel Agustín de Iturbide was considered particularly sanguinary, even when indiscriminate executions were far from uncommon among other royalist officers.[4]

It is impossible to say how rigorously the *bando* was applied against ecclesiastical insurgents. Even the official record contained in the *Gaceta del gobierno de Mexico*, in which the dispatches of the royalist officers were published, is not totally reliable, for reports of summary executions of priests were sometimes suppressed, doubtlessly in deference to public opinion: either the viceroy ordered that the item be omitted from the *Gaceta*[5]

---

[1] For earlier expressions of this policy, see A.G.I., Mexico 1321, Plan de operaciones de campaña, Calleja, 17 Dec. 1810; and Mexico 1635, Venegas to Regency Council, 6 March 1811.

[2] *Bando*, 25 June 1812, párr. 3 and 5.

[3] A.G.I., Guadalajara 317, Audiencia to the king, 16 June 1817.

[4] L. Alamán, *op. cit.*, iv, 348–9. See also W. S. Robertson, *Iturbide of Mexico* (Durham, N.C., 1952), pp. 30–1, 34.

[5] C. M. Bustamante, *Cuadro histórico*, iii, 350, quotes a note by Calleja's secretary to this effect attached to a dispatch from Col. Manuel de la Concha, 27 June 1816, while all the other dispatches from Concha from that same month are published in *Gaceta del gobierno*, 3 July 1816.

or the officer himself failed to mention the incident.[1] One observer estimated that from the start of the rebellion in 1810 until the end of 1815, 125 priests had been executed by the royalists.[2] Another contemporary author spoke less precisely of the 'copious number of precious victims sacrificed for our liberty', concluding that an accurate list could not be made without consulting all the diocesan records in Mexico;[3] but even then it would be incomplete, since the bishops themselves were not always notified.

What is certain is that the general practice was to shoot all prisoners as soon as captured because, according to one royalist officer, if there were no survivors of a skirmish, the officer could exaggerate his victory and gain promotion more quickly.[4] Almost every military operation successful to royalist arms was followed by a report of the number of prisoners captured and executed on the spot, among them ecclesiastics who had not been tried or defrocked.[5] The practice of disregarding the minimum requirements of even a perfunctory court martial could result in the execution of innocent neutrals, who (at least according to the rebels themselves) were not necessarily even sympathetic with the cause of independence, much less active revolutionaries, but simply happened to be in rebel-held territory when the royalists advanced.[6]

A trial, regardless of the loss of immunity, could be an advantage even to bona fide insurgents, for it meant that the

[1] C. M. Bustamante, *Cuadro histórico*, iii, 98, and dispatch of Capt. Félix de la Madrid, *Gaceta*, 24 March 1814; L. Alamán, *op. cit.*, iv, 645, and dispatch of Sarg. José Castro in *Gaceta*, 19 Nov. 1817.

[2] M. Cuevas, *Historia de la iglesia en México*, v, 92, quoting from a manuscript 'Tablas de la Nueva España' cited as being in the Genaro García Collection of the University of Texas Library. However, a recent search by a staff member of the University Library has failed to reveal its whereabouts.

[3] C. M. Bustamante, *Cuadro histórico* (the author's revised version, republished in 3 vols., Mexico, 1961), i, 447.

[4] A.G.I., Ind. Gen. 110, Col. Francisco Crespo Gil to Venegas (in Spain), 16 Aug. 1814.

[5] The following issues of the *Gaceta del gobierno* contain reports on the immediate execution of one or more captured ecclesiastics: 8 Aug. 1812, 5 Jan. 1813, 2 Jan. 1814, 5 May 1814 and 11 Jan. 1815. See also L. Alamán, *op. cit.*, iv, 295, 348, for other examples.

[6] A.G.I., Ind. Gen. 110, 'Aviso al público', José de Herrera, 26 Aug. 1814; 'Proclama del cabecilla Rayón a los europeos', 19 Aug. 1814; and C. M. Bustamante, *Cuadro histórico* (unrevised version) ii, 125.

punishment imposed would be based on a more substantial criterion than the whim of one enemy officer. This was especially true with ecclesiastics. The 1812 *bando* actually discriminated against them (the death penalty was to be applied to lay rebels only from the rank of second lieutenant upwards, but to all ecclesiastics regardless of rank or occupation);[1] but a priest who escaped immediate execution on the battlefield had a good chance of obtaining a less severe sentence if, in the course of his trial, he could convince the court either that he had served only as a chaplain, that he had been compelled to join the rebel forces, or that he was planning to seek an *indulto* when captured.[2]

One author has asserted that 'the insurgent who was able to get one word recorded in a formal trial could consider himself safe'.[3] Although this is an exaggeration (for example, a priest was condemned to death in 1813 who, though claiming to be a non-combatant, had fired on his royalist captors and was in fact a rebel officer),[4] the time factor certainly did work in favour of the defendant, mainly by permitting the spirit of reprisal to dampen. Aside from the major leaders, such as Hidalgo, Morelos and Matamoros, most ecclesiastics brought to trial were spared from capital punishment and sentenced to imprisonment even when they had been convicted of freely bearing arms against His Majesty's forces.[5]

One prisoner who consciously turned a trial to his advantage was a Carmelite friar captured with Hidalgo in 1811. Although one of the leaders of the 1810 uprising in San Luis Potosí (his co-defendants eventually executed in Durango had only been chaplains), he was able to convince one set of judges that he had been a prisoner of the rebels and then to draw out the proceedings for years after the trial had been moved to San Luis Potosí for further investigations, so that the military court

---

[1] *Bando*, 25 June 1812, párr. 7.

[2] See, e.g., A.G.N., Infidencias 86, no. 6, Trial of Anastasio de Benavente, 1814; Infidencias 87, Trial of Fr Felipe Conejo, 1816; Infidencias 76, no. 5, Trial of Rafael Ayala, 1815.   [3] L. Alamán, *op. cit.*, iv, 512.

[4] A.G.N., Infidencias 130, no. 91, Trial of Mariano Ortega Muro, 1813.

[5] See, e.g., A.G.N., Infidencias 169, no. 36, Trial of Fr Manuel Gutiérrez Solano, 1813; Infidencias 177, nos. 35–9, Trial of Francisco Velasco de la Vara, 1814; and Infidencias 94, nos. 10 and 11, Trial of José María Zamudio, 1815.

finally sentenced him to exile, in view of his long imprisonment, rather than to death, which according to law he deserved.[1]

In his *bando* Viceroy Venegas had removed the final vestige of ecclesiastical immunity—the privilege of the canon—but the obstacle of public opinion was more stubborn and could not be eliminated by executive decree. The factor of public opinion had the heaviest influence in the two *audiencia* capitals, Guadalajara and Mexico, and the contrast between the practice followed there and the official policy for military areas was striking: the government never curtailed ecclesiastical immunity in the two capitals beyond the modified system of joint prosecution (i.e., ecclesiastical intervention reduced to a subordinate role) originally adapted from the *Nuevo Código* law during the pre-revolutionary period. Nor was any ecclesiastic ever put to death there, even though one, the insurgent leader Morelos, was formally degraded by the ecclesiastical authorities in Mexico: fearing public demonstrations, the viceroy ordered Morelos to be executed secretly in a small village on the outskirts of the capital.[2]

Though the system of joint prosecution persisted until the end of the war, it did not necessarily function as effectively as it had prior to the rebellion. In fact the delays and ultimate frustration of justice resulting from ecclesiastical intervention in one particular trial—that of eight Creole friars who, along with several militia officers, had plotted to assassinate Viceroy Venegas and deliver the capital to the insurgent forces—had been one of the major causes of the 1812 *bando*.[3] The lay conspirators were convicted and executed within several weeks of the plot's discovery,[4] but the friars were saved from this punishment by the archdiocesan court's refusal to degrade them, despite the determination of the royal judges that they should 'pay with their lives for this execrable crime'.[5]

[1] The records of the lengthy trial of Fr Gregorio de la Concepción, 1811–17, are scattered in A.G.N., Infidencias 68, no. 3; 176, nos. 74–8; and 177, no. 152.
[2] A.G.N., Infidencias 181, Col. Manuel de la Concha to Calleja, 22 Dec. 1815, reporting that the viceroy's instructions had been carried out that afternoon.
[3] P. de la Puente, *Reflexiones sobre el bando de 25 de junio último contraídas a lo que dispone para con los eclesiásticos rebeldes.* . . (Mexico, 1812), p. 115.
[4] L. Alamán, *op. cit.*, ii, 283–4.
[5] A.H.N., Consejos 21212, Auto Junta de seguridad, 12 Aug. 1811.

The hierarchy's intransigence in this case was not as inconsistent with their acceptance of the 1812 *bando* as first appears. Here again their attitude depended on the nature of the crime. None of the defendants was accused of armed rebellion and, although the *Junta de seguridad* had found all of them guilty of conspiracy to the same degree, the *sede vacante* archdiocesan court distinguished between the crime of the one ringleader, whom it agreed to defrock, and that of the other seven, who were merely accessories and who therefore deserved neither degradation nor the death sentence in the opinion of the court.[1]

Considering this distinction invalid, the *Junta* was still pressing for a retrial in the ecclesiastical court when the viceregal *bando* declaring degradation unnecessary was published. But although the *Junta* argued that this clause applied to ecclesiastics guilty of conspiracy as well as those engaged in rebellion, the viceroy declined to carry out the death penalty even on the one friar whom the ecclesiastical court had agreed to defrock.[2] Perhaps he still hoped that the court could be forced into defrocking the other seven; more likely he agreed with one of the *oidores* that the friar's execution so long after the crime 'would be inopportune, and possibly worse'.[3]

Thus the *bando*'s publication, which had been the signal for the execution of other condemned ecclesiastics outside the capital, had absolutely no influence on the fate of these friars, who remained in prison until the government, having abandoned its futile efforts to secure the penalty 'demanded by public vengeance', sent them into exile instead.[4] There had never been any question of applying the death penalty, or the procedure established by the *bando*, in the trials of the other ecclesiastics implicated in the same conspiracy, but to a lesser degree (for example, those failing to denounce the cache of weapons stored in the monastery cells),[5] and those accused of minor forms of subversion, such as 'suspicious conversations',

---

[1] B.N., 20245, Respuesta Promotor Fiscal, 10 Sept. 1811; and A.H.N., Consejos 21212, Auto Junta eclesiástica, 19 Sept. 1811.

[2] *Ibid.*, Auto Calleja, 15 July 1814.

[3] P. de la Puente, *op. cit.*, p. 115.

[4] A.H.N., Consejos 21212, Auto Viceroy Apodaca, 23 Sept. 1817.

[5] A.G.I., Mexico 1476, Causa seguida a los padres Fr Manuel Suárez y Fr Pedro Rivera, 1811.

'seditious sermons', and 'clandestine communication with the enemy'.[1] After a brief joint trial, these defendants were simply sentenced by the viceroy to exile or to varying terms of imprisonment without any prior degradation.

In January 1813, the viceroy introduced one change in the system first established in 1809, which brought the practice followed in civilian areas closer to the policy outlined in the 1812 *bando* for military zones. The new *Constitución política de la monarquía española*, issued in 1812 by the Spanish *Cortes*, had provided a set of judicial safeguards more comprehensive than those of the old law code, among them the right of all citizens to be tried by the ordinary royal courts instead of by special tribunals, regardless of the crime.[2] But Viceroy Venegas, after promulgating the Constitution in New Spain, either ignored the clauses that in his opinion would interfere with the suppression of the revolution or suspended them after a brief trial period.[3] The suppression of the *Juntas de seguridad*, also decreed explicitly in separate communications from the *Cortes*,[4] was in fact carried out, as Viceroy Calleja assured the government.[5] What he failed to mention was that the *Juntas* had simply been replaced by another type of extraordinary tribunal: permanent military courts composed of royalist officers established in all the major cities.[6] Thus exclusive military jurisdiction over all cases of treason as well as rebellion was made uniform throughout the viceroyalty.

This extension of military jurisdiction made little difference in the prosecution of ecclesiastics, who were still accorded a joint trial and, in Mexico at least, the same associate judges from the old *Junta* (*Oidor* Miguel Bataller and *Provisor* Félix Flores Alatorre) continued to conduct these trials. The only

[1] C. M. Bustamante, *Martirologio de algunos de los primeros insurgentes por la libertad e independencia de la América mexicana* (Mexico, 1841), pp. 11–12, 15, 22, 27, 34, from the original files of the Mexican *Junta de seguridad*.

[2] *Constitución política de la monarquía española* (Cádiz, 1812), arts. 247, 261. See arts. 287, 290, 300 for other new judicial safeguards.

[3] For example, liberty of the press, abolished after two months: see below, pp. 233–4, 235.

[4] A.G.I., Mexico 1662, R.O., 26 Aug. 1811; Mexico 1664, R.O., 18 June 1813.

[5] A.G.I., Mexico 1480, Calleja to Minister of Gracia y Justicia, 31 Dec. 1813.

[6] A.G.N., Impresos oficiales 34, no. 23, Reglamento formado para el gobierno de los Consejos de guerra permanentes . . ., Venegas, 6 Jan. 1813.

difference was that a committee of royalist officers instead of the civilian *Junta de seguridad* pronounced the verdict and recommended the appropriate sentence for the viceroy's confirmation.[1]

If anything, the privilege of immunity regained some ground in this period, for the ecclesiastical judge was permitted to participate in the trials of all ecclesiastics in the major cities, even those of captured insurgents. And when the crime was 'atrocious and notorious' enough to warrant the death penalty without question[2]—as in the case of Morelos and his second in command, Matamoros—the defendants were also given a formal degradation trial before they were executed,[3] though the 1812 *bando* had declared this proceeding unnecessary. Less eminent insurgents, as well as conspirators and other subversives, were dealt with according to the old policy of separating them from society, either by imprisonment in the colony or by exile to an overseas *presidio*—the favoured one being Ceuta in North Africa.[4]

3. REACTIONS TO THE ABOLITION OF ECCLESIASTICAL IMMUNITY

During the first years of the insurrection in Mexico the chaotic conditions in Spain and the disruption of sea communications had prevented the Spanish government from exercising much influence over events in the Indies. But after the withdrawal of the French from Spain, the Crown began to re-establish control over the colonial governments, particularly over their methods of suppressing the Creole rebellions. Neither Ferdinand VII

[1] A.G.N., Infidencias 65, no. 3, and 169, no. 110, Trial of Domingo Garfías, 1814.

[2] A.G.N., Infidencias 181, Archbishop-elect of Mexico to Calleja, 22 Nov. 1815, referring to Morelos.

[3] *Proceso del caudillo de la Independencia don Mariano Matamoros* (Publicaciones del Archivo General de la Nación, Mexico, 1918), tried and executed in Valladolid, Jan.–Feb. 1814. For records of the trial, degradation and execution of Morelos in Mexico, Nov.–Dec. 1815, see A.G.N., Infidencias 180 & 181.

[4] See A.G.N., Infidencias 92, no. 9; 58, no. 6; 85, no. 2; 63 (entire); and 171, no. 10, for trials of seditious ecclesiastics, 1813–17. See Infidencias 76, no. 5; 86, no. 3; 94, nos. 10 and 11; and 115, nos. 4–8, for trials of insurgents in the same period.

nor his newly reinstated Council of the Indies was indifferent to the danger of losing these valuable colonies, but they disapproved of the harsh policy the colonial authorities had followed in their efforts to suppress the independence movements. Ferdinand preferred to regain the rebels' loyalty with 'equity, prudence, and clemency',[1] and, in accordance with this general directive, the Council ordered the American officials to follow a new policy of conciliation: reprisals were forbidden in general and especially the wholesale execution of captured rebels, who were to be deported if they could not be securely imprisoned in the colonies.[2]

It is possible that the rigour of reprisals in Mexico would have softened in any case, in response to changing conditions within the colony, for by the time the new viceroy, Juan Ruiz de Apodaca, had replaced Calleja in September 1816 the revolution seemed clearly discredited and almost defeated. The royalist troops had reduced the rebel armies to scattered bands of guerrillas who could cause much damage but were no longer a serious threat to Spanish rule.[3] Royalist officers could afford to be more magnanimous in their victories: they spared the lives of their defeated antagonists more often than not and even granted surrender terms to the defenders of the two rebel fortresses of Mexcala and Cóporo, terms which included a guarantee that the rebels could return freely to their homes and occupations without any harassment.[4]

But the Council's *cédulas*, later reinforced by an order from the Ministry of War prohibiting the punishment of any insurgent without both a proper trial and the viceroy's confirmation of the sentence,[5] were undoubtedly the decisive factors in the return to the milder, pre-revolutionary policies and in the general restoration of the rule of law in the viceroyalty. The timely arrival in early 1818 of the Ministry of War's order saved the lives of a number of recently captured rebel leaders,

---

[1] A.G.I., Mexico 1147, Consulta Council of the Indies, 18 May 1818, quoting from R.O.'s of 1814 and 1815.

[2] A.G.N., Reales cédulas 213, no. 75, R.C. circular, 24 Aug. 1815; Reales cédulas 215, no. 188, R.C., 7 May 1816.

[3] A.G.I., Mexico 1680, Apodaca to Minister of Ultramar, 21 Jan. 1817.

[4] *Ibid.*, Apodaca to Minister of Ultramar, 8 Jan. 1818.

[5] A.G.N., Historia 412, no. 10, R.O. circular, 28 July 1817.

Q

among them Ignacio Rayón, whose death warrants were hastily revoked and replaced with an order for a full trial according to the code of military justice.[1] In general all prisoners were given a formal hearing from then on, and one royalist officer was actually himself prosecuted for violating the new instructions by executing prisoners without the viceroy's approval, though the charges were eventually dropped in view of the officer's long record of faithful service.[2]

There was no question of restoring the privileges of the ecclesiastical insurgents. It was simply no longer considered necessary or wise to execute those who were captured, but this was a general policy and ecclesiastics were treated in exactly the same way as the lay prisoners. Both were tried by a military court[3] (though sometimes with the intervention of an ecclesiastical judge, a practice that had never entirely disappeared[4]) and either deported to another Spanish possession where it was felt they could do no harm, or held in prison until the new general amnesty of 1820 secured their release.[5]

Although it sent no specific condemnation of the abolition of ecclesiastical immunity in Mexico, the Madrid government was sharply critical of this measure, along with the other aspects of the policy of 'sangre y fuego' introduced by Viceroy Venegas and continued by his successor Calleja. This policy was common to all the royalist administrations in America and may even have been applied with greater severity in other colonies,[6] but the Mexican government was unique in issuing a public statement of this policy: the viceregal *bando* of 1812,

[1] J. Hernández y Dávalos, *op. cit.*, vi, 958, Apodaca to Capt. Justo Huidobro, 12 Jan. 1818 and 17 Jan. 1818.

[2] A.G.N., Infidencias 145, no. 13, Trial of Col. José de Armijo, March 1818–July 1820.

[3] See the trial of two captured insurgents, Pablo Delgado (priest) and Mariano Suárez (layman), 1818, in A.G.N., Infidencias 88, no. 1.

[4] A.G.N., Infidencias 102, Trial of José Ignacio Couto, 1817–21; and Infidencias 19, no. 17, Trial of Fr Servando de Mier, 1817–20.

[5] A number of prominent ecclesiastical insurgents were captured and tried in this period: A.G.N., Historia 412, no. 16, Trial of José de Talavera, José Ayala, Pedro Vázquez and José Sixto Verdusco, 1818; Infidencias 146, no. 1, Trial of José San Martín, 1818–21. See also Auto Apodaca, 10 Nov. 1820, ordering the release of Ignacio Rayón, in J. Hernández y Dávalos, *op. cit.*, vi, 1074.

[6] A.G.I., Mexico 1147, Consulta Council, 18 May 1818, referring to the brutality displayed by the royalist officers in Venezuela and Santa Fe de Bogotá.

which was condemned by the Council of the Indies as 'the most inhuman, illegal, and pernicious document to appear in this unhappy epoch'.[1]

Mexican officials had apparently realized that the *bando* would be censured by the Madrid government, which learned of its publication and application only extra-officially or by oblique reference.[2] The issue of the *Gaceta del gobierno de Mexico* in which the *bando* was published never reached Spain,[3] and information on the summary execution of insurgent priests was intentionally withheld.[4] A typical example is the *Relación de méritos y servicios* of the *Asesor* of Durango, containing a detailed account of the part he had played in suppressing the revolution in that intendancy but omitting any reference to the trial and execution of the six ecclesiastics captured with Hidalgo, although he had acted as legal adviser to the governor-intendant throughout the proceedings.[5] Even when specifically instructed to send a report on the *bando* and the immunity of ecclesiastical insurgents, Viceroy Calleja promised to do so, but this report somehow failed to reach Spain also.[6]

Despite the absence of this report, the Council received enough information, both official and unofficial, on conditions in New Spain to condemn the entire viceregal policy as completely contrary to the Crown's interests. The Council's reaction was partly conditioned by the Spanish government's traditional distrust of any flicker of initiative or independence displayed by the colonial authorities, and also by its preoccupation with legality, but the Council based its objections primarily on pragmatic grounds. The almost total exclusion of civil

[1] *Ibid.*, Consulta Council, 18 May 1818.

[2] Its publication was mentioned in letters on other topics, e.g., A.G.I., Mexico 1664, Informe Audiencia, 18 Nov. 1813, párr, 122 and 133. Information on executions was quarried from *expedientes* like the Expediente promovido por haber hallado en Durango un pasquín revolucionario . . ., 1812, A.H.N., Consejos 21215.

[3] A.G.I., Mexico 1147, Note on letter from Venegas to Minister of Gracia y Justicia, 26 Nov. 1812.

[4] See, e.g., A.G.I., Mexico 1482, Notas sobre algunos individuos . . ., 1814, in which Calleja mentions the execution of Matamoros, carried out after his formal conviction and degradation, but not that of other ecclesiastics listed.

[5] A.G.I., Guadalajara 317, Relación de los méritos y servicios de D. Ángel Pinilla, 1815.

[6] A.G.I., Mexico 1146, Minister of Gracia y Justicia to Council, 18 Oct. 1814 and 29 Oct. 1815.

jurisdiction and the indiscriminate provision of the death penalty were contrary to royal law and the principles of justice, but they were also, and mainly, errors in judgement according to the Council. The viceregal policy was based on a premise, that the only solution was 'to annihilate every last rebel',[1] which the Council considered totally false. Far from being even the best solution, the excessive bloodshed and destruction of property resulting from this emphasis on retaliation had resulted in incalculable damage to a colony on whose contributions the prosperity of the metropolis depended ('ya casi el fundamento de nuestra subsistencia');[2] and, instead of stifling the revolution quickly, this policy had served only to provoke more atrocities and stronger resistance from the rebels.[3]

The total abolition of immunity was condemned on the same pragmatic grounds as the other measures taken by the Mexican government. The Council recommended the restoration of ecclesiastical immunity to its pre-war status—that is, the compromise system of joint prosecution decreed in 1795—not because the clergy were necessarily worthy of special consideration, nor even because the viceregal *bando* had violated both royal and canon law, but because the *bando* and the executions it authorized had created such an adverse effect on public opinion, discrediting the government and turning many uncommitted or loyal subjects against the Crown.[4]

It can be argued that the Council's assessment of the viceregal policy as a failure was completely contradicted by the fact that the Mexican rebellion had been defeated (except for a few guerrilla bands) by 1818. But the contradiction is not as complete as it seems. The eventual suppression of the rebellion was the result of successful military campaigns—since 1815 the royalist troops had almost consistently defeated the rebel forces in any major encounter, gradually ejected them from the populated areas, and captured most of their officers, with the consequent dispersal of the leaderless rank and file—and there is no evidence that the terrorist tactics and reprisals, used in

---

[1] A.G.I., Mexico 1482, Calleja to Minister of Gracia y Justicia, 18 Aug. 1814.
[2] A.G.I., Ind. Gen. 110, Consulta Council, 16 Nov. 1815.
[3] A.G.I., Mexico 1147, Consulta Council, 18 May 1818.   [4] *Ibid.*

conjunction with orthodox military operations, had contributed to this success. On the contrary, if the primary aim of the Mexican government in pursuing the policy of reprisals, or 'sangre en mucha abundancia', as one officer put it,[1] was to bring a swift end to the rebellion by deterring would-be rebels as well as frightening those already fighting against the government (intimidation was considered even more important than the actual administration of punishment),[2] then this policy must be judged a failure, as the Council contended. For if anything, it actually lengthened the war by stimulating and strengthening resistance.

Royalist terrorism and repressive measures in general actually worked in favour of the independence movement. As the clandestine organization, *Los Guadalupes*, explained to Morelos: 'The harder the royalists squeeze, the faster our party grows'.[3] When Hidalgo started the revolution in 1810 the number of people in favour of independence was relatively small, but the victims and witnesses of the reprisals committed by royalist troops—civilian inhabitants of towns retaken from the rebels were often executed and their homes sacked as a warning to other non-combatants[4]—soon added considerable strength to the rebel forces. For example, the *Audiencia* of Guadalajara challenged the credit given Brigadier José de la Cruz for capturing the rebel forts in Lake Chapala in 1816 by explaining that Cruz had been responsible for their existence in the first place. The formerly neutral Indians in the area, whose villages he had burned and whose families he had slaughtered, had joined the rebel priest Marcos Castellanos and erected these island forts as bases from which they attacked detachments of royalist troops and all Europeans in the area, in retaliation for the atrocities they had suffered.[5]

---

[1] A.G.N., Infidencias 134, no. 17, José de la Cruz to Venegas, 24 Nov. 1810: 'Mi sistema particular no es el del moderantismo sino el de sangre en mucha abundancia. . . .'
[2] See A.G.I., Mexico 1321, Plan de operaciones de campaña, Calleja, 17 Dec. 1810; and Mexico 1635, Venegas to Regency Council, 6 March 1811.
[3] A.G.I., Mexico 1482, Los Guadalupes to Morelos, 20 Jan. 1813.
[4] A.G.I., Infidencias 117, Bishop Antonio Pérez of Puebla to Calleja, 14 April 1816, protesting this practice. See also, Infidencias 147, no. 13, Instrucción sobre quejas contra comandantes . . ., 1820, a file of complaints about arbitrary executions and other atrocities.

The measures directed specifically against the clergy were no more an unqualified success than the other aspects of the viceregal policy, despite official claims that the 1812 *bando* was a mortal blow to the insurrection.[1] The *bando* may have simplified the royalist military campaigns by enabling the officers to eliminate any insurgent priests that fell into their hands, but its indirect and long-term effects were harmful to the royalist cause. Instead of stimulating a rush for *indultos* among the rebel clergy, as the government had predicted, the *bando* deepened their antagonism as well as turning many neutral or loyal ecclesiastics against the government. The mere arrest of a priest was enough to produce strong reactions from other members of the clergy: one curate compared the arrest of a fellow cleric in his parish, who had been led out of the town in chains escorted by soldiers, to the treatment suffered by Christ in Jerusalem.[2] And another curate warned the viceroy that the clergy could not be expected to remain loyal to a government that did not respect their immunity.[3]

Neither these priests nor the 110 clerics of Mexico City who later drew up a memorial in protest against the 1812 *bando*[4] were originally supporters of the independence cause (in fact, one of the priests who signed this petition held the rank of colonel in the royalist army and had led troops against the insurgents in several encounters),[5] but they insisted that treason could be punished without violating the sacred character of the priesthood. The effect of the *bando* on the royalist clergy was to arouse bitter feelings against the government for its ingratitude in repaying their firm support with a measure that made the whole clergy 'despicable in the eyes of the people', and a sense of solidarity with the insurgent ecclesiastics, whose

[1] A.G.I., Mexico 1664, Oidor Pedro de la Puente to Regency Council, 15 Dec. 1812.

[2] *D.H.M.*, i, 295–6, Miguel Villalobos to Archbishop of Mexico, 28 Dec. 1809.

[3] A.G.N., Infidencias 165, Ignacio López de Luna to Venegas, 14 Dec. 1811.

[4] Representación que hace el clero mexicano al Venerable Deán y Cabildo, 6 July 1812, *D.H.M.*, iii, 'Semanario patriótico americano', 26 July 1812.

[5] See *Gaceta del gobierno*, 26 April 1811, Col. José Francisco Álvarez, to General Calleja, 31 March 1811.

[5] A.G.I., Guadalajara 317, Audiencia to the king, 16 June 1817.

immunity could not be violated without bringing harm to the whole clerical state.[1]

After the *bando*'s publication a number of ecclesiastics decided to join the rebellion, not necessarily to fight for independence but to defend ecclesiastical immunity. As one Creole priest explained, he had abandoned his allegiance to the government when he realized that it was the royalists and not the rebels who murdered priests and sacked churches.[2] Another priest, Mariano Matamoros, who had been an insurgent since 1811, raised a special squadron of dragoons to which he gave as a banner a black flag bearing a crimson cross, the arms of the Church, and the legend 'Morir por la Inmunidad Eclesiástica'.[3]

As an aid to the revolution, the viceregal policy provided the rebels not only with additional recruits but also with valuable material for their propaganda campaign against the government. The rebels themselves did not always respect the sanctity of the priesthood but, although one contemporary author asserted that they killed many priests, giving several examples,[4] it was not a general practice. Except for the two friars slaughtered in Guadalajara along with other European prisoners under Hidalgo's orders,[5] crimes of violence against the clergy were the spontaneous acts of undisciplined rebel hordes. Rebel policy was to execute most royalist officers and any Europeans they captured, but not if they were priests;[6] and unco-operative royalist curates were to be replaced with priests sympathetic to the rebel cause to ensure the allegiance of the parishioners, without, in theory at least, causing the former any physical harm.[7] Because of their generally respectful treatment of the clergy, the rebel leaders were able to condemn the royalist executions as an official policy,[8] use them as the main argument

---

[1] Representación que hace el clero mexicano . . ., 6 July 1812.

[2] A.G.I., Mexico 1477, Clamores de la verdad, Justa condenación del europeo traidor por el fiel americano, 1812, by anonymous Creole priest.

[3] C. M. Bustamante, *Cuadro histórico*, ii, 149.

[4] L. Alamán, *op. cit.*, ii, 81; iii, 164-5.

[5] J. Hernández y Dávalos, *op. cit.*, i, 14, Testimony of Miguel Hidalgo, 8 May 1811.

[6] See A.G.I., Mexico 1482, Ignacio Rayón to Morelos, 10 Sept. 1812 and 2 March 1813.

[7] See, e.g., A.G.I., Mexico 1477, Morelos to Sr Cura de Tiosintla, 22 May 1811 (copy taken from captured rebel papers).

in their exhortations to neutral Creoles to join the insurrection,[1] and include them as one of the major items on the famous rebel list of grievances against the government, the prelude to the 'Plan de paz y plan de guerra' published in 1812.[2]

The insurgents also exploited this persecution of the clergy to the fullest extent in their newspapers, in which the executions of priests were publicized and protection was offered to the clergy of New Spain.[3] Articles in this vein had appeared prior to the 1812 *bando*, but this 'horrendous transgression of the divine immunity of God's ministers'[4] gave them the most convincing proof of their allegations. Attacks on the 'irreligious and impious' Viceroy Venegas, other 'bloodthirsty' royalist leaders, and the prelates who condoned the violations of immunity with their silence,[5] although not necessarily insincere, were calculated to discredit the royalist claim to religious orthodoxy and to stir up popular feeling against the government.

An insurgent author has expressed astonishment that Viceroy Venegas, noted for his astuteness in other matters, could have issued such an 'impolitic' measure as the 1812 *bando*, which in the author's opinion aroused the hatred of the entire nation and gave the 'final impetus to the revolution'.[6] The government was aware of the dangers it risked in pursuing this policy. In 1809 the royal *fiscal* recommended a sentence of exile rather than death for a seditious friar, because the latter penalty, if executed in Mexico where respect for the priesthood was a deeply rooted tradition among the Mexican masses, could

[1] A.G.I., Mexico 1477, Desengaño de la América y traición descubierta a los europeos, Nicolás Bravo, 12 Nov. 1812; Mexico 1483, Proclamación a los criollos habitantes de Veracruz, 30 Aug. 1814.

[2] 'Plan de paz y plan de guerra', by Dr José María Cos, 1812, published in C. M. Bustamante, *Cuadro histórico*, i, 389–400 (printed copies were distributed widely in the colony at the time).

[3] *D.H.M.*, iii, 'Semanario patriótico americano', 26 July 1812.

[4] *Ibid.*, iii, 'Ilustrador americano', 12 Sept. 1812.

[5] *Ibid.*, iii, 'Semanario patriótico americano', 22 Aug., 30 Aug. and 27 Dec. 1812; iv, 'Sud', 25 Jan. 1813, and 'Correo americano del Sur', 6 May 1813.

[6] C. M. Bustamante, *Cuadro histórico*, ii, 148. L. Alamán, though of royalist sympathies, agreed with this assessment of the *bando*'s effect: *Historia de México*, ii, 78.

[8] A.G.I., Mexico 1480, José Sixto Verdusco to Ignacio Rayón, Dec. 1812; Mexico 1482, Morelos to Rayón, 27 Feb. 1813.

have had 'dangerous consequences of much greater tran-
scendence than any benefit derived from the satisfaction of
public vengeance'.[1] In 1811 two royalist bishops suggested that
any execution of an ecclesiastic be preceded by a series of
pastoral letters in which they could enlighten the 'fanatics' who
believed that a priest could not be punished even after he had
been defrocked.[2]

It is doubtful that this indoctrination would have had any
effect, since the formality of degradation meant nothing to the
vast majority of the Mexican population, to whom the immunity of an ordained priest was irrevocable, and any violence
done to his person a terrible sacrilege, regardless of what
judicial processes and canonical ceremonies had preceded it.
It is not surprising, then, that merely the rumour that a captured priest was to be put to death could produce a popular
outcry.[3] Feeling ran especially high in Durango over the fate
of the ecclesiastics captured with Hidalgo: the bishop was
threatened if he failed to save their lives, and an anonymous
broadside was posted on the cathedral doors, warning that:
'Si matan a los padres se subleva la ciudad.'[4]

The threat of violence in Durango was never carried out,
possibly because the governor took the precaution of ordering
the executions performed at midnight in an isolated spot outside the city.[5] But the government was faced with far more
dangerous manifestations of public feeling within the viceregal capital itself. Taking advantage of the recently proclaimed
freedom of the press,[6] a number of prominent Creoles published articles and pamphlets attacking the 1812 *bando* and the

[1] A.H.N., Consejos 21081, Respuesta Fiscales del Crimen y de lo Civil, 27
March 1809.

[2] A.H.N., Consejos 21212, Dictamen Bishop of Puebla, 25 Aug. 1811; Dictamen
Bishop of Oaxaca, 10 Sept. 1811.

[3] See A.G.N., Infidencias 160, no. 94, Archbishop of Mexico to Venegas, 18
Feb. 1813, referring to a trial in Querétaro; L. Alamán, *op. cit.*, iv, 245, referring
to the trial of Morelos in Mexico.

[4] A.H.N., Consejos 21215, 'Exhortación de Jeremías a la puerta del templo
santo', (n.d., Feb. 1812), in Expediente promovido por haber hallado un
pasquín . . ., 1812.

[5] *Ibid.*, Governor of Durango to Nemesio Salcedo, 20 June 1812; Audiencia of
Guadalajara to Governor, 29 Aug. 1812.

[6] A.G.N., Impresos oficiales 34, no. 23, Bando, 5 Oct. 1812, inserting Real
Decreto, 11 Nov. 1810.

government[1] in terms similar to those used by the 110 clerics in their 'Representación' to the *sede vacante* chapter, which had appeared several months earlier in an insurgent newspaper.[2] Considered particularly offensive by the authorities were articles in two popular journals edited by Creole laymen, *El juguetillo* (Carlos María Bustamante) and *El pensador mexicano* (José Joaquín Fernández de Lizardi). The former declared that the officers who applied the *bando* were more criminal than the rebel ecclesiastics,[3] while the latter addressed his protest to the viceroy, whose error in judgement and sacrilegious violation of the law were vehemently criticized.[4]

The rancour and bad feeling already existing in the capital, kindled by these articles and the agitation of the rebellion's undercover supporters (who formed themselves into the group *Los Guadalupes* about this same time), erupted into popular riots on the occasion of the municipal elections which took place in November 1812. The demonstrations combined triumphant processions in celebration of the elections (won exclusively by Creoles, many of whom were clerics who had signed the 'Representación' protesting against the 1812 *bando*) and menacing protests against the government. All the church bells were rung, and the houses of government officials and prominent Europeans were surrounded by torch-bearing crowds jeering 'Death to the *gachupines*', shouting their intention to 'Die for the immunity of the priests', and even cheering, 'Viva Morelos'.[5] One *oidor* requested permission to return to Spain, alleging that he had already received threats of assassination because he had been the only official to defend the viceregal *bando* publicly.[6]

---

[1] See J. Peredo y Gallegos *Discurso dogmático sobre la jurisdicción eclesiástica* (Mexico, 1812); and J. García de Torres, *Vindicación del clero mexicano vulnerado en las anotaciones que publicó el M.R.P. José Joaquín Oyarzábal* (Mexico, 1812), and *El vindicador del clero mexicano a su antagonista B.* (Mexico, 1812).

[2] *D.H.M.*, iii, 'Semanario patriótico mexicano', 26 July 1812. The similarity was probably no coincidence, since García de Torres was reputed to be the author of this 'Representación'.

[3] C. M. Bustamante, *El juguetillo* (Mexico, 1812), issue no. 3.

[4] J. Fernández de Lizardi, *El pensador mexicano* (Mexico, 1812–27), 3 Dec. 1812.

[5] A.G.I., Mexico 1322, Testimonio del expediente instruído en averiguación de los movimientos populares de los días 29 y 30 de noviembre . . ., 1812; Mexico 1664, Informe Audiencia, 18 May 1813, párr. 161–3.

The riots were eventually put down by troops, but the government feared that they were only the prelude to a general uprising in all the capitals organized by the *Guadalupes*, who would have been able to inflame public opinion easily on this 'delicate issue' of ecclesiastical immunity.[1] Whether or not such an uprising was contemplated cannot be determined on the basis of available evidence, but the viceroy and the *Junta de seguridad* were sufficiently alarmed to take the precautionary measures of nullifying the electoral results, reinforcing the capital's contingent of troops, suspending the liberty of the press,[2] and arresting the authors of the incendiary articles and the 'Representatión del clero', who were eventually released after signing retractions of their statements[3] (with the exception of Bustamante, who had fled to join the rebels before he could be arrested).

Public reaction to the abolition of immunity had little direct effect on viceregal policy, except for the decision not to apply its more extreme aspects in the capital where popular protests could have the most dangerous consequences. The 1812 *bando* was never officially revoked and, if the government eventually returned to milder methods of suppressing the rebellion, this change owed more to the success of the royalist military operations and to orders from Madrid (though these in turn had been influenced by popular reaction) than to the pressure of public opinion.

But even though popular reaction to the curtailment of ecclesiastical immunity had little direct effect on the government's actions, it did not cease to be a major influence on the course of the independence movement. The 1812 *bando*, together with the other repressive measures taken by the

---

[1] A.G.I., Mexico 1480, Calleja to Minister of Gracia y Justicia, 20 June 1813; Mexico 1322, Testimonio del expediente instruído . . ., 1812.

[2] A.G.N., Impresos oficiales 34, no. 40, Bando, 5 Dec. 1812; A.G.I., Mexico 1664, Oidor Miguel Modet to Minister of Ultramar, 6 Jan. 1813.

[3] A.G.N., Historia 409, Expediente con motivo de la solicitud de varios individuos del clero . . ., 1812. See also Infidencias 116, nos. 11–12, Trial of José Fernández Lizardi, 1812–13.

---

[6] A.G.I., Mexico 1664, Pedro de la Puente to Minister of Ultramar, 15 Dec. 1812 and 1 Feb. 1813. See his *Reflexiones sobre el bando de 25 de junio*.

royalist régime, had already helped to prepare the ground for the next phase of the movement by alienating a large portion of non-combatants, both laymen and ecclesiastics, who became secret supporters of independence,[1] and the issue of ecclesiastical immunity was to be even more intimately linked with the cause of Mexican independence in this next and final phase of the struggle. The clergy, provoked by new and more extreme attacks from the Spanish liberal régime of 1820, and led this time by the formerly ultra-royalist hierarchy, allied themselves with the military to deal the final blow to Spanish domination and to preserve the privileges they had enjoyed for centuries under colonial rule.

[1] Even in 1813 the viceroy asserted that 'todo americano aspira a la independencia': A.G.I., Mexico 1480, Calleja to Minister of Gracia y Justicia, 22 June 1813.

CONCLUSION

Independence:
The Triumph of Reaction

THE ABOLITION of ecclesiastical immunity during the independence period, decreed by the viceregal government and later confirmed by the Spanish *Cortes*, was a legacy from the Caroline programme of ecclesiastical reform. The direct causes of these decrees and the contexts in which they appeared—the first responding to the military exigencies of a civil war, and the second appearing in the anti-clerical ambience of nineteenth-century liberalism—differed from the regalist and absolutist theories that had influenced the ministers of Charles III. But the measures themselves were the logical culmination of the policy first outlined by these ministers, which was based on the view that ecclesiastical privilege was fundamentally incompatible with the interests of the State.

This new policy of antagonism to the Church, replacing the old Habsburg system of interdependence and co-operation, whose purpose was to weaken the influence and the authority of the Church, must ultimately be judged a failure as far as Mexico was concerned. In all three phases of its development—Bourbon absolutism, military expedience, and liberal anti-clericalism—the policy helped to weaken the colonial régime and in the end contributed to its destruction, while leaving the Church and the clergy in a stronger position than ever.

The role of ecclesiastical immunity in the Mexican struggle for independence has been largely ignored in the historiography of the period. Yet official attacks on this privilege were the basis of serious grievances held against the Spanish government that combined with the political, economic and social causes of discontent to produce and sustain the independence movement in its various stages of development.

The effect of the Caroline ecclesiastical reforms during the movement's long incubation period was not immediately apparent. The rift within the colonial government between the *audiencia* and the *fiscal* and *sala del crimen* over the application of the reforms (echoing a similar division between the Council of the Indies and progressive ministers over their promulgation) had little if any influence on the Mexican independence movement, although the bitter exchanges between the opposing factions reveal the strength of feeling that this issue could arouse.[1] Even if the *oidores* acted out of any particular sympathy with ecclesiastical privilege (and they may simply have been opposed to change in general, regardless of what form it took), they were not prepared to challenge royal authority openly over this or any other issue. Nor were the Mexican bishops prepared to do more than make vehement protests to the Crown over these serious threats to their power and prestige. Far from translating these verbal protests into active opposition to the régime, the bishops were the Crown's most loyal allies during the greater part of the independence period. If the Caroline attacks on ecclesiastical privilege contributed to the growth of a separatist movement in Mexico, this effect must be sought, not in the resistance from royal officials and the ecclesiastical hierarchy, but in the reactions of two groups considered politically unconscious by the ruling classes: the lower clergy and the pious, ignorant masses.

In creating and pursuing the Caroline ecclesiastical policy, the advocates of reform failed to take into consideration two closely related factors in the social life of the colony: the deeply rooted veneration the majority of Mexicans felt for the priesthood and the consequent influence the clergy were able to exert over their ideas and actions. The unsophisticated Creole as well as the Indian neophyte made little distinction between the sacramental functions of a priest and his ordinary condition as a fellow human being. Nor was this distinction encouraged, since a view of the priest as a semi-divine being somehow set apart from the laity in every way was useful in

---

[1] See above, pp. 188–95. For a record of the conflicts over the application of the laws restricting the privilege of asylum, see A.G.I., Ind. Gen. 3025, Expediente general sobre inmunidad de los reos que se refugian al sagrado, 1764–87.

preserving clerical authority over the faithful.[1] The hierarchy wrote with satisfaction of the 'fanatical devotion' of the Indians to their ministers, whose hands they always knelt to kiss and whose advice they blindly followed.[2]

Since ecclesiastical immunity was the most obvious expression of the priesthood's sacred character, any official act which appeared to violate this privilege inevitably created resentment against the government among the Mexican masses. Most of the Caroline reform programme was too subtle a form of regalism to be noted by the general public. For example, only the few who might seek dispensations for canonical impediments too serious for episcopal authority would be aware of the 1778 law requiring the prior fiat of the Council of the Indies for all petitions addressed to Rome.[3] But two measures, the expulsion of the Jesuits and the curtailment of personal immunity in criminal cases, were exceptions. The enforced exile of almost five hundred Jesuits, marched from all points of the viceroyalty under military escort to Veracruz, and the public arrest and imprisonment in the royal jail of a parish priest, were overt attacks on the clergy that even the most naïve witness could recognize.

Widely separated in chronology and superficially unrelated, both events were integral parts of the same policy of strengthening royal control over the clergy. Although ignorant of the inner workings of royal policy, the Mexican masses also connected these two measures, which were both viewed as manifestations of a 'diabolical plan to destroy religion in Mexico',[4] and they reacted in a similar way to both. Just as plagues and droughts were blamed on the expulsion in the 1760's, so people

[1] See A.G.I., Ind. Gen. 3027, Bishop of Puebla to the king, 30 Oct. 1799; and Mexico 1661, Archbishop of Mexico to the king, 25 June 1804.

[2] R.A.H., Col. Mata Linares 76, Chapter of Puebla to the king, 18 Nov. 1799. See also 'De la naturaleza del indio', Juan de Palafox y Mendoza (Bishop of Puebla in the mid-seventeenth century), G. García and C. Pereyra, *Documentos inéditos ó muy raros*, vii, 223–92.

[3] *Decretos reales tocantes a la iglesia* (B.M.), no. 42, R.C. circular, 21 Nov. 1778. See also above, p. 62.

[4] A.H.N., Inquisición 2287, Anonymous letter, April 1768. This *legajo* and 2286-B contain a number of poems and pamphlets in the same tone, recalled by the Bishop of Puebla in his letter to the king, 30 Oct. 1799, A.G.I., Ind. Gen. 3027, where he reports similar reactions.

predicted that similar or worse signs of God's wrath would be delivered on the people of Mexico for consenting to the 'sacrileges' committed in consequence of the law limiting immunity in criminal cases.[1] Resentment was also expressed openly in popular riots occurring in 1767, when mobs tried to prevent the departure of the Jesuits,[2] and at least one in 1799, when a group of Indians tried unsuccessfully to free an imprisoned priest from the royal jail in Puebla.[3]

There is no evidence to indicate either that the curtailment of personal immunity led directly to the early conspiracies and the final outbreak of armed rebellion, or that this rebellion was the realization of anonymous threats made in 1768 to take up arms in retaliation for the expulsion of the Jesuits.[4] These measures were important, not as direct causes of revolution, but as two sources of resentment against the government which helped to gain support for the revolution once it had started.

Both measures and, later, the threat of worse religious persecution at the hands of Napoleon's forces (many Mexicans believed, or professed to believe, that Francophile royal ministers were planning to deliver Spain and the colonies to Napoleon)[5] gave rise to the idea that 'America is the only refuge left for the religion of Jesus Christ'.[6] Further proof of the government's intention to destroy the Church was provided, in the opinion of the Mexican insurgents, by the famous *bando* of 1812 abolishing immunity entirely, which lent support to the rebel propaganda campaign, stimulated further resistance among the masses, and provoked a third wave of predictions of divine vengeance.[7] Comparisons with the expulsion of the Jesuits were revived again. The superstitious discounted coincidence and saw an evil portent in the fact that both the

[1] A.H.N., Inquisición 2286-B, Expediente sobre la propagación de las revelaciones falsas y fanáticas profecías . . ., 1768; and R.A.H., Col. Mata Linares 76, Chapter of Puebla to the king, 18 Nov. 1799.

[2] See above, pp. 131–3, for material on popular reactions to the expulsion.

[3] A.G.I., Ind. Gen. 3027, Testimonio de la causa seguida al Padre Manuel Arenas, 1799.

[4] See A.H.N., Inquisición 2287, 'Los pobres cristianos de Puebla', 1768.

[5] *D.H.M.*, iii, 'Despertador americano', 3 Jan. 1811.

[6] *Ibid.*, 'Despertador americano', 20 Dec. 1810.

[7] See A.H.N., Consejos 21215, Expediente promovido por motivo de haber hallado un pasquín revolucionario . . ., 1812.

bando and the expulsion order had been published at the same hour, on the same date and even the same day of the week, although 45 years apart.[1] Others asserted that the *bando* was influenced by the same enemies of religion, the 'Calvinists and *philosophes*', who had influenced Charles III.[2]

The Bourbon ecclesiastical policy undoubtedly had the most immediate effect on the clergy, whose strong influence over the Mexican laity determined the course of the independence movement more directly than any spontaneous public reaction to the violation of ecclesiastical immunity. For, as has been shown, the Creole clergy provided many of the political and military leaders of the insurrection,[3] which gained the support of the masses, not necessarily because of their own revolutionary convictions but because of their ingrained habit of obeying and following the lead of their ministers. As one viceroy explained: 'They are led astray by persons they regard with superstitious veneration'.[4]

At the end of the eighteenth century, the Mexican hierarchy had warned the king not to be 'deceived by the *apparent* advantages of these measures' limiting ecclesiastical immunity and jurisdiction, predicting that he would eventually have to resort to force to hold his American subjects in subordination, as a result of the official attacks on the Church.[5] Although based on a somewhat naïve interpretation of the causes of the French Revolution—that is, that the monarchy had weakened its own authority and prestige by challenging those of the Church—the bishops' conclusions were in part valid, and their arguments contained several observations on the political situation in New Spain which help to explain the effect of the Caroline ecclesiastical policy on the independence movement.

One bishop warned the king that Mexico was a nation which hid 'a profound malice and irreconcilable hatred towards its conquerors underneath the most humble and abject exterior'.[6]

---

[1] L. Alamán, *Historia de México*, iii, 164.

[2] See, e.g., A.G.I., Ind. Gen. 110, Proclama del Dr Cos, 1814.

[3] See above, pp. 199–200.

[4] A.G.I., Mexico 1322, Calleja to Minister of Ultramar, 15 March 1813.

[5] A.G.I., Ind. Gen. 3027, Bishop of Puebla to the king, 30 Oct. 1799. See also B.N., 12009, Bishop and Chapter of Michoacán to the king, 11 Dec. 1799.

[6] A.G.I., Ind. Gen. 3027, Bishop of Puebla to the king, 30 Oct. 1799.

R

And all the petitioners agreed that Spain had been able to control its colonies for almost 300 years, with only a token contingent of troops, only because the missionaries and secular priests had constantly preached obedience to and respect for God and king. They pointed out that it was unwise of the king to pursue a policy that alienated his staunchest and most trustworthy allies, especially during a period of political unrest: if ecclesiastical influence had contributed to the peaceful subordination of the colony, that same influence could easily be turned to the opposite effect.[1]

The history of the Mexican independence movement reveals how prophetic these comments were. But since the vast majority of subversive and rebellious ecclesiastics in the early phases of the movement came from the lower ranks of the clergy,[2] the original motives for independence must be sought in conditions and measures which would have caused disaffection within that particular sector of the ecclesiastical state. Most of the regalist measures of the late Bourbon period had no more effect on the lower clergy than they did on the great mass of the laity. The curtailment of communications with Rome, royal interference in ecclesiastical legislation, and other methods of subordinating the Church to the State, were disputed between high-ranking royal officials and the hierarchy, and it is likely that the local curate was scarcely aware of their existence.

However, the economic condition of the lower clergy, exacerbated rather than alleviated by certain royal measures, was a major source of discontent and unrest.[3] The alleged *gachupín* monopoly of the higher ecclesiastical benefices provides only a partial explanation for this discontent. The available statistics indicate that Creoles actually predominated in the cathedral chapters in this period[4] (though only one

[1] A.G.I., Ind. Gen. 3027, Bishop of Puebla to the king, 30 Oct. 1799. See Also R.A.H., Col. Mata Linares 76, Archbishop of Mexico to the king, 26 Sept. 1799; Cathedral Chapter of Mexico to the king, 28 Nov. 1799; and B.N., 12009, Bishop and Chapter of Michoacán to the king, 11 Dec. 1799.

[2] See Appendix. See also K. M. Schmitt, 'The Clergy and the Independence of New Spain', *H.A.H.R.*, xxxiv (1954), pp. 289–93; and J. Bravo Ugarte, 'El clero y la independencia', *Ábside*, v (1941), pp. 612–30, vii (1943), pp. 406–9 and xv (1951), pp. 199–218.

[3] See A.H.N., Consejos 21081, Gabriel de Yermo to Junta Central, 12 Nov. 1808.

[4] A.G.I., Mexico 2545, Lista de sugestos para el vacante . . ., 16 Dec. 1807:

bishopric, Puebla, was held by a Creole at the beginning of
the rebellion); and the resentment that the division of benefices
caused was probably limited to the unsuccessful candidates for
vacant canonries—disgruntled office-seekers who, as one bishop
warned, might choose to believe that they had been discriminated against as Creoles and would therefore join a
political movement that promised greater opportunity for
advancement.[1]

But much more important than the division of benefices
themselves was the distribution of incomes, so dispropor-
tionately in favour of the bishops and prebendaries. The incomes
of the different curacies varied also, but even the wealthiest
curate, although better off than most of his parishioners, could
not fail to contrast the opulence of the higher beneficiaries with
his own relative penury, to say nothing of the *vicarios* and
tenientes de cura, who were paid a fraction of the curate's living.
The same disparity existed among the regular clergy: the
ordinary friars resented the luxury which their superiors
(whether Creole or peninsular) enjoyed, in violation of the
monastic vow of personal poverty and often at the expense of
the community's patrimony.[2]

The various Caroline reforms directed against the clergy's
economic immunity, if anything, increased this disproportion
in income. The subjection to royal jurisdiction of all lawsuits
concerning chantries and pious works and the alienation of
their capital[3] had little effect on the bishops and canons, whose
livings were paid from tithes. But the parish priests often

[1] A.G.I., Mexico 2545, Archbishop of Mexico to the king, 28 Dec. 1808; and
Consultas para vacantes . . ., 1805–9, containing records of unsuccessful candi-
dacies of several Creoles who later became insurgents (e.g., José Couto) or conspirators (e.g., José Alcalá).

[2] See A.G.I., Mexico 2743, 2744, 2747–51 for records of the reform *visitas* of
the religious orders in New Spain at the end of the eighteenth century. See also
Mexican Political Pamphlets (B.M.), vii, no. 76, 'Los frailes gordos contra los frailes
flacos', 1823.   [3] See Ch. VII, sect. 3.

18 Creole prebendaries out of a total of 21 in Puebla (also Creole Deans of Oaxaca,
Durango, and Valladolid); Mexico 1664, Informe Audiencia of Mexico, 18 Nov.
1813, párr. 121: 16 Creole prebendaries out of 24 in Mexico, and 9 out of 11 in
the Collegiate Church of Guadalupe; Mexico 1481, Lista de los eclesiásticos de
este obispado, 29 Aug. 1813: the Chapter of Valladolid was divided equally.

depended upon the income from chantries to supplement their salaries, while for the real proletariat of the Church—the vast army of clerics who held no benefice under royal patronage (estimated at four-fifths of the entire secular clergy at the end of the eighteenth century)[1]—these chantries and other endowments for masses were the only source of income. And the regulars, too numerous for their communities' original endowments, often subsisted almost entirely on the revenues from pious foundations.[2]

The loss of income on ecclesiastical endowments that reduced the chaplains and ordinary friars to 'a shameful state of beggary' in this period[3] was perhaps due as much to unsound investments (with returns dwindling as agriculture and commerce became increasingly disrupted) as to the 1804 expropriation decree, which was laxly enforced and eventually permitted to lapse altogether, or to the curtailment of *fuero* in property suits. But the reduction of the annual interest rate on the property that was expropriated, the Crown's failure to pay even the 3 per cent it had promised,[4] and the fact that the beneficiaries could not sue either private defaulters or the Crown in their own *fuero*, enabled the lower clergy to blame their economic ills on the 'rapacious and impious' measures dictated by the Madrid government.[5]

It was also the lower clergy rather than the hierarchy who suffered most from the curtailment of immunity in serious crimes, since it was unlikely that the royal justices would dare arrest a bishop or a canon even if he were accused of a grave crime. However, the new law was applied not only to members of the lower clergy accused of murder and theft, but also to those who clashed with the local royal officials in performing what they considered the duties of their ministry.[6] More important than the fear of punishment was the loss of prestige which, in the clergy's opinion, depended upon special privileges

---

[1] B.N., 12009, Bishop and Chapter of Michoacán to the king, 11 Dec. 1799.

[2] See, e.g., A.G.N., Obras pías 6, Lista de los capitales de obras pías hechas a favor de este convento, sus destinos y réditos, 1779 (the main Bethlemite house in Mexico).

[3] A.G.N., Infidencias 117, Bishop of Puebla to Calleja, 14 April 1816.

[4] *Ibid.*   [5] *D.H.M.*, iii, 'Despertador americano', 3 Jan. 1811.

[6] See above, pp. 180–2.

that set them apart from the laity.[1] The parish priests in particular resented the fact that this law gave their rivals, the royal justices, a new and effective weapon against them in the local competitions for power and influence.

The Caroline programme of ecclesiastical reform was by no means the only stimulus to rebellion among the lower clergy, who were also moved by many of the same forces influencing their lay companions, such as the developing spirit of nationalism and the general Creole ambition for self-rule. But the importance of this factor as a contribution to the independence movement should not be underrated, especially in view of the emphasis the revolutionary leaders placed on their religious grievances against the government both before and after the 1812 *bando*, which strengthened the antagonism of those already partaking in the rebellion and aroused new resistance.

The specific goal of separation from Spain, although perhaps held secretly by the earliest insurgent leaders, was not publicly acknowledged until October 1814 in the Constitutional Decree of Apatzingán,[2] but the aim of defending religion and the priesthood against attacks from the peninsular government was expressed from the beginning of the rebellion.[3] In particular, the 'restoration of the lost privileges and prestige of the priests' was one point in their rather vague political programme on which most rebel leaders could agree.[4]

The effect of the government's attacks on ecclesiastical privilege in the late colonial period and during the course of the 1810 rebellion must be determined largely on the basis of inference and indirect evidence. But the contribution made by the unequivocally anti-clerical decrees of the 1820 Spanish *Cortes* to the final success of the independence movement is a well-substantiated fact agreed upon by contemporary witnesses. By the time the liberal faction in Spain had gained control of

---

[1] B.N., 12009, Bishop and Chapter of Michoacán to the King, 11 Dec. 1799.

[2] A.G.I., Ind. Gen. 110, Decreto constitucional para la libertad de la América mexicana, Apatzingán, 22 Oct. 1814, signed by José Liceaga, José María Morelos and Dr José María Cos.

[3] See *D.H.M.*, iii, 'Despertador americano', 20 Dec. 1810.

[4] J. Hernández y Dávalos, *Colección de documentos*, ii, 195, Rafael Iriarte to Dr Cos, 29 Oct. 1810; A.G.I., Mexico 1482, Morelos to Ignacio Rayón, 27 Feb. 1813; Rayón to Morelos, 2 March 1813; and Proclama convoking the Congress of Chilpacingo, by Morelos, 11 Sept. 1813.

the government in 1820 and reinstated the Constitution of Cadiz,[1] the viceroyalty of New Spain had been almost entirely pacified with the exception of a few isolated guerrilla bands.[2] But the same influential classes in the colony whose support had aided the viceroys to suppress the rebellion turned against the government and united in a successful attempt to bring about the independence they had previously opposed so energetically.

This switch in allegiance was only superficially inconsistent, for self-interest, much more than simple loyalty to the Crown, determined the position of the hierarchy and other privileged classes throughout the period. If the prelates had lent the full weight of their financial and moral support to the Crown, it was because they had identified their interests with those of the Spanish government,[3] and when they became convinced that their welfare was threatened by that same government they did not hesitate to conspire against it.

Although the Constitution of Cadiz had already been promulgated before, there was a vast difference between the political situations in 1812 and 1820. In 1812, the innovations contained in the Constitution had either been ignored or suspended.[4] Both the viceregal government and the conservative classes could hope that the *Cortes* were only a temporary nuisance and that absolute monarchy and the old order would soon be restored, as they were restored after the return of Ferdinand VII in 1814. But in 1820 they realized that even the king could no longer be relied upon to preserve the *status quo* against the increasingly powerful liberal forces.

The liberal government issued a series of decrees in the space of a few months which offended the influential classes, particularly the clergy, much more seriously than the legislation of the *Cortes* of Cadiz. The Church's unlimited right to acquire and own property had been respected in the 1812 Constitution,[5]

---

[1] A.G.I., Mexico 1677, R.O., 25 March 1820.

[2] A.G.I., Mexico 1678, Apodaca to Minister of Ultramar, 18 July 1820.

[3] A.G.I., Mexico 1662, Dean and Chapter of Michoacán to Iturrigaray, 8 Aug. 1808. See also above, pp. 206, 217.

[4] A.G.I., Mexico 1482, Calleja to Minister of Gracia y Justicia, 18 Aug. 1814, explaining why most of the clauses of the Constitution had not been put into effect.   [5] *Constitución de la monarquía española*, art. 172.

but the new *Cortes* prohibited the establishment of any new *capellanías* and pious works.[1] Several of the innovations, such as the suppression of all monastic and hospital orders, the sharp reduction in the number of *conventos* belonging to the other, mendicant orders, and the prohibition of all novitiates,[2] were viewed in Mexico as merely the first steps in the total suppression of the regular clergy.[3]

Another decree abolishing ecclesiastical immunity entirely in what amounted to all criminal cases (any crime that according to any Spanish law, even if no longer in use, could incur any form of corporal punishment)[4] was particularly resented. For, while the 1812 *bando* had been a temporary measure depriving only insurgents of their immunity, the 1820 decree was a permanent law applying to the entire clergy, even those who had loyally supported the government. Nor was the hierarchy to be spared. The bishops were warned specifically that any opposition to the new régime and its principles would be dealt with severely[5] and, as proof that this was no idle threat, the *Cortes* ordered the arrest and confiscation of the property of 69 persons—the Bishop of Puebla included among the several prelates on the list—who had petitioned the king in 1814 to revoke the Constitution of Cadiz.[6]

Clerical and popular reaction to the new régime was not necessarily dependent on the actual enforcement of the anti-clerical measures, for news of the legislative programme under debate in the *Cortes* and rumours of worse to come were sufficient in themselves. Royal officials were aware of the clergy's resentment of the attacks on their property and personal immunity long before these decrees could have reached Mexico and even before some of them were issued in Spain.[7] News of

[1] A.G.I., Mexico 1680, R.O., 27 Sept. 1820.
[2] A.G.N., Reales cédulas 244, no. 283, R.C., 28 Nov. 1820.
[3] L. Alamán, *op. cit.*, v, 37.
[4] *Colección de los decretos y órdenes que han expedido las Cortes generales y extraordinarias desde su instalación* (10 vols., Madrid, 1820–3), vi, 141–2, Decreto, 26 Sept. 1820, promulgated by R.O. of 25 Oct. 1820.
[5] A.G.N., Impresos oficiales 60, R.O., 5 Sept. 1820, inserted in circular order, Apodaca, 24 Feb. 1821.
[6] A.G.I., Mexico 1680, Apodaca to Secretary of Ultramar, 31 Jan. 1821.
[7] L. Alamán, *op. cit.*, v, 41–2, quoting from José Hipólito Odoardo, Fiscal of the Audiencia, to Minister of Gracia y Justicia, 24 Oct. 1820.

the supposedly secret order for the arrest and deportation of the Bishop of Puebla was enough to provoke a two-day riot in Puebla and, though the order was never carried out (the point of the riot and earlier demonstrations was not lost on the viceroy),[1] the bishop not surprisingly became one of the new régime's staunchest and most effective opponents, having warned the viceroy that he had no intention of permitting such a violation of his rights and the sacred dignity of his office.[2]

Royal officials in New Spain, commenting on the transformation of the seemingly pacified viceroyalty into an independent nation, noted that the appearance of these anti-clerical decrees, which in Spain had resulted in riots and other forms of violent opposition,[3] coincided in Mexico with the turning point in the fortunes of the independence movement. But they did not regard this as mere coincidence, for they believed that the Mexican clergy, alarmed by these attacks on their vital interests, were the organizing force behind the *Plan de Iguala*, in which the Creole army officer, Agustín de Iturbide, proclaimed Mexican independence in February 1821.[4]

Opinions differ concerning the exact relationship between Iturbide and the two clandestine ecclesiastical *juntas*, one formed in Puebla under the direction of Bishop Antonio Pérez, and the other in Mexico under that of the peninsular canon Matías Monteagudo. Royal officials believed that the two groups, working in close co-ordination, chose Iturbide as their agent for the destruction of the colonial régime, and several believed that Monteagudo persuaded Viceroy Apodaca to appoint Iturbide commander of the royalist Army of the South, from which position he could deliver military support for their scheme[5] (Apodaca himself failed to mention any such

---

[1] A.G.I., Mexico 1680, Apodaca to the Bishop of Puebla, 24 Jan. 1821.

[2] A.G.N., Operaciones de Guerra 1014, Bishop of Puebla to Apodaca, 13 April 1821.

[3] V. de la Fuente, *Historia eclesiástica de España* (6 vols., Madrid, 1873–5), vi, 193–200.

[4] Similar versions of the clergy's role in the events leading up to independence are contained in A.G.I., Mexico 1680, Apodaca to the Minister of Ultramar, 8 Jan., 31 Jan. and 7 March 1821; and Juan O'Donojú to Minister of Ultramar, 31 Aug. 1821, in addition to the other sources cited below.

[5] A.G.I., Mexico 1680, Resumen histórico de los acontecimientos de Nueva España, 18 Dec. 1821, by Lt. Col. Vicente Bausá; Mexico, 1676, Ciriaco de

pressure when reporting rumours of the scheme,[1] though if he had been duped his silence on this point would be understandable).

Another version, which Iturbide's recent biographer finds more plausible,[2] was offered by Bustamante. He attributed the initiative to Iturbide who, chosen without ecclesiastical machinations as the ablest royalist officer available to defeat Vicente Guerrero and the other rebel guerrillas, devised the plan himself and cleverly gained the support of the clergy, as well as the rebels and other groups in the colony, employing the defence of religion as one of several drawing cards.[3] But whether the clergy manipulated Iturbide or vice versa, there was no disagreement over the fact that Iturbide succeeded where Hidalgo and Morelos had failed because he was backed by the influential classes—mainly the entire clergy, who prepared public opinion in his favour as well as provided him with material aid.[4]

There were some ecclesiastics who believed they could preserve their privileged position without separation from Spain, or who placed loyalty to the Crown above any other consideration, but the overwhelming majority gave their full support to Iturbide's *Plan de Iguala*, which had been printed by one priest and delivered to Viceroy Apodaca by another.[5] Many members of the lower clergy had favoured independence, either actively or in secret, during the first phases of the movement, but now they were joined by the hierarchy. Only one prelate, the Creole Bishop of Durango, openly opposed the *Plan* (though the Archbishop of Mexico was privately hostile and left Mexico in 1823); the rest of the bishops and canons publicly endorsed it, preached sermons and wrote articles in

[1] A.G.I., Mexico 1680, Apodaca to Minister of Ultramar, 31 Jan. 1821.

[2] W. S. Robertson, *Iturbide of Mexico*, pp. 67–70.

[3] C. M. Bustamante, *Cuadro histórico*, v, 93–144, particularly pp. 96–105, 134–44, in which letters are published from Iturbide to Guerrero, the Bishop of Guadalajara, royal officials, and military leaders, seeking support for the *Plan de Iguala*.

[4] *Ibid.*, v, 132; A.G.I., Mexico 1680, O'Donojú to Minister of Ultramar, 31 Aug. 1821; Mexico 1676, Ciriaco de Llano to Minister of Ultramar, 30 Jan. 1822.

[5] C. M. Bustamante, *Cuadro histórico*, v, 108, 127.

Llano (ex-Comandante General of Puebla) to Minister of Ultramar, 30 Jan. 1822.

its praise,[1] and provided elaborate religious celebrations to welcome Iturbide and his army into the major capitals.[2]

Neither Charles III's ecclesiastical policy nor the anti-clerical decrees issued in 1820 can be divorced from the other aspects of the Caroline reform programme and the liberal legislation of the Spanish *Cortes* that alienated other influential classes in Mexico besides the clergy. Caroline attempts to transform the colonial *status quo*—the reduction of trade restrictions and the creation of intendancies, for example—were only pallid forerunners of the innovations introduced by the *Cortes*. The Creole oligarchy's virtual monopoly of municipal administration was challenged by decrees extending suffrage to all but Indians and *castas*;[3] the abolition of *mayorazgos, repartimientos,* and all forms of forced labour threatened the interests of the landowners;[4] and the judicial reforms circumscribing the powers of the *audiencias* and suppressing many of the special tribunals and *fueros*[5] inevitably alienated both the judiciary and those who had enjoyed professional or inherited *fueros*. All these powerful groups had supported Viceroy Venegas in opposing the execution of the 1812 constitution,[6] so that it is not surprising that they should have received the news of its reinstatement with dismay and allied themselves with the military (whose general dissatisfaction with the meagre rewards they had received was intensified when the *Cortes* suspended their recent salary increase) to preserve their privileges and status by securing independence from Spain.[7]

[1] See M. de la Bárcena (Governor of the vacant bishopric of Valladolid), *Manifiesto al mundo de la justicia y necesidad de la independencia de la Nueva España* (Mexico, 1821). See also L. Alamán, *op. cit.*, v, 16, quoting a sermon by Canon José de San Martín, 25 June 1821.

[2] C. M. Bustamante, *Cuadro histórico*, v, Chapters 8–11, describing the advance of Iturbide's forces.

[3] A.G.I., Mexico 1678, Expedientes sobre elecciones de ayuntamientos constitucionales, 1820–1.

[4] A.G.N., Impresos oficiales 43, Bando, 29 Aug. 1820, publishing Real Decreto, 15 April 1820.

[5] A.G.N., Reales cédulas 207, R.C., 10 Oct. 1812, publishing Real Decreto sobre arreglo de los tribunales, 9 Oct. 1812. See also *Gaceta del gobierno*, 3 June 1813, publishing a list of the 'encargos y ocupaciones' taken from the *audiencia* and a list of the suppressed tribunals.

[6] A.G.I., Mexico 1664, Informe Audiencia, 18 Nov. 1813.

[7] L. Alamán, *op. cit.*, v, 35–6. See also Odoardo to Minister of Gracia y Justicia, 24 Oct. 1820, quoted in *ibid.*, v, 41–2.

But the success of Iturbide's revolution also required a broader base of support than the relatively small privileged classes, and in this respect the Caroline and liberal attacks on the clergy's privileges were decisive. They not only antagonized one of the most influential sectors of Mexican society, but they also alienated the pious Mexican masses, who might be totally indifferent to a merchant's loss of his trade monopoly but whose support could easily be enlisted by the clergy for any cause which claimed to defend religion and the Church. Royal officials attributed the general unrest they noted after the 1820 liberal coup in Spain almost entirely to the work of the clergy who, taking advantage of the 'notable piety and docility' of the Mexicans, turned the pulpits and confessionals into 'so many chairs of political doctrine'.[1] Pamphlets and articles appeared denouncing the Spanish government as a 'band of atheists and Jacobins', reporting the preparation of even worse attacks on the Church, and urging the faithful to defend their cherished religion.[2]

The astute Iturbide, who had not hesitated to execute insurgent priests without benefit of trial during the 1810 rebellion,[3] included the preservation of ecclesiastical privileges among the articles of his plan for independence and 'the defence of our sacred religion' as one of the three guarantees,[4] thereby assuring the support of both the clergy and the general public. As one peninsular missionary explained to Ferdinand VII in 1822, Spain had lost its colony because the Mexicans had been persuaded by the clergy that their choice lay between loyalty to the Crown and defending their religion from destruction, their priests from persecution, and their churches from despoliation. He himself had been forced to stop preaching against independence or risk being branded a heretic by 'these fanatics'.[5]

---

[1] A.G.I., Mexico 1680, Resumen histórico, Vicente Bausá, 18 Dec. 1821.

[2] See A.G.I., Mexico 1677, 'Defensa del patrimonio de Jesucristo', Mexico, 1820; 'Defensa de los padres jesuítas por los poblanos', Puebla, 1820; and Mexico 1679, 'El yucateco', Mérida, 31 July 1821.

[3] See *Gaceta del gobierno*, 11 Jan. 1815.

[4] A.G.I., Mexico 1680, 'Plan o indicaciones para el gobierno que debe instalarse . . .', Iguala, 24 Feb. 1821, copy sent by Apodaca to Minister of Ultramar.

[5] *Ibid.*, Fr Mariano López Bravo to the king, 30 March 1822.

The ultimate triumph of the independence movement was inevitable, for, despite the suppression of the first rebellion of 1810, independence had become an increasingly common goal for the majority of Creoles. But the alienation of both the lower clergy and the hierarchy by the anti-clerical legislation of the *Cortes* and the clergy's consequent organization of opposition to the government helped to achieve this goal more quickly and peacefully than otherwise would have been possible: a bare six months and a minimum of bloodshed intervened between the *Plan de Iguala* and the treaty signed at Córdoba on 24 August 1821 which put an end to three centuries of Spanish rule in Mexico.

One author has questioned whether the clergy actually derived any benefit from the independence they had promoted so effectively, since they had merely exchanged the remote liberalism of the Spanish *Cortes* for a home-grown variety, representatives of which were to be found even in the Iturbide administration.[1] But if anything the Church and the clergy were in a stronger position after independence than before, in spite of the periodic but largely self-defeating attacks from short-lived liberal régimes. For the old Habsburg balance of power, which the Bourbons had sought to tip in favour of the State now moved in the opposite direction. The clergy were able to preserve the privileges they had enjoyed before the 1820 liberal coup in Spain, in many respects without even the Caroline restrictions. The enforcement of these reforms had been only partial in any case, and some of them, like the alienation of ecclesiastical property and the curtailment of *fuero* in criminal cases (except for crimes of *lèse-majesté*) had been entirely suspended in practice as the colonial government became increasingly concerned with the more urgent question of its own survival. But while the Church reclaimed its traditional privileges, the State lost its principal check on ecclesiastical power. Neither the Mexican clergy nor the pope ever recognized the new republic's claim to the patronage prerogatives the Spanish Crown had exercised so effectively,[2] a

[1] L. Alamán, *op. cit.*, v, 299.
[2] See J. García Gutiérrez, *Apuntes para la historia del origen y desenvolvimiento del Regio Patronato Indiano hasta 1857* (Mexico, 1941), pp. 281–310.

loss which in the opinion of a modern Mexican author made the clergy 'completely independent and uncontrollable'.[1]

But though the Church had become more powerful, its position was more precarious. The Caroline programme of ecclesiastical reform had been successfully opposed in all its phases: the radical programme originally proposed by the ministers of Charles III had been diluted even before it became law; clerical resistance had prevented the effective application of the modified reforms that did reach the Indies; and the successor to the Caroline programme, the liberal decrees of the 1820 *Cortes*, had been blocked by the overthrow of Spanish rule. But the failure of the Spanish colonial régimes to achieve their goals of curtailing the clergy's power and privilege only postponed the establishment of a secular state and meant that the decisive struggle, when it finally took place, would be much more bitter and violent. The Juárez and Lerdo reform laws of the mid-nineteenth century (which differed only slightly from their Caroline prototypes)[2] and the radically anti-clerical clauses of the 1917 Constitution[3] were the inevitable consequences of the repudiation of the programme of ecclesiastical reform first conceived by the regalist ministers of Charles III.

---

[1] J. Pérez Lugo, *La cuestión religiosa en México* (Mexico, 1926), p. 18.

[2] See W. H. Callcott, *Church and State in Mexico, 1822–1857* (Durham, N.C., 1926), pp. 239–57. The Ley Juárez (1855) abolished ecclesiastical *fuero* in civil suits and serious crimes; the Ley Lerdo (1856) applied the 1804 desamortization decree to all property not used directly for worship.

[3] *Constitución política de los Estados Unidos Mexicanos* (promulgated in 1917; Mexico, 1962), art. 8, nos 1 and 4; art. 27, no. 2; and art. 130.

APPENDIX

Ecclesiastical Participants in the Mexican Independence Movement 1808–20[1]

Hyphens are used in the table below to indicate that the opening and/or closing dates of participation are unknown.

SECULAR CLERGY

Abad y Cuadra, Dr José María	insurgent (1810)
Aguilar, Mariano—teniente de cura (Nopala)	subversive (1810)
Aguilar, Pablo—cura (Ahuistlán)	insurgent (–1812, 1813–)
Aguirre, José María (Guadalajara)	subversive (–1815)
Albis, Manuel (Valle de Santiago)	insurgent (–1817)
Alcalá, Dr José María—canon (Mexico)	member of Los Guadalupes (–1814)
Alcázar, José María (Guad.)	subversive (–1814)
Alda, Antonio	subversive (–1815)
Alducín	insurgent officer (–1814)
Álvarez, José María—sacristán mayor (Oaxaca)	subversive (–1811) insurgent (–1814)
Amador, Felipe	insurgent with Rosains
Amés y Argüelles, Antonio—cura (Coscomaltepec)	insurgent officer (–1818)
Aparicio, Nazario	insurgent officer with Morelos
Araujo, Felipe (Querétaro)	insurgent
Arechonda, José Antonio	insurgent (–1814)
Arévalo, Vicente	insurgent (–1814)
Argandar, Dr José Francisco—cura (Baniqueo ?, Michoacán)	insurgent (–1814–)
Arruti	insurgent officer

[1] Compiled from the sources cited in Ch. IX, mainly the *Gaceta del gobierno de Mexico*; C. M. Bustamante, *Cuadro histórico* and *Martirologio*; the records of trials contained in A.G.N., Ramo de Infidencias; and five *cuadernos* of papers captured from the insurgents in 1814, containing lists of insurgent officers and members of juntas and correspondence, copies of which are located in A.G.I., Mexico, 1482. Another useful source, not previously cited, is E. Martínez, 'Los franciscanos y la independencia de México', *Ábside*, xxiv (1960), pp. 129–62.

Aspeitia, José (Guanajuato) — subversive

Ayala, José Antonio—vicario (Tetela del Río) — insurgent (–1817)

Ayala, Rafael—cura (Ajuchitlán) — insurgent officer (–1815)

Balda, Dr Juan Francisco (Durango) — subversive (1812)

Balleza, Mariano—vicario (Dolores) — insurgent (–1811)

Barrera, Manuel de la — insurgent officer (1814, 1816–)

Belán, Antonio — insurgent (–1811)

Benevente, Anastasio — brigadier general (–1813)

Benites, José — insurgent (–1814)

Berdeja, Mariano — subversive and insurgent (1814–)

Bernal, José María (Mex.) — rebel agent (–1811)

Beye Cisneros, Francisco (Mex.) — subversive (1808)

Bonachea — insurgent (–1814–)

Bravo, José Antonio — collaborator (1813)

Buenabad, José Ignacio (Mex.) — subversive (1814)

Bustamante, Juan — collaborator (1814)

Caamaño, Juan Nepomuceno (Quer.) — subversive (1811)

Caballero, Nicolás (Guad.) — insurgent (–1815)

Cacho, José María — insurgent (–1816)

Calderón, Miguel — insurgent (–1814–)

Calvillo, Pablo—cura (Huejúcar) — insurgent officer (1811–)

Cano, Juan Miguel—cura (Pichátaro, Mich.) — insurgent (–1812–)

Cardeña, Ramón—canon (Guad.) — insurgent spy (–1812)

Carmona, José María (Guan.) — insurgent (–1813)

Carrasco — insurgent officer (–1811–)

Carvajal, Felipe — insurgent officer (–1813–)

Castañeda, Francisco—cura (Valle de Santiago) — insurgent (–1816)

Castellanos, Marcos—cura (Ajijic) — commander of Fort Mexcala (1811–16)

Castilblanque, José Manuel — conspirator and insurgent

Cornide, Gregorio — subversive

Correa, José Manuel—cura (Nopala) — insurgent officer (1811–17)

Cos, Dr José María—cura (Burgo de San Cosme, Zacatecas) — insurgent officer and political leader (1812, 1814–)

Couto, José Ignacio—cura (San Martín Texmelucan) — insurgent officer (1812–17)

Crespo, Manuel Sabino—cura (Río Hondo, Oax.) — political leader (–1813)

Cuevas, Francisco (Puebla) — insurgent (–1816)

Dávila y Bravo, Francisco — insurgent (–1812)
Delgado, Pablo—cura (Urecho) — insurgent officer (–1818)
Díaz, José Antonio (Guad.) — subversive (1814)
Díaz, Manuel (Mich.) — insurgent (–1820)

Espinosa, Domingo — rebel agent (–1812)
Estrada, Isidro—cura (Tenango del Río) — subversive (1812)

Fernández, Manuel (Guan.) — insurgent
Fernández del Campo, José María—cura (Huatusco) — insurgent (–1816)
Flórez, Fernando—cura (Acámbaro) — subversive (1812)
Franco (Guan.) — insurgent
Fuentes Alarcón, Mariano de las—cura (Maltrata) — insurgent (–1812–)

García, Martín (Mex.) — subversive (1816)
García, Pablo (San Luis Potosí) — subversive (1816)
García Cano, José Antonio — insurgent officer (–1812, 1814–)
García Carrasquedo, Martín—canon (Mich.) — conspirator (1813)
García de León, Rafael (alias Garcillita) — field marshal (1811, 1814–)
Garduño, Máximo (Ixtlahuaca) — collaborator (1814)
Garfias, Domingo—cura (Tehuantepec) — insurgent spy (–1814)
Garibay, José de Jesús—teniente de cura (Ario) — collaborator (–1815)
Garnelo, Manuel—cura (Tlapa) — insurgent (–1813–)
Gastañeta, José María — insurgent (1810)
Gil (Quer.) — subversive (1811)
Giménez, José Cayetano — insurgent (–1818)
Gómez, Antonio (Sultepec) — collaborator (1810)
Gómez, Francisco—cura (Toluca) — subversive (1816)
Gómez, Miguel—cura (Petatlán) — insurgent officer (–1813)
Gonia, Ignacio — insurgent (–1816)
González (Xochimilco) — insurgent (–1813)
González, Manuel (Mich.) — conspirator (1809)
Guerra, Miguel — collaborator (–1811)
Guerrero — insurgent officer
Gutiérrez, Cayetano — insurgent
Gutiérrez, José Joaquín—cura (Ahuatlán) — chaplain with Morelos
Gutiérrez, José María—cura (Guamelula, Oax.) — insurgent (–1814)
Gutiérrez de Terán, Juan — insurgent

Herrera, Ignacio (Mex.) — subversive (1812)

Herrera, José Manuel—cura (Huamustitlán)	insurgent officer (–1812, 1814–)
Herrera, Nicolás Santiago—cura (Uruapan)	insurgent
Herrero—cura (Cuernavaca)	insurgent officer
Hidalgo, Ignacio	insurgent (1810–11)
Hidalgo y Costilla, Miguel—cura (Dolores)	*Generalísimo* (1810–11)
Huesca	insurgent officer (–1814–)
Ibarra, José Mariano	insurgent (–1815)
Igartua, José (Guad.)	subversive (1815)
Izquierdo, José Manuel	insurgent officer (1812–20)
Jiménez, Ignacio—vicario (Huango)	insurgent
Jiménez Caro, Tomás (Mex.)	member of Los Guadalupes (–1814–)
Jiménez del Río, Juan	insurgent officer (–1817)
Labarrieta, Dr—cura (Guan.)	insurgent (–1811–)
Lara, Francisco (Mex.)	conspirator and insurgent (–1815)
Larragoiti, José Nicolás	subversive (1812)
Laso de la Vega (Quer.)	subversive (1811)
Lezama, Mariano (Huichapán)	subversive (1810)
Ligueria, Ignacio (Orizaba)	subversive
López, Gregorio (Salvatierra)	insurgent
López, Pablo	conspirator (1811)
López, Vicente (Guad.)	insurgent (–1814)
López Romano	insurgent officer (–1815–)
Lozano	insurgent officer
Luján, Mariano (Mich.)	conspirator (1813)
Llave, José de la—cura (Puebla)	subversive
Macías, José Antonio—cura (La Piedad, Mich.)	insurgent officer (–1811)
Magos, Dr José Antonio	insurgent (–1811–19)
Maldonado, Francisco Severo—cura (Mascota)	collaborator
Marín, Manuel	insurgent (1811–14)
Martínez Conejo, Manuel (Mich.)	insurgent (–1817)
Martínez de Segura—cura (Tetela, Oax.)	collaborator
Marulanda, Luis	insurgent (–1814)
Matamoros, Mariano—cura (Tautetelco)	second-in-command to Morelos (1811–14)
Mendoza (Oax.)	insurgent officer (–1812–)

S

Mercado, José María—cura (Ahualulco)   insurgent (1810–11)
Mier, Servando Teresa de—secularized   member of Mina's expedition
Dominican   (1817)
Miranda, Joaquín (Apango)   insurgent (–1814)
Miranda, Tomás—cura (Malacatepec)   insurgent (–1813)
Moctezuma Cortés, Juan—cura   insurgent officer (–1812–)
(Zongolica)
Monroy, José (Guad.)   subversive (1814)
Montes, Hermenegildo—vicario (Dolores)   subversive (1811)
Montes de Oca, José Antonio—cura   conspirator (1813)
(Tiripitío)
Mora, Laureano   officer with Morelos (–1815)
Morales, José María   chaplain with Morelos (–1815)
Morelos, José María—cura (Curácuaro)   insurgent leader (1810–15)

Navarrete, José Luciano   insurgent colonel (1811–14)
Noces, Benito   insurgent (–1812–)
Norzagaray, Alexo (Mex.)   conspirator (1811)

Oceguera, Ramón—sacristán mayor   insurgent (1810, 1812–)
(Santa Clara, Mich.)
Ochoa, Vicente   field marshal (–1812)
Olivera, Rafael   insurgent (–1816)
Olmedo, José Francisco   insurgent (1810–11)
Oñate, José María (Quer.)   subversive
Orcillés   guerrilla leader (–1811)
Ordoño, Ignacio (Oax.)   insurgent officer (–1814)
Oropesa (Guad.)   insurgent officer (–1812)
Ortega, Mariano de (Mex.)   subversive (1812)
Ortega Muro, Mariano—cura   guerrilla leader (–1813)
(Huitlalpan, Pue.)
Ortiz,   member of Junta de Naulingo
(1812)
Ortiz (Mich.)   conspirator (1809)
Ortiz, Ignacio (Guad.)   subversive (1815)
Ortiz, José—chaplain (Hospital de San   subversive (1810)
Pedro, Pue.)
Ortiz, José María—cura (Zacoalpan)   collaborator

Pacheco, Juan Nepomuceno (Guan.)   subversive
Palacios, Francisco—cura (Chiautla)   subversive (1809)
Palacios, Manuel—cura (Huichapán)   subversive (1809)
insurgent (–1813–)
Palancares, Domingo—cura (Tuxtepec,   collaborator
Oax.)
Pana, Francisco (Guad.)   insurgent (–1815)

Paredes, Mariano — insurgent
Patiño, Mariano (Mich.) — insurgent (–1816)
Pedroso (San Luis Potosí) — guerrilla leader (–1812–)
Peláez, Dr José María—chaplain (Hosp. de Pobres, Mex.) — subversive (1812)
Peláez, Manuel — insurgent (–1817)
Perea, Blas — insurgent (–1812)
Peredo y Gallegos, Dr José Joaquín (Mex.) — insurgent with Rayón (1813–)
Pérez, José (Guad.) — insurgent
Pérez, José Antonio (Quer.) — insurgent chaplain (–1816)
Pérez, José María — insurgent (–1812)
Pérez, Rafael (Guad.) — subversive (1811)
Plata, Francisco (Guad.) — insurgent (–1813)
Ponce, Mariano — officer with Liceaga

Rabadan, — officer with Morelos
Ramírez, José Mariano (Guan.) — officer with Rayón
Ramírez, Juan José — insurgent (–1812)
Ramírez, Dr Manuel (Mex.) — subversive (1812)
Ramírez, Mariano (Guad.) — subversive (1814)
Ramos, José María—cura (Guad.) — insurgent (–1817)
Río, Francisco del (Mich.) — insurgent (–1816)
Riva y Rada, Manuel — subversive (1809)
Rivera, Mariano (Huichapán) — subversive (1810)
Rodríguez, Fabián (Mich.) — insurgent officer (–1812–)
Romero, José Cayetano — insurgent officer (–1815)
Romero, Juan Antonio—vicario (Tlalpujahua, Mich.) — collaborator (–1813)
Rosado, Mariano—cura (Misantla, Pue.) — insurgent (1812–17)
Ruelas, Santiago — subversive (1809)
Ruiz, Antonio — insurgent (–1811)
Ruiz de Chaves, Manuel—cura (Huango) — conspirator (1809)

Saavedra, Ignacio (Mich.) — insurgent officer (–1812–)
Sáenz, Juan (Mich.) — guerrilla leader
Sáinz, Francisco de Paula (Mich.) — insurgent (–1815)
Salazar—chaplain (La Regina mine) — subversive
Salcedo, José María — insurgent officer (1811, 1812–)
Salgado, Mariano—cura (Cuahuayutla) — collaborator (–1813–)
Salto, José Guadalupe—vicario (Teremendo, Mich.) — insurgent (–1812)
Sánchez de la Vega, José María—cura (Tlacotepec) — officer with Morelos (–1812–)
San Martín, José—canon (Oax.) — officer and political leader (1811–18)

Sartorio, José Manuel—canon (Mex.) — member of Los Guadalupes (–1814–)

Serrano, Miguel (Mex.) — subversive (1812)

Sierra Gorda, Conde de—canon (Mich.) — member of Los Guadalupes (–1814–)

Soria—cura (Etácuaro, Mich.) — insurgent

Soria, Francisco—cura (Xiquipilco) — collaborator (1811)

Sota y Cuevas, Juan José de la (Durango) — subversive

Subiano, Manuel—vicario (Ajuchitlán) — subversive (1817)

Suiza, José María — insurgent (–1815)

Tagle, Carlos (Mich.) — conspirator (1813)

Talavera, José Antonio (Oax.) — insurgent officer (1811–17)

Tapia, Mariano de—vicario (Tlapa) — officer with Morelos

Tarelo, José Rafael — insurgent with Rosains

Tejo, Fernando (Quer.) — subversive

Ternero, Francisco (Salvatierra) — subversive

Tirado, José Luis—vicario (Tenango) — insurgent (1810–12)

Torayo, Manuel (Mex.) — subversive (1808)

Torre, José María (Pue.) — guerrilla leader

Torreblanca, José Pablo—cura (Acatlán) — insurgent (–1818)

Torres, José Antonio—vicario (Cuitzeo) — lieutenant general (1811, 1814–)

Torres Lloreda, Manuel (Mich.) — conspirator (1809)

Trujillo, José de Jesús — insurgent (–1815)

Ulloa, Juan Nepomuceno (Jalapa) — insurgent

Uraga, Dr Antonio María—cura (Maravitío, Mich.) — conspirator

Uribe (Mich.) — insurgent officer (–1815–)

Urquijo, Joaquín de—cura (Acayucan) — subversive (1812)

Valderas, Tiburcio (Mex.) — conspirator (1811)

Valdivieso, José—cura (Ocuituco) — chaplain with Morelos (1812–14)

Vázquez, Pedro—cura (Ajuchitlán) — insurgent (–1817)

Vega, José Manuel — insurgent (–1818)

Vega, José María de la—cura (Sola, Oax.) — collaborator (–1811)

Velasco, José Mariano—cura (Texcalicalco) — insurgent (1810–)

Velasco de la Vara, Dr Francisco Lorenzo—canon (Guadalupe) — officer and political leader (1812–17)

Venegas, Alcario — subversive (1816)

Venegas, José María — insurgent (–1817)

Verdusco, José Sixto—cura (Tusantla) — officer and political leader (–1817)

Victoria, Pablo (Guad.)   subversive (1814)
Villanueva, Agustín Mateos de—cura   collaborator (1810)
(Ixtlahuaca)
Villanueva, Toribio   insurgent
Villaverde, Pedro Alcántara   insurgent spy (–1814)

Zambrano, Cristóbal   collaborator (–1814)
Zamudio, José María (Celaya)   insurgent (–1815)
Zavala, Juan   insurgent with Matamoros
Zavala, Matías—cura (Cutzamala)   insurgent officer (–1818)
Zegui (Mich.)   conspirator
Zempoaltica, Cristóbal   subversive
Zimarripa, Fernando (San Luis Potosí)   insurgent (–1812)
Zúñiga, Francisco—chaplain (La   subversive
Valenciana mine)
Zúñiga, José Antonio—cura   subversive (1811)
(Temascaltepec)
Zúñiga, Nicolás—cura (Sultepec)   collaborator

REGULAR CLERGY

Aguirre, José   subversive (1814)
Alcántara, José María—Franciscan (Mex.)   conspirator
Álvarez, José María (Pachuca)   subversive (1816)
Antelo, Francisco—Franciscan (Mex.)   subversive (1811)
Aparicio, José—Dominican (Oax.)   subversive (1809)
Aparicio, José de San Sebastián—   insurgent (–1817)
Carmelite
Arana, Mariano—Franciscan (Quer.)   subversive
Arellano, José María—Mercedarian   insurgent officer (–1813–)
Arenas, Joaquín   insurgent
Ayala, Cristóbal   subversive (1810)
Ayala, Mariano—San Hipólito Mártir   conspirator (1811)
(Mex.)

Belaunzarán, José María—Dieguino   subversive (1815)
(Guan.)
Bernal, Joaquín   chaplain with Morelos
Bustamante, Agustín—Franciscan (Mex.)   conspirator (1811)
Bustamante, Pedro—Mercedarian   insurgent (–1811)

Camargo, Manuel   insurgent
Cano, José Raimundo—Franciscan   insurgent officer (1811–13)
Carmona—Mercedarian   officer with Rayón
Carranza, Gregorio—Dominican   insurgent (–1813)
Castro, Juan—Augustinian (Mex.)   conspirator (1811)
Cea, Esteban—Mercedarian (Pue.)   insurgent chaplain (–1815)

Cervantes, Mariano—Franciscan	insurgent with Morelos
Colosia, Francisco—Dieguino (Mex.)	conspirator (1811)
Concepción, Gregorio de la—Carmelite	insurgent (1810–11)
Conde, Bernardo—Franciscan	insurgent (–1811)
Conejo, Felipe de Jesús—Franciscan (Guad.)	insurgent officer (–1816)
Cueva, Agustín—Augustinian	subversive
Cueva, Pedro de la	conspirator
Chávez, Simón—Bethlemite	insurgent with Rayón
Dávila, Juan	insurgent (–1814–)
Delgadillo, Pablo—Franciscan (Guad.)	insurgent officer (–1811)
Delgado—Franciscan	officer with Verdusco
Díaz, Tomás	insurgent (–1814)
Díaz del Castillo, Manuel (Mex.)	conspirator (1811)
Duen, José Antonio—Dieguino (Mex.)	conspirator (1811)
Escalante, José María—Dieguino (Quer.)	collaborator (1812)
Escobar, Mariano—Franciscan	subversive
Espíritu Santo, José del	insurgent (–1811)
Esquerro, José María—Augustinian	insurgent (–1811–)
Farifán, Agustín	insurgent (–1814–)
Fernández, Manuel—San Hipólito Mártir	insurgent (–1813)
Fernández, Mariano—Franciscan (Mex.)	subversive (1809)
Flores, Pascual	insurgent chaplain
Franco, Carlos	insurgent
Gálvez, Antonio—Franciscan	insurgent chaplain
Gallaga—San Juan de Diós	insurgent officer (1811–)
Garcés, Ignacio—Dieguino (Mex.)	subversive (1812)
García, Francisco—Franciscan	insurgent
Gómez, Tomás—Mercedarian (Mex.)	subversive (1812)
González, Francisco (San Luis Potosí)	insurgent (1811–)
Gutiérrez, Juan	insurgent officer (–1813–)
Gutiérrez Solano, Manuel—Franciscan	officer with Morelos (–1813)
Hernández, Antonio	insurgent (–1816)
Hernández, José	insurgent (–1814)
Herrera, Luis de—San Juan de Diós	insurgent officer (1810–11)
Ibargoyen—Franciscan	insurgent officer (–1812–)
Jesús Niño, Felipe de (Mex.)	conspirator (1811)
Jiménez	insurgent with Rosains
Jiménez, Ignacio—Francisco (Monterrey)	insurgent (–1811)

Jiménez, Pascual	lieutenant-colonel with Morelos
Ladrón de Guevara, Juan—Franciscan (Mex.)	conspirator
Lamano, Manuel	subversive (1812)
Landín, Manuel—Franciscan	insurgent (–1816)
Lechuga, Francisco—Augustinian (Mex.)	conspirator (1811)
Lima, José de—Mercedarian (San Luis Potosí)	insurgent (–1813)
Liñán, Ignacio	insurgent officer (–1813)
Lozada, Alifrio	insurgent (–1813)
Lozano, José—Mercedarian	subversive (1813)
Lugo de Luna, José—Franciscan	insurgent (–1815)
Luna, Felipe de Jesús—Franciscan	insurgent (–1811)
Mancilla—Franciscan	insurgent (1811–)
Manjares, José—Dominican (Oax.)	collaborator (1810)
Manrique, Sebastián—Franciscan (San Luis Potosí)	insurgent (–1811)
Martínez, Agustín (Mich.)	conspirator
Medina, Carlos—Franciscan	chaplain with Hidalgo (–1811)
Melgarejo, Nicolás—San Hipólito Mártir	insurgent officer (–1817)
Méndez, Antonio—Franciscan	subversive
Misieres, José—Augustinian (Mex.)	conspirator (1811)
Monserrate, José	subversive
Monterde, Manuel—Franciscan	insurgent (–1818)
Montero, Juan	insurgent (–1812)
Mora, José Mariano	insurgent (–1816)
Moreisa, Bartolomé—Franciscan	subversive
Morenti—Augustinian	insurgent
Muro, Miguel—Franciscan	subversive
Narváes, Manuel—Augustinian Prior (Zacatecas)	conspirator (1814)
Negreiros, Vicente—Augustinian (Mex.)	conspirator (1814)
Ocaranza, Manuel—Augustinian	insurgent officer
Orcillés, Pedro José—Franciscan	insurgent officer (–1819)
Ornoz, Miguel—Franciscan	insurgent officer
Oroñoz, Luis—Franciscan (San Luis Potosí)	insurgent (–1811)
Orozco, José Domingo—Franciscan	insurgent (–1820)
Orozco, Manuel—Franciscan	insurgent (–1811–)
Orozco, Mariano (Guad.)	collaborator
Otalegui, Antonio—Franciscan	insurgent

Oviedo, Joaquín—Mercedarian Prior (Zacatecas)	conspirator (1814)
Páez, José Ignacio	insurgent (–1812)
Panes, José—Mercedarian	subversive (1814)
Parodi, Antonio—Franciscan	subversive
Parra, Francisco de la—Dominican (Guad.)	insurgent spy
Pedroza, José Antonio—Franciscan	diplomatic agent for insurgents
Perea, Ignacio	insurgent
Pérez, Anselmo—Franciscan	collaborator
Pérez, Gelasio de Jesús—Augustinian	insurgent (–1810)
Pérez Gallardo, José	insurgent chaplain (–1813–)
Pino, José Mariano—San Juan de Diós (Mex.)	subversive
Pons, Tomás—Dominican Provincial (Pue.)	collaborator
Porres, José—Mercedarian	insurgent (–1818)
Pugo, Francisco de (Mex.)	conspirator (1811)
Quevedo, Manuel—Franciscan (Salvatierra)	collaborator (–1813)
Quintana, José Ignacio (Mich.)	subversive
Ramírez, Diego—San Juan de Diós	insurgent officer
Ramírez Arellano, Ignacio—San Hipólito Mártir (Mex.)	collaborator (1813)
Ramírez Arellano, Joaquín—Mercedarian (Mex.)	subversive (1812)
Ramos, José—Franciscan (San Luis Potosí)	insurgent officer
Rascón, Ventura (Mich.)	conspirator
Raso, José—San Hipólito Mártir (Mex.)	conspirator
Río, Antonio del—Franciscan	collaborator
Rivera, Pedro—Augustinian (Mex.)	conspirator (1811)
Robles—San Juan de Diós	insurgent
Robles, Francisco—Franciscan (Saltillo)	subversive (1816)
Rodríguez, José—Mercedarian (San Luis Potosí)	insurgent (–1813)
Rodríguez, Santiago—Dominican	insurgent with Garcillita
Rosendi, Manuel—Augustinian (Mex.)	conspirator (1811)
Rueda, Alvino (Mich.)	subversive
Ruiz, Miguel—Franciscan	insurgent chaplain
Saavedra, Laureano—Dominican	brigadier general (–1812–)
Sabinas, Vicente (Mex.)	conspirator (1811)

Sáenz de la Santa, Melchor—Franciscan — insurgent (1810-11)
Salazar, Juan de—Franciscan — insurgent (-1811)
Salazar, Manuel—San Juan de Diós (Mex.) — conspirator
Salinas, Manuel—Augustinian — insurgent (1812-)
San Hilarión, José de (Quer.) — collaborator (1812)
San Salvador, José de—Mercedarian (Mex.) — subversive (1812)
San Sebastián, José de — insurgent chaplain (-1813-)
Santa María, Vicente de—Franciscan (Mich.) — conspirator (1809) and insurgent (-1813-)
Santa Teresa, Matías de — subversive (1812)
Santísima Trinidad, Bernardino de la—Bethlemite (Oax.) — subversive (1810)
Santoscoy—Mercedarian (Veracruz) — subversive (1811)
Simiano, Pío—doctrinero (Río Verde) — collaborator (1813)
Soria, Ignacio—Augustinian (Mex.) — conspirator (1811)
Sotomayor, Antonio Gabriel — insurgent (-1814)
Suárez, Manuel—Augustinian (Mex.) — conspirator (1811)

Tabaquero, Antonio — insurgent officer (-1812)
Talamantes, Melchor de—Mercedarian (Mex.) — subversive 1808)
Toledo, Mariano—San Juan de Diós — insurgent (-1814)
Travieso, Vicente—Franciscan (Mex.) — conspirator (1811)
Troncoso, Francisco—Dominican — insurgent (-1814)

Vargas, José Antonio—Franciscan — insurgent (1810-11)
Vergara, José—San Hipólito Mártir (Mex.) — conspirator
Villagrán, José María — insurgent officer
Villaseñor, José Bernardo—Franciscan — insurgent chaplain
Villerías — insurgent officer (1810-12)

Zapata—San Juan de Diós (San Luis Potosí) — insurgent
Zea, Manuel—Mercedarian (Mex.) — subversive
Zenizo, Francisco—Dieguino (Mex.) — conspirator (1811)
Zugasti, Manuel—Franciscan (Mex.) — subversive (1809)

GLOSSARY OF SPANISH TERMS

Alcalde del crimen: criminal magistrate; member of *sala del crimen*

Alcalde mayor: local administrative and judicial official

Asesor: legal adviser to an executive official, e.g. a viceroy

Asistente real: non-voting representative of the Crown at elections of regular superiors, *oposiciones* for benefices, and provincial councils

Audiencia: appellate court with legislative and administrative functions

Auditor de guerra: civilian magistrate acting as legal adviser to the viceroy or governor in military cases

Auto: decree or sentence; in plural, testimony of judicial proceedings

Auxilio real: assistance given by the secular authorities in executing ecclesiastical writs and sentences

Bando: viceregal decree

Capellanía: chantry; private ecclesiastical benefice with the obligation of fulfilling stipulated spiritual duties, usually masses for the soul of the deceased benefactor

Capítulo: meeting of a province of a religious order, usually every two years, to elect new superiors

Carta acordada: order issued by a royal council (or sometimes *audiencia*) on its own authority, without the royal signature

Causa de remoción: trial for the removal of an ecclesiastical beneficiary under royal patronage

Cofradía: parish confraternity dedicated to charitable works

Colegio mayor: college preparing students for university degrees

Comandante General: military and executive officer of the Provincias Internas in northern New Spain

Comisario general: superior of various religious orders in the Indies (Franciscans and Mercedarians, for example) under the General but with authority over several provinces

Competencia: jurisdictional dispute

Consulado: organization of merchants with judicial jurisdiction in certain commercial cases

Consulta: report submitted to the king containing the Council's recommendations

Custodio: superior of a small religious community

Dictamen: legal opinion; synonym of *respuesta*

Doctrina: curacy or parish of Indians

Doctrinero: priest in charge of a *doctrina*

Expediente: case; and also file of papers bearing on a case

Familiares: laymen employed by the Church, such as notaries, bailiffs, and choirmasters

Fiscal: a legal officer representing the Crown with the duty of advising the Council or *audiencia* in preparing legislation and making judicial decisions

Fiscal de lo civil: colonial *fiscal* who advised the *audiencia* in civil suits and certain administrative matters

Fiscal del crimen: colonial *fiscal* representing the Crown in criminal cases, usually as public prosecutor

Fuero: the privilege of being tried in a particular tribunal; also the particular tribunal or area of jurisdiction

Fuero externo: pertaining to statute law

Fuero interno: pertaining to conscience

Gachupín: term applied to peninsular Spaniards in Mexico, often in a derogatory sense

Infidencia: disloyalty or treason

Inmunidad local: the privilege of asylum granted to a person taking refuge in a church (often extending to rectories and monasteries as well)

Inmunidad real: the exemptions enjoyed by ecclesiastical property from taxation and secular control

Juez conservador: magistrate (usually a member of the secular clergy) chosen by a religious order to defend its privileges and immunities

Juez de testamentos, capellanías y obras pías: diocesan judge in all suits concerning ecclesiastical property (except tithes); also responsible for the administration of ecclesiastical foundations

Juez hacedor: member of a cathedral chapter with jurisdiction over the collection and distribution of tithes

Juicio de residencia: judicial inquiry into the conduct of an official at the end of his term in office

Mixti fori: pertaining to two or more *fueros* or areas of jurisdiction

Motín: tumult, riot

Oidor: appellate judge; member of an *audiencia*

Oposiciones: competitive oral examinations for office

Partida de registro: entry of a prisoner in a ship's register for transport, usually to Spain, in the custody of the captain

Pase regio: royal authorization for the publication of a papal rescript

Patronato real: royal patronage of the Church which in the Indies involved the rights of presentation and supervision of the Church's administration along with the responsibility to provide material support and protection

Poder económico: inherent authority of the temporal sovereign; executive as distinct from judicial and legislative authority

Presidio: fortified military base

Proceso informativo: a judicial inquiry into a criminal offence for the purpose of gathering information but not preparing an indictment

Provisor: diocesan magistrate exercising the ordinary judicial authority of the bishop

Real acuerdo: administrative or legislative session of an *audiencia* presided over by the viceroy or governor

Real amparo: royal writ granting a pardon or commuting a sentence

Real cédula: royal decree issued by a council

Real orden: royal decree issued by a ministry

Real provisión: decree issued by an *audiencia* with the legal force of a royal *cédula*

Recurso de fuerza: extraordinary appeal to a royal court for redress of a grievance suffered in an ecclesiastical court

Recurso de protección: variation of a *recurso de fuerza* appealing for protection from any grievous act, not necessarily judicial

Regalía: royal prerogative

Respuesta: legal opinion, synonym of *dictamen*

Sala del crimen: criminal court forming subdivision of a major *audiencia*

Subdelegado: official with judicial and administrative authority in charge of a subdivision of an intendancy

Teniente de justicia: royal justice in rural areas subordinate to *subdelegado*

Tribunal de la acordada: royal court in the *audiencia* district of Mexico with authority to dispense summary justice for crimes committed outside the immediate jurisdiction of the municipalities

Vicariato: variation of the *patronato* in which the Spanish king assumed papal authority over the colonial Church

Visita: visitation; tour of inspection and reform of a royal province, diocese or religious order

Visitador: inspector; in the religious orders appointed by the General to investigate and reform a particular province

BIBLIOGRAPHY

I. UNPUBLISHED SOURCES

A. ARCHIVO DIOCESANO DE TOLEDO: Sala 4, Nos. 125 and 127

B. ARCHIVO GENERAL DE INDIAS—SEVILLE

Audiencia de Guadalajara: 242–5, 247, 310, 315, 317, 323-A, 332, 334, 335, 339, 341, 343–5, 348, 356–8, 362, 369, 533, 534, 536, 545, 546, 563, 566, 568, 569

Audiencia de México: 3, 1140–3, 1146, 1147, 1150, 1152, 1159, 1271, 1285, 1289, 1321, 1322, 1424, 1473–7, 1480–3, 1635, 1661, 1662, 1664, 1665, 1675–80, 1691–761, 1885, 2170, 2383, 2531, 2534, 2537, 2538, 2540, 2542, 2544, 2545, 2571, 2604, 2609, 2614, 2616–19, 2621–38, 2641, 2644–8, 2651, 2661, 2665, 2666, 2669, 2672, 2675, 2694, 2696, 2711, 2743, 2744, 2747–51, 3005, 3051, 3053, 3054, 3063, 3064, 3068–3070-A, 3072, 3167

Contratación: 4038, 4059, 4074, 4121, 4194, 4298, 4310, 4344, 4377

Estado: 20, 22, 34, 39

Indiferente General: 15, 60, 62–64, 66, 68, 73, 110, 350, 563, 1653, 1654, 2883, 2915, 2916, 2993–5, 3025–7, 3040, 3041

C. ARCHIVO GENERAL DE LA NACIÓN—MEXICO

Bandos y ordenanzas: 6, 7, 15, 19

Capellanías: 1

Clero regular y secular: 5, 30, 32, 61, 67, 83, 153, 204

Cofradías y archicofradías: 12, 16

Historia: 409, 411, 412

Impresos oficiales: 34, 43, 60

Infidencias: 5, 10, 11, 19, 23, 29, 58, 63, 65, 68, 76, 85–8, 92, 94, 99, 102, 114, 116, 117, 128, 130, 134, 139, 145–7, 160, 165, 169, 172, 177, 180, 181

Obispos y arzobispos: 3

Obras pías: 2, 6

Operaciones de guerra: 1011–14

Reales cédulas: 91, 92, 207, 213, 215, 244

D. ARCHIVO HISTÓRICO NACIONAL—MADRID

Códices: 687, 689, 691, 696, 698, 700, 706, 715, 717, 718, 722, 724, 730, 756

Consejos: 58, 494, 8925, 20675, 20683, 20691, 20716, 20718, 20723, 21081, 21203, 21212, 21215, 51560

Estado: 6438

Inquisición: 2286-A, 2286-B, 2287

E. BIBLIOTECA NACIONAL—MADRID
Sección de Manuscritos: 2706, 3534, 3535, 3650, 4175, 5806, 10653, 12009, 12054, 13224, 19199, 19200, 19709, 20245, 20265

F. BIBLIOTECA DEL PALACIO—MADRID
Colección general: 1439, 1492, 3078
Colección Ayala: 4, 19, 26, 31, 39

G. BIBLIOTECA PÚBLICA DE TOLEDO
Colección Borbón-Lorenzana: 62, 178

H. REAL ACADEMIA DE LA HISTORIA—MADRID
Colección Jesuítas: 28, 86
Colección Mata Linares: 9, 76
Legajos de Jesuítas: 89, 100

II. PUBLISHED SOURCES AND CONTEMPORARY WORKS

ABAD Y QUEIPO, Manuel, Colección de los escritos más importantes que en diferentes épocas dirigió al govierno (Mexico, 1813).
La administración de D. Frey Antonio María de Bucareli y Ursúa (Publicaciones del Archivo General de la Nación, vols. 29 & 30, Mexico, 1936).
ÁLVAREZ DE ABREU, Antonio (Marqués de la Regalía), Víctima real legal (Madrid, 1726).
AMAT Y JUNIENT, Manuel de, Memoria de gobierno de Manuel Amat y Juráent, virrey del Perú, V. Rodriguez Casado and F. Pérez Embid, eds. (Seville 1947, written in 1776).
AVENDAÑO, Diego de, Thesaurus Indicus (2 vols., Antwerp, 1668–77).
BÁRCENA, Manuel de la, Manifiesto al mundo de la justicia y necesidad de la independencia de la Nueva España (Mexico, 1821).
BELEÑA, Eusebio Ventura, Recopilación sumaria de todos los autos acordados de la Real Audiencia y Sala del Crimen de esta Nueva España (2 vols., Mexico, 1787).
BELLARMINO, Roberto, De controversiis christianae fidei (Milan, 1586).
BUSTAMANTE, Carlos María, El juguetillo, periodical (Mexico, 1812).
CABARRÚS, François (Conde de Cabarrús), Cartas sobre los obstáculos que la naturaleza, la opinión y las leyes oponen a la felicidad pública (Vitoria, 1808, written in 1792).
CAÑADA, Conde de la (Juan Acedo y Rico), Observaciones prácticas sobre los recursos de fuerza; modo de introducirlos, continuarlos y determinarlos en los tribunales reales superiores (Madrid, 1793).
Cartas político-económicas al Conde de Lerena, A. Rodríguez Villa, ed. (Madrid, 1878, written in the 1780's).
CASTILLO DE BOBADILLA, Gerónimo, Política para corregidores y señores de vasallos en tiempo de paz y de guerra y para prelados en lo espiritual y temporal entre legos (2 vols., Madrid, 1775, first published in 1574).
Codex Juris Canonici (promulgated in 1917).

Colección de los decretos y órdenes que han expedido las Cortes generales y extraordinarias desde su instalación (10 vols., Madrid, 1820–3).

Constitución política de los Estados Unidos Mexicanos (promulgated in 1917; Mexico, 1962).

Constitución política de la monarquía española (Cadiz, 1812).

COVARRUBIAS, José, *Máximas sobre recursos de fuerza y protección con el método de introducirlos en los tribunales* (Madrid, 1785).

CROIX, Carlos Francisco de (Marqués de Croix), *Cartas del Marqués de Croix* (Brussels, 1884).

Decretales (promulgated by Pope Gregory IX in 1234).

Decretos reales tocantes a la iglesia (collection of printed documents, British Museum).

Decretum Gratiani (compiled *c.* 1140–50).

Documentos históricos mexicanos (collection of printed documents, 2 vols., British Museum).

Documentos para la historia de México (four series in 20 vols., Mexico, 1853–7).

ESPEN, Zeger Bernhard van, *Jus ecclesiasticum universum* (Louvain, 1700).

FERNÁNDEZ DE LIZARDI, José Joaquín, *El pensador mexicano*, periodical (Mexico, 1812–27).

—, *El periquillo sarniento* (Mexico, 1961, first published in 1816).

FLEURY, Claude, *Institution au droit ecclesiastique* (2 vols., Paris, 1676).

FONSECA, Fabian de, and Carlos de URRUTIA, *Historia general de Real Hacienda, escrita por . . . orden del virrey conde de Revillagigedo . . .* (6 vols., Mexico, 1845–53).

FRASSO, Pedro, *De regio patronatu ac aliis nonnullis regaliis regibus catholicis in Indiarum Occidentalum imperio pertinentibus* (Madrid, 1677).

Gaceta del gobierno de Mexico, periodical (Mexico, 1810–21).

GARCÍA, Genaro, ed., *Documentos históricos mexicanos* (7 vols., Mexico, 1910).

GARCÍA, Genaro, and Carlos PEREYRA, eds., *Documentos inéditos ó muy raros para la historia de México* (36 vols., Mexico, 1905–11).

GARCÍA DE TORRES, José Julio, *Vindicación del clero mexicano vulnerado en las anotaciones que publicó el M.R.P. José Joaquín Oyarzábal* (Mexico, 1812).

—, *El vindicador del clero mexicano a su antagonista B.* (Mexico, 1812).

HENRÍQUEZ, Enrique, *De clavibus romani pontificis* (Salamanca, 1619).

HERNÁEZ, F. J., ed., *Colección de bulas, breves y otros documentos relativos a la iglesia de América y Filipinas* (2 vols., Brussels, 1879).

HERNÁNDEZ Y DÁVALOS, Juan. ed., *Colección de documentos para la historia de la guerra de independencia de México* (6 vols., Mexico, 1877–82).

HEVIA BOLAÑOS, Juan de., *Curia Philipica* (Madrid, 1615).

HONTHEIM, Johann von (pseud., Justinus Febronius), *De statu ecclesiae et legitima potestate Romani Pontificis* (Boulogne, 1763).

Instrucciones que los virreyes de Nueva España dejaron a sus sucesores (2 vols., Mexico, 1873).

ISLA, José Francisco de, *Cartas inéditas del Padre Isla* (Madrid, 1957).

JUAN, Jorge and Antonio de ULLOA, *Noticias secretas de América* (2 vols., Madrid, 1918, written in 1749).

272   BIBLIOGRAPHY

LÓPEZ, Juan Luis (Marqués del Risco), *Discurso jurídico, histórico-político en defensa de la jurisdicción real* (Lima, 1685).

—, *Historia legal de la bula llamada In Coena Domini* (Madrid, 1768, written in 1688).

MARIANA, Juan de, *De rege et regis institutione* (Toledo, 1599).

Memorias de los virreyes que han gobernado el Perú (5 vols., Lima, 1859).

Mexican Political Pamphlets (collection of printed documents, 14 vols., British Museum).

Mexican Political Tracts (collection of printed documents, British Museum).

MIER, Servando Teresa de, *Memorias de Fray Servando Teresa de Mier*, Alfonso Reyes, ed. (Madrid, n.d.).

MOLINA, Luis de, *De justitia et jure* (3 vols., Cuenca, 1597–1600).

NAVARRO Y NORIEGA, Fernando, *Memoria sobre la población del reino de Nueva España* (Mexico, 1820).

Novísima Recopilación de las leyes de España (Madrid, 1805).

Nueva Recopilación de las leyes de Castilla (Madrid, 1567).

NÚÑEZ DE HARO Y PERALTA, Alonso (Archbishop of Mexico), *Constituciones que formó para el mejor régimen y govierno del Real Colegio Seminario de Instrucción voluntaria y corrección para el clero secular* (Mexico, 1774).

Obras originales del Conde de Floribablanca y escritos referentes a su persona, A. Ferrer del Río, ed. (Biblioteca de Autores Españoles, vol. 59, Madrid, 1867).

Papeles tocantes e la iglesia española 1625–1790 (collection of printed documents, British Museum).

PEREDO Y GALLEGOS, José Joaquín, *Discurso dogmático sobre la jurisdicción ecclesiástica* (Mexico, 1812).

Precursores ideológicos de la guerra de independencia, 1789–1794 (Publicaciones del Archivo General de la Nación, vols. 13 & 21, Mexico, 1929 & 1932).

Proceso del caudillo de la independencia don Mariano Matamoros (Publicaciones del Archivo General de la Nación, Mexico, 1918).

PUENTE, Pedro de la, *Reflexiones sobre el bando de 25 de junio último contraídas a lo que dispone para con los eclesiásticos rebeldes y al recurso que en solicitud de su revocación dirigieron en 6 de julio a este Ilmo. Cabildo, varios clérigos y cinco religiosos de México* (Mexico, 1812).

Recopilación de leyes de los reynos de las Indias (Madrid, 1681).

REVILLAGIGEDO, Conde de (Juan de Güemes Pacheco y Padilla), *Instrucción reservada que dió el Conde de Revillagigedo a su sucesor en el mando el Marqués de Branciforte* (Mexico, 1831, written in 1794).

RIBADENEYRA Y BARRIENTOS, Antonio Joaquín de, *Manual compendio del Regio Patronato Indiano* (Madrid, 1755).

RICO GONZÁLEZ, Victor, ed., *Documentos sobre la expulsión de los Jesuítas y ocupación de sus temporalidades en Nueva España* (Mexico, 1949).

RODRÍGUEZ DE CAMPOMANES, Pedro (Conde de Campomanes), *Apéndice a la educación popular* (4 vols., Madrid, 1775–7).

—, *Colección de las alegaciones fiscales del Excmo. Señor Conde de Campomanes* (4 vols., Madrid, 1841).

—, *Discurso sobre la educación popular de los artesanos y su fomento* (Madrid, 1775).

—, *Juicio imparcial sobre las letras en forma de breve que ha publicado la Curia Romana* (Madrid, 1768).

—, *Tratado de la regalía de amortización* (Madrid, 1765).

RUYZ DE CABRERA, Cristóbal, *Algunos singulares y extraordinarios sucesos* (Mexico, 1624).

SALGADO DE SOMOZA, Francisco, *De regia protectione vi oppressorum appelatium a causis et judicibus ecclesiasticis* (Madrid, 1626).

SÁNCHEZ, Santos, ed., *Colección de todas los pragmáticas, cédulas, provisiones circulares, autos acordados, bandos y otras providencias publicadas en el actual reinado del Señor Don Carlos IV* (4 vols., Madrid, 1794–1805).

Las Siete Partidas del Rey Don Alfonso el Sabio, published by the Real Academia de la Historia (3 vols., Madrid, 1807, compiled in 1256–65).

SOLORZANO PEREIRA, Juan de, *Política indiana* (Madrid, 1647).

SUÁREZ, Francisco, *De legibus ac de deo legislatore* (Coimbra, 1612).

—, *Defensio fideo catholicae et apostolicae adversus anglicanae sectae errores* (Coimbra, 1613).

TAMARÓN Y ROMERAL, Pedro (Bishop of Durango), *Demostración del vastísimo obispado de la Nueva Vizcaya, 1765*, ed. by Vito Alessio Robles (Mexico, 1937).

TEJADA Y RAMIRO, Juan, ed., *Colección de cánones y de todos los concilios de la iglesia de España y de América* (6 vols., Madrid, 1849–62).

VALLADARES, Antonio, ed., *Semanario erudito*, periodical (34 vols., Madrid, 1787–91).

VILLARROEL, Gaspar de, *Gobierno eclesiástico pacífico y unión de dos cuchillos, pontificio y regio* (Madrid, 1634).

VILLARROEL, Hipólito, *México por dentro y por fuera bajo el gobierno de los virreyes. Ó sea enfermedades políticas que padece la capital de N. España* . . . (Mexico, 1831, written in 1785).

III. SECONDARY WORKS

ALAMÁN, Lucas, *Historia de México* (5 vols., Mexico, 1883–5).

ANCONA, Eligio, *Historia de Yucatán desde la época más remota hasta nuestros días* (3 vols., Mérida, 1878–9).

ANDRADE, Vicente de Paula, *Noticias biográficas sobre los ilustrísmos prelados de Sonora, de Sinaloa y de Durango* (Mexico, 1899).

BANCROFT, Hubert Howe, *History of Mexico* (6 vols., San Francisco, 1883).

BORAH, Woodrow, 'Tithe Collection in the Bishopric of Oaxaca, 1601–1867', *H.A.H.R.*, xxix (1949), pp. 498–517.

BRAVO UGARTE, José, 'El clero y la independencia', *Ábside*, v (1941), pp. 612–30, vii (1943), pp. 406–9, and xv (1951), pp. 199–218.

—, *Diócesis y obispos de la iglesia mexicana 1519–1939* (Mexico, 1941).

BUSTAMANTE, Carlos María, *Cuadro histórico de la revolución mexicana* (6 vols., Mexico, 1843–6).

T

BUSTAMANTE, Carlos María, *Cuadro histórico de la revolución mexicana* (the author's revised version, republished in 3 vols., Mexico, 1961).

—, *Martirologio de algunos de los primeros insurgentes por la libertad e independencia de la América mexicana* (Mexico, 1841).

CALLCOTT, Wilfrid Hardy, *Church and State in Mexico, 1822–1857* (Durham, N.C., 1926).

CASTILLO LEDÓN, Luis, *Hidalgo, la vida del héroe* (2 vols., Mexico, 1948–9).

CHEVALIER, François, *La formation des grands domaines au Mexique* (Paris, 1952).

COLMEIRO, Manuel, *Biblioteca de los economistas españoles de los siglos XVI, XVII y XVIII* (Madrid, 1861).

CUEVAS, Mariano, *Historia de la iglesia en México* (5 vols., El Paso, 1928)

DÁNVILA Y COLLADO, Manuel, *El poder civil en España* (6 vols., Madrid, 1885–7).

DÁVILA GARIBI, José Ignacio, *La obra civilizadora de los misioneros de la Nueva Galicia* (Guadalajara, 1919).

EGAÑA, Antonio de, *La teoría del regio vicariato español en Indias* (Rome, 1958).

EGUÍA RUIZ, Constancio, *Los Jesuítas y el motín de Esquilache* (Madrid, 1947).

ESQUIVEL OBREGÓN, Toribio, *Apuntes para la historia del derecho en México* (4 vols., Mexico, 1937–47).

FERNÁN NÚÑEZ, Conde de (C. J. Gutiérrez de los Ríos), *Vida de Carlos III* A. Morel-Fatio and A. Paz y Meliá, eds. (2 vols, Madrid, 1898).

FERRER DEL RÍO, Antonio, *Historia del reinado de Carlos III* (4 vols., Madrid, 1856).

FUENTE, Vicente de la, *Historia eclesiástica de España* (6 vols., Madrid, 1873–5).

GARCÍA GALLO, Alfonso, *Historia del derecho español* (2 vols., Madrid, 1941).

GARCÍA GUTIÉRREZ, Jesús, *Apuntes para la historia del origen y desenvolvimiento del Regio Patronato Indiano hasta 1857* (Mexico, 1941).

—, *La persecución religiosa en México desde el punto de vista jurídico* (Mexico, n.d.).

GÉNESTAL, Robert, *Les origines de l'appel comme d'abus* (Paris, 1951).

GIMÉNEZ FERNÁNDEZ, Manuel, *El concilio IV Provincial Mejicano* (Seville, 1939).

—, *La política religiosa de Fernando V en las Indias* (Madrid, 1943).

GÓNGORA, Mario, 'Estudios sobre el galicanismo y la "Illustración Católica" en América española', *Revista Chilena de Historia y Geografía*, no. 125 (1957), pp. 96–151.

HERR, Richard, *The Eighteenth-Century Revolution in Spain* (Princeton, 1958).

HINOJOSA, Ricardo de, *Los despachos de la diplomacia pontificia en España* (Madrid, 1896).

HOWE, Walter, *The Mining Guild of New Spain and its Tribunal General 1770–1821* (Cambridge, Mass., 1949).

HUMBOLDT, Alexander von, *Ensayo político sobre el reino de la Nueva España*, Vito Alessio Robles, ed. (5 vols., Mexico, 1941).

KRATZ, Guillermo, *El tratado hispano-portugués de límites de 1750 y sus consecuencias* (Rome, 1954).

LETURIA, Pedro de, *Relaciones entre la Santa Sede e Hispanoamérica* (3 vols., Rome, 1959–60).

LEVENE, Ricardo, *A History of Argentina*, trans. by W. S. Robertson (Chapel Hill, 1937).

LEWY, Guenther, *Constitutionalism and Statecraft during the Golden Age of Spain: a study of the political philosophy of Juan de Mariana, S.J.* (Geneva, 1960).

MCALISTER, Lyle N., *The 'Fuero Militar' in New Spain 1764–1800* (Gainesville, 1957).

—, 'Social Structure and Social Change in New Spain', *H.A.H.R.*, xliii (1963), pp. 349–70.

MALDONADO Y FERNÁNDEZ DEL TORCO, José, 'Los recursos de fuerza en España', *Anuario de Historia del Derecho Español*, xxiv (1954), pp. 281–380.

MARILUZ URQUIJO, José María, *Ensayo sobre los juicos de residencia indianos* (Seville, 1952).

MARTÍNEZ, Elías, 'Los franciscanos y la independencia de Mexico', *Ábside*, xxiv (1960), pp. 129–62.

MECHAM, John Lloyd, *Church and State in Latin America* (Chapel Hill, 1934).

MENÉNDEZ Y PELAYO, Marcelino, *Historia de los heterodoxos españoles* (6 vols., Madrid, 1946).

MERRIMAN, Roger Bigelow, *The Rise of the Spanish Empire in the Old World and the New* (4 vols., New York, 1918–34).

OSORES, Félix, *Noticias bio-bibliográficas de alumnos distinguidos del Colegio de San Ildefonso* (2 vols., Mexico, 1908).

PARRY, J. H., *The Audiencia of New Galicia in the Sixteenth Century* (Cambridge, 1948).

—, *The Sale of Public Office in the Spanish Indies under the Hapsburgs* (Ibero-Americana: 37, Berkeley, 1953).

PÉREZ LUGO, J., *La cuestión religiosa en México* (Mexico, 1926).

PÉREZ-MARCHAND, Monalisa, *Dos etapas ideológicas del siglo XVIII en México a través de los papeles de la Inquisición* (Mexico, 1945).

PORTES GIL, Emilio, *La labor sediciosa del clero mexicano* (Madrid, 1935).

PRADEAU Y AVILÉS, Alberto, *La expulsión de los Jesuítas de las provincias de Sonora, Ostimuri y Sinaloa en 1767* (Mexico, 1959).

PRIESTLEY, Herbert Ingram, *José de Gálvez, Visitador General of New Spain, 1765–1771* (Berkeley, 1916).

ROBERTSON, William Spence, *Iturbide of Mexico* (Durham, N.C., 1952).

RODRÍGUEZ-ARANGO DÍAZ, Crisanto, *El fuero civil y criminal de los clérigos en el derecho canónico* (Rome, 1957).

RODRÍGUEZ CASADO, Vicente, *La política y los políticos en el reinado de Carlos III* (Madrid, 1962).

SÁNCHEZ AGESTA, Luis, *El pensamiento político del despotismo ilustrado* (Madrid, 1953).

SCHMITT, K. M., 'The Clergy and the Independence of New Spain', *H.A.H.R.*, xxxiv (1954), pp. 289–312.

SEMPERE Y GUARINOS, Juan, *Historia de las rentas eclesiásticas de España* (Madrid, 1822).

SHIELS, William Eugene, *King and Church: the rise and fall of the Patronato Real* (Chicago, 1961).

TEJA ZABRE, Alfonso, *Vida de Morelos* (Mexico, 1959).

TORO, Alfonso, *La iglesia y el estado en México* (Mexico, 1927).

ULLMANN, Walter, *The Growth of Papal Government in the Middle Ages* (London, 1955).

VICENS VIVES, Jaime, ed., *Historia social y económica de España y América* (5 vols., Barcelona, 1957–9).

VILLASEÑOR Y VILLASEÑOR, Alejandro, *Biografías de los héroes y caudillos de la independencia* (2 vols., Mexico, 1910).

IV. OTHER USEFUL WORKS

ALAMÁN, Lucas, *Disertaciones sobre la historia de la república mejicana* . . . (3 vols., Mexico, 1844–9).

ALEGRE, Francisco Javier, *Historia de la Compañía de Jesús en Nueva España*, C. M. Bustamante, ed. (3 vols., Mexico, 1841–2).

ALZATE Y RAMÍREZ, José Antonio, *Gazeta de literatura*, periodical (Mexico, 1788–96).

ASTRAÍN, Antonio, *Historia de la Compañía de Jesús en la asistencia de España* (7 vols., Madrid, 1902–25).

AYALA, Francisco Javier de, 'Ideas canónicas de Juan de Solórzano', *Anuario de Estudios Americanos*, iv (1947), pp. 579–613.

BATLLORI, Miguel, *El Abate Viscardo: historia y mito de la intervención de los jesuítas en la independencia de Hispanoamérica* (Caracas, 1953).

BUSTAMANTE, Carlos María, *Continuación del cuadro histórico de la revolución mexicana* (2nd ed., 4 vols., Mexico, 1953–63).

CAVO, Andrés, *Los tres siglos de México durante el gobierno español hasta la entrada del ejército trigarante*, notas y suplemento de Carlos M. Bustamante (4 vols., Mexico, 1836–8).

Colección eclesiástica mexicana (4 vols., Mexico, 1834).

La constitución de 1812 en la Nueva España (2 vols., Mexico, 1912–13).

DANVILA Y COLLADO, Manuel, *El reinado de Carlos III* (6 vols., Madrid, 1891–6).

DÁVILA Y ARILLAGA, José Mariano, *Continuación de la historia de la Compañía de Jesús en Nueva España* (2 vols., Puebla, 1889).

DÁVILA GARIBI, José Ignacio, *Apuntes para la historia de la iglesia en Guadalajara* (3 vols., Mexico, 1957–63).

DESDEVISES DU DEZERT, G., *L'Espagne de l'Ancien Régime* (3 vols., Paris, 1897–1904).

DOMÍNGUEZ ORTIZ, Antonio, *La sociedad española en el siglo XVIII* (Madrid, 1955).

ESQUIVEL OBREGÓN, Toribio, *Biografía de D. Francisco Javier Gamboa, Ideario político y jurídico de Nueva España en el siglo XVIII* (Mexico, 1941).

FISHER, Lillian Estelle, *Champion of Reform: Manuel Abad y Queipo* (New York, 1955).

FUENTE, Vicente de la, *La retención de bulas en España* (Madrid, 1865).

GÁLVEZ, José de (Marqués de Sonora), *Informe general que en virtud de real orden instruyó y entregó el Excmo. Sr. Marqués de Sonora, siendo visitator general de este reino, al Excmo. Sr. virrey Frey D. Antonio Bucarely y Ursúa con fecha de 31 de diciembre de 1771* (Mexico, 1867).

GIBSON, Charles, *The Aztecs under Spanish Rule: A History of the Indians of the Valley of Mexico, 1519-1810* (Stanford, 1964).

GODOY, Manuel, *Memorias de don Manuel Godoy, Príncipe de la Paz, ó sea cuento dada de su vida política* (6 vols., Paris, 1839).

GONZÁLEZ CASANOVA, Pablo, *La literatura perseguida en la crisis de la colonia* (Mexico, 1958).

GONZÁLEZ DE SOCUEBA, Fernando, *Instrucción manual para la más breve expedición de los casos prácticos y disputas de la inmunidad local* (Madrid, 1776).

GONZÁLEZ ZUMÁRRAGA, Antonio J., *Problemas del patronato indiano a través del 'Gobierno eclesiástico pacífico' de Fr. Gaspar de Villarroel* (Madrid, 1961).

GUZMÁN, Martin Luis, ed., *Morelos y la iglesia católica* (Mexico, 1948).

HERA, Alberto de la, 'Las leyes eclesiásticas de Indias en el siglo XVIII', *Estudio Americanos*, xvi (1958), pp. 239–52.

HUMPHREYS, R. A., and JOHN LYNCH, eds., *The Origins of the Latin American Revolutions, 1808-26* (New York, 1965).

KREBS WILCKENS, Ricardo, *El pensamiento histórico, político y económico del Conde de Campomanes* (Santiago de Chile, 1962).

LAFUENTE FERRARI, Enrique, *El virrey Iturrigaray y los orígenes de la independencia de México* (Madrid, 1941).

LAVRÍN, Asunción, 'Ecclesiastical Reform of Nunneries in New Spain in the Eighteenth Century', *Americas*, xxii (1965), pp. 182–203.

LLORENTE, Juan Antonio, *Historia crítica de la Inquisición de España* (10 vols., Madrid, 1822).

LÓPEZ CÁMARA, Francisco, *La génesis de la conciencia liberal en México* (Mexico, 1954).

LYNCH, John, *Spanish Colonial Administration, 1782-1810: The Intendant System in the Viceroyalty of the Río de la Plata* (London, 1958).

MEDINA ASCENSIO, Luis, *La Santa Sede y la emancipación mexicana* (Guadalajara, 1946).

MERINO, Luis, *Las 'Noticias secretas' y el clero colonial (1720-65)* (Madrid, 1956).

MIER, Servando Teresa de (pseud., José Guerra), *Historia de la revolución de Nueva España* (2 vols., London, 1813).

MIRANDA, José, *Humboldt y México* (Mexico, 1962).

—, *Las ideas y las instituciones políticas mexicanas. Primera parte: 1521-1820* (Mexico, 1952).

MORA, José Maria Luis, *Disertación sobre la naturaleza y aplicación de las rentas y bienes eclesiásticos* (Mexico, 1833).

MURIEL, Andrés, *Historia de Carlos IV* (6 vols., Madrid, 1893–4).

MURIEL DE LA TORRE, Josefina, *Conventos de monjas en la Nueva España* (Mexico, 1946).

—, *Hospitales de la Nueva España* (2 vols., Mexico, 1956–60).

MURO OREJÓN, Antonio, 'Leyes del Nuevo Código de Indias vigentes en América', *Revista de Indias*, v (1944), pp. 3443–72.

NAVARRO GARCIÁ, Luis, *Don José de Gálvez y la comandancia general de las Provincias Internas del norte de Nueva España* (Seville, 1964).

NAVARRO Y NORIEGA, Fernando, *Catálogo de los curatos y misiones que tiene Nueva España* (Mexico, 1813).

OCARANZA, Fernando, *Capítulos de la historia franciscana* (2 vols., Mexico, 1933–4.)

OLAVIDE Y JÁUREGUI, Pablo Antonio José de, *El Evangelico en triunfo, ó historia de un filósofo desengañado* (4 vols., Madrid, 1791).

'Representación del cabildo de la ciudad de México, 1771', Rafael Gómez de Hoyos, ed., *Boletín de Historia y Antigüedades*, xlvii, (1960), pp. 425–76.

REYES HEROLES, Jesús, *El liberalismo mexicano* (3 vols., Mexico, 1957–61).

RODRÍGUEZ CASADO, Vicente, 'La orden de San Francisco y la visita general de reforma de 1769', *Anuario de Estudios Americanos*, ix (1952), pp. 209–33.

SARRAILH, Jean, *L'Espagne éclairée de la seconde moitié du XVIIIᵉ siècle* (Paris, 1954).

El segundo conde de Revilla Gigedo (juicio de residencia) (Publicaciones del Archivo General de la Nación, vol. 22, Mexico, 1933).

TEJADA Y RAMIRO, Juan, ed., *Colección completa de concordatos españoles* (Madrid, 1862).

TIMMONS, Wilbert E., 'Los Guadalupes: A Secret Society in the Mexican Revolution for Independence', *H.A.H.R.*, xxx (1950), pp. 453–99.

TORRE VILLAR, Ernesto de la, ed., *La Constitución de Apatzingán y los creadores del Estado Mexicano* (Mexico, 1964).

VALDÉS, Manuel Antonio, ed., *Gaceta de México*, periodical (Mexico, 1784–1821).

VARGAS UGARTE, Rubén, ed., *Concilios limenses (1561–1772)* (3 vols., Lima, 1951).

VELASCO CEBALLOS, Rómulo, ed., *Visita y reforma de los hospitales de San Juan de Dios de Nueva España en 1772–4* (2 vols., Mexico, 1945).

VILLASEÑOR Y SÁNCHEZ, José Antonio de, *Theatro americano. Descripción general de los reynos y provincias de la Nueva España y sus jurisdicciones* (2 vols., Mexico, 1746–8).

VILLORO, Luis, *La revolución de independencia. Ensayo de interpretación histórica* (Mexico, 1953).

WEST, Elizabeth Howard, 'The Right of Asylum in New Mexico in the Seventeenth and Eighteenth Centuries', *H.A.H.R.*, viii (1928), pp. 357–91.

INDEX

279